Culture and Revolution in the Thought of Leon Trotsky

Revolutionary History, Volume 7, no 2
Porcupine Press
Socialist Platform Ltd

Revolutionary History

Editor: Al Richardson

Deputy Editor: Ted Crawford

Continental Contributing Editor: Fritz Keller

Reviews Editor: José Villa

Business Manager: Barry Buitekant

Production and Design Manager: Paul Flewers

Editorial Board: Ian Birchall, Tony Borton, Clarence Chrysostom, Paul Hampton, Baruch Hirson, Mike Jones, Stuart King, Bahir Laattoe, Bozena Langley, Esther Leslie, George Leslie, Sheila Leslie, John McIlroy, John Plant, Jim Ring, Ernest Rogers, Barbara Rossi, Bruno Simon, Phil Walden

ISBN 1 89943 832 7

ISSN 0953 2382

Copyright © 1999 Socialist Platform Ltd

Web site: http://www.compulink.co.uk/~jplant/revhist

E-mail: tcrawford@revhist.datanet.co.uk
        jplant@cix.compulink.co.uk
        paul.flewers@virgin.net

Socialist Platform Ltd, BCM 7646, London WC1N 3XX

Porcupine Press, 10 Woburn Walk, London WC1H 0JL

Typeset by voluntary labour

Printed in Britain by Polestar Wheatons Ltd, Exeter

Contents

Editorial   1

The Culture of the Old World   3

Leon Trotsky, Ibsen
Leon Trotsky, Two Literary Souls at the Mercy of the Metaphysical
    Demon
Leon Trotsky, Poetry, the Machine, and the Poetry of the Machine
Leon Trotsky, On the Novel in General and on *The Three of
    Them* in Particular
Leon Trotsky, Culture and the Little White Bull
Paul Flewers, *Vekhi* and the Retreat from Reason

Impressionism: Trotsky in Vienna   49

Fritz Keller, Trotsky in Vienna
Leon Trotsky, On Death and Eros
Leon Trotsky, A New Year's Conversation about Art
Leon Trotsky, The Vienna Secession of 1909
Leon Trotsky, Two Viennese Exhibitions
Leon Trotsky, On the Intelligentsia
Leon Trotsky, Vienna Secession 1913

The Culture of the Transition Period   105

John Plant, Trotsky, Art and the Revolution
Antonio Gramsci, A Letter to Leon Trotsky on Futurism
Leon Trotsky, For Quality — For Culture!

Culture Under the Dictators   137

Pierre Naville, Trotsky on Art and Literature
Richard Greeman, Did Trotsky Read Serge?
Esther Leslie, Elective Affinities
James T Farrell, A Memoir of Leon Trotsky
Leon Trotsky, Marcel Martinet
Leon Trotsky, The Attitude of Men of Letters
An Interview with Jean Malaquais
Fritz Keller, Stalinism versus Hedonism

The International Federation of Independent   203
Revolutionary Artists

Maurice Nadeau, Trotsky and Breton
Leon Trotsky, You Must Not Whisper
Leon Trotsky, Difficulties With Diego
Clé

Obituaries   219

Work in Progress   228

Reviews   234

André Liebich, *From the Other Shore* (Paul Flewers)
Noreen Branson, *History of the Communist Party of Great Britain 1941-
1951* (Paul Flewers)
David King, *The Commissar Vanishes* (Paul Flewers)
Aindrias Ó Cathasaigh (ed), *James Connolly: The Lost Writings* (Chris Gray)
FA Ridley, *Socialism and Religion* (Chris Gray)
Richard Brenner, *Trotsky: An Introduction* (Al Richardson)
International Communist Union, *Hungary 1956* (Al Richardson)
Jane Rowlandson, *Women and Society in Greek and Roman Egypt* (Al
Richardson)
Marilyn Vogt-Downey, *The Ideological Legacy of LD Trotsky* (Al Richardson)
Hall Greenland, *Red Hot* (Al Richardson)
Ralph Darlington, *The Political Trajectory of JT Murphy* (John McIlroy)
Molly Murphy, *Molly Murphy* (John McIlroy)
Ben Watson, *Art, Class and Cleavage* (Ian Birchall)
Pierre Broué, *Histoire de l'Internationale Communiste* (Ian Birchall)
Sean Matgamna (ed), *The Fate of the Russian Revolution* (Barry Finger and
Jim Higgins)
Alison McLeod, *The Death of Uncle Joe* (Ron Heisler)
Sam Deaderick and Tamara Turner, *Gay Resistance* (John Plant)
Riccardo Anfossi, *La Resistenza Spezzata* (Barbara Rossi)
Carlo Guerriero and Fausto Rondinelli, *La Volante Rossa* (Barbara Rossi)
Tom Behan, *The Long Awaited Moment* (Barbara Rossi)
Elena Aga-Rossi and Victor Zaslavsky, *Togliatti e Stalin* (Barbara Rossi)

Letters   299

Reader's Notes   306

Back Issues of *Revolutionary History*   316

Editorial

R EVOLUTION, 'the carnival of the oppressed', has often been described as a form of mass artistic creativity, and the obvious examples that spring to mind in our century are Agitprop and the poster art of the Russian Revolution. And even if the revolutions of the past had been for the benefit of small minorities, they still drew on the support and participation of wider layers of society, with all that that implied in unlocking their creative potential. The great seventeenth century Dutch painters could hardly have existed without the revolt of the United Provinces against Spain, the first successful and enduring bourgeois revolution in history, and it is obviously impossible to envisage Stendhal and David without the French Revolution and Napoleon.

However, whilst writers and artists often discuss, analyse and directly reflect the revolutions in which they are involved in lively and varied ways, and new forms of expression are often born, it is extremely rare in history for creative figures to stand at the centre of events. It is true that on opposite sides in the English Revolution we have Milton, acting as Latin Secretary to the Commonwealth, and Edward Hyde as a royal councillor. But neither can be said to have occupied so vital a place in the events as Leon Trotsky. Moreover, although Trotsky's main preoccupations were always political, his writings, such as *1905*, *My Life* and *The History of the Russian Revolution* show that he was himself a literary artist of consummate skill. He is thus an ideal guide for exploring the problem of the relationship between culture and politics in the age of permanent revolution.

There is, of course, no consensus about these questions on the editorial board of our journal, and our main aim in this issue is certainly not to lay down a 'line' in the time-honoured Stalinist manner. Rather it is to admit the reader into Trotsky's workshop, where he can watch the ideas slowly taking shape before they appear in his later well-known works. For this reason, we have made a point of weighting our selection of articles towards his earliest period, which is largely neglected in the standard English collections of his writings on art and literature. We have also tried to keep a balance between literature and the major and minor visual arts, between the discussion of general questions and the analysis of particular artists or their work, and between pieces by Trotsky and comments upon his views.

We can only hope that our readers will appreciate our efforts, and join with us in thanking our translators. The measure of our success can only be a lively postbag and a longer subscription list.

Editorial Board
Revolutionary History

Erratum

Pierre Broué has drawn our attention to two errors in *Revolutionary History*, Volume 6, no 4. On page 9, Kumari Jayawardene wrongly describes Lamine Senghor as one of the 'non-Communist nationalists' in West Africa, and an Editor's footnote incorrectly refers to Leopold Senghor, 'a proponent of moderate African Socialism' who later became President of Senegal. Lamine Senghor (1883-1927) was a Senegalese, anti-war veteran who had been in the French army and a postal worker in Paris, and was the first black Communist leader in France and Black French Africa. He died of tuberculosis.

Thank You

We extend our thanks to Wes Ervin for donating to the Socialist Platform Library copies of every internal bulletin of the US Socialist Workers Party up to the mid-1960s, and to Kevin Barry and Frank Fried for providing us with Tariq Ali's *Redemption*, and Sidney Lens' *Unrepentant Radical*.

I: The Culture of the Old World

Our first section concentrates upon Trotsky's comments upon literature translated from the *Sochineniya*, Volume 20 (pp181-204, 210-15 and 308-11) by Bozena Langley, Robert Goldie and Yurii Colombo, to whom we tender our thanks, as we do to Brian Pearce, who checked the translation of the first, fourth and fifth articles. Many of Trotsky's minor gems are politico-literary essays of this type, such as those on Gogol and Céline in Irving Howe's *The Basic Writings of Trotsky* (London, 1964), pp317-24 and 343-55, and on Tolstoy, Essenin, Martinet, Mayakovsky, Malraux, Céline, Silone, Gorky and Jack London in *Leon Trotsky on Literature and Art* (New York, 1977), pp127-66, 174-206 and 217-24. Our selection is taken from Trotsky's earliest writings, because they are less well represented in English, and the short time-span allows us to ensure coherence and provide examples from which to draw conclusions about the formation of his ideas and style.

Approaching this subject was not, of course, a new departure for Marxists. Marx and Engels, *On Literature and Art* (Moscow, 1976) contains a very useful and comprehensive compilation of their views on the whole topic. The views of Engels, Mehring, Plekhanov and Lunacharsky about Ibsen were collected together by Angel Flores and published by the Critics Group in New York in 1937. The New York Critics Group also translated and published Mikhail Lifshitz's 1933 work, *The Philosophy of Art of Karl Marx* (republished, London, 1973), which seeks to extract and synthesise Marx's scattered writings on art. Lifshitz had no access to the *Grundrisse*, and much of the correspondence that we now have available. The fifth volume of Plekhanov's *Selected Philosophical Works* (Moscow, 1981) is devoted to his writings on literature and art, including his article on Ibsen. Plekhanov's lecture from 1912 'Art and Social Life', also included in this volume, illustrates the breadth of his interests, and deals, *inter alia*, with his disputes on art with Lunacharsky and Bogdanov, both of whom were at that time associated with the 'Capri' tendency. Lenin's writings of relevance to our theme have been collected in the anthology *On Literature and Art* (Moscow, 1967), supplemented by the volume *Lenin and Gorky: Letters, Reminiscences, Articles* (Moscow, 1973). Rosa Luxemburg's views on Russian literature before the Revolution can be found in her 'Life of

Korolenko', *International Socialist Review*, Volume 30, no 1, January-February 1969, pp7-31, and Victor Serge later published his own 'Recollections of Maxim Gorki', *New International*, Volume 16, no 4, July-August 1950, pp249-51. Alfonso Leonetti touched on the subject just before he left the Trotskyist movement to return to Stalinism, under the name of 'Ferocci' in 'Art and Marxism' in the *New International* in 1935, and a later attempt at a synthesis was made by Michael Harrington, 'A Marxist Approach to Art', *New International*, Volume 22, no 1, Spring 1956, pp40-9. A good basic general discussion of Trotsky as a literary critic is to be found in chapter 11 of Ernest Mandel's *Trotsky as Alternative* (London, 1995), pp157-64.

Literature remained a consuming passion of Trotsky's life, to which he often returned during times of political exclusion or enforced idleness. During the violent debates between Zinoviev and Stalin during the mid-1920s he is reported to have sat silent, reading French literature.

Leon Trotsky

Ibsen

IT is said that great people do not hold any charm in the eyes of their hangers-on. But, on the other hand, personal acquaintance with great people turned and still turns them into their hangers-on, which can often be concluded on the basis of the relevant documents.

A Norwegian author, John Paulsen,[1] writing in his *Memoirs*[2] about his relationship with Henrik Ibsen, is not an exception to this sad rule. For instance, he quotes, with deep sympathy, the words of his friend, a Norwegian painter, who, after a meeting with Ibsen, said: 'Just imagine, he really did not say anything, but his manners, as he filled my pipe, and his look as he handed it to me, really moved me!' It is hard to imagine a higher level of servility!

On the whole, Paulsen's *Memoirs* provide very little material to give an authentic physiognomy of the famous writer. The facts related by Paulsen are utterly trivial, spiced up in small doses with his home-made philosophy and in large amounts with spiritual flunkeyism before the 'great fellow-countryman'. Keeping in mind that *la plus jolie fille de France ne peut*

1. John Paulsen (born in 1851) was a Norwegian writer, and an author of numerous novels without much success. Paulsen met Ibsen in Munich in 1876, and the latter, thanks to the former's intervention, obtained from the Storthing (the Norwegian parliament) a literary allowance, which gave him an opportunity to live for a certain time in Rome, Paris and Berlin. [Note by *Sochineniya* Editors]
2. The excerpts from these *Memoirs*, printed in parts related to Henrik Ibsen in book III of *God's World* in 1901, prompted me to write the present 'letter'. [Note by Trotsky]

donner plus que ce qu'elle a (the most beautiful girl in France cannot give more than she's got), we shall try to make use of the little that Paulsen offers, together with the much that Ibsen gives in his works.

'When Ibsen, this great sceptic, who shook all our old ideals' – Paulsen can't do without this theatrical pathos! – 'was expressing in a conversation one audacious thought after another, Mrs Lie (the wife of a famous Norwegian writer), brought up in an old religious civil service family, would sometimes disagree with him, quoting scripture.' She apparently regarded Ibsen as 'a revolutionary'. Paulsen himself came to the conclusion that Ibsen was a revolutionary 'only in conversation, and in his works, but not in his everyday life'.

Is Ibsen really a 'revolutionary'?

The respectable lady's opinion about Ibsen was based on a comparison of his views with scripture; Paulsen contrasts Ibsen's 'audacious thoughts' with the miserable codes of his own morality and philosophy. We shall try to bring Ibsen's 'revolutionary' ideas into confrontation with the objective socio-historical conditions. The answer to this question will become clear.

In 1870, Ibsen wrote to Georg Brandes:[3]

'Everything that we are presently feeding upon is mere crumbs from the table of the revolution of the previous century, and the food has already been sufficiently chewed over and over. The concepts demand new content and new commentary. The concepts of "liberty, equality and fraternity" long ago ceased to bear the same meaning as they did during the time of the defunct guillotine. This is what the political revolutionaries do not want to understand, and that is why I hate them. Those gentlemen only desire extraordinary overturns, overturns *from the outside*. But these are all stupidities. The overturn of the human spirit – that is the point!'

Not much revolutionary here, so far.

Paulsen also understands that, although 'liberty for Ibsen is the same as oxygen', nevertheless he doesn't understand it so much in the civil, as in the personal, sense. What does it mean in reality – Paulsen now adds from his own understanding – to have the vote, if not to elaborate one's personal freedom?

Personal freedom? Revolution of the human spirit? But do any social conditions allow the elaboration of 'personal freedom', and can indeed the 'revolution of the human spirit' take place independently of external conditions? Ibsen did not know how to answer these questions. Moreover, he could not even pose them.

---

3. Georg Brandes (1842-1927) was a Danish literary critic, and an historian of literature and publicist.

Ibsen regards social transformations as almost insignificant. Parties, these great cultural forces of the present, only by way of which can one influence society in the desired direction, Ibsen treats with the contempt of a solitary aristocrat of the intellect. 'Party programmes', says Dr Stockman, 'kill every vital truth.' And even more strongly: 'A party? It's a pump, which bit by bit pumps out reason and conscience!' (*An Enemy of the People*) Ibsen starts with individuality, and returns to it. He resolves – or tries to resolve – every social problem within the bounds of the individual spirit. He widens and deepens this flexible individual spirit to super-human dimensions (*Brand*) without even touching on social conditions. In the person of Rosmer, Ibsen wants to 'transform everyone in the country into aristocrats of the spirit, freeing the spirit and cleansing the will' – how decisive! – but Rosmer loses faith even in this cause, and becomes convinced that 'one can't ennoble people from the outside' (*Rosmersholm*).

In his personal life, Ibsen, this 'audacious revolutionary', this 'great minus' as he was called by his countrymen, humbly bows down before the conditions acting *from outside*; with pedantic conscientiousness he subordinates himself to all the conventions of the hypocritically decent lifestyle of his bourgeois surroundings. Only in the creations of his spirit does he stand 'high and free' (though not as high as it seems to Paulsen or to Ibsen himself), but, 'oh, I am not like that in everyday life', he complains with bitterness about himself through the lips of the builder (*Solness*). Just like the builder, he 'doesn't dare, cannot rise as high, as he himself builds'.[4]

This is a weakness, not of his personal individuality, but of his individualist message, his suprasocial morality, or, if you like, his immorality. And if the whole significance of Ibsen was based merely upon this message, then one can confidently say that he would have been of no importance whatsoever.

Ibsen, the creator of great new words and audacious ideas; Ibsen, the prophet of reborn humanity; Ibsen, the spiritual leader of the future... and whatever else he is called, *that* Ibsen does not have a hundredth, a thousandth fraction of the significance of Ibsen, the great depictor of the bourgeois milieu. Ibsen, the artist who denies, the 'great minus', stands immeasurably higher than Ibsen, the symbolist prophet and leader. By nature, Ibsen was not born for the latter rôle. 'I do not remember an occasion', says Paulsen, 'when Ibsen would burst out with enthusiastic expressions, burning words, which would have shown that feelings played

4. Not without a special significance for the characterisation of Ibsen's personality is the fact that having indignantly left his country for voluntary exile, Ibsen demanded – and received – for himself a 'literary pension' from Parliament. It proves to be difficult by efforts 'from within', a mere 'revolution of the spirit', to free oneself 'from without'... if only from financial dependence, so demeaning for the spirit! [Note by Trotsky]

any particular rôle in his spiritual life.' No, he was not a leader. If you free Ibsen's 'new words' from the misty, symbolic outer layer so beloved by many,[5] then the new words in the majority of cases lose both their novelty and charm. This is not surprising. In our present times, when human thought possesses such colossal inherited and acquired wealth, inexhaustible in its variety, a serious, precious new word can be spoken only standing on the shoulders of its great predecessors. Whereas, according to Paulsen, Ibsen 'read very little. He learnt about the latest works of literature and philosophical thought mostly from conversations with others, rather than from his own study.' This self-taught genius, without a systematic education, without a consistent world-view, treated the products of other people's thought with misplaced disdain.

Spiritually akin to him, the self-taught master-builder, the hero of the above-mentioned drama, who has undoubted autobiographical relevance, asks Hilde whether she reads. Hilde: 'No. Never... any more. It's all the same, I don't see the point.' Solness: 'You hit the nail on the head, neither do I.' (*The Master Builder*) This contemptuous attitude towards books, and specifically his ignorance of them, we repeat, did have a far-reaching effect on Ibsen's creative works; he did not give as much as he could have done. However, having forgiven him for his backsliding, let us talk about what he *gave*, let us look at the materials on which he based himself, because he gave a great deal, and worked on material that deserves the most careful attention.

What is the social background against which the personal dramas of Ibsen's heroes usually take place?

It is the peaceful, inert, set-in-one-and-the-same-ways life of the small Norwegian provincial towns, inhabited by the middle sort of bourgeois, which is so moral and decent, so respectable and religious...

Oh! This composed provincial decorum has left a bitter aftertaste in the mouth of the great dramatist, and you can completely understand him, when in an answer to Paulsen's exclamation at the sight of Munich — 'What a big town!' — Ibsen remarks with bitterness: 'One can't even live in a smaller one.'

In these big commercial, industrial and intellectual centres, there is indeed more space and air, fewer conventions, and, most important, less of this morality and decorum which is characteristic of petit-bourgeois towns, suffocating like soot from a bad lamp, sticky like thick treacle, as an atmosphere penetrating every pore and pervading every relationship — family, kinship, love, friendship...

5.   'I knew his writings well', says Paulsen, 'I read them over and over again, but I could not always penetrate their hidden depths... How many Sundays have I sat... racking my brains over some obscure passage.' How absurd his attitude to a work of art appears to us, as though to a puzzle or an apocalyptic revelation! [Note by Trotsky]

The provincial bourgeoisie, eaten to the core by routine and age-long sluggishness, is afraid of any novelties: a new railway line makes him look with fear into the future: 'It was so quiet and peaceful here', before the railway came, complains Mrs Bernik (*Pillars of Society*). If this is the case with the railway, then any new ideas are completely out of order. Why should they be necessary for society? 'The good old ones, with which we all agree, are quite sufficient.' (*An Enemy of the People*)

Not tolerating any novelty, this bourgeoisie could not achieve any originality, independence or even simple distinctiveness. It mercilessly stifled the slightest expression of these qualities. 'You have a passion', its spokesman, the mayor, lectures Dr Stockman, 'for always finding *your own* path, but we shall not allow this in our well-ordered society. Each individual needs to subordinate himself to the whole.'

Whilst the industrial feudatories, under whose heel stand tens of thousands of people, the masters and legislators of the stock exchange, the great 'shakers' of the world market, in short, the all-powerful dictators of the present commercial-industrial world, know only too well their ability to hide their real attitude towards life and people, the middle class, on the contrary, cannot tolerate the nakedness of these relations, and is incapable of facing openly the work of its own hands; it is afraid of the tension of the components of the bourgeois mechanism which are drawing it into its movement, and it tries to soften this tension, lubricating it with the rancid butter of hypocritical sentimentalism. In this immoral great world, 'What price does human life have?', asks the university assistant Rerlund, this personified conscience of local society. 'They treat people's lives there like capital. But *we*, I dare to think, have a completely different moral standpoint.' (*Pillars of Society*) Indeed!

Standing on the borderline between the higher classes of society and the lower ones, the middle and petit-bourgeoisie is not averse to leaning for support on the lower ones, and speaking in their names, but none of this, of course, is done seriously.

Well then, the political education of the nation by way of self-government. 'Haven't you thought about that?', the editor Houstad asks the printer Aslaksen.

'When a man achieves a certain prosperity and must look after it, he cannot think about everything, Mr Houstad', the printer, educated in the 'school of life', answers with excessive frankness (*An Enemy of the People*).

In general, there is a lot to learn from Aslaksen. His motto: '*moderation* — the first virtue of a citizen'. His individuality is completely drowned in his social type; he is strong in the strength of a 'unanimous majority', he does not speak in any other way than in the name of this unanimous majority, in the name of 'small property owners' and house-owners...

These hypocritical liberal principles of moderation which guide Aslaksen pervade the whole bourgeoisie. They compel bourgeois society, with all its hatred of everything novel, original and 'indecent', carefully to avoid taking nakedly repressive measures; any *mimretsovski* principle,[6] 'to grab and never let go', they erase from bourgeois usage. The bourgeoisie acts more indirectly, although no less effectively. In a different political situation, Dr Stockman, as 'an enemy of society', would be subjected to enforced isolation. The educated bourgeoisie acts differently. It boycotts its enemy. It dismisses him from his job (employer and employee are 'free' in their relations), it refuses him a flat, it stops his daughter from having lessons, expels his sons from school, and finally leaves him without work, and only by chance gives in to Stockman by failing to confiscate his flat. 'Without a whip, without an iron bar', it surely achieves its aim. It isolates its enemy almost as surely as if he were sentenced to the 'distant places'.

If a bourgeois of a cosmopolitan type was freethinking, at least until recently, then the provincial bourgeois, on the contrary, always found himself having to defend religion, hoping at the same time for salvation on its part. A pastor plays not an insignificant rôle in many of Ibsen's dramas. Ready to commit an underhand act – abandoning his 'friend' on a ship which is in danger of sinking, to insure himself from being exposed – consul Bernik looks for consolation in... religion. And, it must be said, he finds it. University assistant Rerlund says to him – understandably, in the name of religion: 'My dear consul, you have almost too many scruples. I believe that if you should leave it all to the will of providence...' (*Pillars of Society*)

All the various and often contradictory 'moments' of bourgeois life are kept in a relative balance with the help of the well-tried 'ideological' cement of hypocrisy. Just listen to the man who gave up a girl he loved in exchange for a dowry, without any mercy breaking off with the unhappy singer who was later abandoned by her husband and died in poverty, spreading slanders against his friend to improve his financial affairs, ready to see his friend drown in order to increase his personal wealth; in short, a sort of man already well known to us as a 'pillar of society' – consul Bernik: 'After all, the family is the foundation of society. A cosy house, respectable and loyal friends, a small closed circle, where no perfidious elements can break in.' What is most important, of course, is to avoid 'perfidious elements'.

What this bourgeois sacred 'family home' represents is well known. One writer brilliantly puts these words in the mouth of a bourgeois: 'My home is my castle, and I am the master of this castle!' This often happened, according to Paulsen, even to Ibsen: 'He uses – in books and say-

---

6. From Gleb Uspensky, 'A Shed', *Collected Works*, Volume 1, published by Pavlenkov, p727. [Note by *Sochineniya* Editors]

ings – Paul's severe words, saying that a husband should be the head and master, and a wife his most humble servant.' Even the most exceptional person, like Dr Stockman, this lonely fighter against the vulgarity of the bourgeois majority, says to his wife such a typically bourgeois vulgarity as: 'What foolishness, Katerina! You would do better to busy yourself with your housework, and leave it to me to worry about social issues.'

There is no need, of course, to add that together with the worship of the cult of the family, there calmly went, as if complementing it, the most thoroughgoing debauchery, of course on the side. 'Do you know', says the painter Osvald to the pastor, 'when and where I saw immorality amongst the painters? This used to happen when one of our countrymen, an exemplary father and husband, would arrive here [in Paris] to have a look at the new ways of life. Those gentlemen told us [painters] about such places and things we had never dreamed about.' (*Ghosts*)

To add to the last sketch of this quick characterisation of Norwegian provincial life, we shall quote one interesting anecdote, told by Paulsen. In the theatre of a small Norwegian town, a little-known singer was giving a performance, and the prim bourgeois audience, regardless of its admiration for her, could not decide whether to applaud her. Everyone was afraid that his personal impressions would not agree with the majority's impressions, and everybody with strained attention observed Belhaven, a poet who was a recognised authority, and who, in mockery of the audience, sat completely motionless. Suddenly, Belhaven raised his hands to clap, and the hall resounded with applause: 'The audience was given a signal that it could now trust its impressions and give an outlet to its feeling of admiration!'

That's how dreadful, how stifling the social atmosphere was, quite unbearable for any healthy human being's lungs.

Woe betide anyone in this situation to whom fate gave a strongly expressed originality or high aspirations. He would be condemned to utter loneliness. 'Our great suffering', says Guy de Maupassant, 'consists in this, that we are always *alone*, and all our efforts, all our actions, are directed only to escape from this loneliness.' (*Loneliness*) 'The most powerful man', says our gloomy Norwegian to the contrary, 'is the one in life's arena who stands completely alone.' (*An Enemy of the People*)

This contradiction is to be found in all the writings of the above-mentioned writers who share the same point of departure – a hatred of the bourgeoisie.

Whilst the feeling of loneliness is a constant refrain in the doleful lamentations of Maupassant, this sick singer of the decaying bourgeois society in France, the majority of Ibsen's dramas consist, on the contrary, of a festive hymn, an enthusiastic song in praise of 'the one who stands alone in the arena of social life'.

In a society stifled with bourgeois characterlessness and hypocritical cowardice, Ibsen creates a cult of personal energy, 'blazing with health of conscience: to dare to do whatever you desire the most' (*The Master Builder*).

This cult of a lonely proud force sometimes assumes in Ibsen downright repellent forms. He is prepared to place alongside the socially naive scientist Stockman the financial adventurer Borkman, in whose mouth the author puts the following speech, without any intended irony: 'It is this curse hanging over us, exceptional, chosen natures. Crowds, masses... all these mediocrities... do not understand us.' (*John Gabriel Borkman*)

Ibsen is not interested in the fact that moral force, like any other force, is not determined solely by its magnitude, but also by its point of application and direction. It is typical of Ibsen, as for someone working in the intellectual sphere, that he directs his particular sympathies towards *intellectual* strength. What is the most dangerous enemy of truth and liberty?, he asks through Dr Stockman: 'It is unanimous majority, the accursed liberal majority.' What is the most pernicious lie? It is 'the teaching that the crowd, imperfect and ignorant beings, have the same right to judge, direct and rule, *as the few true aristocrats of intellect*' (*An Enemy of the People*).

These are Dr Stockman's final conclusions, his 'great discoveries'.

Is it necessary to demonstrate that these have no social value? What sort of social system would it be in reality, in which only a few 'true intellectual aristocrats' would 'judge, direct and rule'? And what sort of areopagus would undertake to separate the 'true' from the 'false'?

If the 'crowd' was called upon to decide the question of the veracity of this or that scientific theory or philosophical system, then Stockman-Ibsen would be a thousand times right in his contemptuous opinion about the capabilities of a 'unanimous majority'. Darwin's opinion on the question of biology would be a hundred thousand times more important than the collective opinion of a meeting of a hundred thousand people.

But the field of social practice is a completely different matter, with its deep antagonism of interests, where the point is not the establishment of scientific or philosophical truths, but constant compromises between social forces pulling in different directions. In this field, the suppression of a minority by a majority, as long as it is based on a real relationship of social forces, and is not caused temporarily by artificial means, is incomparably superior to the suppression of a majority by a minority, often carried out under cover of darkness.

Of course, this arithmetical, numerical decision-making of social questions is not an ideal of social solidarity, but as long as society is divided into hostile groups, the superiority of the majority over the minority retains all its deep vital meaning, and the appeal from the 'plebeian spirit' of a unanimous majority to the 'intellectual aristocracy' of a few chosen ones will be left by the supreme court of life as a matter on which 'no action is to be taken'.

In the above-mentioned play, *An Enemy of the People*, two fundamental features of Ibsen's creative work appear: a brilliant embodiment of reality and a complete absence of resources from any positive ideal.

With lively interest, one follows the plot of the drama, how the purely technical, so it seems, problem of a town's sewerage system touches on the financial relations of the town's inhabitants, causing a party to be formed which forces Dr Stockman to move from a chemical examination of water to an analysis of the social environment; holding one's breath, one observes the growing wave of an oppositional mood in the heart of the honest scientist, only in the end to be stopped by an unpleasant surprise, a painful disappointment, when he is confronted by the wretched homily of the 'intellectual aristocracy'.

Oh! Haven't we long heard and don't we still hear this uplifting homily from different directions, and not only from poets, but from economists, sociologists...

For instance, Professor Schmoller,[7] as we all know, stands for social reform: he wants to satisfy the workers' demands. But all of them? Oh, no! There are, apparently, 'justified' and 'unjustified' demands. Egotistical *class* demands are very far from professorial justice. Justified interests are not class interests, but lie outside class, they are extra-class, supraclass, classless. At the basis of class interests lies vulgar economy. Supraclass, justified interests rise above them on the ethico-legal principle of 'distributive justice' (*verteilende Gerechtigkeit*). This universal principle, inaccessible to class pretensions, says that the distribution of material wealth and honours should correspond to the spiritual qualities of people; therefore either incomes should be distributed according to virtue (Mr Schmoller, this is dangerous!), or virtue should be raised to the equivalent percentage level of those people who possess high incomes (Mr Schmoller, this is unattainable!).

The principle of 'distributive justice', this worthy product of philistine perspicacity, would include so many risky aspects, if Professor Schmoller did not define the carriers of this principle as the 'aristocrats of education and spirit' – representatives of liberal professions, officialdom, etc (including, of course, the aristocrats of university chairs). But once done, everything would be fine. Classes taking part in material production, and

---

7. Gustav Friedrich Schmoller (1838-1917) was a German economist, a representative of the historico-moralist school in political economy. The followers of this school oppose the Manchester system, and demand a whole series of economic reforms to soften existing class contradictions. [Note by *Sochineniya* Editors]

thus becoming the carriers of egotistical class interests, disappear once and for all from the universal principle. Classes of material production are as far below 'distributive justice' as the born carriers of this justice are above the realm of material production.

If the 'aristocrats' of university education and the professorial-bureaucratic spirit did not have their own corporate interests, the product of Professor Schmoller's aristocratic spirit would turn out to be, in reality, devoid of the social basis for a supraclass theory... However...

Since 'distributive justice' is to be permanently maintained by the 'aristocrats of education and spirit' and the latter are to be once and for all removed from participation in material production, thus being permanently maintained by the class of material labour, this principle of 'distributive justice' turns out to be a fig leaf that poorly covers the naked shamelessness of professorial-bureaucratic corporate appetite.

Professor Stammler,[8] 'another aristocrat of education and spirit', competing with his colleague, also tries to raise himself above 'social aspirations, brought about by purely subjective impulses caused only by a *given state of things*, to the level of social aspirations, objectively based, justified from an objective point of view'. For this praiseworthy aim, the aristocrat Stammler arms himself with the ideal of 'a society of freely-desiring persons' as the highest point of view in all social judgements, as a formal idea, on the basis of which you can decide 'whether it is an empirical or a desirable social state objectively justified'.

From that moment Professor Schmoller stands above classes. History raises him above the tumult of everyday living struggle and sets him on the judge's throne as one who is a 'freely desiring' man, in order, fully armed with the universal objectively-patented ideal, to pass a merciless judgement and hand down a stern sentence on 'social aspirations, caused by a given state of things'.

Needless to say, Professor Stammler does not think it is worthwhile to get out from his professorial chair, which has become his judge's throne, to participate in the vulgar process of material *production*. Instead, one can be assured that if – what a wonderful dream! – Professor Stammler had been called together with Professor Schmoller to manage the intelligent process of material *distribution*, then the 'freely desiring' man Stammler and 'the aristocrat of education and spirit' Schmoller would

8. Rudolf Stammler [1856-1939 – Ed] was a German lawyer and economist, author of the book *Economy and Law*, devoted to a criticism of the materialist conception of history. The author puts forward law as a fundamental and unchanging category, without which it is unthinkable to understand social economy. The law represents the form of social life, and the economy represents its content. In evaluating social phenomena, it is necessary, first of all, to stress understanding of the goal, not the cause. The setting up of an aim and the choice of means for its realisation is the work of free individuality. [Note by *Sochineniya* Editors]

have acted with so much solidarity and rigour that the carriers of 'social aspirations, caused only by a given state of things', and the representatives of egotistical class interests, deprived of the solid basis of 'ethicolegal principle', would have received a suitable punishment for their lack of Stammler's objectivism and Schmoller's virtue.

No, no one should expect salvation from a corporation of aristocrats of the intellect called upon to 'judge, direct and rule'.

❖　　　　　❖　　　　　❖

We must also say something about Ibsen's women, as he is a writer to whom many are ready to give the title of a 'singer of women'. Ibsen certainly paid a lot of attention when depicting female characters, who are represented in considerable variety in his dramas.

In Ellida (*The Lady from the Sea*) and partially in Marta (*The Pillars*) are personified the dreamy yearnings of escape from a dull life, to where 'the sky is wide... clouds rise higher... the air is freer...', yearnings, which in higher stages become a desire 'to slap the face of all that decorum', not stopping even before a break from one's country (Lona and Dina in *The Pillars*), or with husband and children (Nora). A procession comes before us of Ibsen's women who are self-sacrificing, always living for somebody else and never for themselves (auntie Juliana in *Hedda*, Mrs Linden in *A Doll's House*), unhappy slaves of married and maternal duty (Elena Alving in *When We Dead Awaken*), gentle, morbidly sensitive, affectionate and weak-willed, like Kaja Fosli (*The Master Builder*), or Mrs Elvsted (*Hedda*), and finally, a woman of a *fin de siècle* type, spiritually-broken, highly-strung, decadent Hedda Gabler.

A whole spectrum of psychological types, a whole gamut of spiritual moods! But we cannot agree with Mr A Veselovsky[9] that 'there is in them *every* shade of life, *every* aspiration, hope and weakness of contemporary woman'. No! There is a big gap in this area with Ibsen.

The reality of the last decades has created a new woman, who stands three times as high not only as the Nora who breaks from her husband as a result of an awakened consciousness of her own dignity, but also as the Nora of the later period, who puts all her efforts into a fervent struggle for women's emancipation.

This new woman raises higher than the question of the position of women from a privileged class the social question of the realisation of a form of social life under which there will be no place not only for the subordination of woman by man, but generally for any subordination of one person to another. Hand in hand with man, this woman — not in the

9. AN Veselovsky, a literary historian. [Note by *Sochineniya* Editors] [Aleksandr Nikolaevich Veselovsky (1838-1906) wrote extensively on Slavic, Byzantine and West European literature, and on folklore of various people, and developed original theories on the origins of art. Editor's note]

old rôle of being an inspiration for her husband, brother or son, but as a comrade in arms, equal to them — fights for the realisation of the best ideals of the present time. Ibsen did not know such a woman.

❖   ❖   ❖

Now we have to consider the mystical cult of Ibsen's symbolism as well as the impudent 'critical', 'scientific-physiological' and other accusations aimed at the great Norwegian, in which Max Nordau[10] has acquired such proficiency.

The history of European social consciousness will never forget those slaps, those truly glorious slaps, dealt by Ibsen to the well-scrubbed and combed bourgeois faces, shining with self-satisfaction. Even if Ibsen does not put forward any ideals, and even if his critique of the present is far from always based on an appropriate point of view, nevertheless, with the hand of a master craftsman, he exposed before us the bourgeois soul, and showed how much inner rottenness there is at the root of this bourgeois decency and honesty. When you look at the inimitable portraits of the bourgeoisie created in the best moments of his creative work, involuntarily a thought enters one's head that if in one or two places the brush had been pressed harder and two or three hardly noticeable strokes added, then this social type of highest realism would have become profound social satire.

Vostochnoye Obozreniye nos 121, 122, 126, 3, 4, 9 June 1901

Leon Trotsky

Two Literary Souls at the Mercy of the Metaphysical Demon[11]

ANXIOUS journals are sounding the alarm; the leading Russian press resounds with appeals to wash the mortal sins of positivism, relativism and realism in the refreshing water of metaphysics. These appeals are all the more urgent since young Russian thought has until now almost entirely escaped metaphysical captivity.

10. The remarks by *doctor* Max Nordau about Ibsen's incorrect description of various illnesses, retain, of course, all their validity — but if only the cobbler would stick to his last... [Note by Trotsky] [Max Nordau (1849-1923) was a German writer. Editor's note]
11. See Berdyaev's book and the preface to it by Struve, and issue no 6 of *Mir Bozhi*. [Note by Trotsky] [A reference to Nikolai Berdyaev's first book *Subiektivizm i individualizm (Subjectivism and Individualism)*, St Petersburg, 1901, an attempt to graft Kantian concepts onto Marxism, to which Pyotr Struve contributed a preface. Editor's note]

We are not forgetting, of course, that we have professional metaphysicians on professorial salaries, unsalaried professional metaphysicians and dilettante metaphysicians, and look on all this as 'in the nature of things', for in a cultured society it is thought proper to have in positions of influence not only 'hypocrites, informers and adulterers', as the satirist put it, but many others, too – including metaphysicians. But whilst we have recognised their right to exist, we have had not the slightest inclination to engage with them, or even to read them.

Metaphysical thought had its humble source on the pages of *Voprosy filosofii* [*Questions of Philosophy*], and poured in great harmless torrents through meetings of philosophical societies; but it proved incapable of setting our hearts racing. Some people even express the somewhat flippant opinion that *Voprosy filosofii* is published precisely so that nobody will read it. The metaphysical works of Chicherin,[12] Kozlov[13] and Vladimir Soloviev[14] are considered very clever, possibly, but are of absolutely no use to anyone, or for anything. This latter circumstance even surrounds them with their own peculiar sort of halo.

Today, this attitude to metaphysical problems on the part of 'outsiders' may appear to be wavering.

Mr Struve[15] insistently calls on the vanguard of Russian thought to create 'metaphysical works'. His echo, Mr Berdyaev,[16] declares a resolute

12. Boris Nikolaevich Chicherin (1828-1903) was a lawyer and philosopher, and professor of public law at Moscow University. In his numerous works he attempted to ground his idea of law on the principle of the freedom and independence of the individual. Chicherin's philosophical views are expounded in the works *Positive Philosophy and the Unity of Science* and *The Fundamentals of Logic and Metaphysics*. In these books, Chicherin insistently polemicises against positivism and Darwinism, from the standpoint of a Hegelianism interpreted through the prism of metaphysics. [Note by *Sochineniya* Editors]
13. Aleksei Aleksandrovich Kozlov (1831-1900) was a spiritualist and professor of philosophy at Kiev University, who recognised genuine reality to exist only beyond the world of animate individual beings, and from this standpoint fought against materialism and positivism.
14. Vladimir Sergeevich Soloviev (1853-1900) was a religious philosopher, poet, publicist and critic. He was the forerunner of the god-seeking movement in the early twentieth century.
15. Pyotr Berngardovich Struve (1870-1944) was an economist, sociologist, historian, philologist and philosopher, as well as a publicist, editor, politician and educator. A prominent Marxist in his youth, then one of the leaders of the Russian Social Democratic Labour Party and author of its first programme, he subsequently became a Legal Marxist. He then shifted to idealism, became a leader of the Constitutional Democrats, and a contributor to *Vekhi*. During the Civil War he was Minister of Foreign Affairs in the government of General Wrangel, and was later one of the intellectual leaders of the moderately conservative elements of the Russian emigration.
16. Nikolai Aleksandrovich Berdyaev is a philosopher of the reactionary and mystical persuasion. In the first half of the 1890s, he drew close to the Marxists, but then turned, in his own words, 'from Marxist pseudo-collectivism, from decadent romantic individualism, to the collectivism of a mystic neo-Christianity'. Berdyaev was one of the

struggle for idealism. *Mir Bozhi*,[17] which has zealously devoted itself to the propagation of realist 'self-education', is now – in the person of these writers – making a determined attempt to free itself from 'historical misunderstanding', and to hoist the banner of idealism, buffeted by the metaphysical winds, to an unassailable height...

It is against this background that anxious journals are sounding the alarm.

But does this phenomenon really merit such earnest attention? We think not. At the present time it is not at all evident that the purely *personal* ideological evolution of Mr Struve is indicative of any phenomenon in the sphere of *social* thought. It is possible that something of the kind may take shape in the future – we do not venture to settle the question categorically one way or the other – but for the time being we can be clear about one thing: Mr Struve's voice gains authority from something quite apart from his as yet unformed 'metaphysical creativity'; likewise, though Mr Berdyaev's 'Struggle for Idealism' proved not to be buried in the metaphysical crypt of *Voprosy filosofii* along with Chicherin's *Suschestvo idealizma* [*The Essence of Idealism*] and Trubetskoi's[18] *Zaschita idealizma* [*In Defence of Idealism*], it is to a considerable degree thanks to Mr Struve's deliberate patronage...

At any rate, our sceptical heart, covered in a stubborn realist hide, has so far been beating not a jot faster in view of the approaching metaphysical 'clouds' (Mr Struve's term). For storm clouds, assisted by God and the laws of nature, shed merely utterly harmless *water*!

But, putting to one side the scale of the phenomenon, its *visible* characteristics, and the degree to which it has been instilled with hopes and fears, it would not be superfluous to say a few words on its general, *innate* socio-psychological nature.

Establishing absolute criteria of truth, justice and beauty – in short, of *the meaning of life* – by means of metaphysics (transcendental and transcendent consciousness) is one of those alluring, seductive and captivat-

contributors to *Problemy idealizma* [*Problems of Idealism*] and the collection *Vekhi* [*Landmarks*]. Berdyaev is now in Paris, where he publishes the journal *Put* [*The Way*], which describes itself as 'the organ of Russian religious thought'. [Note by *Sochineniya* Editors] [Berdyaev (1874-1948) subsequently espoused a form of mystical Christian Socialism. Editor's note]

17. *Mir Bozhi* (*God's World*) was a monthly political and literary review which ran from 1892 until its suppression by the Tsarist censorship in 1906. Amongst other topics, it promoted the views of Legal Marxism.

18. Sergei Nikolaevich Trubetskoi (1862-1905) was professor of philosophy at Moscow University and editor of the journal *Voprosy filosofii i psikhologii* [*Questions of Philosophy and Psychology*]. His most important works are *Metafizika v drevnyei Gretsii* [*Metaphysics in Ancient Greece*] and *Ucheniye o Logosye* [*The Doctrine of Logos*] and his philosophical outlook was very close to that of Vladimir Soloviev.

ing illusions that a generalising mode of thought finds it particularly hard to shed.

The objectively established meaning of life, one that is outside time and space and is universally obligatory, is a grotesquely magnified reflection of the temporal, transient states of socio-historical consciousness.

In this respect, metaphysics is a theology without a god which, in common with mystic thought, transports the earth to the heavens, but by using much cruder devices. Here's two examples. A certain medieval abbot from the monastery of St-Germain-des-Prés talks in his theological poem of a *tournament* between Christ and the Antichrist; his tournament takes the form of a jousting contest; the contestants gallop out to the sound of trumpets and cross lances; the spectators include the Mother of God and other holy women, in the guise of 'ladies'.

The feeble imagination of a German *Kleinbürger* (petit-bourgeois) of the 'good old days' depicts the celestial realm quite differently. He turns heaven into a beautiful church with beautiful music, with chairs for the common folk, and stalls and choirs for the nobility. He fits out the church inside and out with all the magnificence at the disposal of the limited arsenal of the philistine imagination. He conceives the pleasures of heaven as simply a bourgeois dance or a *Kiremes* (name-day festival). (See Schlosser's *Die Geschichte des achtzehnten Jahrhunderts* [*The History of the Eighteenth Century*].)

He thus pictures the heavens as merely an expanded and improved version of his studio, shop, bedroom, council chamber, parish church...

Alas! The same thing is repeated in the case of metaphysical 'heavens'.

The undisciplined psyche 'hypostatises' unstable terrestrial phenomena, and transforms them into absolute *categories*, immutable, in defiance of ever-changing time, never ageing, never flagging at their important posts — supreme guardians of morals, knowledge, the law, etc.

Having projected some image or other of terrestrial relations onto the metaphysical screen, thought assiduously erases all the auxiliary lines that connect the crude terrestrial original to its delicate celestial image, painstakingly removes all temporal and local 'colouring' from the affected copy — in short, covers its tracks and attempts once and for all to fix this 'wiped clean' projection *in saecula saeculorum* (for all time) on the screen, as a celestial map of human life, as an immutable 'Baedeker'[19] of intellectual, moral and aesthetic consciousness.

But — alas! — deep in the depths of social existence, the unceasing, spontaneous work of destructive creation and creative destruction carries on, the outlines of terrestrial affairs and relations are becoming blurred, new social forms are taking shape, and the undisciplined consciousness once again hastens to give a grotesquely magnified projection of the new

19. A popular series of travel guidebooks.

picture of social life, and to this end hurriedly scrapes off the traces of previous outlines from the metaphysical screen.

In proposing to mankind their own systems of truth and of the meaning of life, the individualist moralists of the *realist* school do not erase from their constructs the stamp of their subjective provenance: their systems cannot, therefore, lead anyone into temptation, since they are proclaimed to be, and remain, constructs of this or that *individual* who has attained a certain level of 'mental and moral development'. Such systems are only supported by the *degree* of their creator's moral, intellectual, aesthetic, etc, development; in other words, these systems become obligatory for us if we are at the same 'stage of development' as their authors, that is to say, if we belong to the same socio-historical formation.

In such a case, this or that subjective evaluation, bearing no relation to *science* (or, rather, fitting into it as a naked fact, as a cobble-stone 'fits into' the mineralogical record), may be significant in social and party *practice*.

Mr Berdyaev (like Mr Struve) considers the drawing up of an ethical tariff for the legacy of the ages to be an irrational task, and one that flows from a philistine aspiration to ascribe to the cosmos the biases of one's own 'petty brain'.

But what does he himself do? He performs exactly the same 'philistine' work, except that he declares in advance that his head houses not simply a 'petty brain', but the pure crystal of transcendental consciousness. Such 'diversionary tactics' have the convenient effect of allowing him complete freedom from personal responsibility without in the slightest compromising his ability to do just as he pleases.

He projects his *personal* moral evaluation onto the *impersonal* canvas of 'transcendental ethical consciousness', all the while presenting himself not as an observer of socio-historical decay acting on his own agenda, but as a simple novice in the temple of objective truth; having painstakingly destroyed the scaffolding he used to clamber up to the metaphysical heights, he takes cover with his subjective judgements and assessments behind the screens of 'transcendental consciousness'.

The realist mentality, which is firmly embedded in the cultured Russian, whichever 'generation' he belongs to, will not be reconciled to this sort of naive fiction, and real life will not be made a jot more meaningful by these vain metaphysical contortions, which have arrived on the scene many decades too late...

So then, exactly what sort of metaphysical structure is it that Messrs Struve and Berdyaev are attempting to erect to such a giddy height?

Mr Berdyaev assures us that it will be a magical 'castle in the air', an elegant 'tower' built on stone foundations.

But hold on, is it really a *tower?* Will this 'edifice' not prove to be no more than an old, hole-ridden metaphysical... starling-house, so worthless that even the frivolous starlings have abandoned it, incapable of luring in the wise owl of Minerva?

Vostochnoye Obozreniye, no 189, 25 August 1901

Leon Trotsky

Poetry, the Machine, and the Poetry of the Machine

'LET us try', the late Ruskin[20] proposed to his compatriots, 'to leave at least one corner of our country beautiful, serene and wealthy. We will have neither earthworks nor railways, we will have no witless and senseless objects... When we need to go somewhere, we will go in tranquillity and safety, without risking our lives travelling at 60 miles per hour; when we need to transport something, we will carry it on our backs, or put it on the backs of our animals, or take it in carriages and boats.'

England remained deaf to Ruskin's romantic appeals. Is this to be regretted?

We think not!

Do earthworks and railways really destroy beauty, tranquillity and wealth? Do 'witless and senseless objects' (machines) really represent an evil we need to be saved from?

The answer to these questions can only be a resounding *no*.

Putting to one side the social roots of Ruskin's reactionary romantic delusions, we can see that they are based on a colossal methodological misunderstanding: Ruskin drew no distinction between the technical and the social significance of the machine.

We are not about to deny the dark aspects of the machine's rôle in society. Under modern conditions, they are a hammer in the hands of

---

20. John Ruskin (1819-1900) was a celebrated historian and art theoretician, and creator of an original aesthetic teaching. Ruskin attempted to introduce elements of beauty into mankind's humdrum everyday life, into his work and production. These attempts led Ruskin to renounce machines and to advocate the notion of a free and ennobled labour to which all mankind's spiritual strength would be devoted. Renouncing, from this perspective, the modern industrial order, he called for a return to manual labour, and dreamed of a revival of cottage industries and handicrafts. [Note by *Sochineniya* Editors]

the blind machinery of bourgeois exploitation, which uses this mighty hammer to smash human skulls, spines, ribs and muscles. Yet a hammer is still only a hammer: it may be used to smash a skull, but it may also be used to forge knives to cut birthday cakes at family gatherings...

If we place (today mentally, but tomorrow – in practice) the same 'witless and senseless' machine that provokes thousands of curses in harmonious social conditions, then its truly liberating, socio-technological mission will appear before us in all its grandeur.

We can and must rise up against the modern uses to which the machine is put, but to rise up with Ruskin against the machine *an und für sich* [*per se*] is one of the worst types of reaction.

Nevertheless, is the machine not a 'witless and senseless object', and therefore does not any horse or, even, donkey, renowned for its Homeric stupidity, possess undoubted advantages over it?

In fact, we value the horse and the donkey precisely to the extent that they have no will of their own, and uncomplainingly submit to ours. The donkey, which manifests its 'will' and its 'meaning' – in short, its asinine individuality – in fits of classic stubbornness, does not, rightly, receive any encouragement from its driver, who beats the 'will' out of it with a whip.

If this is the case, we should take the argument to its logical conclusion: try to conjure up a picture of the ideal horse (that is to say, one without 'restiveness' and other equine traits) or the ideal donkey (one not infected with the spirit of contrariness), and you will get... a locomotive. In that case, what right do we have to raise our donkey's hooves threateningly against the locomotive?

Whenever 'intelligent living strength' is contrasted with 'the dead machine', we cannot help but be reminded of the deadly ironic words of one of Russia's most intelligent men, NA Dobrolyubov[21] in *Slavyanskiye dumy* [*Slavonic Meditations*]:

Swiftly goes the steamer, yet it is a dead machine that drives it,
A wooden barge makes slower progress, yet it is towed by an
    intelligent being.

Aha! Nine times out of ten, protests against the 'dead' machine are the other side of the coin of spiritual mourning over the obsolescent 'intelligent being' of a pre-industrial idyll...

But perhaps Ruskin is right in stating that travelling on a real horse at the very least possesses the advantage of safety over the furious gallop of that embodiment of the abstract equine idea, the locomotive?

21. Nikolai Aleksandrovich Dobrolyubov (1836-1861) was a literary critic, journalist and revolutionary democrat. He called for a society based upon democratic industrial-agricultural associations.

Alas! In spite of the fact that the speed of 60 miles per hour Ruskin talks about has been almost doubled by the best modern expresses, 'there is only one death (in England and France) per 45 million passengers; more accidents happen, of course, to pedestrians, and it is therefore more "dangerous" to walk than to travel by train — at least, by English or French trains' (*Russkiye Vyedomosti* [*Russian Gazette*] no 132, *Iz khroniki otkrytii i izobretyenii* [*From the Chronicle of Discoveries and Inventions*]).

Another widely credited notion is the idea that the all-pervasive machine sounds the death knell of poetic creation.

For Ruskin, every object retains its poetic charm until we conceive of it as self-sufficient. As soon as we begin to see it as subject to an alien goal — which is always the case with a machine — it loses its aesthetic charm for us. Once we learn that the leaves on a tree are programmed to absorb carbonic acid and excrete oxygen, we become indifferent to them, seeing them as merely some sort of gasometer: they no longer seem to us to be an artless and beautiful gift of nature, but merely a crude and prosaic machine. Is this convincing? Not in the least!

To tear away the mystic veil, woven from unscientific thought, from some sphere of phenomena and to illuminate these phenomena with the light of scientific realist analysis — does this mean to destroy their poetic charm?

No! Whoever is incapable of supporting the French artist who raised a glass to the disgrace of Newton[22] because that genius had supposedly destroyed the charm of the solar spectrum, through explaining the secret of the magical colour spectrum by breaking down the colourless sunbeam, whoever does not share such a crude mystical point of view will never be imbued with Ruskin's mood as manifested in the above reasoning.

In essence, mysticism still nests in our brain cells, and our souls religiously preserve the spiritual heritage of our remote ancestors who made sacrifices at a stump in the Taiga... Indeed, something precious is torn from our hearts when scientific thought, devoid of all sham sentimentality, expels some 'spirit' from its sanctuary and subjects that sanctuary to the full force of physical and chemical laws.

The machine deals a body-blow to this sort of mind-set: through its combination of levers and inclined planes it achieves results whose causes were before shrouded in alluring mystery. It is accused of destroying aesthetics. In fact, it destroys only aesthetic mysticism. We

22. Isaac Newton (1642-1727) was the supreme scientist of the modern age, one of the inventors of infinitesimal analysis, and the founder of modern theoretical mechanics. His discovery of the law of universal gravity, which laid the foundations for all subsequent development of astronomy, is one of the supreme achievements of scientific thought. Newton's other important discoveries included the breaking down of a sunbeam into the colour spectrum, which laid the basis for a whole range of new scientific disciplines. [Note by *Sochineniya* Editors]

are deeply convinced that the machine, as the symbol and embodiment of the tireless struggle of the human genius to free itself from nature, should become an object of sublime – realist, naturally, not mystical – inspiration!

Take your watch out of your pocket, open up the outer cover and peer at the two hands, whose rhythmic movement, imperceptible to the naked eye, subordinates infinite and elusive time to your consciousness; look at the small 'second' hand, which hurriedly yet measuredly runs through its miniature cycle by finely tuned degrees, constantly breaking up time and turning it into chronological dust.

Turn the watch over and open up the back cover. Look closely at the simple, elegant, noble mechanism, which carries out its task with such accuracy that we use it to check the workings of our heart and lungs.

Can this familiar object really not inspire poetic creation? Is it not the magical crystal of human genius? Is this small machine not associated with the most poetic memories of our lives? Have you not waited in tense anticipation for the moment when the hands reach the figure XII, to proclaim the birth of a new year or a new century? Has your heart not skipped a beat as you watch the hands approaching the time arranged by the woman you love for a rendezvous?

But let us return to the comparison of the horse with the locomotive.

You will remember, of course, that oppressive-looking embodiment of genuine, authentic, machineless labour, striking in its aesthetic power, in the shape of the work-horse.

Put one of these emaciated, downtrodden muzhik beasts, with its protruding belly and loose-hanging flanks, digging its weakened hind legs into the crumbling soil of a mountain up which it must drag a 25 pud weight, alongside a locomotive, 'as powerful as the human will, as audacious and light as hope' (Guiot[23]), that steel incarnation of indefatigable technical thought, that 10 000 pud gleaming gigantic monster gliding smoothly on its metal rails, devouring space with the elegant, measured play of its steel muscles, effortlessly carrying along behind it half a mil-

23. Guiot (1854-1888) was a French philosopher and poet. His most important works are *Morals Without Sanction and Duty*, *Problems of Modern Aesthetics*, and *Lack of Faith in the Future*. Morals, according to Guiot, spring from neither selfish gain nor an abstract consciousness of duty, but from a striving after as full and extensive a development as possible of life. Expanding life in all directions, and expanding intercourse with other human beings, is the foundation of altruism and social relations. The value of art also consists in the fact that it is the creative expansion of life. As far as religion is concerned, on the one hand Guiot understood that no dogmatic religion would be possible in the future, but at the same time he believed that the collapse of all dogmatic forms would lead to the extensive development of individual religious creation, by which he understood the aspiration to grasp the supreme connection between all things that lies beyond the limits of strictly scientific knowledge. [Note by *Sochineniya* Editors]

lion puds of freight;[24] put them side by side and answer the question: which of them has poetry on its side?

No, mankind will not give up the machine – thousands of years of history testify to that fact.

Ever since man first walked upright and armed himself with his first weapon, the stick, his whole life has been a protest against the power of nature. In order to elevate himself above it, vanquish it, and win his freedom, man has saddled man, and, whipping his flanks, has driven him ever forwards, down through the ages.

The whole colossal legacy of practical, theoretical and poetic thought that we possess, and of which we are so justly proud, carries the indelible stamp of the power of man over man in the name of liberation from nature. The whole force of theoretical rebuttal, practical struggle and poetic imprecations that is directed against modern forms of social oppression has sprung from the same source – the power of man over man in the name of emancipation from earthly powers.

The task before us now is to liberate man from man, not to subject him once again to the uncontrolled power of nature.

Lifted up by an infinite series of human waves to the heights of modern social questions and ideals, man, the proud and recalcitrant son of nature, having tasted the satanic dream of subordinating nature to the power of his brain and dragging it along behind him, will not give up the machine, for he can only ascend to the mountain kingdom of freedom on a mighty locomotive, not on a winded, emaciated work-horse.

PS: The Siberian papers have recently run a series of reports on the peasants' superstitiously hostile attitude to 'butter-making' machines, emphasising the peasants' 'stupid prejudices' against this useful machine, and explaining that these prejudices spring from their ignorance. But why, then, has this 'ignorance' (which can hardly be disputed) not led to a 'cult of adoration' of the butter-making machine? Because this machine, as well as its undoubtedly useful technical features, obvious to all, conceals a sort of mysterious social power: as a technical category, the separator separates the butter from the cream; as a social category, the same separator insidiously separates the cream from the hungry mouths of peasant children, and the enterprise's profit from labour. It is this second function of the metallic 'enemy' that the peasant's frightened imagination associates with 'a black book from another land', and other devilry.

Vostochnoye Obozreniye, no 197, 8 September 1901

---

24. The Siberian Railway, of course, does not count. [Note by Trotsky]

Leon Trotsky

On the Novel in General and on *The Three of Them* in Particular

IF we consider the various masterpieces produced in the last few years, we could come to the conclusion that the leisurely, content-rich novel, the novel that reminded one of an old-time journey with hired horses, is finally dead... Firstly, we had the long preparations before the journey: the 'prologue'. Then, a long series of 'parts' and 'chapters', just like a succession of stopovers and days of rest, as when a traveller pauses, warms himself up with a glass of tea and gives his swollen limbs a breather. And, finally, the 'epilogue', the crowning moment of the novel and, at the same time, a quiet refuge for the worn-out traveller...

Should the good old novel catch sight of a short story, a sketch, an essay maybe, or a study... it would contemptuously shake one of its many 'heads' at this literary trifle.[25]

I do not know about the reader, but personally I just do not see any reason why we should grieve for this 'degeneration'. Cast my mind back to the short stories and essays written by Korolenko,[26] Chekov,[27] Gorky,[28] Veresaev, Leonid Andreev[29] – of whom I hope to be able to speak soon – and I just refuse to get distressed about this state of affairs.

Sometimes these little innocent sketches and studies stick like splinters in the readers' consciousness.

The artistic pleasure which can be gained from reading a novel can never be so complete as that given by a short story or an essay, for the novel is simply too wide-ranging. It cannot be contained in one gaze; it cannot be read at one sitting... We approach it in different moods. Sometimes it is impossible to link one impression with another, and the physiognomy of the novel as a whole can only fade away because of this.

But an essay, a short story, is quite different. In this case, we swallow the whole work, which then swells terribly in our consciousness, assimilating all the 'sad memories' of the reader's heart.

25. The Russian word for 'chapter' is the same as 'head'.
26. Vladimir Galaktionovich Korolenko (1853-1921) was a well-known Russian writer of short stories.
27. Anton Pavlovich Chekov (1860-1904) was a major Russian playwright and writer of short stories.
28. Maxim Gorky (Aleksei Maksimovich Peshkov, 1868-1936) was a major radical Russian novelist. He opposed Bolshevism in 1917, emigrated, but returned to the Soviet Union in 1931.
29. Leonid Nikolaevich Andreev (1871-1919) was a well-known Russian novelist.

This reminds me of an extremely 'inhuman' way of hunting wolves. With this method, wolves are lured with a 'whalebone' bent in a circle and then frozen. The unsuspecting wolf, used as it is to eating the carcass of cattle, swallows the bait. Later the ring, after thawing inside the animal's stomach, straightens up and kills the wretched beast.

To be sure, the reader actually survives his ordeal, but he is similar to that wolf in other respects...

He, too, thinks of the large carcass of five-part novels as 'real' food, and rather imprudently swallows the concentrated products of literary art... But he should know better! For those sketches and studies penetrate his consciousness, and straighten out with all their elastic strength, just like the whalebone inside the wolf's stomach, and inflict grievous wounds on the reader's soul...

But there is yet another reason that gives the short 'condensed' story an advantage over the long novel. Artistic pleasure is complete when the writer does not oppress our imagination with a multitude of details or a plethora of factual material. For we, too, have a certain degree of imagination and want a share of the initiative. The artist's task consists in awakening this initiative and giving his reasons for independently creating pictures and images. The reader's fantasy must not be put under petty tutelage.

This is why many viewers find that the impressions given by a painter's preparatory, rapidly-sketched studies make so much stronger an impression than his finished work.

And this is also why a short story, in which the hero is presented at his most 'pathetic' moment in his life, produces in the reader an impression more complete and clear-cut than the novel. In the latter, the hero would be first given birth to, then educated and shaped, exposed to light at the proper moment, and only then made to live through a succession of emotional situations, only to die in the end in one or another form of natural death. In these works, the reader's imagination is invariably guided throughout.

So, is the novel finally dead, then?

No, it is not dead, and writing an obituary would be somewhat premature.

Even when Belinsky[30] was still alive, the novella had already come to the fore. This great critic wrote as early as in 1835 that 'the novel has respectfully moved aside, giving way to the novella'. This correct generalisation did not prevent the novels by Goncharov,[31] Turgenev,[32] Dosto-

---

30. Vissarion Grigoryevich Belinsky (1811-1848) was a revolutionary democrat, and one of Russia's most eminent literary critics.
31. Ivan Aleksandrovich Goncharov (1812-1891) was a well-known Russian novelist.
32. Ivan Sergeevich Turgenev (1818-1883) was a noted Russian novelist, poet and playwright.

evsky,[33] Pisemsky[34] and Tolstoy[35] from seeing the light... And we have no reason to assume that in the foreseeable future literature will renounce those synthetic life scenes that can only find room in the endlessly wide field of a novel.

Life becomes complicated, it becomes richer... And literature is forced not to reject old forms for embodying creativity, but rather to create new ones.

The novel survives as a social frame for all the beauties and horrors of life that look at us in isolated images and scenes in the pages of sketches and essays. So, generally speaking, there is no antagonism — indeed there cannot be — between these two literary genres.

The novel fascinates us for its wide social scope, while the short story achieves the same effect, but with the energy of a psychological blow.

But if the novel is dead as a mandatory form, with all its traditional ritual of chapters, parts, prologues and epilogues, it lives on nevertheless as a modern Illiad, as a poem of Reality.

So, the novel is dead: long live the novel!

One must have iron ribs
and an iron heart
to be able to live in this world, or else
live like everybody else, with neither
thought, nor conscience.

(Gorky, *The Three of Them*, p252)[36]

We have heard that, compared with his more voluminous works, such as *Foma Gordeev*[37] and *The Three of Them*, some feel a certain disappointment in reading Gorky's essays and short stories.

Gorky is not to blame. We cannot expect that during the long process of reading a novel the reader will not experience ebbs and flows in his mood, and find his interest both growing and declining. A novel is not

33. Fyodor Mikhailovich Dostoevsky (1821-1881) was one of Russia's most noted novelists and short story writers.
34. Aleksei Feofilaktovich Pisemsky (1821-1881) was a Russian novelist and the author of *A Thousand Souls* (1858), a broad canvas of Russian life.
35. Lev Nikolaevich Tolstoy (1828-1910) was one of the most noted Russian writers of the nineteenth century. A strong critic of the iniquities of Tsarism, his philosophy was pacifist, and tended to idealise peasant society.
36. All the quotations in this piece are taken from Maxim Gorky, *The Three of Them*, London, 1905.
37. Gorky referred to *Foma Gordeev* as a 'novella'. He said the same about his work *The Three of Them* (in *My Life*). Especially amongst writers, it is the hand that rules supreme, so Gorky defines his short story *Twenty-Six and a Girl* as a 'poem'. However, we hope that the most severe teacher of literature would allow us to call the first two works novels... if only so as, on the whole, to agree to include them in the category of *belles-lettres*. [Note by Trotsky]

an essay, and 400 pages are not the same as 20 pages. However, it can be said that novels give us a wider picture of the daily and social milieu than even the best essay can hope to offer.

We need to speak at length, or alternatively very little, of Gorky's most recent novel. I have chosen to say little about it, for various reasons...

The Three of Them is a drama of vain, uncoordinated efforts, of the hopeless single combat with life for a crust of happiness, for a mouthful of joy...

Here is Ilya Lunev, a hawker, with his strong will, his sober and practical mind... For himself, he asks for a 'crystal-clear' life, a modest but full life, sedate and orderly, for good, 'true' happiness... But alas! Some invisible but powerful hand keeps on pushing him where things are at their worst... 'All my life, I've had to poke my nose into all sorts of abomination...', complains angrily Ilya Lunev. Where and who is that invisible enemy, the thrice-cursed enemy that 'pushes him always into what is dank, dirty and evil in life'? Whereas whenever he is perhaps close to that 'pure' petit-bourgeois happiness, it loses all attraction for him, fades away and becomes the incarnation of boredom, absurdity, and triviality... Vain efforts, the taste for life is lost.

And here is Yakov Filimonov, the dreamy and mystical son of an innkeeper. He too wishes for little: to remain unharmed on the small desert island of his chimerical interests and metaphysical inquiries. The difference between Ilya and Yakov is made splendidly clear in a conversation that we will now quote. Yakov, a dreamer and a man full of feeling for all that surrounds him, sees a mystery, an interrogation, in every single thing. To him, an uncultured young man, just like the great mystic Carlyle,[38] fire seems a miracle. 'Where does the flame come from? It appears suddenly, and disappears as suddenly. Strike a match and it burns. Consequently, it always exists. Does it float about in the air then, invisi-

38. Thomas Carlyle (1795-1881) was a British historian, critic and publicist. He began his literary activity writing enthusiastic articles on classical poetry and German idealistic philosophy. He considered history to be the product of the creative activity of great men. In his pamphlets on social themes, Carlyle launched a harsh attack against bourgeois society and its mechanical culture and utilitarian philosophy, the cult of natural sciences and of political economy. He revolted against the soulless selfishness of the bourgeoisie and the principles of Manchester Liberalism. However, this did not prevent him from bitterly attacking the working class, whom he accused of wanting to seize political power through universal suffrage (cf *Chartism*, 1840). Carlyle rejected the great workers' movement that sought power to liberate itself and all humanity, from the standpoint that: 'In the beginning, God created the world on the basis of equality, not of slavery or domination!' Carlyle's work on Chartism became a source of embarrassment even for his staunchest followers. He called for the creation of a new aristocratic class to be drawn from the upper circles of the bourgeoisie and the intelligentsia, believing that this alone could save Britain from growing social chaos, and recreate a mediaeval-like society based on patriarchal relations. [Note by *Sochineniya* Editors]

ble?' Ilya has a totally different attitude to the question. Rather than facing it, he avoids it. 'Where?', he exclaims with irritability, 'I don't know, and I don't want to know! I know that one must not put one's hand into it, but one may warm oneself near it. That's all.'

'It would be nice to go away somewhere from everything', dreams Yakov. 'To sit down somewhere near a wood, by a river, and think it all over.' But he does not know where to go... the bar of his father's inn separates him from the rest of the world... And so he pines away, this meek, mild dreamer... He who since childhood has been 'doomed to drop out of life'...

The third of 'The Three of Them' is Pavel Grachev, a mechanic with an impetuous, spontaneous, 'sensual' personality. He is not one to ponder on the nature of fire like Yakov, or to set himself clear, practical and day-to-day objectives all life long, like Ilya. He simply wants to live with all his fibres and all his nerves, without 'sober' judgements or metaphysical reflections. To live: that's all. 'I have worked hard my whole life long, since I was 10 years old! Let me live in return', he tells someone with insistence. But it is this 'someone' who does not allow him to live his life. 'He' even forces Pavel to share the woman he loves with drunken merchants... And when the wretched woman attempts to 'free herself', and to that end steals the wallet of the merchant who is carousing with her, that mysterious enemy grabs her with the ever-vigilant hand of justice...

So what is life for 'The Three of Them', for Ilya, Yakov and Pavel? A whirlpool, an evil and disgusting whirlpool 'of pillage, robbery, theft, drink, all sorts of vileness and disorder – our lives consist of nothing but that!'. And there is no way out, no light at the end of the tunnel, no salvation... You cannot get out of this dirty stream: 'You must float down the river with everyone else, and you're soaked by the same water. You must live as is ordained for everyone. There's nowhere to hide.'

'Someone' with his colossal and rough hand deforms these men's bodies, crushes, shakes and distorts their souls, cuts off their desires and finally throws them – just like some unwanted puppies – down some narrow and stinking hole...

'Fate is strangling me...', complains Lunev, 'and it's strangling Pashka, and Yakov, and everybody.'

In that picturesque language that is so abundant with all of Gorky's characters, Ilya sums up the conclusions of his life experience: 'Circumstances surround a man and lead him where they will, just as the police lead a rogue.'

All the horror of the situation of these 'three' and the hundreds of thousands like them, is that they have no chance to come face to face with their mysterious enemy... In their consciousness, the cause of their misfortune is fate, chance and an uncontrollable dark force.

This *social fatalism* is the common bracket into which all Gorky's heroes come to be enclosed, without exception and preceded by a plus or a minus sign; all these people, done-for and unwanted, or simply hurt by life.

'But the enemy who was dealing out injuries... was not to be found – he was invisible.' Once again, Lunev felt that his anger, just as compassion, served no purpose... 'I now feel that nothing is worth anything, even to the devil!', says Ilya, although he immediately acknowledges that he 'can't understand'...

None of the feelings he drew from his life experience are illuminated by any conscious attitude toward reality, so they find no place in social work. They are an instance of blind anger, anger for anger's sake – this is the final outcome...

But it would not be right, reader, to draw from Maxim Gorky's novel any pessimistic conclusions, and to end this article on his work on a dejected note.

There is still gunpowder in the flasks of life... Just look at what view presented itself to Ilya Lunev in the cemetery: 'From under the earth, grass and bushes vigorously forced their way to the light, hiding the sad graves; all the vegetation of the cemetery was full of a tense impulse to grow, expand, to suck in light and air, and to transform the moisture of the rich earth into colour, scent and beauty, to caress the heart and eyes. Life conquers everywhere, and life will conquer all.' Life is an all-shattering destroyer, the universal creator, the universal renewer... Glory to young, all-conquering Life!

Vostochnoye Obozreniye, no 56, 9 March 1902

Leon Trotsky
Culture and the Little White Bull

GENTLEMEN, let us build up culture!... How is it done? You don't know? Neither do I, to tell you the truth... But 'at long last the time has come for us to rid ourselves of this Scythian-ness'!... – as said Shchedrin's[39] General Zubatov around 60 years ago: 'We too must, sooner or later, rise to the level of Europe.'

What an incomparable general he was! People could not understand him, for he was so far ahead of his times... But if he were alive now, he

39. Mikhail Yevgrafovich Saltykov-Shchedrin (pseudonym N Shchedrin, 1826-1889) was considered by many to be the greatest satirist of nineteenth-century Russia. A genuine nihilist, both politically and philosophically, he could find little or nothing worth preserving in the Russian society of the time, although he never set forth his notion of how a just society should be organised.

could justifiably believe that the ideas he sowed have risen a hundred-fold. We could say that all recent Russian political journalism is but a powerful echo of this yearning for 'culture' so deeply felt by the general. For already one year, even longer perhaps, this word has been shouted to us from every newspaper column. 'Culture has a great significance!' 'Culture has an absolute significance!' 'Culture has a religious significance!'

In the name of culture, Mr Struve invites us to give up playing oppositionist spillikins, and to close ranks for a crusade against the forces of the left. Then Professor Kotliarevsky,[40] who obviously does not feel the slightest embarrassment in an atmosphere saturated with fumes of the most elementary truths, has sworn with all the authority of an historian to the great value of culture. Messrs Izgoev[41] and Galich happily complement one another in the struggle for the rights of culture. Were it not for the dirty envy of certain intellectuals, explains Izgoev, Roman cucumbers could long have been growing in our tundra... and Fedor Sologub,[42] if one goes by what people write, has even composed a 'presentation' – exquisitely bad, to be sure, but one which nevertheless clearly shows how ugly lack of culture is, that creature that does not change its underwear, uses its fingers to comb its hair and calls a face a mug, while telling us how attractive Jean the page is, as he is not content with embracing his Jeanne, but wants to embrace her whilst observing all the forms and rituals of culture. *Hélas* – as General Zubatov's wife says – *nous sommes encore si peu habitués de jouir des bienfaits de la civilisation!*...

In our country, a solicitor sank his teeth in the town governor's belly during the party held for his name-day: what good is there in such national originality? In our country, Monsieur Sompolov, under the influence of vodka, dared to treat Madame Simias in an unspeakable manner during a theatrical rehearsal... In our tundra, where Roman cucumber could be growing, because of their hunger the exiles are hunting police inspectors... How can one help but exclaim along with His Excellency: 'It's high time, yes it's high time that we got rid of this Scythian-ness!'

40. Nestor Aleksandrovich Kotliarevsky (1863-1925) was a Russian literary critic and academician of the St Petersburg Academy of Sciences from 1909. He dealt with Russian and Western European romanticism, the Russian 'real novel' and literary works of the Decembrists, also looking at the psychological basis of literary phenomena.
41. Aleksandr Solomonovich Izgoev (Lande, 1872-1935) was a Legal Marxist and later a liberal journalist, Cadet activist and a contributor to *Vekhi*. He was expelled with other intellectuals from the Soviet Union in 1922. He then went to Prague and later Estonia, where he died.
42. Fyodor Kuzmich Sologub (Fyodor Teternikov, 1863-1927) was a symbolist poet, short story writer, novelist and dramatist. His work was considered especially representative of the decadent current within the symbolist movement, but his philosophy was idealist. He remained in the Soviet Union, and was chairman of the Leningrad Union of Writers when he died in 1927.

A worthy yet somewhat aimless yearning for culture once upon a time ruled the heart of Foma Fomich Opiskin,[43] he who became dictator of the village of Stepanchikovo. If you recall, there lived in the master's house a young man called Falaley, a cousin of Sologub's Vanka-Kliuchnik. Falaley, a barbarian from the Black Earth Zone, even remained a barbarian in his dreams, for every night he persistently dreamt of a... little white bull. Foma Fomich lost his temper with Falaley. 'How is it possible that you, you oaf, you dirty pig' – he spoke to Falaley like that – 'how is it that you cannot see even in your dreams something noble, for instance, a garden with ladies and gentlemen drinking tea with jam, and playing cards?' But Falaley clung unmoveably to his fixation, and even with all the great prospects offered by culture being paraded before him, he nevertheless stubbornly lay down on his lice-infested sheepskin, and started dreaming... of his little white bull.

The years went by, and Falaley grew up. The little white bull of his dreams grew with him, and as the laws of nature dictate, turned into a fully grown bull. Finally, the time came when it seemed that Falaley, who always went to sleep with a rope in his hand, would try and throw a lasso around the bull's neck and start to live a great life, so much so that Jean the page could be justified in turning green with envy. Indeed, at that time, everyone thought that culture's main task was to take the bull by its horns. But, alas, the bull simply shook its head and turned away. Falaley sullenly scratched his nose, but his dreams remained the same. And those educated ladies and gentlemen, having sipped the last of their tea with jam in the garden, fell into a state of grave perplexity, and began to ask one another: is it true, then, that it all depends on that steer? Is it perhaps that this little white bull is a sign of some kind? Maybe this is a transcendental bull, so if it shakes its tail, it only does it in a superior mystical sense, beckoning us away to other worlds. Tell us, Falaleyushko, what do you see in your dreams? – asked Merezhkovsky,[44] earnestly. But Falaley, who just around that time must have seen in his dreams the beneficial effects of the law of 9 November,[45] just did not possess enough culture even to tell a pleasant lie. Instead, he enigmatically scratched his nose. 'Your Falaley is an idiot', proclaimed Mr Engelgardt,[46] emerging arms akimbo from under a new gate. We must liquidate once

43. A character in Dostoevsky's *Selo Stepanchikovo i Ego Obitateli*.
44. Dmitri Sergeevich Merezhkovsky (1865-1941) was a Russian poet, novelist and political thinker.
45. A reference to the decree of 9 November 1906, the 'Stolypin reform', a programme of land reform formulated by the Russian Prime Minister Pyotr Stolypin which aimed at overcoming peasant discontent and agrarian backwardness through the creation of a class of prosperous, land-owning peasants, and the gradual replacement of the peasant commune by general land ownership.
46. Aleksandr Nikolaevich Engelgardt (1832-1893) was a Russian scientist and writer, and represented the liberal wing of Populism.

and for all such political delirium – states Izgoev: Falaley's salvation lies in culture!

Perhaps the worst thing in a reactionary epoch is the stupidity that spreads in the social consciousness. When the curve of historical development rises, social thinking becomes more probing, more daring, more intelligent. It learns to discern immediately the essential from the superfluous and to assess with just one look the real proportions of reality. It immediately understands facts and links them with the thread of generalisations. It is true that it sometimes breaks out into so-called 'extremes', claiming for example that without parliamentary guarantees one has a high percentage of difficult births, or that without compulsory expropriation quinine loses its medicinal properties. But, all in all, it is right even in its extremes.

It is when the political curve turns down, however, that within social thinking stupidity begins to prevail. It might well be true that, as echoes of the wave of events, there survive within it some generalisations: 'without effective guarantees...', 'the ways that led to Tsushima...', and so on. But the intrinsic content of these statements has vanished, and the precious talent of political generalisation has disappeared without trace. Each problem stands by itself, like a stump in a chopped-down wood. So, stupidity becomes insolence and, showing its rotten teeth, derides any attempt at serious generalisation.

Feeling ground under its feet, stupidity starts to do its stuff. Firstly, it energetically deals with 'the problem of sex'. It thrusts its paws into physiology, aesthetics and psychopathology, it turns everything inside out, and, after spreading its stench, stands aside and waits. It throws itself into foreign policy and gives Stakhovich[47] and Maklakov[48] a mandate to save Serbia. It turns its attention to the woman question, and decrees that man, that beast, should be bridled. It makes a mess of everything. However, it does not lose faith in itself, and even presents the world with its complete programme: *Russia needs culture*. So a unanimity without thought prevails. The *Torgovo-promyshlennaia Gazeta* [*Trade and Industry Gazette*] quotes Struve, Galich quotes 'real' Marxism. Izgoev opts for *Russkaia Starina*,[49] Merezhkovsky for the devil... and *Rossiia*[50] for its conscience. But they all call for one thing: culture.

47. MA Stakhovich was a moderate Tsarist reformer, and leader of the Octobrists in the Duma.
48. Nikolai Andreevich Maklakov (1871-1918) was a member of the Union of Russian People, with links with the Black Hundreds. He held important posts under the Tsar, and had left-wingers arrested in 1914. He was arrested under the Provisional Government, and was shot by the Bolsheviks as a White Guard.
49. *Russkaia Starina* (*Russian Antiquities*) was a monthly journal of historical studies that ran from 1870 to 1918.
50. *Rossiia* (*Russia*) was a liberal daily paper that ran from 1899 until its suppression by the Tsarist censorship in 1902.

At first, one could be justified in believing that social thinking, tired of its own fragmentation, has at last found its life-saving generalisation, its very own formula for action. But this would be false. 'Culture' as a slogan – what is it if not pompous emptiness into which anything can be dumped, and from which nothing can be obtained. Yet is this empty formula not a symptom? If hypocrisy is the tribute that vice pays to virtue, is this call for 'culture' not the tribute that stupidity pays to the re-emerging need for generalisation? This is a question that we have yet to make up our minds to answer in the affirmative.

Kievskaia Mysl, 29 January 1909

Paul Flewers

Vekhi and the Retreat from Reason

THE appearance of *Vekhi* (*Landmarks*) in March 1909 caused a great stir in Russian intellectual circles. This journal, comprised of essays by seven former radicals, was seen as a sharp attack upon the whole tradition of the Russian intelligentsia, and provoked a wave of angry responses from Socialists and liberals alike. Who were the contributors to *Vekhi*? What did they represent? What were the intellectual processes that lay behind its appearance? And how significant was the whole episode for the Russian intelligentsia and for the course of Russian history?

The Rise of Idealism Within the Intelligentsia

The bulk of the Russian intelligentsia at the end of the nineteenth century adhered to a materialist or rationalist philosophical orientation, and thus rejected religion. Moulded, as Leonard Schapiro put it, by the ideas of Chernyshevsky, Pisarev and Mikhailovsky, and later by Marx and Engels, the Russian intelligentsia 'believed passionately in progress, in utilitarianism, in the perfectibility of human society – if the right formula could be found'.[51] Despite the overwhelming adherence to materialism, there was, nonetheless, an idealist wing within the intelligentsia, which was comprised of a number of religious and mystical tendencies. This wing was augmented in the first few years of the twentieth century by the shift of some intellectuals from the materialist outlook of the Russian Marxist movement to an overtly idealist orientation.

Seven members of this trend, all prominent intellectual figures, were

51. L Schapiro, 'The *Vekhi* Group and the Mystique of Revolution', *Slavonic and East European Review*, Volume 35, no 82, December 1955, p56.

to become the contributors to *Vekhi*. Sergei Bulgakov and Bogdan Kistyakovsky were professors, Pyotr Struve had been a leading member of the Russian Social Democratic Labour Party and in 1898 had written its programme, Semyon Frank and Nikolai Berdyaev were literary critics, Mikhail Gershenzon was an historian and editor, and Aleksandr Izgoev was a journalist. They were all born within a short time of each other (1869-77), they were all Marxists in the last decade of the nineteenth century, and, often through a neo-Kantian transition, came to reject it at the turn of the century, and, with the exception of Izgoev, they all adopted a religious outlook, with Bulgakov actually becoming an Orthodox priest.

Towards the end of the nineteenth century, a major debate took place in the Marxian movement. The main protagonist was Eduard Bernstein, a leading member of the prestigious German Social Democratic Party, who considered that capitalism had changed fundamentally since Marx's days, and had overcome its tendencies towards crisis, and that an equalisation of wealth was occurring. Socialism was essentially an ethical question, rather than an historical necessity caused by the contradictory nature of capitalist development. Struve became an ardent supporter of revisionism in Russia, where it was often known as Legal Marxism. He took part in the debate around revisionism within the SPD, and, according to Andrzej Walicki, his critique of Marx was 'much more radical' than Bernstein's, and he 'insisted that Socialism was not a "negation" of capitalism, but rather the inevitable outcome of the natural development of capitalism itself'.[52]

Orthodox Marxists were very critical of the revisionists, not least in Russia. Lenin accused them of 'declaring the idea of the social revolution and of the dictatorship of the proletariat to be absurd... reducing the working-class movement and the class struggle to narrow trade unionism and to a "realistic" struggle for petty gradual reforms', and wishing 'to convert the nascent working-class movement into an appendage of the liberals'.[53] Plekhanov said that the critics of Marxism had 'no need' of the proletarian revolutionary Marx, but '*only* that Marx who... declared he was ready to support the bourgeoisie inasmuch as it was revolutionary in its struggle against the absolute monarchy'.[54] These were harsh but not unfair descriptions.

According to Christian Gneuss, revisionism in Russia became a powerful force within the social democratic movement, and 'for a time revisionism gained the upper hand among the Petersburg revolutionary intelligentsia'.[55] Walicki says that 'Legal Marxism was the first pro-capitalist

52. A Walicki, *A History of Russian Thought*, Oxford, 1980, p439.
53. VI Lenin, 'What Is To Be Done?', *Collected Works*, Volume 5, Moscow, 1977, pp362-3.
54. GV Plekhanov, 'Karl Marx', *Selected Philosophical Works*, Volume 2, Moscow, 1976, p676.
55. C Gneuss, 'The Precursor: Eduard Bernstein', in L Labedz (ed), *Revisionism*, Plainview,

ideology that appealed to the Russian intelligentsia'.[56] Gneuss says that the growth of revisionism in Russia was not so much based upon the perceived disparity between Marx's prognoses and social reality, but upon 'the doubts entertained by many Russian intellectuals, Marxists until then, in the philosophical foundations of Marxism'.[57] Such was the extent of these doubts that Struve and other revisionists attempted to graft Kantian philosophical concepts onto those of Marxism. This was of great consequence. Plekhanov wrote that:

'Kant's transcendental idealism, according to which the external world receives its laws from Reason instead of Reason receiving them from the external world, is closely akin to the theological concept that the world's laws were dictated to it by divine Reason. *Idealism does not establish the unity of thinking and being,* nor can it do so; *it tears that unity asunder.*'[58]

This attempt to merge Kantian and Marxian philosophical concepts rapidly and logically led the revisionists to abandon materialism altogether, and to adopt an outright idealist outlook.

The driving force behind Berdyaev's philosophical evolution away from Marxism to the religious viewpoint to which he adhered for the rest of his life, was his growing feeling that the Marxist movement did not take into account the question of the individual. Looking back years later, he said:

'But I saw with grief that in that camp also there was no reverence for the dignity of personality, and the liberation of the people was too often associated with the enslavement of man and his conscience. At a very early stage I saw the results of this process. The revolutionaries had no love for freedom of the spirit; they denied the rights of human creativeness.'[59]

The revisionists moved rapidly away from the Marxian movement. They soon aligned themselves with the liberals in and around the zemstvo movement. Their contributions to the volume of philosophical studies, *Problems of Idealism*, showed that whilst they were still interested in the plight of the Russian masses, their concern was now based upon a quite different criterion. Bulgakov said that social improvements were to be demanded not on the basis of the class struggle, but on the grounds of

1974, pp39-40.
56. Walicki, op cit, p439.
57. Gneuss, op cit, p39.
58. GV Plekhanov, 'Fundamental Problems of Marxism', *Selected Philosophical Works*, Volume 3, Moscow, 1976, p125.
59. Cited in MA Vallon, *An Apostle of Freedom: Life and Teaching of Nicholas Berdyaev*, New York, 1960, p64.

'the absolute order of moral law, the command of God'.[60] Jeffrey Brooks considers that 'the rejection of materialism and the establishment of a purely idealistic justification for human action marked a decisive step away from political action'.[61]

As social tensions in Russia intensified in the early years of the twentieth century, and the masses were entering into increasingly sharp confrontations with the autocracy, which were to culminate in the revolution of 1905, the idealists were moving further away from the concept of practical political activity, even though Struve had helped form and had become a leader of the Cadet Party, which most of the others joined as well.

Struve and Frank were outspoken in their hostility to the revolutionary upheavals in 1905. Berdyaev, who had initially welcomed the revolution, recoiled at the violence, which he denounced as 'an ocean of barbarism and savagery'.[62] In November 1905, as the revolution was in full swing, Frank and Struve wrote in their journal *Polar Star*.

'In the consciousness of humanity are present a number of eternal ideals: truth, goodness, beauty, holiness, which move it towards scientific, artistic, moral and religious creation. The fruits of this creativity, all the spiritual acquisitions which are replacing one another in the work of generations, make up the living ambience of conscious being, the gradual embodiment of an absolute ideal in the collective life of humanity.'[63]

This marked a further step away from their old positions. On the theoretical side, they were now promoting pure idealism. Human consciousness was no longer predicated upon social activity. Instead, human activity was based upon eternal ideals that were immanent in each human being. Along with this, they were starting to develop an élitist stance. The experience of the revolution was eroding their interest in the plight of the masses, and they were moving away from any concept of popular culture.[64] They were by now considering that a Western European-style parliamentary democracy would be the most satisfactory form of society in which the relationship between the individual and society would be guaranteed. However, as Brooks says:

60. Cited in J Brooks, '*Vekhi* and the *Vekhi* Dispute', *Survey*, Volume 19, no 1/86, Winter 1973, p23.
61. Op cit.
62. Cited in op cit, p35.
63. Cited in op cit, p24.
64. Brooks says that the expansion of the Russian economy was leading to an ever larger intelligentsia, with the employment of more teachers, technicians and agronomists, and this 'could easily be felt as a threat to the hegemony of highly cultivated intellectuals of the *Vekhi* type' (op cit, p36).

'They felt they had found a compromise between the individual and society, freedom and order, but their theory was impracticable in the actual political environment of Russia. Even a liberal struggle to establish a balance of freedom and order in the future was certain to threaten order in the present. By placing absolute value on the activities of an élite group, the creators of culture, Struve and Frank had outlined a rationale for a complete rejection of their earlier commitment to the interests of the masses of the people.'[65]

Vekhi: A Conspectus and Critique

Vekhi appeared in March 1909. The articles which comprised the book were a sustained and intemperate polemic against the Russian intelligentsia. It was clearly provoked by the activities of the intellectuals in the revolution of 1905, and by the failure of the revolution to gain any real social improvements. Considering that the journal was not a joint effort, and that the articles were written independently and without any consultation amongst the contributors, *Vekhi* presents a cohesive entity, with only minor differences existing between one view and another.

Berdyaev looked at the historical experiences which had shaped the outlook of the intelligentsia:

'The Russian intelligentsia has been what Russian history has made it. The sins of our morbid history, of our historical system of government, and of eternal reaction, are reflected in its psychological make-up. An antiquated despotism has distorted the intelligentsia's soul, enslaving it internally as well as externally by negatively determining all of its values.'[66]

Nevertheless, the intelligentsia only had itself to blame, as it 'itself selected the path of the worship of man'.[67] This latter concept was to run through *Vekhi* as a governing principle.

By the time *Vekhi* was published, little appeared to remain of the contributors' former interest in the solution of the terrible conditions of life endured by the Russian masses. In fact, they were bitterly hostile to the intelligentsia *precisely because* the intellectuals proclaimed the amelioration of those conditions as their primary task, indeed, as their vocation. Frank said:

'The symbol of the Russian intelligent's faith is the *people's welfare*, the satisfaction of the "majority's" needs. For him, service to this goal is

65. Op cit, p26.
66. N Berdyaev, 'Philosophic Truth and the Moral Truth of the Intelligentsia', in B Shagrin (ed), *Landmarks: A Collection of Essays on the Russian Intelligentsia 1909*, New York, 1977, p22.
67. Op cit.

man's highest and, generally speaking, sole obligation... Life [for the in-telligentsia] has no objective or intrinsic meaning whatsoever; the sole good in it is material security and the satisfaction of subjective require-ments. Therefore man is obligated to dedicate all his powers to improv-ing the lot of the majority.'[68]

The problem with the intellectuals, he continued, is that they have no principles or absolute values, nor do they have any criteria other than 'the delimitation of people, actions and conditions as good and bad'. They have no concept of good and evil. Worst of all, they believe that their goal, the 'people's happiness', 'can be realised... in an absolute and eternal form'. But as nothing can be done for the masses in the here and now, 'there is no genuine concern for them'. But their oppressors can be hit: the intellectuals' 'great love for mankind of the future gives birth to a great hatred for people' in the present.[69] So, in reality, the intellectuals do not really care for the welfare of the masses, all they are really interested in is persecuting those whom they consider as 'bad', the autocracy.

Bulgakov attacked the radical intellectuals on three fronts. Firstly, for him, the atheism of the Russian intelligentsia was 'hardly a conscious rejec-tion' of religion, but was 'taken on faith', and had therefore adopted 'the characteristics of a naive religious belief, only inverted'. The problem was that the Russian intelligentsia never went any further than a 'superficial assimilation' of Western ideas, and, moreover, had 'adopted them along with the most extreme and shrill forms of the Enlightenment'.[70]

Secondly, the intelligentsia was guilty of chronic self-worship. It was hysterical in its belief that only it could save Russia. The necessity to strive for maximum social demands led to 'self-hypnosis' and 'ideological mania', which themselves led to the ascendancy of 'insane tendencies' and 'heroic self-affirmation'. Moreover: 'There is a little Napoleon in every maximalist, be he Socialist or Anarchist. Amorality... is the necessary consequence of self-worship, here the danger of corruption awaits him, and ruin is inevitable.'[71]

Thirdly, the intelligentsia completely underestimated the question of the individual: 'Extremely unpopular amongst the intelligentsia are the concepts of *personal* morality, *personal* self-improvement, and the devel-opment of the *individual*... The intelligentsia refuses to admit that the individual possesses a vital creative energy...'[72]

68. S Frank, 'The Ethic of Nihilism: A Characterisation of the Russian Intelligentsia's Moral Outlook', in Shagrin, op cit, pp162-3.
69. Op cit, pp158, 168, 170.
70. S Bulgakov, 'Heroism and Asceticism: Reflections on the Religious Nature of the Russian Intelligentsia', in Shagrin, op cit, pp26, 29-30, 33.
71. Op cit, pp37, 38, 42.
72. Op cit, p44.

Berdyaev's attack upon the intelligentsia descended into clerical obscurantism. The 'compassion and pity' of the populists for the peasantry and of the Marxists for the proletariat had 'turned into the worship of man and the people'. It was a 'false love' because 'it wasn't founded on genuine respect for man as an equal and kindred soul through One Father'.[73] This was merely asserted, and Berdyaev did not explain what exactly he meant by it. He then said that the intelligentsia's 'love for an equalising justice, for the social good, and for the popular welfare paralysed its love of truth', and 'it demanded that truth become an instrument of social revolution, of popular welfare and of human happiness'.[74] Berdyaev's quest for the truth now took precedence over the welfare of the masses, although he maintained a loud silence over what constituted the truth, or by whose criterion the truth could be established. Nor, for all his talk of the truth, was he above getting the facts severely wrong.[75]

Struve provided the most outspoken contribution on the political issues raised by the revolution of 1905. For a start, he wrote off all attempts at rebellion or revolt as worthless. The Pugachev revolt merely resulted in the peasantry having 'aggravated their own enslavement', and the republic emerging from the French Revolution 'seemed to appear only for the purpose of ceding its place to a new monarchy'.[76]

He presented a sharp attack upon the rôle of the Russian intellectuals in 1905, and he considered that the offer by the Tsar of a limited constitution on 17 October 1905 should have 'formally concluded' the revolution. Instead, the intelligentsia 'imagined itself to be the master of the historical stage', and went on the offensive. In effect, the intellectuals ruined what chance there was of a satisfactory conclusion of the whole affair. Ruled by a 'renegade ideology and mentality', the intelligentsia talked of finishing off the old regime:

'Such pronouncements were being made before the national representative assembly had even been convened, when the actual mood of the nation as a whole, and, what is most important, its readiness for political life, its political endurance, was not yet known to anyone. No one had

73. N Berdyaev, 'Philosophic Truth and the Moral Truth of the Intelligentsia', in Shagrin, op cit, p10.
74. Op cit.
75. Berdyaev claimed that the Russian social democrats believed in 'the possibility of achieving this aim [Socialism] in Russia even sooner than in the West' (op cit, p14). He produced no evidence to prove this, which is not surprising as at that time only the theoretically and politically isolated Trotsky considered that the seizure of power by the working class was possible, and even then that the survival of any workers' regime was predicated upon successful revolutions in Western Europe. Other Russian social democrats, Lenin included, hoped that revolutionary activity in 1905 would lead to a democratic republic.
76. P Struve, 'The Intelligentsia and Revolution', in Shagrin, op cit, pp139, 147.

ever before called for such extensive political and social changes with such frivolity as our revolutionary parties and their organisations did during the "days of freedom".'[77]

Struve said that the intelligentsia made a 'moral mistake' in radicalising the discontented masses, and considered that: 'At the base of this lay the conception that a society's "progress" can be, rather than the fruit of man's perfection, winnings won from the game of historical chance by appealing to popular unrest.'[78] Struve had certainly travelled a long way from when he wrote the RSDLP's programme in 1898.

Struve was not the only contributor to *Vekhi* who betrayed a tangible contempt for the masses. Gershenzon ended up siding with the government, and, in a passage that would rapidly gain notoriety, called upon it to defend him and his colleagues against the masses:

'This is the way we are; not only can we not dream about fusing with the people, but we must fear them worse than any punishment by the government, and we must bless that authority which alone with its bayonets and prisons manages to protect us from the popular fury.'[79]

Throughout *Vekhi* there is a yawning gap. For all their bemoaning the intelligentsia's lack of absolute values and principles, in many places it is extremely difficult to ascertain just what the contributors really mean. Many of the appeals to absolute ideals are so abstract that they could mean practically anything the reader wishes. Struve did not explain what he meant by his call for the intellectuals to educate themselves and the masses in politics. Nor did Berdyaev explain what he meant by his call for 'a new consensus... on the basis of a synthesis of knowledge and faith', and for 'an organic union of theory and practice, of moral truth as truth and moral truth as justice'.[80]

77. Op cit, pp146-7. Moreover, 'the intelligentsia introduced into this struggle a virulent fanaticism, a murderous logic of conclusions and constructs; without a hint of a religious idea' (op cit, p148). Gershenzon, on the other hand, did not see the intelligentsia as such an influential force. He considered that the intelligentsia had historically been torn away from the people, and this had 'doomed the intelligentsia to total impotence before the authority that was opposing it' (M Gershenzon, 'Creative Self-Cognition', in Shagrin, op cit, p72).

78. Struve, op cit, p150.

79. Gershenzon, op cit, p80. He was obliged to qualify this intemperate outburst, but the damage was done. As Plekhanov said on another occasion: 'I realised more and more the usefulness of the old and tested rule that any writer should unswervingly observe, namely, that one should first carefully peruse the proofs of one's articles and only *then send them to the printers*, since corrections made *after publication of an article* rarely help matters.' (GV Plekhanov, 'What Should We Thank Him For?', *Selected Philosophical Works*, Volume 2, op cit, pp344-5)

80. Berdyaev, op cit, p21.

If the mystical aspects of the contributions are excised, we are left with the following. Firstly, the intelligentsia is irresponsible because it is atheistic and self-worshipping; secondly, the well-being of humanity is unobtainable; thirdly, the quest for their well-being merely leads to destruction; fourthly, the masses are incapable of sensible political activity; and fifthly, the intelligentsia should not encourage the masses to become involved in politics. The course recommended by the majority of *Vekhi*'s contributors is simple: improve oneself through the adoption of a religious belief. Bulgakov is emphatic with his call for intellectuals to substitute faith for reason:

'Not competing with Providence and not identifying, consequently, his own or anyone else's individual effort with the fate of history and mankind, the Christian hero or ascetic... sees his own activities primarily as the fulfilment of his duty to God, as a Divine commandment directed toward him. He is obligated to fulfil it with absolute thoroughness, and is equally obligated to develop all possible energy and selflessness toward seeking out what is that comprises his duty and obligation.'[81]

So, in what appears to be a religious version of a caricature of the duties of a Marxian party member, the intellectuals were advised to throw themselves into their duty, whatever it may be, and, in the process of doing it, try to discover just what that duty is. At least with the intelligentsia's aims of satisfying the needs of the masses, an intellectual knew from the start what the task was, and why he or she had taken it on in the first place.

Only Struve gave a more practical solution. He called on the intelligentsia to renounce its 'dissociation' from the state. Economic development, he claimed, would enable it to 'reconcile itself to the state' and it would then 'organically and spontaneously enter into the existing social structure'.[82] This was the only practical solution for the problem of the intelligentsia that was presented in *Vekhi*, the only one rooted in material conditions.[83]

Responses to *Vekhi*

The publication of *Vekhi* caused a veritable storm of activity amongst the intelligentsia. The first edition, which appeared in March 1909, was soon

81. Bulgakov, op cit, p48.
82. Struve, op cit, p152.
83. Although the contributors to *Vekhi* were hostile to Bolshevism, only Struve took an active part in the struggle against it, and he became a leading member of Wrangel's White administration during the Civil War. Berdyaev would have nothing to do with anti-Bolshevik forces, which he considered to be no better than the Bolsheviks. Most of the contributors were in exile by the mid-1920s.

sold out, and further editions appeared in May, July and September 1909, and in early 1910. Altogether, around 23 000 copies were printed.[84] Meetings to discuss it took place all over Russia for a year after its first appearance. Nikolai Poltoratzky says that at a 'most conservative estimate', between 250 and 300 articles concerning *Vekhi* appeared in 1909 and 1910.[85] Three books consisting entirely of criticisms of *Vekhi* were published, one by left-wing liberals and Mensheviks, another by Socialist Revolutionaries, and a third by Cadets, and another three books challenged many of the ideas expressed in it. *Vekhi* was subjected to a barrage of condemnation. Very few people amongst the intelligentsia were in favour of it. Only the far right was happy to see former radicals turning upon their erstwhile colleagues.[86]

The Russian liberals were very hostile to the collection. One of the Cadets' journals pointed to what they saw as its main weakness:

'Where is there any battle of ideas here, when they proclaim that we are moral lepers? Is it appropriate to talk of a battle of ideas when they preach to us humility, repentance and renunciation of our errors? This is more in the nature of a sermon, but would it not be better to leave that sort of thing to the church?'[87]

The Cadet leader Milyukov considered that *Vekhi* was providing 'the ideological slogan of all reaction'.[88] The Menshevik leader Martov considered that *Vekhi* was just the latest in a series of liberal journals that were attempting 'to snap the threads traditionally joining it [liberalism] with revolutionary and Socialist ideologies', and promoting ideas 'appropriate for a *ruling* class, or more precisely a class which tomorrow must become the ruling one':

'Liberalism is attempting to become on principle monarchist, nationalist and anti-democratic in its political conceptions, counter-revolutionary in its legal views, strictly individualistic in the sphere of economics, and national-soil in its attitude to the state and the church.'[89]

In December 1909 Lenin considered *Vekhi* to be an 'encyclopaedia of lib-

84. C Read, *Religion, Revolution and the Russian Intelligentsia 1900-1912*, Basingstoke, 1979, p7.
85. N Poltoratzky, 'The *Vekhi* Debate and the Significance of *Vekhi*', *Canadian Slavonic Papers*, Volume 9, no 1, Spring 1967, p92.
86. Schapiro, op cit, p66. Richard Pipes, however, says that reactionaries rejected *Vekhi* because three of its contributors were from a Jewish background (R Pipes, *Struve: Liberal on the Right, 1905-1944*, Cambridge, 1980, p112).
87. Cited in B Kagarlitsky, *The Thinking Reed*, London, 1989, p33.
88. Cited in Brooks, op cit, p45.
89. Cited in Read, op cit, p150.

eral renegacy', and declared: '*Vekhi* is a most significant landmark on the road of Russian Cadetism and Russian liberalism in general towards a *complete break* with the Russian liberation movement, with all its main aims and fundamental traditions.'[90] Lenin considered that the liberals sympathised with the movement for democracy so long as it remained small and 'did not set in motion the real masses', as this enabled 'the upper section of the liberal bourgeoisie to climb a little nearer to power'. But the liberals turned their back upon democracy 'when it drew in the masses, who began to realise their *own* aims and uphold their *own* interests'. Moreover, he considered that *Vekhi* was worthwhile because it revealed 'the whole spirit of the *real* policy of the Russian liberals and of the Russian Cadets'. He considered the Cadets' disavowal of *Vekhi* to be a fraud.[91]

Both Lenin and Martov were being rather unfair, as the ideas expressed in *Vekhi* were rejected by the liberals as well as by the left. Brooks says that by conflating *Vekhi* with the liberals, Lenin was attempting 'to tar those social democrats who wanted to join with liberals in a united front'.[92] In the political downturn and confusion in the wake of the defeat of the revolution, Lenin was trying to prevent the Social Democrats from making concessions to the liberals, and to ensure that the former retained their political independence.

According to Christopher Read, who is sympathetic to the *Vekhi* project, or at least to its political consequences, by their refusal to address in any serious way the criticisms that it made of them, the intellectuals merely proved the validity of the collection:

'Only a handful of commentators seemed to understand the issues *Vekhi* raised. Its hopes that a creative self-assessment might be started were cruelly dashed beneath the waves of self-congratulation and complacency which it revealed in the intelligentsia. Though there was considerable disagreement as to what the intelligentsia tradition meant and what values the intelligentsia in fact stood for, the participants did not hesitate to defend the fundamental revolutionary orientation of the intelligentsia, and to scorn the idea that Christianity or a religious sensibility was in any way necessary.'[93]

To be fair, however, both the tone of *Vekhi* and the manner in which it stigmatised the entire intelligentsia were guaranteed to provoke primarily an angry response, and most intellectuals would be unable to find a point of contact with its mystical and obscurantist ap-

90. VI Lenin, 'Concerning *Vekhi*', *Collected Works*, Volume 16, Moscow, 1977, p124.
91. Op cit, pp126, 130.
92. Brooks, op cit, p42.
93. Read, op cit, p151.

proach, as any discussion between idealist and rationalist viewpoints is extremely difficult. [94]

Nonetheless, *Vekhi* clearly had touched a raw nerve. That such a generally low grade polemic could provoke such a furore shows that beneath their almost unanimous dismissal of the questions that it raised, the liberals and Socialists alike were experiencing a severe crisis of confidence, as the Tsarist regime had not only survived the revolution, but had managed to consolidate itself and its hold over Russian society.

Problems of Russian Marxism

Some of the remarks made about the radicals, both in *Vekhi* and in other works by its contributors, must be taken seriously. In this respect, it is worth looking at criticisms made of Russian Marxism, not from a liberal or conservative approach, which would of necessity be hostile to its aims and methods, but from those on the Marxian left itself.

One of the major factors behind Berdyaev's break from Marxism was that its Russian protagonists, as he later put it: '... adopted primarily not the determinist, evolutionary scientific side of Marxism, but its messianic myth-creating religious side, which gave scope to the stimulation of revolutionary will, and assigned a foremost place to the proletariat's revolutionary struggle as controlled by an organised minority, which was inspired by the conscious proletariat [sic] idea.'[95]

Boris Kagarlitsky, a present-day Russian Marxist, says that whilst Berdyaev's description of Bolshevism did not apply to Lenin, Trotsky, Sverdlov and Bukharin, 'it is fully applicable to the rank and file Bolsheviks who put the party line into practice', and that even with Bukharin

94 Trotsky recognised that there could be no reconciliation between idealism and rationalism. He also recognised that there was a causal connection between the *Vekhi* contributors' rejection of the materialist concept that morality is socially determined and their shift into idealism and, in some cases, clerical obscurantism. Many years later, when polemicising against radicals who were attempting to base their politics upon some form of eternal moral principles, he wrote: 'Petty secular priests speak about eternal moral truths without naming their original source. However, we are justified in concluding: since these truths are eternal, they should have existed not only before the appearance of half-monkey, half-man upon the earth but before the evolution of the solar system. Whence then did they arise? The theory of eternal truths can in nowise survive without God... Heaven remains the only fortified position for military operations against dialectical materialism... At the end of the last century in Russia there arose a whole school of "Marxists" (Struve, Berdyaev, Bulgakov and others) who wished to supplement the teachings of Marx with a self-sufficient, that is, supra-class moral principle. These people began, of course, with Kant and the categorical imperative. But how did they end? Struve is now a retired minister of the Crimean Baron Wrangel, and a faithful son of the church; Bulgakov is an orthodox priest; Berdyaev expounds the Apocalypse in sundry languages.' (LD Trotsky, *Their Morals and Ours*, London, 1974, p8)

95. Cited in Kagarlitsky, op cit, p36.

'Marxist determinism bears a marked resemblance to religious fatalism'. He also says that the earlier criticisms of Berdyaev and his colleagues of Russian Social Democracy 'cannot be dismissed as lacking foundation', particularly 'their vulgar materialism... their scorning of spiritual values... [and] their insufficient interest in the individual'.[96]

Isaac Deutscher gave a graphic description of the crude conception of Marxism that was held by many of the Bolshevik activists, the committee men, and which were applicable to those in other Marxian organisations:

'They accepted certain basic formulas of Marxist philosophy, handed down to them by popularisers of the doctrine, as a matter of intellectual and political convenience. These formulas seemed to offer wonderful clues to the most complex problems – and nothing can be as reassuring to the half-educated as the possession of such clues. The semi-intelligentsia from whom Socialism recruited some of its middle cadres enjoyed Marxism as a mental labour-saving device, easy to handle and fabulously effective.'[97]

There were problems with the theoretical works of the leading Russian Marxists at that time. It is not surprising that many intellectuals accused Marxism of misunderstanding the question of the individual when Plekhanov's well known work on that subject is taken into consideration.[98] The underlying philosophical basis of Lenin's major attack upon idealism, *Materialism and Empiriocriticism*, was criticised by later Marxists. For instance, in the mid-1930s, Franz Jakubowski considered that Lenin tended towards 'metaphysical, naturalistic materialism' with his concept of social consciousness reflecting social being, as it 'opposes consciousness to its object', which resulted in this consciousness becoming 'a supra-human consciousness'.[99] In other words, however much

96. Op cit, pp30, 36.
97. I Deutscher, *Stalin*, Harmondsworth, 1966, pp127-8. Reflecting in 1960 upon his days as a young Marxist in Russia, the old Menshevik David Dallin said that he and his comrades, who were drawn from a wide social span – university and technical students, salesmen, workers and craftsmen – constituted a 'semi-intelligentsia', who eagerly adopted a 'primitive interpretation' of Marxism on studying a few Marxian and Darwinian books, and were convinced that they had 'the perfect philosophy' which had 'the answers to all questions' (DJ Dallin, 'Social Change and Soviet Foreign Policy', *From Purge to Coexistence: Essays on Stalin's and Khrushchev's Russia*, Chicago, 1964, pp182ff).
98. Rather than giving a materialist explanation of the social processes that result in a certain individual playing a significant rôle within society, Plekhanov almost completely dismissed the significance of the individual. See GV Plekhanov, 'On the Question of the Individual's Rôle in History', *Selected Philosophical Works*, Volume 2, op cit, pp283ff.
99. F Jakubowski, *Ideology and Superstructure*, London, 1978, p72. For other Marxian critiques of Lenin's book, see Karl Korsch, 'Problems of Marxism and Philosophy' in

Lenin was trying to oppose idealism, he was actually making concessions to it.

If *Vekhi* is seen as a critique of the vulgarised forms of Marxism that were common amongst the Russian intelligentsia, then it has a certain if limited value. However, the contributors to *Vekhi* considered that the corrupted image of Marxism they were attacking was the genuine article, and those who have hailed *Vekhi* since then have not demurred from this erroneous assessment. As a critique of Marxism in particular and of rationalism in general, *Vekhi* was and remains a miserable failure.

A Lost Opportunity or an Episode of Relative Insignificance?

Some conservative authorities have seen *Vekhi* as a lost opportunity for the Russian intelligentsia. Poltoratzky says:

'On the spiritual foundations of the emerging new *weltanschauung* of *Vekhi* a new ideology and a new policy could have been built... However, tragically for subsequent Russian history, neither the spiritual foundations of the new world outlook represented by *Vekhi*, nor the political conclusions... were adopted by the Russian intelligentsia.'[100]

This is unrealistic. The ideas expressed in *Vekhi* represented such a sharp break from those traditionally associated with both the liberal and Socialist wings of the Russian intelligentsia, that they were quite unacceptable to the vast majority of Russian intellectuals. *Vekhi* was élitist in that it considered that the masses were incapable of sensible political activity. Its concentration upon self-improvement as the primary task facing intellectuals gave the impression that it was, on the one hand, indifferent to the plight of the masses, and was, on the other hand, abdicating from the fight for social improvement. Its only practical suggestion was Struve's call for the intelligentsia to fall in behind the Tsarist regime, a proposal that would be firmly rejected by liberals and Socialists alike.

In retrospect, it is clear in one sense that despite the veritable storm of criticism that it provoked, and despite Richard Pipes' assertion that echoes of the whole affair 'were still reverberating decades after',[101] in the

his *Marxism and Philosophy*, New York, 1970, and Anton Pannekoek, *Lenin as Philosopher*, London, 1975. All these first appeared in the 1930s. For his part, Lenin, after an intensive study of Hegel during the First World War, more or less admitted the vulgar nature of early twentieth century Marxism, including his own, when he said that 'none of the Marxists understood Marx!!' (VI Lenin, 'Conspectus of Hegel's Book *The Science of Logic*', *Collected Works*, Volume 38, Moscow, 1972, p180).
100. Poltoratzky, op cit, pp102-3. Pipes (op cit, p114) expresses much the same sentiments.
101. Pipes, op cit, p106.

long run *Vekhi* was of no great significance. It represented no more than a shift on the part of a few Russian intellectuals away from radicalism, rationalism and political activity towards élitism, passivity, idealism and even clerical obscurantism. The overwhelming majority of the intelligentsia was hostile to the political aspects of *Vekhi*, and was baffled by its religious and mystical pronouncements. Although it brought into relief weaknesses in the traditional theories and outlooks of the intelligentsia, it had little effect upon it then or since (the fact that *Vekhi* was championed by those Soviet dissidents who adopted a mystical and religious stance[102] only underlines its marginal character). Moreover, even though Berdyaev's writings were translated into many languages, their obscurantist nature relegated the appeal of most of them to small circles of Western intellectuals.

Despite the angry response of the Russian intelligentsia to *Vekhi*, and despite the fact that it touched a raw nerve, the mystical and élitist ideas expressed in *Vekhi* had nothing positive to offer Russian intellectuals in the struggle against Tsarism, or in respect of the problems that would emerge under the Provisional Government in 1917 and the ensuing Soviet regime. On the other hand, however, the retreat from rationalism on the part of the contributors to *Vekhi* was by no means exceptional, as irrational trends of thought have regularly emerged, often in response to a perceived failure on the part of a rationalist current. Today, rationalism is on the defensive as irrational trends – be they New Age philosophies and fundamentalist religions, the rejection of the idea of progress on the part of many ecologists, the promotion of biological determinism by some feminists, or the repudiation of all-embracing theories by postmodernists – lurk in many a corner.

Although the ideas expressed in *Vekhi* are no more relevant to Russia today than they were when the journal was first published, the intellectual flux following the collapse of the pseudo-rationalist Stalinist regime in the Soviet Union could permit the rise of a culture of irrationality in which such ideas could enjoy a new round of popularity.

102. One of the contributors to the collection assembled by Aleksandr Solzhenitsyn in the mid-1970s said: 'The path of heroic spiritual striving is the only path that can lead man – and the whole of society – to freedom. The authors of the *Vekhi* (*Landmarks*) anthology wrote of these things 70 years ago... but few understood them at the time. So is it not time, after almost 200 years of obsession with the "social idea" to turn to this path...?' (AB, 'The Direction of Change', in A Solzhenitsyn (ed), *From Under the Rubble*, London, 1975, p148)

II: Impressionism: Trotsky in Vienna

We introduce this section, mainly devoted to Trotsky's writings on the visual arts, with a brief review article by our Contributing Continental Editor dealing with the time of Trotsky's stay in Vienna, where the majority of these pieces were written. In addition to the obituary of Georg Scheuer that he wrote for us (*Revolutionary History*, Volume 7, no 1, pp175-7), he has also provided us with another article in our fourth section, and we are sure our readers will join with us in expressing our thanks. He is well known for his book *Gegen den Strom*, a study of factional conflict within the Austrian Communist Party up to 1945 (Vienna, 1978), as well as articles on the 'Bolshevisation' of that party (*Die Internationale*, fourth series (12), 1978, pp66-83), Trotskyism in Austria (*Cahiers Léon Trotsky*, no 5, January-March 1980, pp115-33), and the European working-class movement in the Second World War (*Internationale Tagung der Historiker der Arbeiterbewegung*, no 20, 1984, pp154-84). Another useful introduction to this period in Trotsky's life is that by Ian D Thatcher, 'Trotsky and *Kievskaia Mysl'*, *Irish Slavonic Studies*, no 14, 1993, pp87-102.

The rest of this section is made up of articles Trotsky wrote, mostly for *Kievskaia Mysl*, and translated from Volume 20 of the *Sochineniya* (pp275-85, 301-8, 327-42, and 463-85), for which we express our gratitude to Yurii Colombo, Craig Brandist, Brian Pearce and Robert Goldie. Many of them have recently been reprinted in the Russian edition of Trotsky's *Literature and Revolution*, along with some of those already available in English in the Pathfinder collection *Leon Trotsky on Literature and Art* (New York, 1977). Two articles on our list have already appeared in English, but our own translations are wholly independent. 'A New Year's Conversation About Art' was translated by Ian Fraser and published in the *International Socialist Review* supplement to the American *Militant*. The essay 'On the Intelligentsia' first appeared in a truncated form translated by Philip Rahv and Irwin Weil in *Partisan Review* magazine, and was reproduced in a pamphlet put out by the Revolutionary Communist League in 1970 (*International Bulletin Series*, no 2). Our version here reproduces the article in full in English for the first time. In spite of the coincidence of title, it is not the same as the contribution on the same subject translated by Brian Pearce which was first published by the Socialist Labour League in

Fourth International, Volume 1, no 3, Autumn-Winter 1964-65, pp105-11, and subsequently released in pamphlet form, a much shorter and less satisfying treatment of the same theme. A later fragment, 'Trotsky's Views on the Rôle of Students, Intellectuals', was first printed in the Danish *Studenter arbeiterbladet* on 9 December 1932 (reprinted in *Fjerde Internationale*, March 1937, and translated into English in *InterContinental Press*, Volume 10, no 41, 13 November 1972).

The particular Russian context of these articles is illustrated by Paul Flewers, 'Socialism and the Intelligentsia: The Ideas of Jan Machajski in Historical Retrospect' (*New Interventions*, February 1995), and in his article on *Vekhi* in the previous section. But the relationship between the intelligentsia and Socialism as a whole was a favourite topic of discussion amongst classical Marxists, such as in Kautsky's article printed in a previous number of *Revolutionary History* (Volume 1, no 1, Spring 1988, pp26-7) which should be read along with Trotsky's own. A more recent discussion is George Novack's 'Marxism and the Intellectuals', *New International*, Volume 2, no 7, December 1935, pp227-32.

Fritz Keller

Trotsky in Vienna

L EON Trotsky spent two periods in the capital of the Austro-Hungarian Empire prior to the First World War. The first time, after the autumn of 1902, was after he had fled from Irkutsk in Siberia, to where he, as one of the responsible leaders of the South Russian Workers Union, had been deported, together with his first wife and comrade-in-arms, Alexandra Lvovna Sokolovskaia. He was again in Vienna from 1907 until the beginning of the First World War in 1914. He was once more an émigré, having escaped from an indefinite tsarist exile (katorga), to which he had been sentenced for his political activities as the President of the Soviet of Workers' Deputies of Petersburg during the Russian Revolution of 1905.

Ever since then, a multitude of anecdotes have circulated in Vienna about Trotsky's life in exile. One of them, for example, tells that some time in 1917, when the first rumours about an approaching revolution in Russia did the rounds of the population, a departmental head of the Austrian foreign ministry told his chief, Prince Windischgrätz: 'Revolution in Russia? Who shall head it? Maybe this Herr Trotsky, always playing chess in the café Zentral?'[1] This seemingly jovial observation of Trotsky

---

1. Gottfried Heindl, *Und die Größe ist gefährlich*, Vienna-Berlin, 1969, p181. The story is

by the Austrian secret state police is repeated in other anecdotes. Another rumour that was widely disseminated abroad by the conservative press claimed that Trotsky's licence to publish *Pravda* was connected with his assumed function as a confidant of the police.

Another tale claims that Trotsky, whom Max Eastman attested could not be trusted with financial matters, came across his Viennese grocer as a prisoner of war, crying: 'Mister Bronstein, Mister Bronstein!' The first reaction of the leader of the Red Army, when he recognised who had called to him, was spontaneously to feel for coins in his pocket, and to ask: 'Do I owe you anything?'

Alongside these more or less serious anecdotes, Trotsky's autobiography *My Life* was the sole source for his years in the metropolis on the Danube, because not one of his biographers, fascinated by his rôle either as a triumphant revolutionary or an outcast prophet, has carried out any investigation of his own in this particular area.

This gap is now filled with the appearance of a dissertation by Alfred Mansfeld.[2] This study assesses the historical validity of some of the above anecdotes. There is not the slightest trace of evidence in the archives of Trotsky's acting as a police confidant. Mansfeld also shows that Trotsky's own warning in the introduction of *My Life* should be taken seriously:

'Since I have submitted to the necessity of writing about myself — nobody has as yet succeeded in writing an autobiography without writing about himself — I can have no reason to hide my sympathies or antipathies, my loves or my hates. This is a book of polemics.'[3]

Under immense ideological pressure from the Stalinist school of falsification, which wanted to portray him as an anti-Leninist traitor from the very beginning, the portraits in his autobiography of the Austro-Marxist leaders, to take one example, were very negative:

'Otto Bauer, Max Adler and Karl Renner... These people were not revolutionaries. Moreover, they represented the type that was furthest from that of the revolutionary... I was surprised to find that these educated Marxists were absolutely incapable of applying Marx's method as soon as they came to the big problems of politics, especially its revolutionary

also reported by Julius Deutsch, *Ein weiter Weg*, Zurich-Leipzig-Vienna, 1960.

2. Alfred Mansfeld, *Der junge Trotzki unter besonderer Berücksichtigung der Wiener Jahre 1907-1914 (The Young Trotsky with Special Regard to the Years in Vienna, 1907-14)*, PhD Dissertation, University of Vienna, 1997, pp181. Part of it was published in the *Archiv 1992 – Jahrbuch des Vereins für die Geschichte der Arbeiterbewegung*, Vienna, 1992, and in the *Cahiers Léon Trotsky*, no 51, October 1993, pp5-18.

3. LD Trotsky, *My Life*, Harmondsworth, 1970, p xxxvii.

turns... In practice, Rudolf Hilferding remained a literary official in the service of the German party – and nothing more.'[4]

Mansfeld has discovered and studied all the articles which Trotsky published between 1907 and 1914 in the newspapers *Neue Zeit, Vorwärts* and *Der Kampf.* He could not find even one polemical sentence against any of the Austro-Marxists, with the sole exception of an article criticising the extreme exponent of chauvinism and imperialism on the right wing of the Social Democratic Party, Karl Leuthner. On the contrary, all the documents show that Trotsky maintained close fraternal relations with the entire centrist leadership of the Austrian Social Democrats. He admired Max Adler, Otto Bauer and Karl Renner. In the case of Hilferding, this relationship can be characterised as something more than merely fraternal. In his correspondence with him, which is deposited in the International Institute for Social History in Amsterdam, Trotsky addressed him using the titles 'Teurer Genosse' ('Admired comrade'), 'Lieber Hilferding' ('Dear Hilferding'), 'Lieber Freund' ('Dear friend'), 'Mein lieber Freund' ('My dear friend'), and 'Lieber Finanzkapitaltheoretiker' ('Dear financial-capital-theorist').

These findings cannot be interpreted in the sense that Mansfeld gives, of accusing Trotsky of lying. Trotsky also wrote of the Austro-Marxists: 'They were well-educated people whose knowledge of various subjects was superior to mine. I listened with intense and, one might almost say, respectful interest to their conversations in the "Central" café.'[5]

What Mansfeld discovered merely permits future historians to draw a sharper dividing line between Trotsky's political opinions in the period when he played the rôle of a conciliator between the Bolshevik and Menshevik factions, and his later opinions, than Trotsky did himself.

Leon Trotsky

On Death and Eros

THE air was heavy with the combined smell of coffee, tobacco and a mass of human bodies. It was already two in the morning. The Café d'Harcourt, the most lively café along the St-Michel[6] was appallingly overcrowded. People pressed round the small tables, bumping into each other with their elbows and knees. The pavements were half-

4. Op cit, pp212-3.
5. Op cit, p213.
6. Boulevard de St Michel, a street in Paris.

blocked by extra chairs added outside. From theatres, from cabarets, from the street and God knows from wherever else, students, shop assistants, journalists and local girls had come to crowd the café: the motley *Bohème* of the Latin Quarter.[7] People smoked, drank, came in and went out, and collided with one another without apologising. The crush created a sort of absurd physical intimacy. People trod on the little piles of sawdust that would be used to clean up the place the morning after. The *grisettes* toured around the tables with the typical gait of their trade. The waiters, their white aprons stained with wine and coffee, were tired, but preserved the faultless automatism of their movements. Without ceremony, they pushed through the crowd, wearing the disgusted expression of persons who see the same show every day.

'All right', said a Russian lecturer who was still quite young, 'but these days you are too quick to dismiss intellectuals, decadent literature, the problem of sex, and fear of death... This won't do. Let's take it that I am a philologist, and on social issues I am a dilettante, but I decidedly, once and for all, refuse to conceive that it is the responsibility of a ministry to solve the problem of sex.'

'Quite so, but did I make you such a promise?'

Five or six Russian men were sitting around a tiny table. All of them wanted to take part in, or at least listen to, the discussion. The table was dirty, on its marble surface coffee stains mixed with tobacco ash made big puddles, whilst burnt matches and cigarette butts were piling up in the ashtrays, the dishes and even the glasses.

'You did not say so explicitly, but nevertheless it is the logical conclusion of your argument. According to you, *A Man's Life, Eleazar,*[8] Wedekind[9] and Artsybashevism[10] stand in direct opposition to all plat-

7. The student quarter of Paris.
8. *A Man's Life* and *Eleazar* are works by Leonid Andreev in the last period of his artistic activity. These works probe deep into his anguish and pessimism, in which death is always in the foreground. Leonid Nikolaevich Andreev (1871-1919) was born in Orel, and was a famous writer, particularly between the two Russian revolutions. His literary style, characterised by irrationality and expressionism, clearly shows his pessimistic view of existence. After the October Revolution, he moved to Finland, from where he was able to launch freely his attacks against the 'Communist dictatorship'. [Note by *Sochineniya* Editors]
9. Frank Wedekind (1864-1918) was a German playwright, and one of the first dramatists to recognise in his works the rôle played by sex and sexuality in modern social consciousness. His works were repeatedly censored in Imperial Germany.
10. Mikhail Petrovich Artsybashev [1878-1927 – Ed] was one of the most representative writers of the idealist literary trend that emerged in Russia after the defeat of the 1905 revolution. The recurrent themes in his work were the preaching of anarchic individualism, an appeal to freedom from all social responsibilities in the name of a life devoted to enjoyment, and a cult of erotic pleasure. Artsybashev's oeuvre, particularly *Sanin*, enjoyed great success amongst the intelligentsia, and led to the emergence amongst the young and literary circles of a particular trend known as

forms, and especially to yours. It's a matter of one or the other. But this is dreadfully arbitrary and strained. As far as I understand you – and not only you, but also those who think like you – you are not iconoclasts, you do not deny either love or art. You do not affirm, publicly at least, that politics has the right to take over the whole of a human being. But aren't you beginning to deny that problems of sex take up a substantial portion of our life? And death, death too, takes up a substantial particle of it – I mean the thought of death, the sinister light that it casts on our actions, or ultimately, if you like, simply the fear of death. The decadent movement, that greatly blamed art of our times, knows of these two moments almost exclusively: the ecstasy of the union of two bodies, and the parting of the soul from the body. Of course, life is more than that, but you must admit that these themes, too, have some value.

'What do you counterpose to this? Enlarging the Duma's control over the budget? Please excuse me, but that by itself is feeble, even feeble to the highest degree, and even if you add universal and equal suffrage and all the socialisations... Please, do not misunderstand me: these are all issues for which I have a sincere and warm sympathy. But even so, I will say here, to your face, that on the most intimate scales of my conscience, all your appeals do not balance the mystery of death. Probably I would not have said this to you in public, simply so as not to attract ridicule, but here and at this late hour, when our nerves are so tense, the usual automatic associations are weakened and we pay more attention to our inner impulses, I have dared to be so bold... The fact that all here present will die, that all mankind will perish, and that the entire globe will break up and revert to dust – this, damn it, has some significance even compared with the expenses of the ambassador to Tokyo, even juxtaposed with the question of how we should produce and distribute... Do you understand me?'

'I have understood you...'

'Just a moment! In the past, people possessed a most authoritative reconciliation between lifetime "service" and the certainty of an unavoidable end. This reconciliation was provided by faith. But today, who or what provides us with this reconciliation? Historical materialism, perhaps?'

'Perhaps...'

'Nonsense. At best, historical materialism seeks to explain the origin of this or that social mood (eroticism, mysticism) by the struggle between different forces in society. Whether it does this well or badly, I don't care. But I, to whom you offer your dubious explanations, shall die nevertheless, and as for all the perspectives your historical materialism spreads

'Artsybashevism' or 'Saninism'. [Note by *Sochineniya* Editors]

before me, even if I believe in them for the sake of my spiritual life, I still set them in the perspective of my inevitable death. So I must ask — where will I find reconciliation and salvation, not from death, of course, but from that psychological split that death continuously generates? Where indeed, if not from mysticism? *Nowhere.* We must recognise this, in all honesty. But since I am not a suitable person for mysticism, that suicide of reason, I turn to art. Art understands me, and does not reject me. It knows my long hours of crazed sleeplessness, those times when one sees the bottom of the abyss of non-being. It knows the tiring contradictions of my soul, and finds colours and sounds for them. I realise this is only a substitute. But what do *you* offer me? Objective analysis? Arguments about necessity? Immanent development? The negation of negation? But all these things are so terribly inadequate, not for my intelligence, but for my will. And you want to bind me psychologically, morally and religiously to them! You will grope about in my soul for a religious noose, hook it onto your historical materialism, and then drag me away. As for me, I will joyfully let myself be dragged away, I will even cry 'Hosannah!'. Yet, in fact, you do not even search: you mock us. "Taking into account the net increase of the discount rate on the New York stock exchange, on the one hand, and, on the other, the consolidation of French reaction around the Clemenceau[11] ministry...", there; that's all you can offer. But it is so little, so insultingly little... The sun will go out, won't it? I ask you: won't it? This too is an objective process, in fact more clearly so than anything else. Here you have two instances of objectivity. On the one hand, the discount rate somewhere or other on some patch of a little planet; on the other, the steam driving the entire machinery of our world is going to run out...'

'Well, let us assume it has not entirely run out yet', the journalist under attack objected cheerfully. *'Garçon, un grogue americain, s'il vous plaît!'*

'If not today, in 200 000 years, then. In principle, the issue is just the same. The important point here is that social objectivity, under which you, if you will excuse me, wish so unceremoniously to conceal my personality, is itself, as a lid, crushed from above by a most desolate cosmic objectivity. And the gentleman from the intelligentsia, looking at these two lids and remembering well that the third "lid", that is, personal death, simply cannot be avoided (and this not in 200 000 years time, but considerably sooner), will up and say: "Go to hell, all of you!" He will then put his hat on askew, and proceed to a bad place. So much for your New York rate! So much for your Clemenceau!'

Everyone burst out laughing.

'As for me', a shy blond young man in his twenties said to the jour-

11. Georges Clemenceau (1841-1929) was a French radical politician, and Prime Minister during the First World War.

nalist, 'if you will allow me, I would like to say something about the so-called "anarchism of the flesh" that you spoke of so scornfully in your talk today. What you call it does not matter, of course, but I think it is, nonetheless, an honest and courageous attempt to find an answer to a huge and tragic question. First of all, it is an invitation to consider the matter simply, to free ourselves from wholly illusory, but no less terribly tormenting, contradictions. If you like, it is a new rehabilitation of life, which is necessary from time to time in a society that – like a spider – spins out of itself a web of prejudices and false morality. Nowadays, satirists zealously pick out examples of excesses and monstrosities from the new literature. As if every struggle – be it political, social or religious – cannot help but create its own exaggerations. But, all the same, its core is healthy and progressive...'

'Gentlemen!', began the journalist who, after a public lecture which was followed by a fervent discussion, still felt like a shell fired from the muzzle of a cannon, 'I find it essentially impossible to accept battle on the ground you have chosen. If you please – you are asking me to create, just in passing, a religious doctrine such as would help a member of the intelligentsia to transcend the shell of his individuality and overcome the terror of death and pretentious scepticism, a doctrine capable of linking mystically his "subconscious", the soul of his soul, to the great epoch in which we live. But, please excuse me, this would make a mockery of my viewpoint. It would be as if I listened to a scientific lecture on the historical origins of the Bible, and then expected the speaker to tell me on the basis of the Apocalypse the date of the Second Coming. *Mais ce n'est pas mon métier, messieurs,* I could say to you, this is not my job, and that's that. However, I will try – not to object to what you have said, for that's not possible – but to set my feelings on this matter in opposition to yours. Let's start like this. You say that you cannot get by without mysticism or, at least, some sort of substitute for it. But look: we do get by. And there are hundreds of thousands, millions, many millions of us... Our numbers swell by the day. Please try to understand: we have no need whatsoever for mysticism. By the whole cast of our thinking and feeling, we cannot, we will not, we don't agree, and we are unable to believe in the witch of Kiev. And you know, as I do, that in the end this is what the question comes down to. Berdyaev started from great mystical heights, but nevertheless ended up believing in a witch with a broomstick and a tail, and now, along with the official Lebedev (do you remember, in Dostoevsky?[12]), he firmly asserts that disbelief in the witch "is a French idea, a frivolous idea". But you, most esteemed professor, have got stuck halfway. Reason is pushing you towards us, but in your feelings, you are with Lebedev...'

12. One of the main characters in Dostoevsky's novel *The Idiot.*

'Allow me', interjected the lecturer, as if suddenly struck by an idea, 'I admit that for you mysticism is replaced by the struggle, its fervour, its heat, its attack. I admit that. But the new man, who will not inherit your struggle, how will it be with him? His thought will be free, his soul serene, and he will have plenty of leisure. Suddenly he will up and ask: *But what comes after?* And, as he will find no answer, he will hand you back your "ticket of admission".'

'First of all, you were wrong to interrupt me. Secondly, you very unskilfully construct the man of the future in your own image. Thirdly, let me tell you frankly that I have yet to spend one sleepless night thinking of the feelings of the man of the future. Let him make his own order within himself: as for us, we shall be content with having left to him a good economy outside himself. But today, this isn't the real issue. The issue is that you, or, to be more precise, those with whom you dare not agree, refuse to believe in the very possibility of a man of the future bereft of the crutches of mysticism. Whether you are aware of it or not, you are reiterating Renan.[13] "With the help of chimeras", he says somewhere, "we have been able to stimulate the gorilla to surprising moral efforts; and when we don't have any more chimeras, the artificial energy they called forth will disappear too." Translated into your language this means that, scared by the cooling of the sun, man will wear his brain askew and will proceed to some disgusting place. But this is no more than a slander on mankind. It is in this that we clearly see the cynicism of the little intellectual *bon-vivant*, who presumes to think that only the false baits and lures placed on the hook of history can save mankind from relapsing into savagery. In this disdainful social cynicism, coupled with portable mysticism and eroticism – and, for the pessimists of Poshekhone,[14] just smutty talk – I do not see development from man to superman, but rather a regression, from the philistine to the gorilla, albeit a philosophising gorilla. We seek and find the guarantee of future development – this once and for all! – not in the experiences of the individual soul, but in the irresistible, profoundly realistic pressure of the masses, free from all chimeras!'

'"Social life is in its very essence practical life", a great, great materialist said in the last century. All that is mysterious, all that leads theory into mysticism, finds a rational solution in human practice. And, from the other side, a very prominent individualist decadent arrived at the

13. Joseph Ernest Renan (1823-1892) was a French philosopher and historian of religion, chiefly noted for his *Life of Jesus* (1863) which was a radical attack on traditional Christian beliefs.
14. From the title of Shchedrin's *Old Times in Poshekhone*. The author intended this to be the first volume in a cycle of autobiographical short stories. In this book, he depicts the social and political landscape of the era of serfdom, as well as a history of his own family.

same idea from the opposite extreme. "Modern *industriousness*, that noisy trader in time, proud of itself, so stupidly proud", he says, "above all educates and prepares one for *unbelief*." You must understand that only a subjective consciousness that is leisured and tired of its own idleness constructs an "insoluble conflict" between social obligation and the obligation to die. Social practice knows of no contradiction here, and we see that, as century follows century, the old generations clear the way for the young and those that have not yet arrived. We want to nourish this instinctive creativity with an intense consciousness. We want this, not because it is demanded by God, by morality or by love for future generations, but because it is this that makes our own life more beautiful, richer and more meaningful. But it is precisely here that, according to you, the tragedy begins: the break between the subjective and the objective, the revolt against the social burden by a personality that has become conscious of itself. Is this true? Is it true for everyone? Is it true for many? Look around you, I say this again to you: you are a handful, we are numberless...

'Realistic activity and mysticism exhausted from idleness! This antithesis finds a confirmation in classes, in groups, and in single individuals. I say bluntly: in our epoch a person who lives a sedentary life (sedentary in every sense of the word), if not an utter dullard, invariably ends up with ideological indigestion. Only wide-ranging practice, activity, only will to action can guarantee him the right mental balance. Allow me to tell you briefly a little parable. The air was calm and unmoving, the sails hung lifeless, meditating on their purpose, and grumbling about the pointlessness of the universe. But then a strong wind began to blow and filled the sails. They no longer theorised about their purpose, but happily began to carry it out, taking the ship into the open sea. It may be that my parable is a bad one, but the sense of it is clear.

> Oh, solve me the riddle of life,
> The tormenting primordial riddle...
> Tell me, what is the meaning of Man?

Asks the passive contemplator, whose will hangs aimlessly like a sail in dead calm.

> Where has he come from? Where is he going?
> Who dwells up there on the golden stars?
> *And a fool waits for an answer.*[15]

15. Heinrich Heine, 'The North Sea 1825-1826', *The Complete Poems of Heinrich Heine*, Boston, 1982, p154. Christian Johann Heinrich Heine (1797-1856) was a famous German poet.

Heine says of him... But I have not finished my parable. Amongst the sails, there were some that were torn, either by nature or due to the passing of time, how it doesn't matter. The storm whistled through their holes, but they did not fill. Angry at their own uselessness, they turned from philosophising and lamentation to cynical *blaming of the world*. And this is a mortal sin, forever unforgivable!

'You take under your wing these people who are spiritually full of holes. You say we do not give them anything. That modern art, which we attack, at least gives them a substitute for faith. If you like, this is true: in Impressionism, timidly mystical, hinting at something or other, where "religious" instincts (that is, in simple terms, human, social instincts) take pleasure end in themselves, without seeking any external manifestation a kind of masturbation of the soul! This art not only indulges the intelligentsia's lack of will, but systematically intensifies it... In a German philosophical pamphlet published only a few days ago, I came across an observation, more or less in these terms: "Art is almost as immoral as opium. It gives the spirit ephemeral satisfaction, and emasculates it in relation to the postulates of the real world, the first of which demands that we must be satisfied with the world in its reality." For contemporary literature, this is terribly true. This literature turns its back on the great real world, and rather than finding satisfaction in its reality, sows only an irresponsible sense of disgust with the world. There is in this literature a sort of debilitating aristocratism, as in Versilov,[16] who feebly complained that reality always smells like a boot... When I say that we must be satisfied with the *reality* of what exists, you, of course, will not think that I mean that we must be satisfied with *what exists*. Just the absolute opposite: a great and persistent protest against what exists only becomes possible when we accept the world unconditionally, in its incontrovertible reality. And, from the other side, mystical self-elevation above the world actually means reconciling oneself with what exists, in all its real ugliness. I say this to you from the bottom of my heart: when reality's nasty-smelling boot grinds to dust all those philosophical and aesthetic disciplines that are not of this world, I can feel nothing but malicious *schadenfreude*. I reject your literature, but not because it is symbolic, or impressionistic, or mystical, and not even because in the main it is bad literature, but because it is infected by the leprosy of despair, because in its hateful desolation it is blasphemy, a base and cowardly blasphemy against the sovereign Boot of reality (I pronounce the word boot with a capital B). This blasphemy is not directed against what exists, before which such art grovels in the dirt, but against what is real, actual, in other words against mankind itself, in its future victories over itself, against mankind's great tomorrow! This is why, in my best hours, when I rise above myself, above

16. A character in Dostoevsky's *A Raw Youth*.

the petty Russian intellectual of the Ides of the Third Duma,[17] when in thought and feeling I join in the anonymous creative tenacity of the millions, I do not accept — do you hear, I do not accept — a single drop of your literary opium...

'I know, I know what your objection will be: what should I care about mankind and its future, since perhaps I shall be dead before this day is over? This is all there is to the wisdom of scepticism and all the bragging about it by the hammer-wielders of cynicism. And know this: it is a feast, a real feast for my *schadenfreude* when I hear the mystical yelping of dogs scalded by the boiling terror of death, and I think: and yet you will die! You want to spit on the spirit of life because you fear death — and yet you will die!'

'*Schadenfreude* is not an answer', muttered the lecturer.

'My dear man, whoever said that I intended to answer them? Let them bury their carrion. We don't need them. We have understood: *We don't need them*. And we are proud in this certainty that we can do splendidly without them!'

Everyone felt that the conversation had ended in a cul-de-sac, and smoked in silence.

'And yet you have not answered me...', said the pale young man, breaking that embarrassing silence.

'Ah yes, the "anarchism of the flesh", wasn't it? You know, what applies to anarchism in general holds for this too: *er glaubt zu schieben und er wird geschoben* (it thinks it moves, and yet it is moved). Anarchism sweetly believes that it is implacable and destructive. But it does no more than slavishly copy what exists. It opposes to economic anarchy as a fact economic anarchy as an ideal. The same goes for "anarchism of the flesh". Just think, what courage it is indeed, to reject morality, aesthetics, even the hygiene of love. And yet this is no more than a dirty copy of a dirty reality...'

The entrance door revolved, and a whole swarm of *grisettes* entered the crowded room, with their faces smiling like mummies, and their clothes like coloured screens thrown over naked bodies. One woman detached herself from the group and slowly made her way to the table where the Russians sat. She listened for a long time and with indifference to the sounds of foreign speech, then, still indifferent, went away.

'That girl', said the journalist as she was going away, 'is a true, albeit forced, priestess of the anarchism of the flesh, an irresistible teacher of sexual morality. Gentlemen, this is not meant as a paradox, and today is not the first time the idea has occurred to me. Where does a young man learn the art of love? From these girls. It is there that he gathers his first,

17. The Third Duma, which assembled in November 1907, was notorious for its docility towards the tsar.

indelible and inextinguishable impressions. It is there that he learns to take love without any psychological commitment – not to the woman, the other person, but *to himself*. It is there that, if you will let me say this, that his sexual personality is formed. Later, he will carry with him the *grisettes'* atmosphere, and his lover, or his wife, will learn from him the manners, the ways and the morality of the *grisettes*, if she hasn't already learnt all that from his predecessor, that is.

'Friedrich Nietzsche,[18] your fellow-philologist', he went on addressing the lecturer, 'said somewhere that "Catholicism made Eros drink poison: Eros did not die from it, but turned into vice". What are your modernists doing? They are rejecting what official Catholicism has taken under its wings: monogamous marriage, registered, signed and sealed, the legal production of children on the basis of a legitimising license. This is what they reject. But what do they stand for? Perhaps for the old cheerful and self-assured Eros (please note: if he ever existed)? Never! Their modern Eros has run the gauntlet of the Middle Ages. They poisoned him with the prejudices of asceticism, and eventually just exhausted him with work, fed him abominably, and infected him with rickets, scrofula and debility. They didn't kill him, but they turned him into vice. This Eros, poisoned by the Middle Ages, an habitué of all brothels and hospitals, is their wretched deity!'

'Excuse me, please', chipped in the young man, who had listened to him with painful attention, 'but now, it seems to me, you are arguing like a professional moralist. In agreement with the official inspectors of our souls, you decide *what* is virtue and *what* is vice, and then say: here is a rule for good sexual practice for you, act according to it. But this too is neither very bold, nor very original.'

The young man blushed, and everyone smiled slightly.

'I must have expressed my ideas very badly', said the journalist mildly, 'if you have misunderstood me to that extent. What I find insufferable in our present-day literature is precisely its moralising, even if this is moralising turned on its head. The anarchism of the flesh, Artsybashevism, amounts to a never-ending and boring sermon: *do not fear, do not harbour any doubt, do not feel ashamed, do not have any scruples, grab what you can...* And since they moralise, I have the right to ask what the *principle* of their moralising is.'

'Their principle is freedom and harmony of the personality.'

'Freedom and harmony, yes indeed. I could cavil and say to you that these words are void of any content. After all, what are freedom and harmony? But I accept your formula, and it is precisely from this angle that I believe I have the right to say that Saninism is the most criminal

18. Friedrich Nietzsche (1864-1900) was a German philosopher, chiefly known for his *Thus Spoke Zarathustra* (1883-84).

pillaging of the personality... You want harmony? Whether or not you can set this longing of yours for personal harmony in a social perspective, you must admit that harmony without completeness, without retention of all that we have won through the torments of historical development, harmony attained through surgically removing all contradictions and through psychological oversimplification is absolutely unacceptable, even if it weren't a hopeless utopia. *Dans le véritable amour c'est l'âme qui enveloppe le corps* (in true love, it is the soul that envelopes the body). On the stem of sexual love such psychological flowers have grown as we neither want nor dare give up. For otherwise what we should get would be the "harmony" of the cattle-yard.'

'*La séance est close, messieurs!*' (The meeting is over, gentlemen!), said a waiter, ironically, to the Russians sitting around the table, pointing to the near-empty room and the lights which had already been switched off in various corners. '*À demain, s'il vous plaît...*' (Till tomorrow, please.)

Odessiskie Novosti, no 7510, 6 May 1908

Leon Trotsky

A New Year's Conversation About Art

VIENNA, Herrengasse. The Café Central, Silvesterbend. All the halls are crowded, bright lights, noise, ladies' hats, exhausted waiters, punch and grog. *Prosit Neujahr!*

Some members of parliament are playing cards at a long table. By looking at them, no one could guess that on their shoulders rests the burden of state institutions. They play every night, and with the fast-approaching new year they see no reason to break their established routine... Nearby, a group of journalists from the gutter press sit with their half-naked ladies. We see partly-emptied wine glasses, jokes cracked in turn, and grateful laughs that come in regular volleys from the women. Hubbub. People come and go. *Prosit Neujahr!* Everyone wants to celebrate in one way or another the fact that the planet has become older by 365 days...

In a corner, near a turned-off fountain, there sat a German doctor, a Russian journalist, a Russian revolutionary who had emigrated in the seventies, a Hungarian woman painter and a Russian woman musician. They had been there for a whole hour, and their conversation sometimes widened, sometimes split up, touching on the Turkish parliament and the ruins of Messina,[19] and then, after two or three more zigzags, settled on painting. They asked each other's opinions about the exhibition of the Russian painters.

'My God!', exclaimed the doctor, turning to his Russian companion. 'Whatever have you given us, gentlemen? With all the many experiences you have had in the last few years, in that marvellous country of yours, surely if you cannot renew art, then who can? I must admit that I went to that clumsy building on the Karlsplatz full of great expectations. And then what? You have brought to us the very same things we see every year here at home, at the Secession,[20] albeit in smaller quantity and, pardon me for saying it, with an inferior quality. In all your exhibition there is nothing of your own, save perhaps for a couple of drawings by Bilibin,[21] and then not even very significant drawings at that. Is it not perhaps as I have put it?'

'I could not agree with you more!', said the emigré, in his support. Judging from the papers, nowadays in our country they talk about the "national principle", not only at liberal meetings, but some people also very tiresomely twitter away about it in all the little restaurants frequented by the decadents. And with what results? International products that are below the average quality of the market... We have home-made colourism as an end in itself, inwardly empty Impressionism, childish and without belief, for everything is borrowed. It is indeed remarkable! The homeland of Impressionism and stylisation is Paris; not only we Russians but also you Germans have fed, and are still feeding, on French suggestions. Meanwhile, in no country does Impressionism[22] hold such a

19. The Young Turks' coup d'état in 1908 gave Turkey a parliament for the first time. Messina was totally destroyed by an earthquake in 1908.
20. An annual art exhibition held in Vienna by the Painters' Society. In the second half of the nineteenth century, it gathered representatives from the fields of architecture, sculpture, painting and decorative art, in an attempt to create a new art form, independent of old styles. As the name suggests, the Secession was a reaction against the naturalistic art of the previous age, and as such it was closely linked with symbolism and the decadent movement in poetry, and with Impressionism in painting. The Secession, or the Vereinigung Bildender Künstler Österreichs, was also an artists' association founded in 1897 in Vienna. The first president was Gustav Klimt [1862-1918 – Ed]. The Secession rejected the conservative attitude towards the arts of the Künstlerhaus, and favoured a more experimental approach. [Note by Sochineniya Editors]
21. Ivan Yakolevich Bilibin (1876-1942) was a Russian graphic artist, stage designer and artist. On the basis of his study of the traditional Russian popular book art, he elaborated a distinctive graphic orientation and an original style, as reflected in his series of works on Northern landscapes and illustrations for fables.
22. A current in painting that originated in France during the second half of the nineteenth century, and was highly influential on German and Russian painting. The main aim of the Impressionist painter was to depict direct visual sensations, the transmission of sunlight and the play of colours in the open sky. This last principle

modest place in art as it does in France today. There, Impressionism has hardly got into circulation. But in some Charlottenburg *bei Berlin*, you must go through a stylised door if you want to visit even the lowest of pubs. And why? Well, because the Germans are infinitely poorer than the French in terms of aesthetic culture, artistic traditions and conservatism of form. Moreover, their power of resistance is also lower. As far as we Russians are concerned, in these matters we are as adaptable as putty. "In Germany I am a German" – wrote once Dostoevsky about the Russian intelligentsia – "a Frenchman in France, a Greek with the ancient Greeks and, thereby, I am a true Russian and I serve Russia in the best possible way."

'Or something along these lines, anyway... But Dostoevsky made a fatal mistake, like all our believers in Russia's independent development. The universal personality that he dreamed of proved to be no more than historical lack of personality. This was clearly to be seen when the old compact way of life tottered and began to break into pieces... For the intelligentsia, the time had come to display at last their national physiognomy, but, alas, this turned out to be like a blackboard all covered with ready-formed foreign characters... As you know, I have been living abroad for over 30 years now, and I constantly observe the Russian intelligentsia from the side. Here is my firmest conclusion: you have come too late, mother dear![23] You won't create a national physiognomy, in any field whatsoever.

At this point, the old emigré switched from German to Russian.

'To take an example, Struve is now sounding the horn of Slavophilism', he said, turning to the journalist, but if we just take a look, we can notice straight away that he is copying slavishly the German National Liberals, with only one difference: the Gothic alphabet has been replaced by the Cyrillic... Benois[24] demands that a Petersburg cabaret be called not 'cabaret', not '*Ueberbrettl*', but by the 'good old Russian term *balagan*', and he swears that it's enough to carry out this national reform, and 'then we'll have music like never before'.

---

of Impressionism was described by Zola: 'We need the sun, we need air, a young and shiny painting. Let the sun come in, and present objects in the true splendour of daylight.' Impressionism developed against the highly detailed technique of the naturalistic school, against the 'blackness' and 'soppiness' of their paintings, set in enclosed environments, and went on to enrich European painting with a series of great advances in pictorial technique. One of the best and most exhaustive collections of Impressionist art can be seen at the Moscow Museum of Western Art (formerly the Shukinskaia Gallery). [Note by *Sochineniya* Editors] Emile Zola (1840-1902) was the author of *Germinal* and *J'accuse*. [Editor's note]

23. An allusion to Mother Russia.
24. Aleksandr Nikolaevich Benois (1870-1960) was a Russian sculptor, illustrator, contemporary painter and art critic. He studied the customs of eighteenth century Russian and French art, and painted a whole series of works depicting that age.

The journalist nodded. The musician made a move as if to say something, but stopped herself. The doctor sucked a bit on his Virginia cigarette, and furrowed his brow uncertainly: it was obvious that he had not grasped the idea.

'Our exhibition is yet another case in point. Even Roerich,[25] with all his Slavic primitivism, wears the national spirit like a cardboard mask, beneath which one can perceive the cosmopolitan decadent. And I am not even saying anything about the others!'

'Still', began the doctor, 'from the exhibition there clearly emerges a certain, if you like, national characteristic of your intelligentsia: their extreme nervous instability. For me, as a professional psychiatrist, this is inexhaustible material. I have paused before several pictures with a sense of attentive astonishment. Anisfeld,[26] with his blue statue, is alone worth a treasure! Then come Messrs Yakulov[27] and Milioti.[28] The philistine shrugs his shoulders and says: "This man has taken a big bucket of blue paint and smeared it over this enormous headless statue. Why on earth did he do that? Evidently to *épater le bourgeois*, to bowl me over!" But this is nonsense. I am not a fan of the artistic creations of your Anisfeld; however, I say that the cause of his abuse of the blue paint must be sought not in some malign will on his part, but rather in some abnormality in his optic nerve. It's just that he *sees* things in this way, that's all. And if he has any admirers, that means that his is a typical disorder. Who knows, maybe in this abnormality the source for new aesthetic discoveries may be found. It is a prejudice to believe that our eye is unchanging; it develops through a selection of useful abnormalities. The

25. Nikolai Konstantinovich Roerich (1874-1947) was a Russian painter specialising in work with historical and landscape themes. He was also an archaeologist and traveller, Secretary of the Society for the Promotion of the Arts, and Director of the society's school. He became a member of the Secession in 1908.

26. Boris Izraelovich Anisfeld [1879-1973 – Ed] is an Impressionist painter belonging to the Union of Russian Painters. He currently lives in America. In the main, his paintings reflect purely colouristic concerns. He exhibited his works in the Union galleries in Moscow, Kiev and Petersburg, as well as in the famous Art of the World gallery, open during 1898-1905 and 1912-22. In its beginnings, this art establishment gathered painters and designers engaged in a whole series of original tasks in the field of design, and greatly contributed to the development of Russian graphic art. As for content, in the main, the works of these painters proposed archaic pictorial and stylistic models (Benois, Roerich, Bilibin, Somov, Dobuyinsky, Lansere). The Union of Russian Painters was created in Moscow in 1901. Originally called the Union of the Thirty-Six Painters, it was the organisation of Impressionist painters who defined themselves as purely pictorial, and set themselves colouristic tasks. [Note by *Sochineniya* Editors]

27. Georgi Bogdanovich Yakulov (1884-1928) exhibited at the Union galleries, as well as at the Art of the World and Blue Rose galleries.

28. Nikolai Dmitrievich Milioti (1874-) was an Impressionist painter who exhibited at the Union, Art of the World and Blue Rose galleries.

whole problem lies in finding out whether a particular abnormality of the optic nerve lies on the main road of our psycho-physical evolution, or if it constitutes a deviation from it.'

'But excuse me, doctor, remonstrated the Hungarian, you are simply reducing art criticism to neuropathology!'

'I dare to think that this is to the advantage of both', replied the doctor. 'Take the Impressionists: in some we find startling, sometimes unbearable, combinations of colours, whilst in others we see an equally startling parsimony with colour. Do you know what is behind all this? Daltonism, colour-blindness! Do not shake your head ironically... It is true that this question has been relatively little explored, but in all the cases I have personally studied, I have always discovered some organic or functional abnormality of the eye or the ear to be the source of new artistic forms and aesthetic experiences. Essentially — note this — every art follows the path of the fixation and generalisation of fortunate personal abnormalities.'

'So then, doctor, does this mean that our eyes, and yours, are colour-blind too?

'Undoubtedly, insofar as the corresponding ways of receiving colours overcome our recognition of them. In varying degrees and forms. We must not be afraid of words: an *abnormality* becomes the *norm* when the flow of development takes it up and fixes it as a general property.

'All this may well be true', the journalist was the first to reply. 'But your theory explains just as little of the evolution of painting as does chemistry, when it gives us the formulae of the colours used by the decadents. You remain without an answer to the main question: why is it precisely now that the "impressionistic" method of perceiving coloured surfaces has triumphed? Or, to use your language, why is it that precisely *these* abnormalities have become fixed, and not others? The answer is to be sought in the social setting, in the conditions of historical development: not in the structure of the eye, but in that of society. And here I say without hesitation: Impressionism, with its colour contrasts and colouristic anaemia, would be unthinkable outside the culture of the big cities. For this culture we need cafés, cabarets, the smoke of cigars, and lastly the transformation of night into day, thanks to artificial light that kills all colours. A peasant won't understand this art!... You say that a peasant doesn't understand any art? Let us presume that this is so. But let's now take a cultured peasant, nay, a peasant of genius, our Tolstoy. I do not know the structure of his eye, but I know that of his soul, and I can tell you that Tolstoy would turn his back on this art... Even if you could show beyond all doubt that the nerve-centres of Russian intellectuals display severe defects, or that their eyes and ears are abnormal, you still would not help me one bit to understand such phenomena as the sudden explosion of erotic aestheticism, or the work of Andreev, or of those Anisfelds and Yakulovs. Intellectuals should be grabbed not by their ear — although, maybe, there's nothing against doing that too — but by their soul. And their soul is a social soul, a soul conditioned by historical destiny... Even our dreams draw their content from the social milieu: the shoemaker sees a last in his dreams, the executioner a rope. And this holds even more for the "dreams" of poetry and painting!...'

Two points of view had clashed, the psycho-biological and the socio-historical, and each wanted to dominate, without admitting the possibility of coordination. Further argument had become fruitless, and therefore irritating. As always happens, with their intuitions, the first to understand this were the women, who had hardly taken part in the discussion — again, as always.

'And you, did you go to the *Kunstschau*?' — the musician asked the journalist.

'No! And unless it proves strictly necessary for me to go, as part of my job, I shall not go.'

'And why not?'

'You see, visiting art exhibitions is a terrible act of violence that we perpetrate on ourselves. This way of experiencing artistic pleasure expresses a terrible barracks-capitalist barbarism. Each single painting', continued the journalist half-jokingly, half in earnest, 'contains a whole series of internal aesthetic contradictions, let alone an entire exhibition... You disagree? Well, let's take a landscape, for example. What is it? A piece of nature, arbitrarily amputated, that has been framed and hung on a wall. Between these elements, nature, the canvas, the frame and the wall, a purely mechanical relation exists: the picture cannot be infinite, for tradition and practical considerations have condemned it to be square. So that it should not crease or buckle, it is framed, and so that it should not lie on the floor, people hammer a nail in a wall, fix a cord onto it, and hang up the picture by this cord. Then, when all the walls are covered in pictures, sometimes arranged in two or three rows, people call this an art gallery or exhibition. And we are then forced to swallow all this in one gulp: landscapes, genre scenes, frames, cords and nails...'

'Why, this is like Tolstoy's critique of opera...'

'So, what do you actually want?', enquired the painter. 'The suppression of painting, perhaps? Or only of all exhibitions?

'Both more and less than that... I am very distant from Tolstoy's rationalism... But I want painting to renounce its absolutism and reestablish its organic link with architecture and sculpture, from which it has long been detached. This separation did not happen by accident, oh no! From that time, painting has undertaken a very long and instructive journey. It has conquered landscape, has become inwardly mobile and intimate, and has developed an astounding technique. But now, enriched with all these gifts, it must go back to its mother's bosom, architecture... I want paintings to be connected not by cords but by their artistic significance to walls, to a cupola, to the purpose of a building, to the character of a room... and not hanging like a hat on a hat-stand. Picture galleries, these concentration camps for colours and beauty, serve but as a monstrous appendage to our colourless and unsightly daily reality. Please excuse my, at first sight, very crude analogy, but my thoughts turned to it without wishing to. Our culture knows of another kind of concentration camp, those buildings where caresses are concentrated. From time to time, men run to such places, for they are oppressed by love, and pay an entrance fee just as we pay an admission fee when we hurry to exhibitions, oppressed as we are by our need for colours and forms. There, one hour of concentrated love, here one hour of concentrated beauty. Such a monstrous accumulation of paintings and sculptures, of epochs and styles, of colours, ideas and moods, could only be created by our accursed age, of grey cubical houses, factory-chimney smoke and black top hats. If only flowers could grow from the tarmac of our streets, if only tropical birds came to rest on the iron balconies of our houses, or emerald-green waves lapped at our windows, if only at evening the sun would sink into the sea and not hide behind the Gerngross signboard,[29] there would be no place for picture galleries... But I do not ask you to step back in time, far from it! We cannot, nor will we, have flowers or birds on our tarmac. Moreover, we shall not give up the tarmac of civilisation, as Tolstoy futilely asks. So, we only have one possibility left: we must fight for the great synthetic art of the future: we have erased the primitive richnesses of colours and forms in order to replace them with new ones, "artificial" and – I am profoundly convinced – infinitely more perfect. But this new beauty has not yet materialised, it is diffused in fragments, splinters and hints. I stand by my belief that a piece of nature put inside a wooden frame is but a temporary and crude substitute.'

'Just a moment, just a moment... Aren't your arguments arbitrary? You reject all that there is, but where do you see these elements of a new art, these fragments and hints of yours?'

'Everywhere! What is Impressionism, after all? The last word of "independent" painting, that is, painting hung on a wall. In its methodology, Impressionism is the same as a mosaic, except that it uses patches and strokes of colours rather than little coloured stones. When it destroys lines and contours, when it breaks down colours into their constituent parts, the new art strikes a mortal blow to independent painting, and in so doing opens up a new outlet for painting towards architecture. I shall not name a whole series of Impressionists who have been pushed

29.   A department store in Vienna, the name translates as 'would-be-great', or 'wannabe'.

toward decorative painting precisely by this new technique, for you know them better than I do. But see these Anisfelds, Miliotis, Krymovs:[30] they all yearn for the decorative purposes and categorical imperatives of architecture. Here we have a "nocturne" in green, here a "prehistoric landscape"... These are not pictures, just as a splinter of glass from a Gothic church cannot be called a picture. Rather, it is a simple piece of canvas on which the artist has tested out various colour combinations; it is but a model for a cupola, or perhaps for a window blind... You will tell me that these artists are not dictating any laws. Agreed. But here for you is a great and uncontroversial name: Turner.[31] Some months ago, I looked again and again at his works in the Tate Gallery in London. His *Evening Star* and his *Waterloo* are not paintings, but waves of the most delicate colours, lit by a mysterious light. There are no lines, everything is immersed in a golden mist. For painting, Turner is not sufficiently material: he waits and seeks a noble architectural setting. In my final opinion, Turner is the destroyer of independent painting, just as Wagner is the destroyer of absolute music...'

'Fine', said the doctor, who was calmly sucking on his Virginia cigarette, as though savouring the blow he was about to strike. 'But do you know – and this fact has been established beyond any doubt – that Turner was in fact astigmatic?[32] Lines did not exist for him, just coloured surfaces... Here we are again with abnormalities of the eye as a basis for artistic individuality!'

'This does not concern me, doctor... I see Turner on the canvas in front of me, and I enjoy him. This means we have something in common, something that goes beyond Turner and his abnormalities, something extra-personal, social. A sort of social-aesthetic bond.'

'You wouldn't be astigmatic too, by any chance?'

'No... I don't think so.'

'I beg your pardon, but I am not so sure of that. Come to see me tomorrow, and I will test your eyes.'

Everyone burst out laughing. The doctor had his revenge, and the conversation, which had become rather one-sided, regained its balance..

'In the words of my friend, I find a lot that is paradoxical', said the old emigré with a smile, 'but to a journalist much can be forgiven. How-

30. Nikolai Petrovich Krimov (1884-) mainly exhibited his works at the Blue Rose, Union and Art of the World galleries.
31. Joseph Mallard William Turner (1775-1851) was a famous English landscape artist. As a colourist, he worshipped light as well as light and clean colours. He thought of nature as a play of colours, and in his works the outlines of objects could scarcely be made out from the boundaries of colour shades. [Note by *Sochineniya* Editors]
32. Astigmatism (near-sightedness) is a visual abnormality caused by an insufficient refraction of light rays in the eye, with the result of an inadequate focusing of the shape of objects. This abnormality causes a decrease in the quality of sight, and makes objects seem out of focus and faded. [Note by *Sochineniya* Editors]

ever, his central idea seems entirely correct to me. The synthetic art of the future! Beauty, not shut up in special institutions, but penetrating all aspects of our existence, a noble combination of nature, architecture and painting, a new *syssitia*,[33] just like the Spartans used to have, but in new conditions, enriched with all miracles of technology. Music as an accompaniment to thought and action. Life in the forum, as art, as the highest form of creativity...'

'But, gentlemen, synthetic beauty is only conceivable on the basis of synthetic *social* justice. Man must become the collective forger of his own historical destiny. Then he will be able to discharge the bulk of his workload onto the shoulders of his metallic slaves, and become the master of the elemental force of the subconscious in his own soul, and devote all his strength to creating new and splendidly sculptured forms of cooperation, love, fraternity, sociality... Leisure is necessary to man. We must have "the right to be lazy"!'

'Gentlemen, let us drink to this carefree, happy and brilliant idler of the future! *Prosit Neujahr*, my friends.'

Kievskaia Mysl, no 358, 30 December 1908

Leon Trotsky

The Vienna Secession of 1909

NOT so long ago, Russian artists exhibited pictures in these same halls where Austrians now make their annual inspection of their paintings and their sculpture. There was very little of Russia then, and there is very little of Austria on this occasion. It is not that we demand of art a display of the 'national face' in artistic style. There was most likely no small amount of 'stylistic' nationalism in the Russian exhibition (Bilibin, Roerich); it is also there in this, the next exhibition of the Secession. But in this case national style just provides a ready-to-use style worked out in the past, motifs for ornament, colour combinations. The use of all forms of 'archaism' is even the most indispensable feature of modernism. The turn to archaism, however, even if it is not only external, gives the impression of a temporary excursion into the past where the artist forgot something, or hopes to find something he overlooked. This is not the main road of art. One artist needs the artistic naiveté of historical childhood as a fresh means for expressing his psychological

---

33. A Greek word meaning the public tables at which, in ancient Sparta, all the citizens dined together, like messes in an army.

threadbareness. Along with scraps of a national style, others try to restore the life which gave rise to that style; they delve into the historical past or, even deeper, into the realm of fairy-tale and myth. Invariably, the distant past reigns over the recent past, and certainly not over the present. If the artist wants to enter into life as a whole, he goes deep into the ages. But amid that living history, which is happening before his eyes, he feels more lonely than in the primordial forests of mythology. This general impression is not one that you had first at the Viennese Secession; but it is once again confirmed here.

Albin Egger-Lienz[34] occupies the most important place in the exhibition. Remember his name, sooner or later you will do so all the same. A Tyrolean from a village near Lienz, the son of a church artist, from 1895 Egger wholeheartedly entered into the heroic past of the Tyrol. This year he exhibited only what he had just completed, a large mass picture marking the centenary of the Tyrolean uprising against Bavaria. Close to the left edge of the canvas, but in fact in the centre of the picture, stands Haspinger, the Capuchin friar. He fought against the French whilst still a student; as a member of a secret society of Tyrolean patriots, he was in the front lines of the heroic uprising of 1809. A hood is over his head, a cross is held aloft in his left hand, his right hand holds a sabre. Behind him are the Tyrolean rebels armed with guns, axes and mattocks, tense faces and bodies, all seized by the same impulse, a fearsome human wave! What grips you about the picture straightaway is its internal unanimity. Large canvasses usually break up one's attention, making the eye move from place to place, and overwhelming with details. There is nothing superfluous in Egger. He does not linger over details. The colours are without nuances, and the shadows of figures are only schematically outlined. The whole canvas — faces, arms, bare knees, clothes, the ground beneath their feet — is kept within a few brick-coloured tones. The drawing is confident, bold, almost crude. But the result is that all the obstacles and contradictions of the large canvas are overcome: it is gathered, concentrated, and the figure of the heroic friar easily becomes the centre of your attention, as the dramatic and artistic node of the picture.

Another of Egger-Lienz's works, 'Two Sowers',[35] is painted in the same severe tones. One, the 'good' sower, the Christian, is that same Tyrolean peasant, but not in that elemental effort of the uprising, but on a peaceful field, a hard-working, stubborn lover of the land. Behind him, marking his steps, is the sower of evil, naked, a copper-red devil, scattering weeds where the wheat has been sown. This devil is wonderful, waving his arms freely. You do not see the devil's mug, but from his back you see

34. Albin Egger-Lienz (1868-1926) was an Austrian painter. He studied in Munich, and was a member of the Secession during 1909-10.
35. This painting was later reworked and renamed 'The Sower and the Devil'.

that he possesses unmistakable strength. Looking at his copper-coloured skin, his athletic shoulders, his powerful neck, tireless and ill-boding, you cannot but say to yourself – the enemy of mankind is very powerful, and it is hard to believe that Mr Merezhkovsky[36] could get the better of him one to one.

In the same hall where six of Egger-Lienz's canvasses are concentrated (the other four are less significant), there are three pictures by the Cracow artist Vlastimil Hofmann.[37] Of these the most interesting is 'Madonna'. It is very much a peasant Madonna, Polish, in Polish peasant costume. She has a big, many-coloured shawl over her head and around her shoulders, with, under this, another, smaller one, enclosing her cheeks and drawn together under her chin. Her quiet, beautiful, simple peasant face really shines out from this frame. In her arms is a very delicate and frail boy, as if after some serious illness, a fair-haired boy, with a little bird. He is Christ. From under red, inflamed eyelids, the boy-Baptist[38] gazes at him with fanatical eyes. Finally, from the right corner of the picture, a city boy in an overcoat, with a soft hat in his hands – perhaps the artist's son – looks at Christ. This frail, doomed little Jesus, this pale-faced John and this gentle, almost indifferent Mary remain long engraved on the memory.

Apart from these three pictures, we found nothing of significance in the exhibition. The fantasist Rudolf Jettmar[39] donated two centaurs abducting a woman. A good old centaur, his grey head inclined towards the body of the victim of abduction, and a good woman: her face shows horror, and at the same time she is almost trustingly pressed against the mighty old one, as if seeking protection from his own self. There are several interesting landscapes, technically rich and with a mood like that which the late Leistikow[40] taught how to draw. Rudolf Nissl's[41] good 'Stroll', Friedrich König's[42] superbly sun-drenched 'Park', Anton Nowak's[43] good Tyrolean landscape. But it is also full of canvasses such as

36. Dmitri Sergeevich Merezhkovsky (1865-1941) was a Russian poet, novelist and political thinker.
37. Vlastimil Hofmann (1881-1970) was a Czech artist. Born in Prague, he studied in Cracow and Paris, and was a member of the Secession from 1908 to 1918.
38. That is, John the Baptist as a boy.
39. Rudolf Jettmar (1868-1939) was an Austrian painter who was regarded as an important exponent of European symbolism. He studied in Vienna and Karlsruhe, and was a member of the Secession from 1898 until his death.
40. Walter Leistikow (1865-1908) was a German artist, and was a founder of the Berlin Secession.
41. Rudolf Nissl (1870-1955) was an Austrian painter. He studied in Munich, and was a member of the Secession from 1897 to 1939.
42. Friedrich König (1857-1941) was an Austrian artist. He studied in Vienna and Munich, and was a member of the *Klimtgruppe*, and a member of the Secession from 1897 to 1939.
43. Anton Nowak (1865-1932) was an Austrian genre and portrait painter. He studied in

you see at every exhibition and forget as one impression forces out another. There are several pleasant portraits – such that without knowing the subject, one involuntarily exclaims: 'This must be a good likeness!' Adolphe Levier[44] sent his portrait of Mr N from Paris. It is almost a type rather than a portrait. A man of hardly-definable age with cold, clever eyes, sensual cheekbones and a hard mouth sits in a garden chair. Behind his thin lips he must have predatory teeth, the jaw of a cultured wolf with which he has already managed to bite and chew a good many in his lifetime. He appears to be an aesthete, but without enthusiasm, who believes in nothing, who worships only himself – a genuine type of international nihilist, such as has supplanted our own old 'nihilist', who was not really a nihilist but a romantic, believing in much, and worshipping much. The forerunner of this well-groomed animal amongst us was Velchaninov, who – do you remember? – reasoned: 'However their social structure may be cracking up, however people and thought may be degenerating, I, all the same, will have this fine and tasty dinner to which I am sitting down, and so I am prepared for anything.'

In the sculpture section, first place belongs to Josef Müllner's[45] huge horseman. This frozen, wild horse is beautiful, with its started-back ears and keen muzzle. And the nude rider is also beautiful, a youth becoming a man. He has put his hand to his forehead in a salute, and ardently gazes into the distance. There lies no beaten track further on, one must find one's own way. There is the unmoving horse, with no bridle, and the unmoving horseman; but in the immobility of the stone you see *Sturm und Drang* – a fortunate path, a beautiful horseman.

Anton Hanak[46] donated several large works in the Untersburg marble that is mined in Tyrol. We lingered only before his 'Mother'. She has placed her protective hand on her abdomen in which new life is felt. Her head is blind and deaf to everything that is outside her. She does not sense the looks of strangers that are cast upon her nakedness. A sort of reverential attention to her own depths at once hypnotises and animates her.

Also worthy of mention is the Viennese sculptor Alfred Hofmann's[47]

Vienna, and was a member of the Secession from 1897 to 1939.
44. Adolfo Levier (1873-1953) was an Italian painter. He studied in Munich, and was a member of the Secession from 1905 to 1918.
45. Josef Müllner (1879-1968) was an Austrian sculptor whose work adorned many public buildings in Vienna. He studied in Vienna, and was a member of the Secession from 1906 to 1911.
46. Anton Hanak (1875-1934) was an Austrian sculptor whose work often resembles that of Auguste Rodin. He studied in Vienna, and was a member of the Secession from 1906 to 1910.
47. Alfred Hofmann (1870-1956) was an Austrian sculptor. He studied in Vienna, and was a member of the Secession from 1906 to 1939.

'Turandot'. It is that princess who set her suitors riddles, and put to death those who failed to find the solution. The artist has managed an enigmatic brow and enigmatic eyes, sensual lips and a sensual chin, a combination of the Sphinx and Messalina.[48] That is, perhaps, all. If we now move from individual works to the collective physiognomy of the exhibition, then most of all, we must repeat what we said at the beginning of this letter: painting stands apart from all that makes up the soul of the present epoch. This is, of course, true in relation to art in general, but of paintings it can be said with terrible conviction. The artist goes into the forest, to the mountains, into the distant past, into the caverns of myth, and seeks there connections with life that are not here, around him. In his isolation he first enlarges his creative freedom, but soon that rich in technique but internally ravaged 'freedom' becomes more bitter for him than any tyranny. And in our eyes, the painting more and more renounces its independence and seeks subordination. It becomes exceptionally attentive towards *decorative* motifs, it strives to fuse with *architecture*. There are a lot of purely decorative works at the Secession. There are five cartoons for wall paintings by Ferdinand Andri,[49] there is a large decorative oval by Karl Schmoll,[50] there is 'The Slave' by Engelhart,[51] drawn directly on a clay square. But more expressive and more profound of that same tendency are the remarkable works of Egger-Lienz. His 'Haspinger' and his 'Sowers' undoubtedly represent the highest level of contemporary wall-painting. Movement of the air, depths of perspective, play of light — this you will search for in vain here. He is not afraid to present his figures on a single plane, and to remove air and shadow from them. But nonetheless do his stocky, solid, self-assured figures live their fascinating life.

Artists are more and more often discarding the paintbrush in favour of the chisel, or putting it into the service of architectural plans. Architecture wants to take painting and sculpture under its wing, to give them shelter and warmth for a new life. Perhaps, we are now seeing just the first steps towards a new synthetic art.

Kievskaia Mysl, no 118, 30 April 1909

48. Valeria Messalina was the wife of the Roman Emperor Claudius, notorious for her dissolute life.
49. Ferdinand Andri (1871-1956) was a minor artist and member of the *Klimtgruppe*. He studied in Vienna and Karlsruhe, and was a member of the Secession from 1899 to 1909.
50. Karl Schmoll von Eisenwerth (1879-1947) was a painter and designer from Stuttgart.
51. Joseph Engelhart (1864-1941) was a leader of Viennese naturalists whose conflict with the *Klimtgruppe* in 1905 led to a division within the Secession. He studied in Vienna and Munich, and was a member of the Secession from 1897 to 1939.

Leon Trotsky

Two Viennese Exhibitions

ONE is in the old House of Artists (*Künstlerhaus*), the other – in a rather absurd, manneredly oversimplified stone cube, topped by a small green fez, in the Secession building. The word 'Secession', once a symbol of revolt, appears in manneredly oversimplified hieroglyphs on the grey cover of the catalogue, whose simplicity is also rather forced, whilst the catalogue for the 'House of Artists' exhibition carries the burden of tradition even on its cover, in the form of three venerable but utterly bored muses – painting, sculpture and architecture.

This year, the Artists' Union is celebrating the fiftieth anniversary of its existence, and the exhibition itself is called a 'jubilee' exhibition. Half a century is not a short time in art. But Secession, too, is already approaching the middle of the second decade of its innovation. In 1897, 12 young artists rebelled against the old corporation, which in art was diligently toiling away in an academic rut, and in economic matters was even more diligently cultivating obsequiousness, Byzantinism and favouritism. The stone cube with its lace fez of gilded tin was already standing on the Karlsplatz in 1898, not far from the old House of Artists...

'Secessionism' was not a local Viennese phenomenon – it was not even initiated in Vienna – but was a Europe-wide phenomenon. The revolution in painting was merely a reflection of the revolution in life. Giant cities had grown up and bled the countryside dry, sucking into themselves all that was talented, vigorous and bold. Life became an irrepressible whirlwind. Movement triumphed over 'matter', which overflowed into effective energy. Ever-changing form pushed content into the background, and form, too, drowned in the subjective stream of impressions. A new type of human being took shape, and found his new expression in impressionist art.

The Berlin professor Georg Zimmel[52] recently talked to us here in Vienna about this new art and this 'new soul', in his brilliant lecture on Rodin.[53] The 'new soul' is constantly in motion, and this movement has

---

52. Georg Zimmel (1858-1919) was a famous philosopher and sociologist, and a professor at Berlin University. His most important works are *Die Probleme der Geschichtsphilosophie* [*The Problems of Historical Philosophy*], *Soziale Differenzierung* [*Social Differentiation*] and *Philosophie des Geldes* [*Philosophy of Money*]. [Note by *Sochineniya* Editors]

53. Auguste Rodin (1870-1919) was a celebrated French sculptor. Rodin's work, by his own admission, wavered between the harmony of classical sculpture, with the serene perfection of its forms, and the severe majesty of Michelangelo, filled with passionate struggle. Rodin's most famous works are *Primordial Man*, *The Thinker*, *The Citizens of Calais* and *Thought*. [Note by *Sochineniya* Editors]

no central direction or doctrine. Diverse not only at two barely separated moments in time, but also at one and the same time, it is never alike unto itself. It is *always* diverse. The soul of the Renaissance era was also in motion. But this motion was smooth and even, between two extreme moments of peace. People of the Renaissance wavered between faith and unbelief, between Christianity and 'paganism', between virtue and vice, and between *yes* and *no*. The modern soul knows not such limits. It mixes up and dissolves everything within itself. Its every state is merely a stage on a journey from the unknown to the unknown. It combines within itself all contradictions, its *yes* merely sets off its *no*, it believes and does not believe at one and the same time, and it loves goals without paths and paths without goals. And Rodin succeeded in expressing this permanently contradictory, disquieting, constantly shifting soul in the most unyielding and inert material – stone.

Whilst I was listening to the Berlin professor's nervous speech about the 'new soul', my mind involuntarily wandered to the late Paul Singer[54] – such a weighty, imposing, solid figure. Here was a man who knew nothing of paths without goals, or goals without paths! His goal was set out once and for all in his party's programme, and his path was clear and straight. Though he dissolved himself in the party, he always remained his own man – a unique, unbending individual. Did Singer possess this 'new soul'? Or Bebel,[55] so like a tautly drawn bow or a tense spring of action – in the name of the same goal for half a century? Or was the soul *they* displayed not 'modern'?

On the other hand, we have the American Carnegie,[56] or the Berliner Aschinger, who sits at the centre of a monstrous telephone-telegraph-stock-exchange web, and, pulling first one wire, then another, controls a turnover of millions that turn into thousands of millions. These new souls also, we must assume, have absolutely no affinity for moral and aesthetic platonism, with its paths without goals and goals without paths.

Zimmel's description abandons overboard both Aschinger and Bebel, the polar opposites of modern culture, and is reduced to group self-description. Zimmel's 'new soul' is, in fact, the soul of the intelligentsia of the cities, Impressionism is its art, and aesthetically camouflaged indif-

54. Paul Singer (1864-1911) was a member of the Central Committee of the German Social Democrats, and a contemporary of Bebel and Liebknecht Senior. Coming from a rich bourgeois family, in the 1880s he broke off all links with liberalism and the bourgeoisie, and soon became an extremely popular leader of the Berlin workers. He was a talented party organiser. He was a member of the Reichstag from 1884, and frequently chairman of German *Parteitags* and international Socialist congresses. He was staunchly 'orthodox' in a time of revisionism. [Note by *Sochineniya* Editors]

55. August Bebel (1840-1913) was a leader of the German Social Democratic Party, which he represented in the Reichstag from 1871 and chaired from 1875 until his death.

56. Andrew Carnegie (1835-1919) was an impoverished Scottish immigrant into the USA. He made a fortune in finance and manufacture, and was a philanthropist.

ference is its social morals. Nietzsche is its prophet, *Simplizissimus*[57] is its satire, Zimmel is its philosophical satirist, and Sombart[58] is its economic satirist.

In the first period of its self-definition, the new intelligentsia, which had then loudly severed its links with tradition in all areas of philosophy, morals and art, looked for support in society. But it did not take long for it to overcome its own social tendencies through refined individualism. 'I understand everything', the repository of this 'new soul' might say about himself, 'but I value this understanding that I possess far higher than I do the practical conclusions to which it commits me. For me, human history is only interesting inasmuch as it is resolved in my cerebral hemispheres; the history that is being made today on the streets is too much of the masses for my liking, and is therefore alien to me. Do not think that I love mental tranquillity, or yearn for the old completeness of forms (except at times, possibly, at odd moments!); on the contrary, eternal motion and spiritual disquiet are my element; but what I do very much value, apart from anything else, is... bodily tranquillity.'

Having severed its short-lived and superficial links with society, the new art became firmly entrenched on paths without goals. It very soon left behind its period of daring, brought its technique to heights that were striking in the variety of its devices, and exhausted itself. The gold on the Secession dome peeled off, the tin grew slightly rusty, and, moving from the exhibition of the 'rebels' to the exhibition of the 'slaves to routine', it is difficult to distinguish what it is, exactly, that separates these two camps.

What is immediately striking about both exhibitions is the overwhelming preponderance of landscapes and portraits, that is, of the most individualistic types of art. Portraits, like landscapes, are expressions of the *solitary* soul. And it has to be admitted that today's artists have learned how to infuse their portraits with a degree of intimacy that is lacking in the works of even the best of the Old Masters. Their female portraits, at which the old artists proved less successful than male portraits, are especially good. The external energy connected with a man's social rôle (warrior, priest, judge, burgomaster...) was reflected in the portrait and gave the face significance. Women did not have this social rôle, which is why the old female portraits are so flat. But today's artists, intimists, 'Underground' people, in the words of Dostoevsky, have learned to bring out not the external energy of the warrior or burgomaster (on the contrary, *this* they have lost the art of doing), but the inner concentration of the face, and its concentration on its own mental experiences

---

57. *Simplizissimus* was a famous liberal German humour magazine.
58. Werner Sombart (1863-1941) was a prominent anti-Socialist economist who criticised Marx's labour theory of value.

and modulations of feeling. The face is almost completely dissolved in the mood, so that the viewer has to make a creative effort in order to put the face back together again – and this pleasurable creative work itself becomes a source of pleasure. The Parisian Alfred Roll's[59] 'Woman with Poppies' is beautiful – and not because of the refined lips and nostrils of her thin face, nor because of the delicate curve of her chin and neck, but because of those invisible currents of melancholy *joie de vivre* that not only animate the face, but also make it *change its mood* before your very eyes. Shmoll von Eisenwerth's woman with flowers, on the steps of a stone staircase, goes even further in this direction. Her facial features are only barely visible through the haze of pensiveness. Melancholy pensive-ness shrouds her whole figure, and can even be sensed in the curve of her hand, the folds of her dress, and the steps of the staircase. Two more of Eisenwerth's paintings are painted in the same intimate tones: a slender girl on a veranda in the early hours of dawn – all expectant, almost fear-fully expectant; and a woman shrouded in a green penumbra, in a state of frozen alarm ('Awaiting Spring' and 'In the Summer-House', respec-tively). Both of them – both Roll and Eisenwerth – are in the Secession exhibition.

This ability of the new portrait-painters to draw out the soul's inner-most experiences through the veneer of stateliness, bellicosity, erudition or 'nobility' makes many of the portraits of cardinals, judges, professors and ministers extremely akin to secret caricatures. Luckily for their distin-guished clients, there are still a great many portrait-painters able to place a general jauntily on a black horse, magnificently to exaggerate an admiral's cloak, to endow the lawyer's forehead with a Roman pleat, and to paint all the diamonds of a commercial advisor's wife with the professional thorough-ness of a Lombard valuer. But it should be noted that most of these por-traitists are still concentrated in the old, patronised corporation...

The soul that loves paths without goals is a stranger to both passion and power. On the other hand, it is often no stranger to a *yearning* for power, primeval wholeness, even coarseness. The Secession exhibition contains many portrayals of the powerful body and elemental passions – but the images of passion are fatally lacking in passion, and the images of power lack power. Rudolf Jettmar's Hercules looks like a circus strong-man, and the mighty dragon is like a scarecrow stuffed with straw. Hein-rich Zita[60] depicts 'unbridled power' in the form of a young centaur. His method is the same as Rodin's: part of the figure is concealed in the raw material, as if in the bowels of Mother Nature. You can see the block

59. Alfred Philippe Roll (1846-1919) studied in Paris, and was famous for his landscapes, portraits and paintings of animals. He was a member of the Secession from 1897.
60. Heinrich Zita (1882-1951) was an Austrian sculptor, and was a member of the Seces-sion from 1913 to 1939.

from which the chisel liberated the beautiful image, having got rid of superfluous material, and, since the figure is incomplete, you complete it yourself by mentally reproducing the creative process. But in the Viennese sculptor's majolica centaur, the embodiment of unbridled power, you see behind the well-developed muscles neither unbridledness nor power, but only the artist's attempt to impart them both. Grom-Rottmeyer[61] exhibited the ornamental canvas 'Strength and Guile'. Guile is represented by a naked woman, whilst power is signified by a gloomy-looking knight – similar to the ones that stand at the entrances to waxworks or moving-picture houses. 'Power' fares no better in the 'House of Artists'. Wieland's blacksmith, exhibited by Wollek,[62] attests far more to brutish coarseness than he does to power.

The overwhelming majority of the works exhibited, particularly in Secession, are landscapes (forests, mountains, seas, parks, old castles), portraits and sketches, corners of old towns, interiors and still lives. Once in a while, the landscape is enlivened by a figure, but it is normally that of a peasant, a constituent part of the landscape. Interiors depict the corner of an apartment, a fir-tree on a carpet, covered in trinkets, an alcove in the dwelling of a Lower-Austrian peasant, or part of a room in rococo style; people were only just here: everything is still marked by the imprint of their lives, but they themselves are no longer here. If there is an urban street, it is always old, narrow, in semi-darkness, or without people; the darkened stones here testify to the centuries that have been lived in them. If there is a harbour, it is always shown on Sunday, when the ships are at rest, without people. There are many churches at twilight, where the praying figures only reinforce the impression of peace, solitude and isolation from the world. Here there is a smithy: a hearth, bellows, an anvil, hammers – but no blacksmiths. If people are depicted, they are never in their working environment, never in their social function, but at rest, on a public holiday, or at play. We have a village square on Sunday or a market in a small town, where people shift about senselessly, chat and listlessly buy things. But all this is dwarfed by the number of landscapes, portraits, interiors and still lives (*Stilleben*), where there is a cucumber lovingly traced out on a glass plate, a Japanese doll, and a sliced lemon...

Sculpture has no place in either landscapes or interiors: whether it likes it or not, it is compelled to deal with *man*. The same has to be said of the sculptured portraits as of the painted portraits: they are often beautiful in their communication of intimacy in the soul. The bodies are not as perfect or as divinely proportioned as in classical sculpture, but

61. Hermann Grom-Rottmeyer (1877-1953) was an Austrian artist. He studied in Vienna and Munich, and was a member of the Secession from 1910 to 1939.
62. Johann Georg Wieland (1742-1802) was a German sculptor who concentrated on church interiors; Carl Wollek (1862-1936) was an Austrian sculptor.

they are incomparably closer to us, softer, more delicate, more human. The achievement of Rodin, the greatest Impressionist – to subordinate the whole body, from the little toe up, to the movement of the soul – entered sculpture and enriched it. But sculpture seems to be looking around helplessly, not knowing what it should do with this wealth. In Secession, sculpture is barren to the utmost degree, though in the artists' jubilee exhibition it is represented somewhat better. But in both exhibitions the poverty of the creative project is staggering. The bronze 'Well-Wisher' in a long frock-coat, high stockings and be-ribboned shoes bows affectedly. The satyr pours wine. The skittles-player prepares to roll the ball. Siegfried admires the sword he has forged. The shot-putter prepares to throw the hammer. 'Night' comes with a wire hoop decorated with tinsel stars. The storyteller tells fairy tales. There is a child with a cat. There's Perseus. There is the inevitable 'abundance', in the form of a girl laden with fruit, and female bathers, of course. A travelling musician looks back at a dancing goose. A fist-fighter throws down a challenge. There's Ganymede, Diana...

However often our native aesthetes in this period of stagnation may repeat that *form* in art has exhausted itself, we will never believe it. In sculpture we will value not only Rodin, who managed to find completely new forms in the most inflexible of arts, but also the great Belgian Meunier,[63] who, without breaking with form, conquered a new content for sculpture.

Classical sculpture reproduced the human body in a state of harmonious peace. Renaissance sculpture mastered the art of movement. But Michelangelo[64] used movement to express the body's harmony more vividly. Rodin, on the other hand, made movement itself the subject of the sculpture. In Michelangelo the body creates for itself its own individual movement, whereas in Rodin, on the contrary, movement finds for itself the body it needs. But Rodin did not extend sculpture's grasp. This was done by Meunier, who introduced into sculpture *the worker at work*. Before him, sculptured figures were standing, sitting, sleeping, dancing, playing, fighting, resting, praying, loving, but never *working*. When a man is at rest, when he is dancing, loving or praying, his body is self-sufficient unto itself. Rodin subordinated the body to movement, but to *inner* movement, the movement of the soul living inside the body itself. Love,

63. Constantine Meunier (1881–1905) was a Belgian realist sculptor, and author of unaffected, monumental and majestic depictions of labour and working life. [Note by *Sochineniya* Editors]

64. Michelangelo Buonarroti was one of the greatest artists of the Italian Renaissance, a sculptor, painter and poet, and creator of the frescos in the Sistine Chapel in the Vatican, which depict scenes from the Old Testament and are crowned by a picture of the Last Judgement. All Michelangelo's works bear the stamp of enormous power and passion. The most famous of Michelangelo's sculptures are *David*, *Moses* and the *Tomb of the Medicis*. [Note by *Sochineniya* Editors]

thought, grief – these are Rodin's themes. During work the body is sub-ordinated to a goal that lies *outside* itself, it ceases to be self-sufficient unto itself, and becomes a tool. Moreover, the artificial tools of labour extend the body's natural field. All this excluded physical labour from the sphere of sculpture. Meunier succeeded in showing that the exertions of labour, directed at a resistant material, do not destroy the body's whole-ness, but, rather, give it new expression; in extending the body's field, labour does not destroy that field; in turning the body into a tool, it makes the tool, too, an animated part of the body. As Zimmel would put it, Meunier discovered the *aesthetic* value of *labour*. An immense, as yet untouched realm unfolded before sculpture.

Meunier's aesthetic discovery had deep social roots. Whilst labour was the lot of slaves, either legal or moral, it remained beyond the threshold of art. Only the social awakening of the 'subject' of labour, the working class, turned labour into a problem for science, philosophy, morals and art. Meunier aesthetically resolved this problem. But the further devel-opment of sculpture revealed all the more clearly that an aesthetic solu-tion alone was not enough. Having shown *how* to reproduce the exertions of labour in sculptured material, Meunier was unable, of course, to draw tight the social and moral bonds between the world of art and the world of physical labour. Disconnectedness remained as strong as ever. Whilst social life was unravelling from itself contradictions unprecedented in world history, and lining up the powerful social movements of these con-tradictions, art retreated ever more into the fragile shell of the new soul, and, retreating before the onslaught of social passions, deserted com-pletely the great field of collective human life, and went into voluntary exile – into landscapes, portraits, still lives and interiors, into idyll and mythology... Although three-quarters of modern artists are pupils and inhabitants of cities, you will not find the city, with its marvels of tech-nical power, with its collective sufferings, passions and ideals, in their paintings or sculptures. In both exhibitions, I found only two works that reflected the new life of the towns. Karl Schulda depicted the construc-tion works of a huge building on Mariahilferstrasse (in Vienna). Olaf Lange produced the colour engraving 'The Appeal'. In Karl Schulda's pic-ture, the outlines of woods stand out dimly against the twilight, and against these woods dimly slip the figures of faceless workers, mere hu-man silhouettes. This is how working people appear to one who casts a fleeting glance at them *from the sidelines*. In Lange's engraving, a mass of people is moving beneath a bridge; working men and women, children – a whole stream of humanity. Part of the bridge is destroyed, and an 'appeal' is being given out from the bridge. The whole composition is muffled, as if the artist himself was only dimly aware of where the crowd was heading, and to what the appeal was directed...

This small canvas and this small engraving reveal even more clearly the themelessness and, to put it bluntly, the poverty of today's fine arts – a poverty that exists in spite of all the richness of forms and techniques. Something larger has to come together beyond the boundaries of art, in the very bowels of our society, if art is to return from its exile, be enriched with the drama of the working and struggling man, and, in turn, enrich his labour and his struggle...

❖   ❖   ❖

Let us make a few remarks on individual works in the 'House of Artists'. The famous Munich artist Defregger[65] exhibited the large painting 'The Adoration of the Magi', in which both Mary and the shepherds look like some of Defregger's Tyrolean peasants. There is an interesting idea behind the work exhibited by the Viennese artist Kasparides.[66] A field of battle is strewn with the naked corpses of fallen warriors. In the evening gloom, a spectral Christ towers above the field, dark and reproaching. A warrior stands facing him, humbly yet impertinently... In Jacob Epstein's greengrocer's shop, the artists has assembled a group of unskilled labourers, seemingly during their lunch break. It is hot, their bodies are sweaty, and their parched lips greedily press themselves to a juicy water-melon; one of the customers, evidently an inveterate clown, is holding a juicy conversation with the young shop-girl; all around lie magnificent water-melons, pomegranates and pumpkins, whilst the others, having sought shelter from the heat, merrily suck in the water-melon juice and listen to the proprietress' vigorous laughter. The Dresden artist Max painted a frightened boy ('Der Aengstliche') with a thin little face, eyes wide open in terror, a thin, tensely stretched little neck, his little fingers separated in a spasm of fear. What is it that has frightened him? A ghost? No, it must be a stern shout from his father, or an even more menacing glance from his teacher. Fathers and teachers are more terrifying than any ghosts. Alexander Rothaug's triptych tells the old tale of the beautiful Helen in paint. The Greeks are on one wing, the Trojans are on the other. Their bodies are dark-complexioned, grown coarse from the sun and the wind, their gazes are concentrated, and their muscles are tensed; there are dead and injured. Between the two wings, Helen, the cause of the war, faces the viewer. Naked, beautiful, serene, she is unhurriedly fastening the gold buckle on her tunic.

There are a number of paintings of the 'Byzantine' school in the jubilee exhibition, such as the four muzzles of the emperor Franz Joseph's[67]

65. Franz von Defregger (1835-1921) was an Austrian painter who specialised in peasant genre scenes, portraits and interiors.
66. Eduard Kasparides was an Austrian artist, who, along with many of the members of the Secession, was a member of the Haagen Society, which discussed problems of modern art.
67. Franz Joseph Habsburg (1830-1916) was Emperor of Austria.

'favourite' horses. There are patriotic battle scenes and edifying historical pictures, specially commissioned by the heir to the throne Franz Ferdinand,[68] a man of martial and clerical disposition, for his new palace. An inscription next to one of these edifying works openly states that its aim is to 'refute widespread Protestant accusations of the Catholic emperors' cruelty'. In the room next to the one that houses this commissioned work of Catholic apologetics hangs a small canvas by Leo Delitz, 'In the Confessional'. A young peasant woman is piously confessing her sins, whilst the priest, avidly listening to her with one ear, is extraordinarily reminiscent of a tom-cat in spring. I looked for the explanation that this picture was painted to refute the criminal narratives of the *Decameron*[69] on the morality of Catholic priests, but there was no such inscription. Obviously, explanations are called for only when the picture itself is not sufficiently persuasive. Whether or not these printed commentaries are of any help I do not know – that is up to the clients to decide.

Kievskaia Mysl, no 145, 27 May 1911

Leon Trotsky

On The Intelligentsia[70]

I

THESE were foul years, the years of the victors' triumph. But the most awful thing that happened (and is still happening) was not, in fact, embodied in the victors themselves. Those who hung on to the victors' coat-tails have been much worse. But even worse for the spirits were

68. Archduke Franz Ferdinand (1863-1914) was heir to the Austrian throne. His assassination in Sarajevo sparked off the First World War.
69. The *Decameron* was one of the greatest works of the Italian Renaissance, written by Giovanni Boccaccio (born 1313). The *Decameron* is a collection of one hundred novellas – rollicking, often obscene stories that are good-natured satires on the clergy and, especially, monks, which paint a vivid picture of life in the author's day. [Note by *Sochineniya* Editors]
70. This article was written in the form of a challenge to the study-circle Messianism of the intelligentsia's coffee houses, which even from a great distance (Petersburg, Moscow – Vienna) has become unbearable. The article languished for a long time in the files of *Kievskaia Mysl*; the editors could not make up their minds whether or not to print it. The political revival that began in 1912 refreshed the atmosphere, and the article saw the light of day, although with severe cuts. It is in this shortened form that it is printed here. [Note by Trotsky, June 1922]

yesterday's 'friends' and half-friends – those who moralised, indulged in *Schadenfreude*, relished the turn of events, or sniggered into their sleeves.

The dismal nightmare of recent years was not Menshikovism but Vekhism.[71] Newspapers, thick journals, collections, speeches, salon conversations – everything smelled of Vekhism. You could wash your hands with coal-tar soap, but this smell would still haunt you, even at night.

Nobody liked Saltykov during these days. It was a question not simply of changing literary tastes, but of the moral character of the age. They did not like him because they were afraid of him. His images of the scoundrel – 'the dominant influence of the modern age', the victorious cad, 'the liberal marching in step with baseness' – were unbearable for an age that was embellishing Menshikovism with Vekhism.

When Mr Milyukov,[72] taking advantage of the depressed public mood, announced in *Ryech*[73] that he would henceforth finally cast off the 'donkey' from his back, he (Mr Milyukov, of course) was thereby merely formulating the essence of the process that was occurring simultaneously in all sections and groups of the intelligentsia – not only on the Olympus of the Cadets. Leonid Andreev[74] and Balmont,[75] Merezhkovsky and Chaliapin,[76] and the Chukovskys,[77] Galiches, Zhilkins,[78] Posses,[79] Engelgardts and Minskys[80] – all in one way or another cast off from their backs some 'donkey' of their former passions, sympathies and hopes.

And thousands of nameless people followed in their footsteps. Taking different paths and turnings – unbridled individualism, aristocratic scepticism, crude anarchism, Merezhkovskyism and unprincipled satirical mockery – everyone aspired to 'culture'. Everybody was fed up with the intelligentsia's old asceticism – they wanted clean linen and a bathroom in their apartments. Galich called this yearning for clean linen 'a religion'.

A peculiar type of talentless journalist appeared, one who neither had

71. A reference to the retreat into philosophical idealism and the political paralysis exemplified by the contributors to the journal *Vekhi*.
72. Pavel Nikolaevich Milyukov (1859-1943) was an historian and a leader of the Constitutional Democrat or Cadet Party.
73. *Ryech* was the Cadet's daily paper. It ran from 1906 until its suppression by the Soviet government in 1917.
74. Leonid Nikolaevich Andreev (1871-1919) was a well-known Russian novelist.
75. Konstantin Dmitrievich Balmont (1867-1942) was a noted Russian poet, and an adherent of the Modernist trend.
76. Fedor Ivanovich Chaliapin (Shaliapin, 1873-1938) was a popular operatic bass vocalist. He abandoned his democratic ideals after 1905.
77. Chukovsky was the pseudonym of Nikolai Vasilievich Korneichuko (1882-1969), a noted Russian writer, journalist and literary critic.
78. Ivan Vasilievich Zhilkin was a journalist and a member of the Second Duma.
79. Vladimir Aleksandrovich Posse (1864-) was a Social Democratic writer, and ran *Zhizn (Life)*, which became the mouthpiece of Legal Marxism.
80. Minsky was the pseudonym of Nikolai Maksimovich Vilenkin (1885-1937), a Russian poet who favoured individualism in art.

nor wanted to have any ideas of his own, but who knew how to stick his tongue out at the past. We all remember how often during those three long years we would read articles by Izgoev's group, and say to ourselves: 'All right... we will wait... we'll just have to learn to wait...'

But it became clear: the reason we were condemned to suffer the ignominy of Vekhism's imprisonment of social thought was that the intelligentsia remained alone on the open stage – with its newspapers, journals, almanacs, satires and literary taverns, and with its feebleness – once again alone, when it should have realised, and have seen with its own eyes, that genuine, authentic, real history is created not by itself, but by other, larger forces. It became clear just how unreliable were the intelligentsia's own reserves of moral fibre...

But such is the ironic nature of history: it was in this very period of near-universal self-denial and retreat from previously-held positions that the cliquish self-importance of the intelligentsia reached its highest intensity. Never had it taken up so much space, and in the most diverse camps – from Octobrism[81] to Marxism; never had it been the focus of so much attention, nor been so concerned with itself, as in these recent years. Never before had it indulged in such self-congratulation, narcissism and pretension. It studied itself from head to foot, and there was surely not one gesture, nor wrinkle of the soul, which it would not record about itself with narcissistic thoroughness. I am religion! I am culture! I am the past, present and future!

As we know, Mr Ivanov-Razumnik[82] has based an entire philosophy of history upon this megalomania. For him, the Russian intelligentsia, as a classless, ideologically pure group, burning with a sacred flame, is the mainspring of historical development. It is conducting a great struggle against 'philistine ethics', and conquering new spiritual worlds which the philistines can only assimilate slowly and in small doses. It is tireless, and with pilgrim's staff in hand marches ever forwards towards new worlds. And, according to Ivanov-Razumnik, this self-sufficient movement of the intelligentsia determines the course of Russian history. And Mr Merezhkovsky has even promised us that the Russian intelligentsia, armed with religious dogma, will save the entire world from the coming boorishness. And there are some who believe him. What are the roots of this self-styled messianism? What are the causes of the striking tenacity of the intelligentsia's arrogance? Is it a reflection of a higher calling, or simply the national trait of Khlestakovism?[83] No, it is merely the ideo-

81. The Octobrists represented the interests of big industrial capitalists and landowners. Their name was based on their support for the manifesto issued by Tsar Nicholas II on 17 October 1905.
82. Vyacheslav Ivanovich Ivanov-Razumnik (1866-1919) was a Russian poet, Slavophil and Nietzschean philosopher.
83. Khlestakov is a leading character in Gogol's *The Inspector General*, an arch-swindler

logical reflection of that fatal curse of Russian history, Karataevism.[84] It
is merely a supplement to the meekness of Alyosha Gorshok.[85]

For although Ivanov-Razumnik has been superficially persuasive in
presenting the entire history of our social thought as the self-sufficient
history of the intelligentsia, it is not simply a case of falsifying history. It
is, of course, a falsification, and a monstrous one at that. But the point is
that this falsification reflects an important and tragic fact that is a burden on the whole evolution of our society. The name of this fact is
backwardness, poverty, cultural pauperism.

II

That we are desperately poor with the accumulated poverty of a thousand
years needs no proof. History has shaken us out of its sleeve into a bleak
environment, and scattered us thinly over a vast plain. Nobody offered us
another place to live: we have had to toil away on our allotted strip. Asiatic invasions from the east, relentless pressure from a wealthier Europe
to the west, a state leviathan swallowing up an excessive share of the
people's labour — all of this not only deprived the working masses of
their share, but also dried up the ruling classes' sources of sustenance.
Hence their slow growth, and the barely perceptible veneer of 'cultural'
deposits over the virgin soil of social barbarism. The Russian people were
oppressed by the nobility and clericalism just as severely as were the
Western peoples. But we never experienced the complex and closed-off
way of life — the gothic lacework of feudalism — that developed in
Europe on the foundations of class supremacy, because we simply did
not have the material resources. We are a poor nation. For a thousand
years, we lived in a humble log cabin, whose cracks were blocked up with
moss — would it have been proper to dream of pointed arches and gothic
turrets?

How pitiful is our nobility, cheated by history! Where are its castles?
Where are its tournaments, its crusades, standard-bearers, minstrels,
pages? Where is chivalrous love? It does not exist — it is all completely
empty. Perhaps it is because the Mstislavs[86] and the Trubetskois[87] threw

and braggart.

84. Platon Karataev is a character in Tolstoy's *War and Peace* who exemplifies the long-
suffering submissiveness of the peasantry.

85. Alyosha Gorshok is the title character of a posthumously-published story by Tolstoy.
Of peasant origin, he works as a servant in the city, and lives and dies without utter-
ing a word of protest against his miserable fate.

86. There were several ancient Russian princes with the name of Mstislav. Mstislav
Vladimirovich (-1036) ruled Tmutarakan and Chernigov, and fought against the Kazars
and Poland, extending his domains on several occasions. Mstislav Vladimirovich (1076-
1132) ruled Novgorod, Rostov, Smolensk and Kiev at various times, and fought against

everything that offended them under the table in revenge... this was all their chivalrous honour was capable of.

Our bureaucracy, drawn from the nobility, displayed all the historical wretchedness of that nobility. Where are its great powers and names? Even at its peak, it was never more than a third-rate imitation of the Duke of Alva,[88] Colbert,[89] Turgot,[90] Metternich[91] and Bismarck.[92]

Examine every other aspect of our culture, and it is the same story. Poor Chaadaev[93] yearned for Catholicism, which he saw as a refined religious culture that had managed to concentrate within its heart enormous moral and intellectual forces. With the hindsight of history, he saw Catholicism as the highroad of human development, and felt lost on the country lane of Nikon's[94] reforms. Catholic Europe produced the Reformation — a powerful movement setting the boundary between mediaeval and modern history. The burgher, hatched from a feudal shell, rose up against the automatism of the Catholic church, and strove to establish a more intimate relationship between himself and his God. This was a spiritual revolution of colossal significance, and marked the emergence of a new type of individual — at the beginning of the sixteenth century! What can our history show that even comes close to the Reformation? Nikon's reforms?

How striking are the differences between cultural types when viewed through the prism of urban history! The mediaeval European city was the

many neighbouring states. Mstislav Mstislavovich Udaloi (-1228) governed Novgorod, Galich and Torchesk at various times. He fought against the Poles, Hungarians and rival princes, but when defeated by the Tartars at the Kalka River in 1223, he destroyed the Dneiper bridges and left the Russian troops to their fate.

87. There were several Russian princes of that name — Dmitri Timofeevich Trubetskoi (-1625), Aleksei Nikitich Trubetskoi (-1680), and Nikita Yurievich Trubetskoi (1699-1767) — who were all important political and military figures.

88. Fernando Alvarez de Toledo y Pimental, Third Duke of Alva (1507-1582) was notorious for his repressive policies as Governor of the Netherlands (1567-73), where he set up the Council of Blood.

89. Jean Baptiste Colbert (1619-1683) was Louis XIV's finance minister.

90. Anne Robert Jacques Turgot (1727-1781) was the famous political economist and Controller-General of Finance who was dismissed by Louis XVI when he attempted to put in order the finances of the *ancien régime*.

91. Klemens Wenzel Nepomuk Lothar Metternich, Fürst von Metternich-Winneburg-Beilstein (1773-1859) was the reactionary Austrian foreign minister (1809-1848) who attempted to hold back the tide of nationalism and liberalism in Europe.

92. Otto Eduard Leopold Bismarck, Graf von Bismarck-Schönhausen (1815-1898), the 'Iron Chancellor', was the chief minister of the Prussian state, and was largely responsible for the unification of Germany.

93. Pyotr Yakovlevich Chaadaev (1794-1856) was a Russian philosopher who criticised Tsarism, and later turned to mysticism.

94. Nikita Minim Nikon (1605-1681) was patriarch of the Russian Orthodox Church who sought to subject to it the state. He fell into disfavour with the Tsar, and suffered exile.

stone cradle of the third estate. The guilds, workshops, municipalities and universities paved the way for a whole new epoch with their assemblies, elections, processions, festivals and debates; it was there that the precious skills of self-government were developed; it was there that the concept of the individual arose — a bourgeois individual, it is true, but still an individual, not a snout that every policeman was at liberty to punch. When the third estate felt constrained by the old corporations, all it had to do was translate the new relationships that had arisen in the cities to the state as a whole. And what of our cities, which are barely classifiable even as mediaeval? They were not centres of commerce and artisanship, but merely military and aristocratic excrescences on the body of the Russian countryside. Their rôle was parasitic. They contained landowners, servants, soldiers, bureaucrats... Instead of self-government, they had Skvoznik-Dmukhanovsky[95] or Count Rastopchin.[96] In the reign of Peter the Great, Saltykov[97] advised reclassifying the merchant classes, that is to say, the very people whom Skvoznik had called arch-cheats and arch-rogues, as barons, patricians and counts. Patrician Kolupaev and Burgher-Count Razuvaev! This sort of bureaucratic masquerade was played out throughout Russia, but it neither covered nor concealed our social poverty. During Peter's reign, workshops were imposed by the police, but these workshops did not produce an urban guilds culture. The poverty of our bourgeois-democratic traditions is thus rooted in the character of our pre-capitalist cities, and is simply an extension of the primitive character of our class traditions.

Russia is a poor country, and if we look back we can see that she has a poor history. This lack of social personality, this slavery of a spirit impotent to rise above the herd instinct, our Slavophils wanted to immortalise as 'meekness' and 'humility' — the best attributes of the Slav soul. The Narodniks wanted to make the country's economic primitiveness the source of social miracles. And, finally, our newly constituted subjectivists, crawling on their bellies in the same social and political squalor, are turning history into the apotheosis of the intelligentsia.

Since the eighteenth century (and even earlier than that), our whole history has unfolded under increasing pressure from the West. The two groupings that have been most swiftly 'Europeanised' are becoming increasingly hostile to each other, but both are equally part of the social

95. Skvoznik-Dmukhanovsky is the leading character in Gogol's *The Inspector General*, the local autocrat, a bribe-taker and swindler.
96. Fedor Vasilievich Rastopchin (1763-1826) was the Commander-in-Chief of Moscow in 1812, and was alleged to have started the burning of the city to prevent it falling into Napoleon's hands.
97. Fedor Stepanovich Saltykov (-1715) was sent abroad by Peter I to study advanced technology in order to help the Tsar's Westernisation programme, and was an advocate of social and economic reform.

superstructure, and are equally removed from the economic and social depths of the lives of the common people. The first grouping is composed of those in charge of the material technology of the state, who are subject to the most pressure from the West, and whose powers of resistance are minimal. The second grouping is a new stratum, composed of those whose consciousness has been shaped by European influences — the intelligentsia. These influences penetrated incomparably more slowly amongst the masses, who were plunged in darkness as if at the bottom of the ocean, even though the surface waters were already reflecting the rays of the rising sun... The intelligentsia has been a national antenna thrust into European culture. The state both needs it and fears it; at first it forcibly educated it, but then held a riding crop over its head. Since the time of Catherine II, the intelligentsia has become ever more hostile to the state, the privileged classes, and the propertied classes in general. We know what the underlying social causes of this hostility are: the poverty, coarseness and ugliness of a regime and society moulded by men like Arakcheev[98] and Khlynov.

'Forgive me, but I do not like that trait in you', says one of Ostrovsky's[99] characters of the merchant Khlynov.

'Which trait, may I ask?'

'Your swinishness.'

Indeed; how can swinishness be loved by one whose intellect has absorbed higher things? In the light of new European concepts, achievements and ideals, the old Russian 'traits' must have stood out ever more glaringly and unbearably. This is why the younger generation of the nobility, who stopped merely vegetating and entered the sunlit atmosphere of European ideology, completely cut themselves off, after practically no inner struggle, from their class traditions and inherited 'faith'. Having measured the spiritual chasm separating their new consciousness from the semi-zoological existence of their fathers, they became puffed up with ideological arrogance. But this arrogance was merely the obverse side of their social weakness.

Culture binds people together and imposes constraints; it is conservative, and the richer it is, the more conservative it is. In Europe, every new idea cutting its way through the solid body of the old culture was met by the deadening resistance of the old outworn ideology, and by a keen rebuff from entrenched interests. In struggling against this resistance, the new idea gained in strength, captured the minds of ever wider social circles, and finally triumphed as the banner of new classes and strata

98. Aleksei Andreevich Arakcheev (1769-1834) was one of the most reactionary representatives of the Tsarist regime.
99. Aleksandr Nikolaevich Ostrovsky (1823-1886) was a playwright who helped to develop the theatre in Russia. His works often exposed the seamy practices of merchants.

struggling to establish their own place in the sun. In subordinating the rebellious idea to their own requirements, the new classes bound and restricted it socially, depriving it of its absolute meaning. Yet it was under this banner of the 'restricted' idea that social development as a whole took great leaps forward. It was thanks to its organic origins that the new idea acquired social stability and, having triumphed, itself became a conservative force.

New ideas appeared to us 'from that shore'[100] as ready-made products of an alien ideological evolution, as finished formulae — like corals slowly deposited in the ocean by some natural process, which women receive ready-made as adornments for their necks. Of the first periods of borrowing there is nothing to be said. Pseudo-classicism, romanticism and sentimentalism, which in the West stood for whole epochs and classes, profound historical reshufflings and experiences, became in the aristocratic salons of Moscow and St Petersburg merely formal stages of literary evolution. Later on, however, when the ideas ceased being merely coral adornments and became the inspiration for the intelligentsia's actions, actions sometimes of an heroically self-sacrificing nature — in that more mature epoch our historical poverty created an enormous discrepancy between the ideological premises and the social results of the intelligentsia's efforts. Hammering nails into walls for hours on end became the Russian intelligentsia's historical calling.

To avoid spending all one's time getting drunk and playing at cards in the debauched and inebriated atmosphere of the 'dead souls', some great ideological concern was needed that would attract all one's moral strengths like a magnet, and keep them in constant tension. To avoid taking bribes and to stay away from the company of grafters and bribe-takers, some deeply-held principles were needed setting one apart from one's milieu and turning one onto a renegade; it required joining the *Carbonari* or, at least, the Freemasons.[101] To marry against daddy's wishes, you had to become a materialist and a Darwinist, that is to say, firmly to comprehend that man is descended from the apes, and that daddy therefore stands closer to the apes on the ascending genealogical ladder than does his son. To concern yourself with Roman law or the surgeon's lancet demanded, in principle, that you read forbidden literature and arrive at the unshakeable conviction that without political freedom the lancet would turn out to be a blunt and rusty hunk of iron. To struggle for a constitution, the intelligentsia needed the ideal of Socialism. Finally, it had to deny the worth of all 'transient' political values before the su-

100. A play on the title of Herzen's book *From Another Shore*, written when he was in exile in Europe.
101. Trotsky uses the rather derogatory term *'farmason'*, which was used to describe not only masons, but freethinkers, political oppositionists and generally unconventional people.

preme tribunal of 'Duty' and 'Beauty' — for the sole purpose of making it easier to reconcile itself with the regime of 3 June.[102]

Thus we have a fatal discrepancy between ideology and worldly social practice — glaring evidence of its own poverty which the intelligentsia, however, treats as justification for its unbridled arrogance.

'Look', they say, 'at the kind of people we are: special, chosen, "anti-philistine", seekers after the City of the Future... Our people, if truth be told, are savages — they do not wash their hands or rinse their ladles; but the intelligentsia has suffered crucifixion for their sake, and has concentrated in itself all the people's yearning for truth; for a century and a half it has dedicated its whole life to shining like a bright beacon for the people.' The intelligentsia has been substituting itself for political parties, classes, and the people. The intelligentsia has experienced entire cultural epochs — on behalf of the people. The intelligentsia has chosen the paths of development — for the people. Where has all this titanic work been going on? Why, in the imagination of this same intelligentsia!

III

The class culture that the old Russian 'intellectual' renounced was primitive, and incapable of subordinating to itself the growing forces of individual consciousness. He easily liberated himself from this culture, after barely any struggle, under the influence of ideas engendered in another, higher, more valuable culture. Having torn himself away from his class roots, this class splinter became a renegade, and therefore felt himself to be absolutely 'free' in his choice of ways and means. He was finished with the past, and saw the future as a large blank sheet. From this arose the boundless subjective radicalism of our repentant noblemen and seminary students, and this, too, is the source of the intelligentsia's delusions of grandeur. In Dostoevsky's novel *A Raw Youth*, Versilov looks at Europe, as Herzen did, with a semi-contemptuous longing. 'There', he says, 'the conservative is struggling merely to make a living, and the store clerk pours out his kerosene merely to earn his morsel of bread. Only Russia lives *not for itself, but for the sake of an idea*... Russia [that is, its intelligentsia — LT] has been living for almost a century with absolutely no thought for itself, but for Europe alone.' The same Versilov says that 'Europe created the noble types of Frenchman, Englishman, German, but it still knows next to nothing of the European man of the future. And it would seem that she does not yet want to know. This is understandable, *since they are not free, whereas we are free*. In all Europe, I alone, with my Russian melancholy, have been free...'

102. On 3 June 1907, the Tsar's government dissolved the Second Duma, an act that was followed by the arrest of the Social Democratic deputies, and illegally changed the electoral law to the disadvantage of the workers and peasants.

Versilov cannot see that, unlike the European conservative or clerk in the kerosene store, he is 'free' not only from the fetters of his class traditions, but also from any possibility of social creativity. The same faceless environment that gave him his subjective freedom also looms before him as an objective barrier.

In Europe, with its cultural order and deliberate certainties, you walk on the pavement, on the highway — wherever you are told that you may walk. You will not find absolute 'freedom' there. In their basic outlines, the activities of parties and leaders are predetermined by the objective state of affairs. This is not the case with us, where the intellectual is not, in his own mind, bound by anything. 'They' in Europe are bound by plans, regulations, textbooks and programmes of class interests, whereas I, amidst my social steppes, am absolutely free. But here's an odd thing: the absolutely free Russian intellectual took three steps, and ignominiously got lost amongst a mere three pines. So he returned to learn from Europe, taking her latest ideas and words, and then again rebelling against their stipulated, limited, 'Western' meaning, adapting them to his absolute 'freedom'; in other words, he empties them of meaning and returns to the starting point, having described a circle of 80 000 versts around himself. Put another way: 'He repeats the same old lies enough for two men.'

'Your deny me', says our barbarian society to the aristocratic intellectual who has ascended to the realm of 'freedom', or to the rebellious priest's son, 'but I in turn deny you. Look how friable, viscous and shapeless I am — you'll never catch hold of me. I can neither bind you spiritually nor discipline you, it's true; that is your "freedom". But as sculptural material to model your ideals I am useless. You are on your own, and I am on my own. Make your history without me.'

> We have people, but no society:
> Russian thought matured in solitude,
> And it wanders around aimlessly.

Versilov's 'freedom' has meant no more than this freedom of thought to wander aimlessly. It is the sort of absolute freedom possessed, for example, by Morozov[103] of the Narodnaya Volya,[104] who spent his time in prison in Shlisselburg trying to solve the riddles of the Apocalypse — this

---

103. Nikolai Aleksandrovich Morozov (1854-1946) was a leading Populist. He was a member of Zemlya i Volya (Land and Freedom) and then the Narodnaya Volya (People's Will), and was a member of the First International. He was given an indefinite prison sentence in 1881, and was released during the revolution in 1905. He took a great interest in science and the history of religion.

104. The Narodnaya Volya (People's Will) was a conspiratorial populist terrorist organisation that was formed in 1879. It suffered considerable repression after its members assassinated Tsar Alexander II in 1881.

is the 'freedom' that hangs like a curse over the whole history of the Russian intelligentsia.

❖   ❖   ❖

'What does it matter that my words are not translated into action?', the Russian intellectual might say about himself. 'My thoughts and my words have been my actions, and I bequeath them to posterity!' But in the realm of world thought, the Russian intelligentsia has been merely an adopted child: it has lived on what has already been accomplished, contributing nothing of its own. It has always had at its disposal an enormous choice of ready-made literary movements, philosophical systems, scientific doctrines and political programmes. In any European library, it has been able to observe its spiritual growth in a thousand mirrors — large, small, round, square, flat, concave, convex... This has taught it the technique of self-observation, and refined its intuition, flexibility, receptiveness and sensitivity — the feminine attributes of the psyche; yet it has also cut at the roots of the physical strength of thought. This permanent possibility of receiving an idea easily and immediately, with scarcely any effort, along with a ready-made critique of that idea, and a critique of that critique, could not but paralyse independent theoretical creativity. 'Our minds', Chaadaev once remarked brilliantly about the Russian intelligentsia, 'are not furrowed by the indelible traces of successive intellectual movements, because we borrow our ideas ready-developed.' The result is that we often produce an appalling intellectual hash, a continuous series of theoretical misunderstandings, and the most unexpected home-brewed philosophies. 'Our best heads', wrote Chaadaev, 'contain more than mere frivolity.' Turgenev maintained that the Russian not only possesses a cap, but is also crack-brained. Chaadaev himself fell victim to his yearning for consistency, which unfortunately for him proved to be something worse than frivolity.

One cannot but be irritated at the sight of the smugly respectful historians and portrait artists of our intelligentsia. For a century and a half it has been utterly selfless, ideological to the core, living 'for thought', 'for Europe' — and what have we given to the world in the fields of philosophy and social science? Nothing, absolutely zero. Try to name one Russian philosopher whose greatness is beyond dispute; Vladimir Soloviev, who is usually remembered only on the anniversary of his death? Soloviev's lacklustre metaphysics not only failed to enter the canon of world thought, but even in Russia failed to produce anything even close to a philosophical movement. Messrs Berdyaev, Ern[105] and Vyacheslav Ivanov[106] borrowed something from Soloviev... but very little.

105. VF Ern was a reactionary philosopher, with clerical and Slavophil tendencies.
106. Vyacheslav Ivanovich Ivanov (1866-1949) was a Russian Slavophil poet and playwright, and a theoretician of symbolism.

Mr Gart,[107] a philosopher and former Octobrist, losing his head at the unbridled manner in which the military martinets rob, the reactionaries commit excesses, and the Octobrists grovel, searches helplessly for a categorical imperative that would fit in perfectly with 'the general Russian character' (including the character of the martinets), fit in with its good-naturedly undisciplined podginess, give it a sense of inner discipline, and wean it off the habit of bribe-taking. 'Where is the imminent Slavic Kant?',[108] asks his puny forerunner. Indeed, where on earth is he? He does not exist. Where is our Hegel? Where is anyone of equal greatness? In philosophy we have nobody but third-rate disciples and faceless imitators.

We have had plenty of 'original' social utopianism, and even today we have more than enough of it. But what have we contributed of our own to the treasury of social thought? Narodnism [populism], the Russian surrogate of Socialism? It is nothing more than the ideological reaction of our barbarism to the capitalist progress that is corroding it. It is not a new achievement in world thought, but merely a small chapter in the spiritual history of historical provincialism.

Where are our great utopians? The greatest of them was Chernyshevsky,[109] but even he, weighed down by the wretchedness of his social environment, remained a disciple, and never developed into a teacher. Herzen,[110] Lavrov[111] and Mikhailovsky[112] will never in any sense enter the history of world Socialism; they are completely dissolved in the history of the Russian intelligentsia. Perhaps only Bakunin[113] has inscribed his name in the book of the European workers' movement, but to accomplish that he had to cut himself off completely from his roots in Russian society, and even then he represents not an essential component of that European movement, but a transient episode, and even then not even one that in any way represented a step forward. What remains now of Bakuninism? A few prejudices in the workers' movements of the Latin countries, nothing more...

To be sure, at this point we could mention the name of Tolstoy, but even this is hardly a convincing argument. Tolstoy, with his cord tied around his waist and with his hemp sandals, has indisputably entered the

107. Gart was a frequent contributor to the reactionary press.
108. See Gart's *Why is Russia Unstable?*, St Petersburg, 1910. [Note by Trotsky]
109. Nikolai Gavrilovich Chernyshevsky (1828-1889) was a prominent Russian revolutionary democrat and utopian Socialist, scientist, writer and literary critic.
110. Aleksandr Ivanovich Herzen (1812-1870) was a pioneer of the revolutionary movement in Russia and a theorist of Populism.
111. Pyotr Lavrovich Lavrov (1823-1900) was a noted Narodnik theorist.
112. Nikolai Konstantinovich Mikhailovsky (1842-1904) was a literary critic and publicist who contributed to the rise of the Narodnik movement.
113. Mikhail Aleksandrovich Bakunin (1814-1876) was one of the foremost theoreticians of Anarchism.

canon of world thought, but not because of his social philosophy, merely because he himself was such a towering figure. His 'teachings' were, and remain, subjective forests of his mind; they are of great biographical value, but after the European religious reformations and European revolutions, and after the nineteenth-century European social doctrines, what did he have to say that was new?

Let us say it again: the history of our social thought has up to now made not even a small dent in the history of human thought. This may be small comfort to our national self-esteem, but historical truth is not a servant of national self-esteem, and we would do better to invest our national self-esteem in the future than in the past. The celebrated General Benkendorf[114] once said that 'Russia's past was astounding; her present is more than magnificent; and as to her future, it is greater than anything that could be conjured up by even the most passionate imagination'. Our opinions are completely at odds, of course, with those of the intelligentsia's admirers who think like Benkendorf, and turn Russian history into the history of a Chosen People. But we do not think like General Benkendorf — from which it does not follow, it must be hoped, that we do not believe in Russia's future...

But we are firmly and unshakeably convinced that the greatness of our future will be transformed from a hazy fantasy into reality only to the extent that history erases the 'original' traits of our 'astounding' past and 'more than magnificent' present. But our old, classless, Messianic intelligentsia is the crowning glory of these original traits — in the theoretical sphere characterised by 'something more than frivolity', but in practice by its impotence.

❖   ❖   ❖

The lack of historical traditions and distinct political groupings led inevitably to a lack of personal moral stability. In a disintegrating, 'ahistorical' environment it is far easier to sacrifice one's life for an idea than to hold to that idea consistently throughout one's life. And it must be admitted that the light-hearted criticism of the Russian intelligentsia — that 'up to the age of 30 they are radicals, and after that — scoundrels' — is not without a grain of truth. However crude Goncharov's caricature of a nihilist in *The Precipice* may be, there is nothing implausible in the fact that he repents and becomes a Cadet. The character of the Gracchus[115] candidate who 'falls prey to his environment' and becomes a tax inspector has only recently been retired from his rôle in Russian fiction.

114. Aleksandr Khristoforovich Benkendorf (1781-1844) was Tsar Nicholas I's chief minister, headed the gendarmerie and the Third Section (the secret police), and was largely responsible for the Tsar's reactionary policies.

115. Caius Gracchus (154-121BC) and Tiberius Gracchus (162-133BC) were brothers and popular tribunes of the Roman people. They were both assassinated.

How did the best of them manage to stand their ground and survive? Through terrible moral exertions and concentrated asceticism, and by becoming social renegades. With no social ground to stand on, moral stability could only be achieved through ideological fanaticism, merciless self-limitation, mistrustfulness and suspiciousness, and unflagging monitoring of one's own purity. 'The Russian will jump into the fire rather than betray his faith', said the archpriest Avvakum.[116] The roots of the Old-Believer-type fanaticism and zeal for the letter at the expense of the spirit that are sometimes displayed by the most extreme elements of our intelligentsia are to be found, not in the peculiar contortions of the Slavic brain, but in the social conditions of old Russia. As for the consistency of the intelligentsia's faith, it goes without saying that its refusal to swallow mosquitoes does not prevent it from quite happily gulping down two-humped camels.

'I am a Yid, and I will not sit at the same table as philistines!', wrote Belinsky.[117] Nevertheless, for all the moral coherence of his personality, Belinsky was more than once forced to change his opinions radically. Ideological implacability, a noble trait in any fighter, is in itself too weak a guarantee of endurance if it is not constantly supported by the objective implacability built into the very mechanics of social relations. Frequent and abrupt changes of opinion, a common phenomenon amongst Russian intellectuals (and not only those who become tax inspectors once they turn 30), is merely the inevitable concomitant to Versilov's concept of absolute freedom, the freedom of thought 'to wander aimlessly'.

These changes in outlook could have a subjectively tragic quality (Belinsky), a comically banal quality (Berdyaev), an intellectually undisciplined quality (Struve), a semantically superficial quality (Minsky and Balmont), or a renegade quality (Katkov[118] and Tikhomirov[119]), but their historical cause was one and the same: our social wretchedness.

❖   ❖   ❖

Writing of the Decembrist uprising,[120] Count Rastopchin ironically

116. Petrovich Avvakum (1621-1682) was a dissident priest who was burnt at the stake for opposing Patriarch Nikon's church reforms. Those who opposed the reforms were known as the Old Believers.
117. Belinsky, a staunch critic of the backwardness of Tsarist society, was not Jewish, which made his use of the pejorative term 'Zhid' to describe his alienation from that society more striking.
118. Mikhail Nikiforovich Katkov (1818-1887) was a Russian journalist and assistant Professor of Philosophy in Moscow who had been a liberal in the 1840s, but subsequently became a supporter of Tsarism.
119. Lev Aleksandrovich Tikhomirov (1852-1923) was a leading Narodnik who renounced his previous convictions in 1882, and became a monarchist and a spokesman for the proto-Fascist Union of Russian People.
120. An unsuccessful conspiracy organised primarily by progressively-minded aristocratic

commented that in France the 'rabble' made a revolution in order to make itself equal to the aristocracy, whereas our aristocracy made a revolution in the interests of the rabble. Mr Ivanov-Razumnik uses Rastopchin's paradox to emphasise the anti-class, purely idealist character of the Decembrists. To what degree the Decembrists' idealistic radicalism corresponded with their class interests is another question; what is certain is that the Decembrists acted as the Russian intelligentsia has often acted ever since, that is to say, they attempted to *substitute* themselves for mature classes that did not yet exist. They acted 'as a proxy' for bourgeois liberalism.

This substituting of itself for non-existent or feebly developed classes, which has masked the intelligentsia's social weakness, is now becoming an ideological necessity and political profession for the intelligentsia. Firstly, the aristocratic intellectual substituted himself for the 'rabble', then the non-aristocratic Narodnik substituted himself for the peasantry, and, finally, the Marxist intellectual substituted himself for the proletariat. Gleb Uspensky, himself a non-aristocratic Narodnik, exposed the Narodnik movement's intellectual masquerade with brilliant perspicacity. However, a further two decades were to pass before the real-life peasantry displayed its true colours; only then was the intelligentsia's love affair with the Russian peasant dealt a mortal blow...

But even when an idea developed in line with general historical development, it was so far ahead of that development in time, under the influence of the West, that the bearer of that idea, the intelligentsia, became connected to the country's political life not through the class that it wanted to serve, but merely through the 'idea' of that class. So it was with the first circles of the Marxist intelligentsia. Only gradually did the spirit become flesh.

❖   ❖   ❖

In 1905-06, large social entities appeared on the historical stage – classes with their own interests and demands; at a stroke, Russian events forced themselves into world history, evoking a powerful response in Europe and Asia; political ideas ceased to appear as incorporeal spirits that had wafted down from the ideological heavens; the age of the intelligentsia's acting as a proxy for other classes was over, as it had reached the end of its historical life. But it is remarkable that it was only *after* those momentous years that the intelligentsia's bacchanalia of self-exaltation went into full swing; just so does the lamp flare up most brightly just before it is extinguished.

It is nonsense to suggest that after the colossal upheavals of those

army officers against Tsar Nicholas I. The armed rebellion planned for 14 December 1825 collapsed, and the conspirators were severely punished.

years history has been reversed. The bureaucracy may have gone backwards; but the bureaucracy, though it controls many things, does not control the course of history. The ahistorical character of the masses has gone for good, never to return; and along with it has gone the intelligentsia's apostolism.

After three years of smug prostration, the intelligentsia has begun to straighten up again; hurrah! But it would be naive to believe that it can ever again return to the epoch preceding the 1905 revolution. History does not repeat itself. However great the intelligentsia's significance may have been in the past, henceforth it can only play a secondary and subordinate rôle. Its heroic substitutive rôle belongs to an era that is passing into oblivion.

It is pointless for one who believes in the future to worship the past. The past will never return. And this is a good thing, because the future is better than the past − if for no other reason than that it rests on the foundations of the past and draws on its experience, and is therefore stronger and more intelligent than the past.

Kievskaia Mysl, nos 64 and 72, 4 and 12 March 1912

Leon Trotsky

Vienna Secession 1913

I VISITED the spring Vienna Secession only at the end of June, almost on the eve of its closure. Apart from myself, some family excursion from Galicia wandered around the halls: a Polish gentleman, ladies and their children... They were very noisy, all ate sweets and in general behaved as if they were in the Gerngross department store. There had been, of course, more of the public there in April and May, but just then there were few. It seemed to me that the Secession's empty halls were very eloquent during the two or three hours that I spent there. What place does painting occupy in present-day life? Is it a large one? Who does it grab powerfully these days? Who needs it?

As always, there were interesting works at the Secession this time. The most prominent Viennese artist Rudolf Jettmar exhibited two large pictures. The more important of them is 'The Tower of Obstinacy' (or of 'Audacity': 'die Türme des Trotzes'). It is an empty landscape, but obstinate towers naturally grow out of it in the background − straight, with no windows, stone boxes which reach high into the sky. In the foreground lies a naked woman − in a pose that could as easily express leisurely voluptuousness as weary despair: the face is hardly visible. Leaning very slightly over her – attentively and, it seems, with love – is a strong man. The face of an old woman sitting nearby is stubborn and long-despairing, and a naked infant is resting against the old woman. I do not know whether the caption beneath this scene is connected with the particular locality, or whether it simply dramatises the landscape, in which obstinate passion is combined with hopelessness. The picture leaves behind it an impression of the significance of the idea and the bitter taste of perplexity.

Two artists, Grom-Rottmeyer and Harlfinger,[121] exhibited a whole room, with walls and ceiling, although without furniture: their task was to create an apartment intended to 'serve as the setting for fateful events in a family' – obviously a family not mentioned in the catalogue. The walls of the octahedronic apartment are painted with depictions symbolic of fidelity, love, valour and the three measures: distance, depth and height; on one of the walls for some reason there are four caryatids; the whole thing is crowned with a ceiling of coloured glass. Before us, therefore, was something like a domestic temple, but alas! – in this temple no sense of domestic gods grabs one. The symbols are banal, and remind one of allegory, and the coloured glass with its stylised dragons, lions and whales could just as well serve as the surroundings in the foyer of a modern hotel, or the domestic temple of an unknown stockbroker; it would have most likely been more in place in the hotel.

Wladislaw Jarocki,[122] a painter from Lvov, exhibited the beautiful 'Huzul'. The idea is almost simply ethnographic: three girls and a young man in bright clothes walk past the viewer in the snow – this picture is true artistry in its irresistible aesthetic cogency and human significance. These Huzuls are not drawn from nature but *from within*. Such is their strong self-confidence, and so powerfully is that self-confidence expressed in the language of line and colour that to us it begins to seem as if the Galician Huzuls only begin to bear their present genealogy from this canvas. And at the same time, it is so physically clear, that they are from a different epoch, a different culture from us. Between 'harmonious' birds [*tëlka*][123] who know of no accursed questions and those women who devote their lives to the political emancipation of their sex stand sometimes these sharply observed Huzul girls – who are undoubtedly nearer to the birds [*tëlka*] than to Miss Davison.[124] And this lad with hair cut in a

121. Richard Harlfinger (1873-1948) was born in Milan, studied in Vienna and Munich, and was a member of the Secession from 1906 to 1939.
122. Wladislaw Jarocki (1879-) was a Polish artist, an adherent of the Young Poland current, and stood in the tradition of the Secession.
123. The Russian *tëkla* means 'bird', or 'chick' in the rather derogatory sense of referring to a woman.
124. A reference to Emily Davison, the suffragette who threw herself under the King's

fringe, in a high lambskin cap – is a jester, dancer and hard-worker – you see this '*Mishanka*' (according to Uspensky)[125] is the most wonderful child of nature; but dress him in an Imperial-and-Royal Austro-Hungarian jacket and put a rifle in his hands, and without batting an eyelid he will shoot down Hungarian workers who demonstrate for universal suffrage. From this young Huzul, fatal in his own way, who compliments those beautiful women, no doubt exclusively in Ukrainian, one's thought imperceptibly passes to the '*Mishanka*' who follows stealthily the smuggler's route to Volochisk.

Otto Friedrich's[126] 'Cycle of Rhythms' occupies a room of its own, and should adorn the entrance to a music room. It is difficult to state the 'content' of pictures in general, and especially those where paint and lines are meant to serve as the embodiment, not of painted, but of musical images, or, more correctly, combine one with the other. Is this task legitimate in general? One can argue about this as much as one likes. But Otto Friedrich has shown that he has done this legitimately, for it is aesthetically convincing. His growing collection of nude figures on five canvasses: nebulous and touching children's bodies, supple adolescent bodies, nobly passionate women's bodies, and strong, intense men's bodies, despite the complexity of composition, speak in a language of clear and pure harmony. Whilst the images of the domestic temple (in which a commercial councillor will entrust his daughter to a colonel of the general staff) are external allegories, where courage is represented by a man in armour who wields a sword, and fidelity by a man who is bound to a post and pierced by a javelin, the 'rhythms' of Friedrich are not replaced by conventional signs, but directly inspire the viewer with the inner rhythmicality of the depiction itself, the harmony of line and colour.

The talented Armin Horowitz subordinates his idea to architectural wholes. But his idea is incomparably simpler: his canvasses are sketches of wall paintings for some public hall showing the cycle of seasons. In lively and cheerful colours (tempera), Horowitz throws onto one small spring background lovers by a fountain, a young gardener, thoughtful by a flower bed; a girl driving a hoop, an old woman who has alighted from a carriage for a walk; silhouettes of soldiers passing by, mating rabbits; a maiden (the daughter of the master) puts a flower into the buttonhole of an old gardener; just as on the general winter background he draws Pierrot, in a top-hat with a fur coat on top of ragged multicoloured trousers, on his knees in the snow before an enigmatic Columbine; a snow-man; a

horse at the Derby in June 1913.

125. Most likely a reference to the Russian novelist Gleb Ivanovich Uspensky (1840-1902), who wrote mainly about peasant life. 'Mishanka' is the pet name for Mikhail.
126. Otto Friedrich (1862-1937) was an artist of the Hungarian school who settled and exhibited in Munich. He was a founder member of the Secession in 1897.

chilly girl, muffled up to her nose in her old mother's shawl; an old worker warming himself with his pipe; skaters; the silhouette of a ski-jump, and so on. Despite the fact that these various phenomena of spring and winter actually happen in different geographical and social dimensions, so to speak, in Horowitz everything is placed together, in the spirit of popular symbolism (for example, the famous 'ages of man': childhood, youth, manhood, age); you feel nothing is forced: figures are not simply combined by the artist's will, but by inner connection of the whole (in all their variety) of their springtime and wintertime experiences, in other words: an artistic work is before us.

II

Before beginning to look at things in a European way with their slanting eyes, the Chinese taught European art to look at the world in a Chinese way, without perspective, that is, outside the space that visually devours things, on one plane, where all the outlines of bodies that are important for the artist appear clearly visible, or in a conventional perspective which is not subordinated to geometrical demands, but instead gives the artist the possibility of deriving all the lines most valuable to him from the objects. Franz Wacik[127] exhibited several interesting small works in this 'Chinese' style. However, whatever may be the advantage of this style, in its pure form it would be too naive for our mature eyes. Instead, it harmonises perfectly with fairy-tale and biblical stories. Such are Wacik's inspired forest motifs, such also, though drawn differently, is 'Madonna in a Vineyard' by Maximillian Liebenwein.[128]

This Liebenwein exhibited a large canvas on which there is the lustful bull from Olympus who abducted Europa, about which we have already spoken. The bull is very monumental, but the stone folds of its neck look like a statue, and do not permit us to believe that this dull beast could be capable of risking amorous adventures. Europa, in a short tunic, sits astride Zeus, and despite her youth treats this unusual adventure without particular concern, and without arousing any concern for her on the part of the spectator. Since then, Europa has aged a lot, and written in her diary a large number of novels about bulls, not always Olympian. There are undoubtedly interesting technical details (good are the fantastic circles which cross the water from the forelegs of Zeus!), but the picture bears the impression of superfluity — for, essentially, it makes no impression.

Such pictures are in the majority at the exhibition, and it is therefore

127. Franz Wacik (1883-1938) was a Viennese artist. He studied at Streblow, and was a member of the Secession from 1910 until his death.
128. Maximilian Liebenwein (1869-1926) was an Austrian artist. He studied in Vienna and Karlsruhe, and was a member of the Secession from 1901.

rather boring... If we leave aside the already mentioned interesting (but nothing more) examples of wall paintings, and pass over the inevitable quantity of ungifted canvasses, then it turns out that there are almost no pictures in the genuine sense, that is, those who could contend for an independent existence. There are expressive sketches of gypsy girls by Wieden,[129] some successful portraits, the winning melancholy intimacy of the Stuttgart artist Karl Schmoll, 'Woman with a White Rose', so much like our own Boris Zaitsev,[130] a good still-life (for example, an apple in bright colours contrasted with a dead red flower), but all this seems an endless 'first attempt', a provisional trial of strength of new painting techniques. But there are no pictures. And the viewer, not the specialist, but not the indifferent idler either – will inescapably be finally left in depressing perplexity.

❖   ❖   ❖

Modernism in painting, which was accused by representatives of the old academic piety of malicious far-fetchedness and false mannerism was, in fact, a life-giving protest against the old style which had outlived itself and turned into a pose. The first stage of the revolution was Naturalism, which contrasted 'ungilded' nature to the sugary retouching school. The logic of naturalism's own development reached a cross-roads: either to carry its principles through to the end and dissolve itself into photography, or better still, cinematography, or consciously to place the perceiving and creating personalities, with their organic senses, nervous systems and psyches, between nature and the screen. Naturalism transcended itself and became Impressionism, which did not at all give up its fidelity to nature and its truth to life, but, on the contrary, precisely in the name of this truth, in its eternally changing colours and outlines, raised its banner of revolt against the settled forms, and demanded freedom for the truth of subjective perception. Whilst the old academic style said 'here are the rules (or images) according to which nature must be depicted', and naturalism said 'here is nature', then Impressionism said 'here is how I see nature'. But this 'I' of Impressionism is a new personality in new circumstances, with a new nervous system, with new eyes, a *modern* person, and that is why this painting is modernism, not fashionable[131] painting, but modern, *contemporary*, emerging from contemporary perception. The urban eye became complex, and, like all life, it broke away from dead-end and immobile visual beliefs and standing prejudices, and became used to colour combinations which were earlier considered discordant. It became

129. Ludwig Wieden (1869-1947) was an Austrian artist. He studied in Vienna and Munich, and was a member of the Secession from 1906 to 1939.
130. Ivan Kondratievich Zaitsev (1805-1887) was a Russian portrait painter.
131. There is a pun in the original here between *modernizm* (modernism) and *modnyi* (fashionable).

accustomed to them and loved them. Is this good or bad? The question is senseless. Is it good or bad that along with the sun and moon there appeared the gas lamp and the incandescent bulb, which occupy a much larger place in our lives than the moon and little less than the sun? Children in a present-day town grow up in a new atmosphere, and for them the 'stylised', flat figures of contemporary posters are as natural as was in its time were the kobza-player in the oleographical supplement to *Niva*. The immobility of academic form, which long ago lost its soul, left only one path for painting: concentration on the 'content' or, more precisely, on the plot, to give the canvas significance and interest – pious, moralising, or sensual-stimulating, or romantic-dreaming, or patriotic-pathetic content. The revolt against academicism was naturally transformed into a revolt of self-sufficient artistic form against content, as an indifferent fact. Such was the purely aesthetic logic.

It found its foothold in social logic. The lack of a homogenous, harmonious, aesthetically educated milieu appeared the objective reason which pushed the Impressionists towards a hermit's outlook, and instilled social neutrality in them, in the interests of artistic self-preservation, an aesthetically motivated indifference. Painting repudiated 'literature', morals, propaganda – it returned to its own point of departure: to the eye.

That idea that the *content* of art is in its form, an idea which has been so thoroughly explained to the Russian public in recent years, only means at its indisputable core that art begins where impressions of nature, living experience, ethical ideas or social conflict find their *artistic* reproduction. But that does not at all mean that it is a matter of indifference for us *what precisely* finds artistic embodiment. A person, including a modern person, is a certain complex psychological unity, and he remains true to himself only when he demands that painting, too, must give him an aesthetic-transforming interpretation of that which troubles him as a social-moral personality. Looking at a beautiful and newly drawn onion, at parrots in a cage, or at innumerable female 'loins', he comes to the conclusion that contemporary painting is only exercising its sensitive brush on indifferent and occasional themes – and is preparing to paint its real picture. The canvases at the exhibition seem preparatory sketches. Sketches may be interesting as the rough drafts of skill, but this interest is particular, for a narrow circle. People do not live, did not live, nor will they live by the world-outlook of the eye, and therefore painting cannot but feel its orphaned isolation.

We have lived through a year which has seen a dreadful conflict amongst the Balkan peoples, a year of uninterrupted anxiety in Europe, a year of political strikes in Belgium, a year of heroic recklessness by English suffragettes, and a year of the ceaseless growth of the social struggle around which all contemporary society turns. But none of this is reflected in a single brush-stroke at the Secession exhibition. Neither our last year, the previous one, nor our decade, nor the whole epoch has permeated it. With new methods, Impressionism merely repeats and turns over old motifs. Painting languishes in the contradiction between the modernism of form and archaic, indifferent content. Serious artists cannot but feel they are in a cul-de-sac.

In the art of line and colour, as in all other spheres, contemporary life has given us enormous technical achievements. But in order to turn them into joy for people, profound changes in the organic fabric of contemporary society are necessary. However, this conclusion takes us beyond the limits of painting.

Kievskaia Mysl, nos 171 and 172, 23 and 24 June 1913

III: The Culture of the Transitional Period

This section has been kept to a minimum, for Trotsky's considerable output on this topic during the 1920s is already well represented in English in *Literature and Revolution* (Ann Arbor, 1960), as well as in such collections as *Leon Trotsky on Literature and Art* (New York, 1977), and *Problems of Everyday Life* (New York, 1977).

Background material to his thought during this time is provided by sections in full-length books such as Isaac Deutscher's 'Not by Politics Alone...', a chapter in *The Prophet Unarmed* (Oxford, 1978), pp164-200; Baruch Knei-Paz's 'On Art, Literature and Philosophy', chapter 11 of *The Social and Political Thought of Leon Trotsky* (Oxford, 1979), pp445-75, and the largely hostile treatment in Dmitri Volkogonov, 'Culture and Revolution', a chapter in *Trotsky: The Eternal Revolutionary* (London, 1996), pp218-34. Of the countless shorter articles, we should particularly note Paul Siegel, 'Art and Revolution', *International Socialist Review*, Volume 31, no 6, September 1970, pp18-25; Granville Williams, 'The USSR: Socialism and Culture 1917-32', *The Marxist*, Volume 3, no 3, pp45-52; Tom Owen, 'Trotsky on Art and Revolution', *Workers Press*, 1 September 1990; and Ruaridh Nicoll, 'Art from Russian Time of Turmoil', *Guardian*, 2 February 1998. The various articles on this topic appearing with some frequency in *Marxist Review* are little more than centos put together from Trotsky's own writings. They include Nick Axarlis, 'The October Revolution and Art' (Volume 1, no 4, July 1986, pp39-48); Martin Booth, 'Trotsky on Art and Revolution' (Volume 5, no 7, August 1990, pp16-20); Mike Vale, 'Leon Trotsky and Art' (Volume 5, no 8, September 1990, pp22-4); Mike Driver, 'The Russian Revolution and Art: An Outline' (Volume 6, no 10, October 1991, pp24-6); and William Westwell, 'Art and Revolution' (Volume 9, no 9, September 1994, pp16-20). A more satisfactory treatment can be found in Alan Wald's presentation to the Wupperthal Symposium of March 1990, 'Leon Trotsky's Contributions to Literary and Cultural Theory', expanded into a full-length article, 'Literature and Revolution: Leon Trotsky's Contribution to Marxist Cultural Theory and Literary Criticism' in the *Journal of Trotsky Studies*, no 2, 1994, pp17-41; more conveniently consulted in H Ticktin and M Cox (eds), *The Ideas of Leon Trotsky* (London, 1995), pp219-32.

Background material on the visual arts during this period is exceptionally rich, and only the merest selection can be represented here. In terms of full-length books, Vladimir Tolstoy, Irina Bibikova and Catherine Cooke, *Street Art of the Revolution: Festivals and Celebrations in Russia, 1918-33* (reviewed by Fiona McCarthy, 'Put Out More Red Flags', *Observer*, 11 March 1990) deals with the more participatory aspects. Articles include Ann McDonald, 'The Development of Russian Painting', *The Marxist*, Volume 3, no 2, pp24-9; 'A Guest Contributor', 'Posters of the Russian Revolution', *Marxist Review*, Volume 4, no 3, March 1989, pp9, 16-17; 'A Guest Contributor', 'Marc Chagall and the Russian Revolution', *Marxist Review*, Volume 13, no 8, August 1998, pp21-3; and Andrea Tierney, 'Socialist Realism', *Marxist Monthly*, Volume 4, no 7, May-June 1992, and no 8, July 1992. Especially perceptive are Rachel Lever's discussions, 'Art in Bolshevik Russia 1917-24', *Workers Republic*, no 17, Spring 1967, pp15-22, and no 18, May-June 1967, pp15-23; and 'Class, Culture and Stalinism', *Workers Liberty*, no 12-13, August 1989, pp36-46, of which the second is richly illustrated. Trotsky's appreciation of the famous cartoonist and poster artist Moor (DS Orlov) can be found in 'To a Hero of the Pencil and the Paintbrush', an order issued to the War Council on 25 July 1922, *How the Revolution Armed*, Volume 4 (London, 1981), p261. *Art as the Cognition of Life: Selected Writings 1911-1936* (Michigan, 1998), the best collection of writings by AK Voronsky to have appeared in English, came into our hands too late to be reviewed for this volume. Nevertheless, it is appropriate to welcome its appearance here, and to draw it to the attention of our readers. It presents several of the most important documents contributed by a major ally of Trotsky's to the discussions over literature with the emergent bureaucratic trends in the Bolshevik party. In this context, Robert Maguire's *Red Virgin Soil: Soviet Literature in the 1920s* (Princeton, 1968) gives what is probably the best account of Voronsky and his current.

Trotsky was also keenly interested in technological forms of culture such as radio, photography, the phonograph and cinema, as shown in his essay 'Radio, Science, Technique and Society' (*Problems of Everyday Life*, pp250-63), and 'Vodka, the Church and the Cinema' (*Problems of Everyday Life*, pp31-5) shows that he was aware of the need to make use of film culture. Before the cultural policy of Stalinism put an end to autonomous cultural organisation and debate, photographic and film culture occasioned excited political debate in the Soviet Union. A reprint of Trotsky's essay, originally published in *Pravda* in 1923, can be found in Richard Taylor and Ian Christie's edition of *The Film Factory: Russian and Soviet Documents, 1896-1939* (Harvard UP, 1988), pp94-7, along with other considerations of the questions raised by technological culture.

Trotsky's theories on 'proletarian literature' came under attack from such as NN Punin at the time (see 'Literature Without Revolution', *Journal of Trotsky Studies*, no 3, 1995, pp47-52), and have been heatedly debated ever since. An interesting symposium on the topic appeared in the literary review *Monde* in August and September 1928, to which contributed André Breton, Maurice Parijanine, Benjamin Péret, Henri Poullaile and Victor Serge (reprinted in the *Cahiers Léon Trotsky*, no 47, January 1992, pp101-11). Modern appreciations illustrated from both contemporary literature and the visual arts include David Walsh, 'Bolshevism and the Avant-Garde Artists', *Fourth International*, Volume 20, no 1, Winter-Spring 1994-95, pp110-49; and 'Die ästhetische Komponente des Sozialismus', *Gleichkeit*, no 5/98, 29 April 1998. Three contributions by Cissie Lodge, 'The Russian Avant Garde', *Labour Review*, Volume 7, no 3, October 1983, pp24-9; 'Soviet Constructivism', a review of Christina Lodder's *Russian Constructivism*, *Labour Review*, Volume 7, no 6, January 1984, pp45-7; and her review of Vladimir Markov's *Russian Futurism* (London, 1969) appearing in *The Marxist*, Volume 8, no 2, pp30-2 should also be noted. Chris Pike's edition of *The Futurists, the Formalists and the Marxist Critique* (London, 1979) includes Nicholas Gorlov's essay, 'On Futurisms and Futurism (Concerning Comrade Trotsky's Article)' on pages 169-80. Maurice Parijanine's interview with Trotsky in April 1932, 'Proletarian Literature', appears as an appendix to the Pathfinder edition of Trotsky's works of his last exile (*Writings of Leon Trotsky 1932*, New York, 1973, pp347-55).

Useful further discussions include Trent Hutter, 'Trotsky's *Literature and Revolution*', *International Socialist Review*, Volume 19, no 1, Winter 1958, pp26-8; Michel Lequenne, '*Littérature et Révolution* et ses critiques', *Quatrième Internationale*, twenty-third year, no 24, first quarter 1965, pp51-7; and Cliff Slaughter, 'Trotsky on Literature and Revolution', *Workers Press*, 27 and 28 August 1970, reprinted in *Fourth International*, Volume 7, no 1, Winter 1970-71, pp36-41); and 'Literature and Revolution', *Marxism, Ideology and Literature* (London, 1980), pp86-113, 217-8). Poetry is dealt with in Viktor Shklovsky, *Mayakovsky and His Circle* (London, 1974); and by José Revueltas, 'So That Mayakovsky's Suicide not be Repeated', *International Socialist Review*, Volume 31, no 1, January-February 1970, pp38-44. James Meek has recently spread the extraordinary accusation that Essenin was killed by Blumkin on Trotsky's orders ('Trotsky Blamed for Murder of Russia's Greatest Poets', *Guardian*, 22 June 1998). The fortunes of Anna Akhmatova's poetry during the Stalin period are conveniently summarised in RJ Waterhouse, 'Anna Akhmatova', *The Times*, 19 November 1998. EH Carr provides important accounts of the struggles over literature and their relationships with other factional struggles. See in particular *Socialism in One Country*, Volume 2, Chapter 14 for the 1923-26 period (the context for *Literature and Revolu-*

tion), and *Foundations of a Planned Economy*, Volume 2, Chapter 55 for 1926 and onwards, when the bureaucratic state's ascendancy put an end to all cultural discussions.

Whatever the drawbacks of Trotsky's analyses, they are plainly well ahead of a diet hashed up from Stalinist Socialist Realism or the effusions of China's misnamed 'Great Proletarian Cultural Revolution'. But since much of the discussion about Trotsky's views in thinking left-wing circles consists of adulation, we have made a point of introducing this section with a critical essay by John Plant.

We are again much in debt to Yurii Colombo for providing us with a translation of Antonio Gramsci's correspondence. It first appeared as an appendix to chapter four of the Russian edition of *Literature and Revolution*. A different translation appears in Antonio Gramsci, *Selections from Cultural Writings* (London, 1985), pp52-4, but we have included it here to place it within the context of Trotsky's writings. Our version has been very carefully checked against the Italian original. Our thanks are also extended to Simon Pirani for his translation of our third item below.

John Plant

Trotsky, Art and the Revolution

Some Cautionary Notes

The following article was written for a discussion group organised by some ex-members of the Workers Revolutionary Party (*Workers Press*) and others during 1994, which concerned itself with the Stalinist and post-Stalinist states. The text as originally circulated has been amended to exclude some unjustified remarks about Paul Siegel. In the course of the discussion, Rex Dunn wrote an extended article opposing several of the points made by Alan Wald and the author. The interested reader is encouraged to contact Rex Dunn for a copy of his work at 13c Coleridge Road, London N8 8EH.[1]

APPARENTLY by coincidence, *Workers Press* of 27 August 1994 dealt twice with Russian cultural matters. Peter Fryer commented approvingly on Alan Wald's article in the *Journal of Trotsky Studies* on Trotsky's writings on culture, and Rex Dunn reviewed the exhibition

1. I have made no attempt to standardise transliterations of Russian names from different sources. I assume any reader so determined as to be able to read this text will be able to cope with such minor blemishes.

of Russian avant garde books at the British Museum, also drawing on Trotsky's *Literature and Revolution*. This coincidence drove me to try to set out some thoughts (and specifically questions) on culture and Bolshevism, and the Russian avant garde in particular, that I had been discussing with comrade Sam Levy for a number of months.

The phenomenon usually called the 'Russian avant garde' was one of the most remarkable cultural developments in human history – a period of intense innovation in most of the fields of creativity, comparable in its richness, complexity and diversity to the Renaissance, but possessing unique features. Moreover, it was only one aspect of a tremendous upsurge of artistic activity in Russia in the early part of the twentieth century, which arose from a very specific combination of social, economic and cultural conditions.

Attempts to study and analyse its history are bedevilled by its interaction with the Bolshevik revolution. This often leads art historians with only a superficial knowledge of the revolution, and students of the revolution with little or no understanding of cultural history, to define invalid connections between the avant garde and the revolution, in effect to categorise the avant garde as 'revolutionary art', or as some cultural consequence or aspect of the revolution.

In fact, the avant garde began and was substantially established as a cultural current several years before 1917. Its end was eventually brought about by Stalinist cultural policies in the early 1930s. In the intervening period, many artists associated with the avant garde supported the revolution, responded to it, worked with it and benefited from it. Others left Russia either in disagreement with the revolution (apparently the case with David Burliuk), or unable to work under the stresses of War Communism and the New Economic Policy. The avant garde was in no sense a coherent political movement; neither did it have a unifying philosophical base. Different currents within the avant garde argued fiercely about philosophical and cultural matters, almost incessantly publishing manifestos, and grouping and regrouping around theoretical statements and projects. In *Literature and Revolution*, Trotsky criticised this pattern as 'utopian sectarianism', as Rex Dunn has pointed out.

Rex Dunn focuses on this aspect of the avant garde's activity, and comes close to blaming the avant garde for its eventual suppression by Stalinism, saying 'these debates reveal that the Russian avant garde was cursed with an Achilles heel', and later that 'it was this increasingly doctrinaire and therefore sectarian approach to art which constituted the most dangerous weakness in the Russian avant garde'.

One way of refuting Rex Dunn's position here is to point out that repression under the Stalinists (and currents in the bureaucracy which were emerging before Stalin assumed power) fell with equal force on other currents in Soviet cultural life, including those which did not produce groups or manifestos, and which could not be tarred with the brush of 'sectarianism'.

It should also be pointed out that the manifestos and theoretical statements, especially those produced by the visual artists, often had a very short 'shelf life'. However resounding and forceful their language, they rarely established permanent new groupings, and were often written specifically to announce or promote exhibitions or magazines. It is easy to be misled by the proliferation of such manifestos and statements into overestimating the importance attached to them by their signatories, and to draw the conclusion that the avant garde artists were part of a mad hot-house of sectarian bombast. In practice, membership was quite fluid amongst the groupings, and cooperation was more common than open quarrels. The important disagreements and developments in artistic thinking were much fewer in number than the short-lived regroupings, and some of them (particularly Tatlin's divergence from the 'mainstream' of the avant garde) remain very inadequately documented.

It is also important to reassert that the avant garde (comprising mainly the futurist, suprematist and constructivist currents) was only one element in the cultural upsurge in Russia in the first third of the twentieth century. Pasternak, Stravinsky, Tsvetaeva, Bakst, Shostakovich, Bunin, Stanislavsky, Meyerhold, Eisenstein – all these were active during the same period as the avant garde. When we look at the cultural policies, achievements and theories of the Bolshevik government, this huge resource of creative energy and talent is one of scales against which they must be measured.

But this statement is not intended to hold up a distorting mirror to the face of Bolshevism. To try to understand the significance of the cultural riches being created in Russia around the time of the revolution, it is also necessary to have some impression of the immense inequalities in cultural life, and consequently the scale of problems which the Bolsheviks were tackling. The 1897 census in Russia found that only a third of all males and 14 per cent of females were literate, and this probably underestimated the situation, since it was based only on European Russia. Conditions in Asiatic Russia were often considerably worse (Trotsky's accounts of his escape from Siberia give some flavour of this). But even ignorance, poverty and illiteracy must be considered as dynamic rather than static elements. Lunacharsky's 'Red Train of Propaganda' encountered an insatiable hunger for books in the countryside and outlying towns, and their sudden availability provoked the setting up of reading groups and classes amongst the poor. Even amongst the rich, some 28 per cent were illiterate. So the cultural upsurge was not merely confined to the wealthy cities, and to Petrograd in particular, it was even inaccessible to many of the wealthy. In fact, there was a tendency for the cosmopolitan merchant traders to assume a cultural hegemony (purchasing and exhibiting paintings from Paris), succeeding the liberal currents in the aristocracy who had sponsored projects such as the 'World of Art' movement early in the twentieth century.

Inevitably, there was a wide range of responses to the October Revolution amongst the artists and the intelligentsia, but largely as a result of Lunacharsky's efforts, many sections of them were won to a position of some sort of support for the revolution. Consequently, the momentum of artistic development was not only maintained in the period after October, but increased. Naturally, this period was not without its problems and conflicts, and Trotsky's *Literature and Revolution*, published in 1924 as the Stalinists were beginning to establish a firm grip on the state power, is the text to which most Trotskyists turn for an understanding of it.

One of the mysteries about *Literature and Revolution* is its silence on Lunacharsky and his work as People's Commissar for Education from 1917 to 1929. In this capacity he was to all intents and purposes responsible for the policies of the revolution towards the arts. He reformed the art schools and colleges, established the system of national museums, financed the preservation of institutions such as the Bolshoi Theatre, and commissioned numerous works from the new generations of artists and writers. Classic literature was nationalised, and cheap editions were produced to meet the demand from the poor. One might reasonably have expected from Trotsky, in his writings on cultural matters, some appraisal of the work of the revolutionary government and its commissar, but you will search in vain for any, at least in those texts which have been translated into English thus far, including Trotsky's obituary of Lunacharsky of 1934.[2]

Perhaps the kindest interpretation that can be placed on Trotsky's silence on Lunacharsky would be that he did not wish to render Lunacharsky's political position vis-à-vis Stalin any more difficult by allowing his enemies to associate him with the Opposition. Lunacharsky's *Silhouettes* had been published in 1923. It consisted of pen portraits of leaders of the revolution, and, significantly, made no mention of Stalin. This prompted a great deal of criticism and adverse comment, even at such an early stage in the ascendancy of the Stalinists, and the book was withdrawn from public sale a year later. I do not know of any documents which support this interpretation of Trotsky's silence, and it could not probably account

2. LD Trotsky, *Portraits Political and Personal*, New York, 1977, pp104-7. See also A Yeramov, *A Lunacharsky*, Moscow, 1975. Although from a Soviet source, it presents biographical information not easily available elsewhere. It is not mentioned in the notes to *Portraits Political and Personal*, which state that there is no biography in English.

for a silence extending longer than 20 years. It remains a question for future study, and is not without its importance in the development of a revolutionary Marxist cultural policy.

Lunacharsky's line on cultural policy does seem to have been in substantial agreement with elements of Trotsky's on the central question of the 'Proletcult'. As commissar, Lunacharsky appears to have resisted all the demands of the competing schools to be recognised as the sole representatives of revolutionary culture, and to have encouraged a rich diversity of forms of expression. He shared with Trotsky an opposition to the Proletcult leader Bogdanov's concept of the 'manufacture' of a new, proletarian culture in a 'laboratory', whilst he encouraged Proletcult's work in establishing theatre groups, art studios and other ventures in working-class areas.

Trotsky's failure to discuss the actual, concrete policies and achievements of the Bolshevik government is therefore one of the limitations of his book of which readers should be aware, before too readily accepting Alan Wald's description of it as 'a masterwork'.[3]

It is also fair to say that Literature and Revolution does not celebrate, or even recognise, the richness and variety of artistic work that was being created. Trotsky limits himself to a discussion of literature, as if it was possible to isolate literature from the rest of artistic activity. As the British Museum exhibition (which Rex Dunn reviewed) demonstrates, writers, designers, artists and photographers worked together on projects and publications, exchanging ideas and developing similar attitudes. Trotsky's concentration on literature, almost to the exclusion of all other forms of expression, provides the contemporary reader with only a blinkered view of the achievements and problems of culture in the revolutionary period.

Trotsky also seems not to have considered in his writings on culture the emergence of large-scale festivals as an element of the developing pattern of culture. This gap is surprising and, at this stage of studies, unaccountable. In these festivals the theories of the avant garde were put into effect, with street decoration, drama, readings and other activities. For example, the catalogue of the recent Moscow retrospective exhibition of Tatlin includes a photo of the famous Monument to the Third International in a Leningrad Mayday parade. Nor does Trotsky discuss or evaluate the propaganda and education work undertaken by many of the avant gardists in developing new and forceful graphic techniques of communication.

In the second issue of the Journal of Trotsky Studies, Alan Wald presents a useful general view of Trotsky's writings on cultural matters. He points

3. See Alan Wald, 'Literature and Revolution: Leon Trotsky's Contributions to Marxist Cultural Theory and Literary Criticism', Journal of Trotsky Studies, no 2, Glasgow, 1994.

out one key difference between Trotsky's stance and that of the majority of critics and writers – namely, that Trotsky was operating from a position of involvement, and of committed activity, not of armchair contemplation. Indeed, many of Trotsky's writings on literature were drafted on his famous military train, during intervals in his intense military work. Perhaps this is why Rex Dunn describes Trotsky as a 'spare-time critic'.

Wald argues from this that Trotsky's contributions to discussions about literature should be judged in the context of his 'central preoccupations and political objectives at various moments of his career'. This is not an unreasonable proposal, although one might ask what could be a more 'central preoccupation' than culture – that is, the quality of conscious existence – to a revolutionary, but it is not one which Wald pursues.

Perhaps this is an unfair criticism of Wald given the present state of our knowledge of the circumstances in which and the purposes for which *Literature and Revolution* was written. *Literature and Revolution* has been in print for the last 20 years, but the introductions to it have not sought to place the work in an historical or political context, to explain why Trotsky felt it necessary to direct his attention to cultural policies at the particular time he did and not at others. Of course, we know of some other occasions when he wrote on art and culture, but never with the same energy and focus.

At the time *Literature and Revolution* was written and published, there were limitations on Trotsky's ability to express himself, and the seriousness of his differences with the leadership majority was not well known outside inner-party circles. The *Platform of the Forty-Six* had been refused publication, as had some of his letters to leading bodies in the party. He was not, however, completely silenced; *The New Course* was published, initially as a series of articles in *Pravda*, and later as a pamphlet. In the December 1923 Appendix to *The New Course*, Trotsky also refers to serious problems with his health obstructing his participation in party discussions.

In such circumstances, one might surmise (and it can be no more than surmise pending the availability of evidence) that Trotsky would have sought both direct and indirect ways of raising the issues of central concern to him. The growing strength of the concept of 'proletarian culture', one of the main targets of Trotsky's criticism in *Literature and Revolution*, is closely linked with the slowing down of the revolution, and the disaster of the failure of 1923 in Germany in particular. Trotsky rejected the programme of 'proletarian culture' for a number of reasons; the most 'Trotskyist' of his reasons was that it should not be expected that the proletariat would have the time to create its own culture. The world's transition to Socialism would take decades, but those decades would be filled by wars and the struggle for power. The proletariat would not have the luxury, which the bourgeoisie had enjoyed, of long periods of class dictatorship in which its culture could develop. The end of these struggles would not then be the stabilisation of the dictatorship of the proletariat, but the active dissolution of the proletariat into the Socialist community. The aim of the revolution, then, was not to establish a proletarian culture, but a human culture.

The growth of a powerful movement for a 'proletarian culture' would therefore become a negative force, limiting and delaying the extension of the October Revolution. Its appearance was connected with the growing strength of those tendencies opposing the extension of the revolution – the bureaucracy, the rightists and the Stalinists. This, I propose, is the 'strategic' reason for Trotsky's specific and urgent concern with cultural matters at this time. What Wald refers to as the 'ambiguities' of *Literature and Revolution* are aspects of Trotsky's as yet incompletely developed break with the positions of the rapidly degenerating Communist Party and Comintern, which he still hoped could be revived, and in whose state he continued to see the continuation of October.

Wald describes a pattern of development in Trotsky's cultural writings, in which his later writings, culminating in the collaboration with Breton in 1938, show a substantial (and welcome) movement towards a libertarian position. I concur with Wald in the recognition of this shift, and in welcoming it.[4] I find, however, that Trotsky's lately-found cultural libertarianism did not extend so far as to promote a re-evaluation of some of the positions he took in *Literature and Revolution* which left him substantially in line with the Stalinists.

There are accounts to be settled with *Literature and Revolution* which need clearer language than Wald's diplomatic reference to Trotsky's 'ambiguities' of 1924. In addition to the avant garde, Russia at the time of the revolution was blessed with a number of the finest poets of the twentieth century – amongst them the Acmeists. One of the most significant Acmeists, Tsvetaeva, soon came to oppose the revolution and supported the Whites, and returned from exile to die under the Stalinist repression. The other major Acmeists, Mandlestam and Akhmatova, attempted to stand apart from the revolution, neither opposing nor supporting it. They were amongst the first to learn the consequences of not being approved of by the state.

Akhmatova was one of the very first poets to suffer from Soviet censorship. As early as 1921 one of her poems, written in 1917, about her decision to stay in Russia in the face of the risk of German occupation,

---

4.   I must add that *Culture and Socialism* of 1926, which Wald does not discuss, disrupts his otherwise viable groupings of Trotsky's cultural writings.

was only permitted to appear in print after severe mutilation. And in connection with this poem and its censoring arises one of the many puzzling questions about *Literature and Revolution*. Trotsky appears to refer to it with grudging but distinct approval in his chapter on fellow travellers: 'Akhmatova has some strong lines on why she did not go away. It is very good that she did not go away. But Akhmatova herself hardly thinks that her songs are of the revolution...'

What are we to make of this? Was Trotsky perhaps taking his distance from the censorship? If so, his position was so indirectly expressed as to be incomprehensible to contemporary readers (or at least to this one).

To help the reader arrive at an assessment of how far the revolution needed to interfere with artistic expression, here are Akhmatova's 'strong lines':

> When in suicidal anguish
> The nation awaited its German guests,
> And the stern spirit of Byzantium
> Had fled from the Russian Church,
> When the capital by the Neva,
> Forgetting her greatness,
> Like a drunken prostitute
> Did not know who would take her next,
> A voice came to me. It called out comfortingly,
> It said, 'Come here,
> Leave your deaf and sinful land,
> Leave Russia forever.
> I will wash the blood from your hands,
> Root out the black shame from your heart,
> With a new name I will conceal
> The pain of defeats and injuries.'
> But calmly and indifferently,
> I covered my ears with my hands,
> So that my sorrowing spirit
> Would not be stained by those shameful words.[5]

The first eight lines were not permitted to be printed in the 1921 edition. Elsewhere in *Literature and Revolution*, Trotsky is much less gracious towards Akhmatova:

'One reads with dismay most of the poetic collections, especially those of the women. Here, indeed, one cannot take a step without God. The lyric circle of Akhmatova, Tsvetaeva, Radlova and other real and near-real po-

---

5. Included in Roberta Reeder (ed), *The Complete Poems of Anna Akhmatova*, Edinburgh, 1992, which contains a useful short biography and other material.

etesses, is very small. It embraces the poetess herself, an unknown one in a derby or in spurs, and inevitably God, without any special marks. He is a very convenient and portable third person, quite domestic, a friend of the family who fulfils from time to time the duties of a doctor of female ailments.'

This is a form of expression which approaches thuggishness in its exuberance. And the contemporary reader cannot fail to discern a tendency in Trotsky to be sharper in his arguments *ad mulierem* than in those *ad hominem*.

Perhaps in the senior common room of a university, or in the columns of some conservative literary journal, this style of criticism might raise a sardonic smile. In 1924, however, Trotsky still carried substantial authority, although his position in the leadership of the Communist Party was crumbling under the Stalinists' attacks, whilst the targets of his criticism were virtually powerless. Moreover, Akhmatova and other Acmeists were under public attack from many directions. Her former husband, divorced some years before, had been shot, accused of taking part in a counter-revolutionary plot, the 'Tagantsev Affair'. The pronouncements of literary critics had been as aggressive as Trotsky's since 1921. Chukovsky (on whom Trotsky sheds some vitriolic scorn in *Literature and Revolution*) described Akhmatova as 'a nun who crosses herself as she kisses her beloved'. Others took up the theme, and denounced her work as unworthy of consideration in a revolutionary Communist society. Trotsky's denunciations were therefore neither extraordinary nor original. Nor did they differ in content or vocabulary from denunciations that continued to be heaped upon Akhmatova for the rest of her life, through the darkest periods of Stalinist repression. And nor did Trotsky take any opportunity during the 1930s, when she was banned from publication and her son arrested, to amend his line on Akhmatova. Indeed, he would have found it difficult to achieve such a radical change of line as to permit himself disagreement with Zhdanov's description of Akhmatova in 1946 as 'part nun and part harlot', having come so close to the same vocabulary himself.

Mandlestam also suffered from official disapproval, although he received some degree of unofficial protection from Bukharin and Lunacharsky. It is hard not to consider that Trotsky was a party to the conspiracy of silence against Mandlestam. Even when attacking the Acmeists, Trotsky does did not use Mandlestam's name. The absence of Mandlestam from *Literature and Revolution* is as huge and obvious a gap as that created by the absence of Solzhenitsyn from the official accounts of Russian literature in the Brezhnev period. The enthusiasts for *Literature and Revolution* have some serious explaining to do.

In Trotsky's sporadic writings on cultural matters after *Literature and Revolution*, most notably in the section in *Revolution Betrayed*, he continues to defend the positions he took in 1924, and does not recognise either the scale of destruction of independent artistic thinking which the Stalinists had achieved by 1936, or the enormous value of what had been lost. In *Revolution Betrayed* (Section 3 of Chapter 7, dealing with Nationality and Culture), he spares a sentence for Soviet films, but not even that much for painting, design, architecture and music combined.[6]

To attempt to draw some of the threads together – I have not spared much energy to praise *Literature and Revolution*, not because it deserves none, but because it has had plenty. I have argued that Trotsky failed to perceive the value of the avant garde in Russia, and that this was in large degree a consequence of his belief in the superiority of literature, and of classical literature in particular. I have also sought to demonstrate that some of Trotsky's methods of argument and selections of subject matter were improper, and that despite a considerable movement towards a 'libertarian' line during the 1930s, he never changed or corrected these positions. I have also attempted to implement Alan Wald's proposal that Trotsky's writing on culture should be evaluated in relation to his political preoccupations and objectives – at least insofar as the writing of *Literature and Revolution* is concerned. This has prepared the ground for further consideration of the nature of the culture and society which was formed by Stalinism.[7]

6. In *Culture and Socialism* he gives some indications of the reason for his preference for literature over the other arts, and especially over music. In criticising the artistic theories of Tolstoy (and according to Brian Pearce, by implication, of Bukharin), he describes as 'reactionary' all 'attempts to approximate all forms of art to music', on the grounds that they have 'always signified a depreciation in art of the rôle of the intelligence in favour of formless feeling'. But this aspect of Trotsky's contributions on artistic theory was not dealt with by Wald, and is also outside the scope of this note. Extracts from *Culture and Socialism* can be found, along with *Class and Art* (May 1924), in LD Trotsky, *On Literature and Art*, New York, 1977. Both of these pieces were previously published as pamphlets by the Socialist Labour League/Workers Revolutionary Party.
7. As well as works cited in the text or previous notes, readers are recommended to investigate the following.
    Roger Pethybridge, *The Social Prelude to Stalinism*, London, 1977. See especially the chapter on illiteracy.
    Nadezhda Mandlestam, *Hope Against Hope* and *Hope Abandoned*, London, 1976 and 1973. Memoirs of the poet by his widow.
    Elaine Feinstein, *Marina Tsvetayeva*, London, 1989.
    Rex Dunn, 'Russian Avant Garde Revisited', *Workers Press*, 27 August 1994.
    Susan Compton, *Russian Avant-Garde Books 1917-1934*, London, 1994. Written to accompany the exhibition reviewed by Rex Dunn.
    Susan Compton, *The World Backwards: Russian Futurist Books 1912-1916*, London, 1978.

Antonio Gramsci

A Letter to Leon Trotsky on Futurism

HERE are my replies to your questions on the Italian futurist movement. Since the war, in Italy, the futurist movement has utterly lost all its defining features. Marinetti[8] now pays scant attention to the movement. He got married, and prefers to devote his energies to his wife. The futurist movement currently comprises royalists, Communists, republicans and Fascists. Recently, a new political weekly entitled *Il Principe* [*The Prince*] has been established in Milan. This publication supports, or attempts to support, the very same theories which Machiavelli preached in the sixteenth century for Italy, that is, that struggles splitting local parties and leading the nation to chaos can be ended by an absolute monarch, by a new Cesare Borgia, who should simply behead all the leaders of the struggling parties. The magazine editors are two futurists, Bruno Corra[9] and Enrico Settimelli.[10] As for Marinetti, despite his arrest in Rome in 1920 during a patriotic demonstration after his very forceful speech against the king, he actually contributes to this weekly.

The most significant figures of prewar futurism have all become Fascists, save for Giovanni Papini,[11] who has actually turned Catholic and has written a history of Christ. During the war, the futurists were the most ardent supporters of 'war to the final victory' and imperialism. Only one Fascist, Aldo Palazzeschi,[12] expressed his opposition to the war. He broke with the movement, and, although he happens to be amongst the more interesting writers, as a man of letters he now keeps silent. Generally speaking, Marinetti has always exalted war, and published a manifesto in which he tried to show that war is the sole means for cleansing the world. He took part in the war, as the captain of an armoured car unit, and his latest book, *l'Alcova d'acciaio* [*The Steel Alcove*] is an enthusi-

8. Filippo Tommaso (Emilio) Marinetti (1876-1944) was an Italian prose writer, novelist and poet, and was one of the ideological founders of futurism.
9. Bruno Corra (1892-) was an Italian artist and journalist.
10. Settimelli's first name was actually Emilio. He was an artist and futurist. Together with Marinetti and Corra he wrote the manifestos *The Futurist Synthetic Theatre* (1915) and *The Futurist Cinema* (1916).
11. Giovanni Papini (1881-1956) was a journalist, critic, poet and novelist, and one of the leaders of futurism. He later converted to the Roman Catholic Church.
12. Aldo Palazzeschi (real name Aldo Giurlani, 1885-1974) was a futurist writer of poetry and prose.

astic celebration of the use of the armoured car in the war. Marinetti has also written a pamphlet entitled *Oltre il comunismo* [*Beyond Communism*], in which he states his political ideas, if indeed we can use the word 'ideas' for the sometimes ingenious but ever peculiar fantasies of this man. Before my departure, the Turin branch of Proletcult[13] invited Marinetti to the opening of an exhibition of futurist paintings, and asked him to explain the meaning of these works to the workers belonging to the organisation. Marinetti gladly accepted the invitation, and, after touring the exhibition together with the workers, said he was satisfied that he had received a practical confirmation of the fact that, as far as futurist art was concerned, workers' artistic sensitivity was far superior to that of the bourgeoisie. Before the war, futurism was very popular amongst workers. The magazine *Lacerba*[14] had a circulation of 25 000 copies, four-fifths of which went to workers. During the numerous futurist arts events, in the theatres of the largest Italian cities workers took the futurists' side, and defended them against the attacks of the semi-aristocratic and bourgeois youth, who often came to blows with them.

But Marinetti's futurist group is no more. One Mario Dessy, a man

13. In the summer of 1920, during the Second Congress of the Communist International in Moscow, the All-Russian Soviet of the Proletcult, with the support of Anatoly Lunacharsky, promoted the establishment of a provisional international bureau of the Proletcult, which would be represented in all European countries. In the case of Italy, the Istituto di Cultura Proletaria (Sezione del Proletcult Internazionale di Mosca), was created in Turin in January 1921. Gramsci actively supported the initiative. Although he declined to take a prominent position on the ICP's provisional committee, as he wanted to allow 'non-intellectuals' to gain experience in the activity, in 1921-22 Gramsci was in full agreement with the ideas of the Proletcult, and the contents and initiatives of the ICP were markedly influenced by it. Through the party and its daily paper, he also sought to give maximum publicity to the activities of the ICP, and to link them to the party at large. He firmly believed that in preparation for the revolution, the proletariat as a class should equip itself with every means to carry out its historical tasks, and struggle to restore fully the values of civilisation. Despite facing increasing difficulties under the Fascist regime, the ICP had a membership numbering several hundred, comprised of individuals, trade unions, factory committees, etc. Amongst its highly popular and well-attended initiatives were conferences, courses, plays and concerts, visits to museums and exhibitions, amongst which was the one on 2 April 1922 to which Marinetti was invited. Initially, Gramsci considered that Marinetti and the futurist movement were a revolutionary intellectual force, in the sense that they sought to destroy bourgeois culture and old-fashioned practices and conventions, such as style and form, particularly in the field of language. Gramsci admired their boldness in trying out new artistic and cultural forms, and urged the proletariat to be just as bold and to create its own culture, totally distinct from that of the bourgeoisie. The ICP also announced in 1922 that a monthly newsletter, *Proletcult*, would be published, but nothing came of it. The ICP also tried, with very limited success, to establish branches in other Italian cities, but it had ceased practically all activity in the same year.

14. A literary journal published in Florence between 1913 and 1915 which espoused futurism, and called for Italy to intervene in the war.

without any intellectual or organisational qualities, now edits his old magazine *Poesia* [*Poetry*]. In Southern Italy, and especially in Sicily, there still are several small futurist publications, and Marinetti sends his articles to them, but these are nothing more than magazines edited by schoolboys, who clearly mistake their ignorance of Italian grammar for futurism. The strongest cell amongst futurists is made up of painters. In Rome, there is a permanent gallery exhibiting futurist works, which is managed by a failed photographer, one Anton Giulio Bragaglia, a cinema agent and theatre impresario. Amongst the futurist painters, the best known figure is Giorgio Balla.[15] Publicly, D'Annunzio has never had a position on futurism. One must remember that when it first emerged, futurism was very much opposed to D'Annunzio – indeed one of Marinetti's first books was entitled *Le dieux vont, et D'Annunzio reste*. Although during the war the political programmes of Marinetti and D'Annunzio were virtually identical, the futurists have remained strongly against D'Annunzio. They showed little interest for the Fiume movement,[16] although later on they actually took part in the demonstrations organised around it.

It can be argued that after the signing of the peace the futurist movement has utterly lost its distinguishing features, and has dispersed into various currents created and built after the turning point marked by the war. The young intellectuals have nearly all become reactionaries. Workers, who had seen in futurism the elements of a struggle against the old Italian academia, so immobile and divorced from the popular masses, must now struggle arms in hand for their very freedom, and they have little interest in any old polemics. In the large industrial centres, the Proletcult programme, which seeks to awaken the creative spirit of workers in the field of literature and art, is absorbing the energies of all those who still desire or are able to deal with these problems.

Moscow
8 September 1922

15. Balla's first name was actually Giacomo. Balla (1871-1958) was an artist and a founder of the futurist movement in painting.
16. Gabriele D'Annunzio (1863-1938) was a writer and poet, and was the leading figure of the decadent movement in Italy. He was heavily influenced by Nietzsche's ideas on the superman. On 12 September 1919, at the head of some renegade military units, he took control of the town of Fiume (Rijeka) in response to the rejection by the Paris Conference of the Italian request of 7 February 1919 that it be annexed to Italy. This independent initiative by the 'Poet-Soldier' posed a problem for Mussolini's personal authority and the Fascist movement, in its open challenge to the authority of the Italian state.

Leon Trotsky

For Quality — For Culture!

Translator's Introduction

This article was one of a collection written by all the senior leaders of the Russian Communist Party for the special issue of *Pravda* published on 7 November 1925 to mark the eighth anniversary of the Bolsheviks' seizure of power. It has been translated from Volume 21 of Trotsky's *Sochineniya*.

The year of 1925 marked a turning-point in the New Economic Policy. After its initial successes in restarting industry and agriculture after the ruination brought by world war, revolution and civil war, the NEP began to suffer the problems inherent in the compromise with private business activity on which it was based. In particular, the better-off peasants, nicknamed kulaks, were increasing their economic power-base; a poor harvest in 1924 raised the prospect of grain shortages in the towns for the first time since the Civil War, and the state was forced to abandon low fixed grain prices and buy at high prices from the better-off peasants.

These problems formed the background to the conflict that erupted in the party, in which the right wing, broadly grouped around Stalin and Bukharin, advocated further concessions to the well-off peasants, and a new opposition coalescing around Zinoviev and Kamenev towards the end of the year called for an end to the concessions, and opposed the formula of 'Socialism in One Country'.

As the disputes mounted — first around the economic issues raised in Preobrazhensky's *The New Economics*, which was subject to a withering attack by Bukharin; then around Bukharin's infamous call in April to the well-off peasants to 'enrich yourselves'; then around the Platform of the Four (Zinoviev, Kamenev, Sokolnikov and Krupskaya) issued in September, demanding open discussion of the questions in the party; then at a Central Committee plenum in October at which the dispute was thrashed out openly — Trotsky distinguished himself by his silence. Having been witch-hunted after the defeat of the 1923 Opposition, made a humiliating statement of submission to the Thirteenth Party Congress in May 1924, left the Commissariat of War in January 1925 and been appointed to the Council of National Economy, and in July issued a statement disavowing Max Eastman's publication of Lenin's 'Testament', Trotsky made no comment on the Zinoviev-Stalin conflict when it came out into the open in September and October. His writings of this period, the most notable of which was the book *Towards Capitalism or Socialism?*, make no reference to the internal party disputes. Only after the Fourteenth Congress of December

1925, and after Stalin's manoeuvres in early 1926 to emasculate Zinoviev's base of support in Leningrad, did the latter become reconciled with Trotsky. Only in May 1926 did they launch the Joint Opposition; the conduct of the NEP and the issue of 'Socialism in One Country' were central to its platform. (Standard accounts of the disputes of 1925 and Trotsky's part are in EH Carr, *A History of Soviet Russia*, Volume 5, pp189ff, and Volume 6, pp52-75, 108-52, and in Isaac Deutscher, *The Prophet Unarmed*, Oxford, 1979, pp223-59.)

The article that follows was written just after the October plenum at which the Stalin-Zinoviev dispute came into the open, and five months before Trotsky re-entered the fray against Stalin. It is interesting perhaps because it shows the acuteness with which Trotsky, despite his aloofness from the Stalin-Zinoviev conflict, felt the contradictions of NEP that underlay it. It certainly shows his capacity for understanding those problems in their broad historical and cultural context.

Simon Pirani

E IGHT years of dictatorship, that is, of an *exclusive* regime. And in that time − economic expansion! How is such a thing possible? Because that dictatorship trampled on and destroyed only those forces that were already at death's door; it by and large found means by which to cooperate with those forces that could not yet be replaced. This is the indefatigable vitality of the proletarian dictatorship: it is ruthless not because it is arbitrary or motivated by blind passion, but because it is based on a scientific assessment of the historical process, and does not run ahead of that process if the necessary preconditions are not present.

The Great French Revolution gave us the classic model of pre-proletarian revolutionary dictatorship, in the form of the terrorist regime of the Jacobins. Babeuf and Blanqui[17] fought to bring a Socialist content to the idea of revolutionary dictatorship. This great heritage passed to Marx. But he went further, and once and for all brought Socialism together with the class struggle within bourgeois society. From the tradition of revolutionary dictatorship arose the programme of the *proletarian dictatorship*.

Marx was the first to teach us to approach society as it really is, as an organic product of economic development. Historical society, as we have

17. Gracchus Babeuf (1760-1797) was amongst the most extreme radicals in the French revolution, and, when imprisoned first by Robespierre and then by the Thermidorians, elaborated egalitarian Communist doctrines. He was executed for his leading rôle in an unsuccessful conspiracy against the Thermidorian government. Louis Auguste Blanqui (1805-1881) was a French revolutionary, a utopian Communist who advocated conspiratorial methods and led the conspiratorial Société des saisons; he stood on the extreme left of the 1848 revolution, and served many years of imprisonment for his actions.

known it, is the organisation of production, based on exploitation. The fact that the bourgeoisie organised relations of production at a higher level than its predecessors was a precondition for its advance. Marx taught that no social system leaves the scene without having exhausted the possibilities for development contained within it. From this, it follows that the replacement of one ruling class by another is by its very essence bound up with new ways of organising society. All genuine social revolutions, whether bourgeois or proletarian, are conceivable only under conditions in which the rising class unites the whole nation around itself, against that class which stands at the head of the outmoded economic system. The proletarian revolution in each separate country is at the same time a national revolution, for the proletariat cannot conquer and hold power, let alone use it to transform society, if it does not itself become the axis around which can be drawn all the nation's vital elements, that is, its overwhelming majority. Such are the first letters in the ABC of Marxism.

Once it takes power, the proletariat takes possession of the nation's historical inheritance – and it is not given the option of rejecting any part of that inheritance at any specific moment. True, the Soviet power at the stroke of a pen renounced the payment of debts on the old [Tsarist] loans. But in the final analysis, these loans were only an insignificant part of the country's historical liabilities. A far greater part of these liabilities consisted of poverty, ignorance, superstition, alcoholism, prostitution and, above all, the contradiction between town and country. None of this could be cleared from the account by means of a decree. The years directly following the taking of power showed us in harsh practical terms what we already knew in theory: that the proletariat is not arbitrarily opening a fresh account. It does not start with a clean sheet. No, it takes over the social mechanism on the move, with all the stratifications and contradictions left by history. The vanguard of the proletariat, which directly exercises the dictatorship, cannot order the mass of the people who are caught up in the webs of the past, 'abandon the old economic methods and relationships, until I remake everything anew'!

Our task is posed in a different way: the building of the new society is necessarily combined with maintenance of those functions of the old society whose termination would leave great masses of people without heat, without water, and without bread. *From this* stems the problem of the *smychka*.[18] This is not a cunningly contrived tactical device, but a basic problem of the revolution. It flows from the circumstance that, by the very act of exercising its dictatorship, the proletariat takes on responsibility – not formal, that is, juridical or 'moral', but practical, material, direct responsibility – for living human society, with all its vital needs that

18. This word, meaning 'link' or 'contact', was used in the discussions of the 1920s to designate the necessary bond between workers and peasants.

cannot be postponed. The task of the transition period is to coordinate the building of the new society with the use of habitual, and so far irreplaceable, market methods of meeting need and consumer demand. The problem of the *smychka* in its most generalised form is not a national peculiarity, still less an exception to the principles of Marxism. It is a fundamental and inevitable consequence of the existence of proletarian dictatorship as a transitional state form that is rebuilding human society – a society whose structure includes huge, heterogeneous strata from the past. In contradistinction to the Blanquists, that is, to those who understand dictatorship idealistically and mechanically, who simply counterpose Socialism to the old society in general and therefore remain utopian, the Marxist conception of dictatorship inevitably presupposes the Leninist formula of the *smychka*.

Moreover, the word *smychka* has not only a national sound but also a national content. Lenin formulated this central aim of the transitional period for application to a society that lags far behind historically, where the contradiction between town and country is especially enormous, where the proletariat comprises a small minority of the population, and where the great majority are disparate small-scale producers – peasants or handicraftsmen – little touched by culture. This Leninist formula, like the whole Leninist policy, is deeply national. But this means only that it applies internationalist methods to the specific conditions amongst a particular people at a particular time. Without this there can be no politics. However, if the *smychka* is the national concretisation of the fundamentals of the Marxist conception of dictatorship, it is also a development of this conception on an international scale. For only from the experience of the Soviet republic, illuminated by this Leninist formula, will the international proletariat understand and achieve, as it must, the new tasks that will fall to it from the first hour of the taking of power.

In those countries where the proletariat comprises the clear majority – although that is in no way a necessary precondition for proletarian dictatorship, as we now clearly understand – it will also be obliged, from the first moments after the seizure of power, to develop the necessary connections between socialised[19] and unsocialised parts of the economy. In its most developed form, the problem of the economic *smychka* with the artisans, peasants and small traders will have a different specific weight; its precise form depends on the social structure of each nation. But it will have a greater or lesser significance in all countries. In a country such as England, where the workers comprise the overwhelming majority of the population, the problem of the *smychka* immediately takes on an international character: the English proletariat must resolve, to-

19. Trotsky uses the words 'obobshchestvlennye', which could be translated as 'socialised' or 'collectivised'.

gether with the peasants of India, Egypt, etc, to conduct on the basis of voluntary agreement those economic relationships which at present have a forced, colonial character.

❖   ❖   ❖

As the oppositional class in the old society, the proletariat passed a great test by overthrowing the old lords and masters. But straight after this, in its capacity as a ruling class, it faced a new test.

The working class had to come into its own as the holder of power at the same time as it was laying the foundations of new state organisations and defending the society it was leading from domestic and foreign class enemies. The building of the state apparatus and the revolutionary army was the proletariat's first great test as a ruling class. The new state and the new army reflected the nation that was being rebuilt. The Soviet constitution guaranteed for the proletariat the leading rôle in the workers' and peasants' state. The Communist proletariat formed the core of the Red Army, but that army's ranks were filled above all by the peasant masses. In the state apparatus, just as in the military organisations, we have a *smychka* of two classes — the leading and the led. The proletariat has proved in practice that it is able to lead, and it is able to defend. In this way, it guaranteed the most basic preconditions for completing our Socialist tasks.

Further ahead lie questions of the economy, and, interwoven with them and based upon them, questions of culture.

From the first, the revival of industry depended on the availability of foodstuffs and other provisions, and of raw materials — that is, on the rural economy. The problem of the *smychka* was presented in its *economic essentials*; it was at that very moment that Lenin's well-chosen word [*smychka*] came into circulation. At that time, the *smychka* had a primitive content: it meant exchanging one thing for another thing, in order to save someone from death by starvation or to prevent the last factory in an area from grinding to a halt. But from there grew a more regulated exchange of industrial products for agricultural ones. The development of such relationships has been a most important factor of the last few years. Now the problem of the *smychka* increasingly focuses on the exchange of agricultural equipment and machinery for raw materials produced for industry in the countryside. And here heavy industry enters directly into the chain of the *smychka*, providing an essential link in the form of the construction of agricultural machinery. Only to the extent that this task is carried out will strong foundations be laid for productive cooperation in the countryside, that is, for Socialist agriculture. That work is still ahead.

If by taking Perekop[20] and purging the Soviet territory of its enemies,

20. The battle of Perekop on 7-10 November 1920 resulted in the defeat of the last sig-

the proletariat proved conclusively that it had a strong grip on military affairs; then by bringing industry close to its prewar level of production, it demonstrated irrefutably its ability to manage the economy. The significance of the control figures produced by Gosplan[21] is not only that they show, in outline, the elements of our rapidly-improving economic balance-sheet — which is an accounting question — but also that they emphasise, above all, the growing preponderance of Socialist elements over capitalist ones in industry, trade and finance. Precisely this, and only this, justifies *from a Socialist point of view* the broader scale of capitalist and semi-capitalist relationships in the countryside. These relationships bring with them new dangers — and after the resolution of the latest Central Committee plenum on the issue[22] no reminders are needed of that. But these dangers can be overcome — if all the necessary political, administrative-economic, fiscal and other measures are taken — only under conditions of a gigantic development of state industry and a development of

nificant White army on Russian soil, that of Wrangel, and is usually counted as the end of the Russian Civil War. The Perekop isthmus connects mainland Ukraine to the Crimean peninsula, where Wrangel's army of 32 000 was based. Wrangel faced an offensive by five Red armies, totalling 133 000 men, led by Mikhail Frunze, who in 1925 went on to become Commander-in-Chief of the Red Army. The Whites were routed; Wrangel, aided by France, left Sevastopol on 14 November.

21. The state planning commission.
22. The plenum of the party Central Committee held in October 1925, mentioned in the introduction, was dominated by the conflict between the Stalin-Bukharin leadership and the supporters of Zinoviev, based in Leningrad, who would subsequently join Trotsky and former members of the 1923 Opposition in the Joint Opposition of 1926-27 (for an account of the discussion, see EH Carr, *A History of Soviet Russia*, Volume 5, pp305-11). The resolution to which Trotsky refers dealt with party work in the countryside. It was proposed by Molotov, who was loyal to Stalin and Bukharin, but also incorporated some points made by Zinoviev; Carr describes it as a compromise between the Stalin-Bukharin and Zinoviev factions in the party. The resolution warned both of a 'neglect of the interests of the village poor and an underestimation of the kulak danger', and also of a neglect of the middle peasants and a breach of the *smychka* between the proletariat and peasantry. According to a footnote in the volume of Trotsky's collected works in which the article 'For Quality — For Culture!' was reprinted, he was referring especially to a passage in the resolution which stated: 'The notable widening of social differentiation in the countryside has given an impetus to the activity of social groups within the peasantry. The kulak has become more active. The mass of middle peasants has become more active. And the poor peasants have also become more active, but, being least prepared for the struggle under these new conditions, they lag behind other sections of the peasantry in their activity and organisational level. The growing influence of the kulaks was noticeable in a number of places in the last election campaign for the soviets; so was the inability of party organisations to rally the poorest layers in the countryside, in order to work together with the middle layers to guarantee in the soviets and cooperatives a clear preponderance of the poor and middle layers.' The resolution went on to propose special meetings of poor peasants to defend their interests in subsequent soviet elections.

its capacity not only to put clothes on the peasant's back and shoes on his feet, but also to transform the economy in which he works.

This great task has yet to be tackled. So far we have built the *rough foundations* of our state, army and economy; *finished construction* is still ahead.

❖   ❖   ❖

On this eighth anniversary of the October Revolution, it would be appropriate to remind ourselves most forcefully that the historical worth and reliability of every social formation is defined in the final analysis by the productivity of labour it is able to achieve. This is the most important and objective criterion. Of course, we flatly reject teleology, the idealistic notion that humanity proceeds towards goals precisely worked out in advance. But the fact remains that human society – partly spontaneously, partly consciously – travels constantly towards increases in the productivity of labour: this 'goal' is not determined from without, but grows out of the material conditions of existence of society. This is the main difference between humanity and the world of animals; it is also the fundamental and, in the final analysis, the most accurate criterion of all historical development.

'Progress', understood as humanity's supposedly constant ascent, is an idealistic chimera, at least as far as the last few thousand years are concerned. Development actually goes in a zigzag fashion. Downturns and long periods of collapse follow surges of development. Capitalism assured a large measure of stability to social progress precisely because it put the development of the productive forces at the centre of attention. But capitalist society knows not only fast-moving alternation of industrial upturns and crises, but also long periods of decline. The world war was a serious reminder of this. Capitalism prepared the technological preconditions for planned and all-sided progress, but has itself been unable to make that progress. Above all, it was unable to raise agriculture up to the level to which it has raised industry. Capitalism heaped onto the backs of the least developed peoples the great weight of crop farming and herdsmanship, preferring to use its own industrial primacy to exploit them. Overcoming this worldwide contradiction between town and country is the same as overcoming the contradiction between West and East, between the exploiting nations and the oppressed colonies. Only Socialism will be able to do this. And not by chance has the first proletarian revolution unfolded in Russia, the great meeting-place of the capitalist West and the colonial East.

Our relationship with the East is one of the most important guarantees of our success. But in respect of technology and culture it is with the West that we, and the whole East with us, must compare ourselves. So great have been our economic successes that they have taken us — against the furious resistance of our enemies — into the world economic system. But the very connections we have established with the capitalist system have brought into sharp focus our great technical and cultural backwardness. Socialism is a much higher social form than capitalism, which it is replacing — and not only because it clears away exploitation and prepares the ground for social equality. These criteria, taken in isolation, are not the decisive ones. We do not want equality in poverty and ignorance, and anyway that is unrealisable. Inequality arises from want. We have seen from the living experience of our peasantry, albeit only in the last few years, that slavery to nature is no less severe than class slavery. We are striving for Socialism because it will prepare the way for equality on the basis of technical developments, material prosperity and a high level of culture.

Whilst reviewing the achievements of the last eight years with rightful satisfaction, we must nonetheless evaluate these achievements accurately on the scale of the world economy. We have not yet attained the prewar quantity of goods produced, still less have we attained prewar quality. We have every reason to expect that in the next 12 months we will get right up to the prewar level in terms of quantity, and, partly, in terms of quality. But the prewar level is called 'prewar' for a reason: because it was severely tested during the war — and we know the results of that test all too well. Whilst Germany, surrounded on all sides by enemies, held out for four years on account of its industrial might, every single day of the war exposed all the more harshly the inadequacies and shortcomings of Russian industry, notwithstanding the support it received from the strongest of wartime allies. The war delivered a fatal verdict on the economic backwardness of old Russia. Let us not forget that within the new social forms, we have so far not even returned to the economic level achieved of old.

It is true that the balance of forces has changed to an exceptional degree in our favour. Europe is incomparably weaker today than it was before the war; on the other hand, Soviet forms of organisation give us the possibility to use the available material resources with immeasurably greater expediency. Furthermore, there are great political resources available both to us and to the Communist International. Only thanks to these factors has Russia not become a colony in the last eight years — a fate towards which it was moving inexorably in 1914-17. But facts are facts. From a technical point of view, we are the most backward country in Europe. The productivity of labour in the USSR is lower than in any of the advanced capitalist countries; our consumer goods are more expensive, and they are of a lower quality. All this can and must be measured by accurate comparative statistics, which will become the most reliable 'index' of the tasks we have to carry out in the future – not only economic tasks, but also cultural ones.

❖   ❖   ❖

Our construction work, especially its economic aspect, has until now rested primarily on old technical skills. All aspects of our work have been conducted up until now at that level of culture attained under the old regime. In terms of politics and the social order, we took a leap of great historical significance. In other respects, we have moved forward incomparably more slowly. In the economy, in terms of the production of material values, we have not even caught up with the old. The development of society does not proceed uniformly on all tracks – that is just one of its contradictions. But now we have reached the stage at which we must level up the fronts of production and culture with the social-political front. We have exhausted the knowledge, methods and skills – both productive and cultural – that we inherited from the past. From here on, there are scarcely any roads laid out by capitalism – indeed, hardly any footpaths. To go forward, we will need to build highways, to lay new technological foundations, to teach ourselves new skills, to eradicate illiteracy, to raise qualifications, to learn and learn again from our enemies, and to raise our level of culture. We need a heightening of cultural 'quality' in all aspects of our activity. We need to move the nation – or rather, family of nations – led by the proletariat up to a higher form in history's school. We will achieve this only by an intensive effort with regard to every aspect of human culture.

Hegel's law of the transition of quantity into quality also works in reverse: quality is transformed into quantity. In considering our economic life as a whole, we can test the force of this law by experience. In the last year of the Civil War and the first year of the New Economic Policy, when the whole country had run out of supplies and was getting by on leftovers, no one would have dared to inquire about quality. We needed more goods, whatever the quality! But to the extent that additional quantities of goods came into circulation, production itself automatically improved. An extra bale of poor-quality cotton improved the work of the half-dead textile factory; an extra pud[23] of rotten flour or a dozen poor-quality pencils improved the organisation of teaching at a school that had previously stopped all together. And so on down the line. The quality of work was raised by virtue of the increase in quantity, but only to a certain level.

Once the unbearable famine in all aspects of the economy and culture had at least partially subsided, we could start to make a critical self-appraisal. The country began to say, through the voices of its advanced

23. A measure of weight, about 16 kilos.

elements: we work clumsily, carelessly, expensively and badly. The issue of how to put our work onto a scientific basis began to interest wider circles of people. Production meetings began to be held. The question of the quality of production, both material and spiritual – including the output of offices and not only of factories – moved more and more into the foreground. Not for a minute has the aim of increasing the quantity of material benefits been moved to the background; on the contrary, it is making itself felt like never before. Everything is in short supply. There is not enough of anything. But the fight for quantity itself depends at every stage on the question of quality. To increase the productivity of labour, we need better technology, more scientifically organised production, better raw materials, and a higher level of training. The more completely we bring into circulation these scarce resources, the more it will become clear that the pursuit of quantity lies through quality.

The electrification programme relies on old reserves, above all the old engineers. But this resource has nearly run out. The completion of electrification now depends directly on how our schools succeed in training new engineers, technicians and labourers. More than that: the development of the electricity network raises directly the question of us having village teachers who will be able to explain both to pupils and their parents what electricity pylons really mean for us, and, in this way, ensure that they are properly guarded. The work of the village school, in its turn, raises the question of cheap and sturdy textbooks, of paper supplies, of pencils; it raises again the far-from-resolved question of our publishing and typesetting industry. And further: this *smychka* of town and country raises again the question of the means of communication, of highways, of the country roads and bridges.

Improvements in the quality of agricultural machinery – its ability to sustain wear and tear, ease of operation, and effective spare parts supply – will heighten the peasantry's trust in our domestic machine-building industry and increase demand. Improvements in the quality of grain, flax fibre and so on will naturally increase the volume of exports. Improvements in the technique of newspaper production – more durable paper and more legible typefaces – will increase the number of readers with every issue. Improvements in the literary-political content of the press – greater vitality and many-sidedness, stronger organic connections with its audience – will bring to it new readers. A simple improvement in the quality of food in the public canteens will speed up the transformation of the closed-in life of the family as an economic unit. A consistent fight against various negative tendencies amongst our young people, above all a lack of discipline and a slackness of all kinds, goes forward by raising the quality of personality. The means for this are scientific learning, technique, literature (real, not ersatz, literature), sport, etc. So in all respects, in all areas of life, the question of 'quality' becomes the key to our new culture.

❖   ❖   ❖

At each new stage, the basic tasks of the Socialist organisation of society confront us in a new fashion and, most importantly, with ever greater concreteness. Today, the question of all questions is this: how do we escape bureaucratism, deathly indifference and suffocating red tape? The state economy embraces a huge variety of themes, people and processes — and this means that those who are giving directions are exceptionally far away from those that are carrying them out. Socialism aims to overcome hostile competition in industry, the duplication of effort, unnecessary friction, and unnecessary movement of goods backward and forwards; in a word, it aims to overcome anarchy in the economy and in all cultural and social practices — by means of leadership, based on planned accounting and worked-out perspectives. But our Socialist cures harbour within them their own diseases, which we may justifiably — and without in any way understating their harmfulness — call infantile diseases. The great difficulty consists in achieving a combination of active personal concern with the social planning of the economy. In this respect, we have already achieved some great successes, above all in that we have to a certain extent — far from completely or perfectly, but to a certain extent — tied the level of wages to the productivity of labour. But we are far from achieving our aims in this regard.

The rottenness of bureaucratism consists of its disregard for the real tasks in hand and its evasion of what really needs doing, its sliding away at a tangent from what is essential — in the very times that compel us, as never before, to get to the essence, to the living heart of the matter, in every problem, big or small. A circular hard on the heels of another circular, itself followed by a further circular, solves nothing — even though we cannot do without circulars. Rather we need the cog-wheels of concern and responsibility, both individual and collective, to interlock closely. Such a system cannot be created in a finished form — it needs to be worked out and developed day by day. The construction of a Socialist economy is the continuous creative work of society. Such creative work as ours, on such a large scale, must include an element of experimentation, that is, the production of prototypes, the testing of different systems of inspection, incentives, material and moral rewards and punishments, mutual indemnities, etc. We must not allow routine to settle down and harden; we must force openings in it that will let in better-worked-out methods, and allow new creative possibilities to arise. All this work will be driven forward by the striving of the masses for a better life, for security of material well-being, for a higher spiritual level, for everything that strengthens the body and enriches the consciousness, and that lifts and inspires thought – in a word, for culture.

In relation to the peasant, as a small-scale commodity producer, our aims consist in gradually, through a series of intermediate steps, bringing him – with all his proprietorial interest in both the quantity and quality of his production – into the system of socialised production.

The main lever to achieve this is Socialist industry. Its future success will enable it to set itself the task of giving a helping hand to agriculture. This is the new stage of the *smychka*. In the early years, industry gave hardly anything to the peasantry, time and again demanding loans from it. The muzhik's advances were used to kindle the factory furnaces. When the wheels of industry began to turn a little, it began for the first time to supply the peasant as a consumer, whilst hardly engaging with peasant industry as such. That peasant industry began to revive and live on the strength – or with the weakness – of the past. The *smychka* was principally a relationship of consumers: bread went to the workers, woven cotton products went to the peasants. But now that is insufficient for both sides. The town needs from the countryside ever-increasing quantities of raw materials for industry. The countryside demands from the town equipment, machinery and electrical energy. Industry, albeit slowly, is approaching its greatest task: to take agriculture in tow, and to pull it out of the terrible conditions that Marx and Engels once called the 'idiocy of rural life'. The tug of industry is tied to the barge with a tow-rope; the tow-rope needs to be strong enough not to break. The mechanisation of agriculture, the introduction of the principle of the *smychka* into the process of production, must be our tightly-woven steel cable by which heavy industry will tug agriculture.

Every tractor is another tug on that rope by industry, to pull the peasant economy from the swamp of strip-farming and the senseless waste of labour power. According to our projections, the countryside needs to receive about 20 000 of these tractors in the present financial year. Even that is not many, but it is something. We note, also, that it means 20 000 tractor-drivers and thousands of repair stations staffed by qualified workers. The tractor is a tug on the tow-rope not only in the technical, but also in the cultural sense. A Communist on a tractor is the best leadership that can be provided in the countryside of tomorrow. Industrialisation of agriculture will provide the natural basis for the introduction of proletarian leadership in the life of rural areas. 'Patronage' exercised by a proletarian corps of tractor-drivers, mechanics, repair workers, which the town selects carefully and sends to the countryside, will be incomparably more powerful than those forms of patronage, often artificial and not always successful, to which the town is compelled to resort at present.

However, we must not forget that of those 20 000 tractors planned for delivery this year, the lion's share will have to be imported. Soviet industry will be able to produce only 2000 tractors in the coming year. There is nothing dreadful in that; our industry will first and foremost provide the countryside with the most simple machines, and mass production of tractors will follow in due course. Nonetheless, the figures – approximately 2000 of our own tractors and 18 000 imports – are a measure of the grandiose and as yet unfulfilled tasks before us. The tow-rope really must be not a capitalist one, but a Soviet one, a steel cable marked with the hammer and sickle.

It will be possible to carry out this gigantic task only by raising qualitatively our technique, and by improving the organisation of industry and our administrative and cultural work. This is a new stage, which requires higher qualifications for everyone and in everything. This cannot be done except by combining personal concern and responsibility with the organisation of collective control.[24] The manufacture of good boots, ploughs and pencils – like the training of competent engineers, technicians, qualified workers, teachers, commanders and state officials – will be guaranteed only if it is done under the pressure of active collective control, strong demand and skilful selection. The struggle against red tape and bureaucratic falsehood must be internally integrated into relationships in society. Consumers, organised in cooperatives, must be able to exercise control over producers. Industry must be able to control the training of technicians in special departments. The peasants must be able to submit the agronomist trained at the Timiryazev Academy[25] to final and decisive examinations. Every branch of industry stands in relation to other branches as a consumer and a recipient of goods. Elements of mutual control must be elaborated within this chain of mutual interdependence and developed out of it. To organise this control, armed with the most effective methods; to replace hostile competition with competition leading to common improvement; to awake inventiveness, rewarding and stimulating it, whilst waging a pitiless war on the method of doing things secretly; to teach Socialist labour morality neither by unadulterated propaganda nor by administrative prescription, but by the thought-out combination of interests and, where necessary, their counterposition to each other in social and industrial relationships – these are the methods and ways forward we have in view. To work on behalf of the consumer – that is the key. The trade unions must become organisations, not only of producers, but of consumers. In its struggle for better conditions of life for the workers that it organises, the metalworkers' union must demand

24. The word control, here and subsequently, is used to render the Russian word 'kontrol'. It means inspection, checking, organising, managing, similar to the word 'control' in the phrase 'quality control', rather than 'control' in the sense of domination or rule.
25. One of Moscow's leading institutes of agricultural sciences.

cheaper clothing items, boots made of better leather, better schools and more competent medical aid staff. Only by the combination and counterposition of different organisations and social groupings can we achieve real, living, and not bureaucratic, control.

❖ ❖ ❖

Every person can do the same job better, or worse. This depends on all sorts of factors. One of them – and now the most important one – is personal concern. Another, of higher quality, is an inner spirit of responsibility. Of the latter, military regulations say: act behind your superior's back as you would before his eyes. Internal discipline does not fall from the sky; it is a crystal of social opinion in individual consciousness. A person works better when he knows that he is being asked to work better, and when he is disposed to ask the same of others. The heart of the matter is public opinion, the demands and criticisms it makes of all of us, its vigilant control, and its cultural activity.

A private businessman works with personal concern and 'the bosses' eye'. We need to develop and exercise personal concern far more effectively than the private businessman, for we have incomparably more grounds and more opportunities to do so – in the sense of getting from ourselves what is best, of the highest standard, most effectively and enthusiastically done. It is always harder to work with the so-called bosses' eye. That must be replaced by collective control. Our ability to make this control active, prompt and flexible will depend on the level of culture of those exercising the control and those subject to it.

But will it not take a number of generations to raise our level of culture? Of course Socialist culture is still very far in the future. We are still going through the preparatory, and therefore most difficult, stage of our education. We are still acquiring the most basic information, knowledge, methods and skills. When these have all become commonly accessible, the development towards Socialism will be on the right track. Just as in the economy, so in this respect the hardest period is *the period of primitive cultural accumulation*. But it should not be thought that we will have to wait decades for the fruits. Our efforts, and our successes too, will proceed in concentric circles: from thousands of people to millions; from millions to tens of millions.

In our view, the demand for *the best* will become sharper and more generalised as the possibilities of achieving it become more evident. We can count on that. Initiative and the example given by a vanguard minority can perform miracles, if the methods of that minority are in step with the experience of the masses. The struggle for culture implies a daily, stubborn, persistent, unyielding rejection of uncultured behaviour in all its forms: slovenliness, lack of expertise, carelessness, irresponsibility, and inattention to work or to other people. It is not a question of simply agitating for culture – pure agitation will get you nowhere – but in one's own economic activity and day-to-day cultural life taking up the struggle for 'quality'. Do not allow anything to slip past. Do not close your eyes, or turn a blind eye, to anything. Present yourself and others with the highest possible demands in every situation. Hold every chicken's egg up to the light for inspection; pull every weed out of the vegetable garden. The spirit of personal responsibility and professional honesty will grow in parallel with the formation of a Socialist public opinion – which is not a lifeless superstructure on top of the economic base, but the economy's most important piece of equipment.

We will need to a much greater extent even than we do now, the cultural and technical help of our European and American friends. Foreign delegations, coming here to see how we live and being able to compare the truth to the lies that are told back home, do an extremely important political job, strengthening both the international position of our [Soviet] Union and the position of the working class in their own country. But alongside these *political* delegations, we will need a growing number of 'delegations' concentrating on *technical* and *industrial* problems. Let highly-qualified workers, technicians and engineers, individually or in groups, come to visit us, to see how we work – and let them help us to work more effectively. This kind of foreign 'intervention' would be most welcome, and would add to the work done by our engineers, technicians and workers on study trips abroad. Both the stem and branches of our economy need to have grafts of advanced technology and productive culture; the stem is already quite strong enough to withstand the effect of such a grafting operation.

In all aspects of our work without exception, the years ahead must be ones of intensive improvement and demanding study. With justifiable anger we speak of the wastefulness of strip-farming in the peasant economy – but in the factories we are also suffering, essentially from the most awful types of industrial strip-farming left behind from the capitalist economy. We mercilessly censure the archaic three-field system, which impoverishes the soil and condemns the peasant population to poverty. But many branches of industry are dominated by methods which are flesh of the three-field system's flesh. Spare parts that do not fit and non-uniform materials are to be found in our industrial enterprises for the same reason that many school-leavers speak, read and write Russian very badly; for the same reason that our offices are sometimes nightmares of red tape; for the same reason that the stairways and corridor floors of our public buildings are often covered in cigarette ends and spit. All these are problems on different levels, but of the same kind: we have a low level of culture. We have yet to take the overwhelming majority of the population through the school of basic practical knowledge which has already become customary in the leading capitalist countries. Here, as in other questions, we do not need 'the least trace of false idealisation', to use Lenin's phrase. We need to rebuild our economy from the bottom to the top. We need to train, retrain and train once more. We need to equip ourselves better, to provide better leadership, and to carry out our tasks better. We need to learn from capitalist Europe and America. Let there be no trace of false idealisation! And not a trace of despondency either!

Our historical tasks are not measured by calendar years or anniversaries. The ninth year of Soviet power will continue the work of the eighth. But at the same time, there is a reason to state that the eighth anniversary of the revolution coincides with a clearly definable sea-change in all our economic and cultural work. For eight years we have worked hastily, putting up the rough scaffolds. Of course, this will not change overnight; in far too many areas of work we are still awaiting the first, even 'rough', blow of the shovel. But at the same time in the key branches of the economy and culture, it is now time to talk about putting up the finished structure.

All this cannot be achieved by enthusiasm alone. The enthusiasm of the masses is an invaluable force, which has showed its effectiveness in the past, and in the future will be in even greater demand. But what we need today, above all, is self-possession, systematic methods and consciously regulated persistence. These qualities do not negate enthusiasm – on the contrary, combined with it they promise historical results on an unprecedented scale.

In two years time, we will have completed the first decade of Soviet rule. They must be two years of steep ascent. Our enemies will increase the economic, if not military, pressure on us. The resistance to that pressure – alongside the growth of the revolutionary movement in the West – can only be an increase in the tempo of our economic and cultural advance. The issue of tempo is the issue of our defence, of our self-assuredness, and of our victory.

CENTRO STUDI PIETRO TRESSO

Archive of the Italian and International Trotskyist Movement

The Centro Studi Pietro Tresso was founded in October 1983 by militants and comrades of different political orientations, to collect and publicise material relevant to the Italian and international Trotskyist movement. The Centro Studi is not an intellectual debating club, but aims to investigate the past in order to help build a revolutionary movement in the present and future.

Write to: Centro Studi Pietro Tresso, c/o Paulo Casciola, Via Firenze, 18-06034 Foligno PG, Italy.

IV: Culture Under the Dictators

Since most of Trotsky's output on literature during the time of his last exile is well represented in the Pathfinder series of his writings, this section partakes more of the nature of a symposium. Ian Birchall translated from the French and annotated the first, fifth, sixth, seventh and eighth items, and we are grateful to Maurice Nadeau for his permission to publish our first short selection, along with his own contribution in our next section. Naville's death in 1993 produced many obituaries, including those by Rodolphe Prager, *Rouge*, 29 April; Malcolm Imrie, *Guardian*, 19 May; François Forgue, *Informations ouvrières*, 19-25 May; Jeremy Stubbs, *Independent*, 3 June; and Ian Birchall, *Socialist Review*, September, as well as a major appreciation by Nadeau, Rousset and Martinet, 'Hommage à Pierre Naville', *Critique Communiste*, no 132-134, Summer 1993, pp6-17. Trotsky's appreciation of French literature in general occupies an entire issue of the *Cahiers Léon Trotsky*, no 25, March 1986; and the essays by Claude Boyard, 'Trotsky, Céline, *Le Voyage au bout de la nuit*', pp47-64; and Hilaire Touvet, 'Trotsky, de Zola à Jules Romains', pp81-6, are particularly important.

We thank *Informations ouvrières* for the right to publish François de Massot's valuable interview with Jean Malaquais, which should be read along with Trotsky's two short letters to him (19 June and 9 August 1939, *Oeuvres*, first series, Volume 21, pp226 and 380), and the review he wrote of *Les Javanais*, 'A Masterly First Novel', 7 August 1939, *Leon Trotsky on Literature and Art*, pp225-34. Malaquais' *War Diary* was published in English during the war by Doubleday-Doran (cf the review by 'RF' in *New International*, Volume 8, no 8, August 1944, p272).

We are in no less of a debt to Esther Leslie, Fritz Keller and Richard Greeman, whose essays appear here in print for the first time. A preliminary article also touching upon Esther Leslie's theme was written by Enzo Traverso, 'Walter Benjamin et Léon Trotsky', *Quatrième Internationale*, no 37-38, August-October 1990, pp97-104, reprinted in the *Cahiers Léon Trotsky*, no 47, January 1992, pp55-63. Those who wish to explore Greeman's work further should refer to the brief introduction to his article 'The Victor Serge Affair and the French Revolutionary Left' published in *Revolutionary History*, Volume 5, no 3, Autumn 1994, pp142-74. Nor can David Cotterill's translation of *The Serge-Trotsky Papers* (London, 1994) be at all neglected.

And without the help of Alan Wald, we would not have been able to obtain a copy of James T Farrell's reminiscences, 'A Memoir of Trotsky', which originally appeared in *The University of Kansas City Review*, Volume 23, no 4, June 1957, and are reprinted here with the permission of *New Letters* (formerly the *UKC Review*) and the Curators of the University of Missouri-Kansas City. They should be read along with Wald's own articles 'Farrell and Trotskyism', *Twentieth Century Literature*, no 22, 1967, pp90-104; 'James T Farrell and *Studs Lonigan*', US *Militant, International Socialist Review* supplement; his re-edition of Farrell's *A Note on Literary Criticism* originally written in 1936 (Colombia University Press, 1992; reviewed by Paul Siegel, 'James T Farrell: "Literature is an Instrument of Social Influence"', in the US *Socialist Action*, February 1994; and his later full-length study, *James T Farrell: The Revolutionary Socialist Years* (New York, 1978). Wald's obituary of Farrell appears in 'James T Farrell: 1904-1979', US *Militant*, 14 September 1979; *InterContinental Press*, Volume 17, no 34, 24 September 1979, pp903-4. Another by Robert Houston, 'James T Farrell: The Last of America's Left Writers', *Socialist Challenge*, 14 February 1980, should also be noticed. More recent studies include Edgar M Branch's *Studs Lonigan's Neighbourhood and the Making of James T Farrell* (reviewed by Patrick M Quinn, 'Where Studs Lonigan Came From', *Against the Current*, March-April 1997).

Farrell remained loyal to the Trotskyist movement for some years after the other literary giants had departed. His account of Dewey's visit to Trotsky was published in Sidney Hook's edition of *John Dewey: Philosopher of Science and Freedom* (New York, 1950), and his 'Portrait of Leon Trotsky', which first appeared in *Partisan Review*, October 1940, can now be consulted in Alain Dugrand's *Trotsky in Mexico* (Manchester, 1992), pp57-61. But he was more or less driven out of the movement by the growing dogmatism of the SWP. When Albert Goldman and Felix Morrow criticised that party's postwar perspectives, Farrell came to their support using the pseudonym of O'Neal, only to earn a rebuke from Cannon for assuming that 'someone who has the virtue and merit of writing novels is entitled to give advice to our party on how to conduct its politics' (James P Cannon and Albert Goldman, 'The Party and the Intellectuals', *New International*, Volume 9, no 5, August 1945, pp144-8; James P Cannon, *Letters from Prison*, New York, 1973, pp141-3). The tone of Cannon's replies was so unpleasant that they were omitted from the first edition of the *Letters* (James P Cannon, *The Struggle for Socialism in the American Century*, New York, 1977, pp316, 450, n139). And whilst continuing to play an important part in the SWP prisoners' defence committee, Farrell was further repelled by the extravagant cult then being woven around Cannon by Joseph Hansen. So from then on his contributions to the Marxist appreciation of literature appeared in Max Shachtman's *New International*. They include 'Stalinist Literary Discussion' (Volume 12, no 4, April 1946, pp112-5), 'A Comment on Literature and Morality' (Volume 12, no 5,

May 1946, pp141-5), 'American Literature Marches On' (Volume 12, no 7, September 1946, pp218-23; no 8, October 1946, pp243-7), and 'The Literary Left in the Middle Thirties: From *Proletarian* to People's Front' (Volume 13, no 5, July 1947, pp150-5).

A full picture of the extent of Trotsky's literary influence at this time cannot, of course, be formed without studying the rest of Wald's contribution, and in particular his introduction to the special issue of the *Cahiers Léon Trotsky* entitled 'Trotsky and the Intellectuals of the United States' (no 19, September 1984, pp4-16), which also contains his appreciation of Herbert Solow (pp41-67), and should be consulted along with his later piece 'Trotskyism, Anti-Stalinism and the US Intellectuals in the 1930s – An Ambiguous Legacy', *International Marxist Review*, Volume 3, no 2, Autumn 1988. Earlier articles on kindred themes include 'Mike Gold and the Radical Literary Movement of the 1930s', *International Socialist Review*, Volume 34, no 3, March 1973, pp34-7, and 'The Responsibility of Intellectuals', *International Socialist Review*, Volume 35, no 2, February 1974, pp24-31, an extended review of David Caute's *The Fellow Travellers* (London, 1973). His full-length books include *The Revolutionary Imagination* (Chapel Hill, 1983), on John Wheelwright and Sherry Mangan, and his major work, *The New York Intellectuals* (Chapel Hill, 1987; cf the reviews by Tom Kemp, 'New Light on History of American Trotskyism', *Workers Press*, 31 October, 7 and 14 November 1987, and *Labour Briefing*, 8-21 February 1989). Additional information of some value is provided by Saul Bellow himself in 'Marx at my Table', *Guardian*, 10 April 1993, and by Andrew Hemmingway, 'Meyer Schapiro and Marxism in the 1930s', *The Oxford Art Journal*, Volume 17, no 1, 1994, pp13-29.

In a more general context, Gen Doy's *Materialising Art History* (London, 1998) refers to Trotsky in passing, as well as including quite a lot of material on the French photographer and surrealist Claude Cahun, and a few remarks about Ken McMullen's film about Trotsky's daughter Zina, made in 1985. The work of Claude Cahun is also discussed by Rose Jennings, 'Out of the Closet', *Independent*, 8 October 1994; and by Val Williams, 'Photographs from the Edge', *Guardian*, 13 October 1994.

The collapse of the Soviet Union has now revealed much more information about the Stalinist persecution of the writers, and Vitaly Shentalinsky's *The KGB's Literary Archive* contains the first crop of results. Important reviews of this book include those by Louis Coutourier, *Rouge*, 3 February 1994; Craig Raine, *Sunday Times*, 10 December 1995; Robert Winder, *Independent*, 16 December 1995; Sally Laird, *Observer*, 24 December 1995; André Novrozov, *The Times*, 28 December 1995; Rosa Mora, *Independent*, 8 January 1996; 'PHB', *Sunday Times*, 2 February 1996; and Vivian Yates, *Marxist Monthly*, October-November 1997, pp435-9. The wretchedness of the apologists for this terror among the French intelligentsia who were involved with the Popular Front is touched upon by Janine Robrieux, 'Gide, Trotsky et l'URSS', *Cahiers Léon Trotsky*, no 25, March 1986, pp93-104. Victor Serge's protests now available again in *16 Fusillés à Moscou* (Éditions Spartacus) have lost none of their value over the years. In 'The Writer's Conscience' (in David Craig (ed) *Marxists on Literature*), Serge gives a picture of the troubles suffered by writers under the Stalin regime. Craig's collection also presents, by way of a grim curio, Zhdanov's 1947 condemnation of the publishers of Akhmatova and Zoschenko.

The official culture of the Stalin period, on the other hand, is now largely discredited. Bukharin's report on poetry to the 1934 Congress of the Writers Union is discussed by 'Benjamin Biro' (Ken Tarbuck) in 'Bukharin and Socialist Realism', *Bulletin of Marxist Studies*, Volume 2, no 1, Winter 1969-70, pp26-30. More modern treatments by William Feaver, 'Life Washes Whiter on the Stalin Line', *Observer*, 26 January 1992; and Tom Lubbock, 'Always Look on the Right-Left-Side of Life', *Independent*, 26 January 1992, focus more narrowly on Socialist Realism itself, whilst Angela Tierney, 'Agitating for Happiness: Soviet Art in the Stalinist Era', *Marxist Monthly*, Volume 5, no 5, January-February 1994, pp234-7, provides a general survey. The tragedy of the Soviet theatre is discussed by Benedict Nightingale, 'The Voices Stalin Couldn't Gag', *The Times*, 1 January 1999.

Pierre Naville

Trotsky on Art and Literature

Pierre Naville (1904-1993), who had been a member of a surrealist group, spent some time with Trotsky in Prinkipo. In his book *Trotsky vivant* (Éditions d'Aujourd'hui, Plan de la Tour, 1975), he presented numerous recollections of Trotsky. The following extract deals with some of Trotsky's views on art and literature.

IN 1929, I had published in *la Vérité* an article on Panaït Istrati,[1] dealing with his book *Vers l'autre flamme*,[2] where he was one of the first to denounce Stalin's policy towards the Opposition. Trotsky sent me a rather ill-tempered letter: a whole page on Istrati, when there were so many burning questions! I explained to him that Istrati was a 'symptom'.

1. Panaït Istrati (1884-1935) was a Romanian writer who sympathised with the Left Opposition, but later went over to the extreme right.
2. In fact, of the three volumes of *Vers l'autre flamme*, one was by Victor Serge, and one by Boris Souvarine.

Later, at Prinkipo, he asked me: 'And Istrati? Could we win him over?' Unfortunately, Istrati had returned where he came from, a kind of mystical dreaming. A few years later, when Gide published his *Back From the USSR*,[3] I was surprised that Trotsky didn't respond to it.[4] The work justified it, and Gide's readership deserved it. But nothing came from Coyoacan. I think Gide himself was somewhat disappointed. He told me around this time – in his doubtful, tentative manner – about a plan he would perhaps put into practice: a journey to Mexico, which would have given him the opportunity of meeting Trotsky there... But the trip never happened. I had spoken to LD of the failure of this attempt, and (as usual) he very unfairly blamed me for it. To tell the truth, Trotsky did not like Gide: everything in him bristled up at the art and thought of the author of *Paludes*,[5] which led him to underestimate the author of *Back From the USSR*, seeing him as an aesthete...

Rosmer was one day talking to LD about Proust, without himself being sensitive to the art of this novelist, and even less to his intentions. The reaction came immediately: 'What are these people without will? These characters who let themselves drift? There may be art there. Doubtless, artistic gifts exist. But no will! That is extraordinary.' Clearly LD was an opponent of 'art for art's sake', as well as of the 'unmotivated action'.[6] Without admitting it, he adopted the point of view that Tolstoy set out so naively in *What is Art?* And he admired Tolstoy, as he admired Balzac, for having moulded life, that is, will. In Malraux, he regretted only that will was 'running in neutral'. It should be added that what concerned him was not a preoccupation with realism, but quite the opposite: will is what transcends current reality, which is oppressive, routinised and even spineless.

It was for the same reason that he disliked Dostoevsky, even though he praised his language. Rosmer recounts: 'I once said to him: "You must admit that Dostoevsky expresses something specifically Russian. After all, doesn't this taste for lying exist to some extent?" Trotsky got angry: "No, not any more than with other peoples. It's an error, a hypocrisy of European literatures. There are invertebrates everywhere."' LD had read a little Proust, a bit of Giraudoux. But he turned up his nose: all those people lacking will! They describe decadent milieux, it's no accident that they

3.   A Gide, *Retour de l'URSS*, Paris, 1936; English translation, *Back From the USSR*, London, 1937.
4.   Pierre Naville's brother, Claude Naville (1908-1935), also a Trotskyist, wrote a critical but not wholly negative study of Gide's politics, *André Gide et le communisme*, Paris, 1936.
5.   Gide's second novel, published in 1895; translated as *Marshlands* (London, 1953); a 'book about nothing' in the tradition of Flaubert – the main character is writing a book called *Paludes*.
6 .   '*L'acte gratuit*', a major theme in Gide's work.

achieve literary success. No will! In Malraux, it was the opposite that had attracted him: there were self-willed people, revolutionaries. Unfortunately, a number of them were also adventurers.

❖   ❖   ❖

I was not much inclined to investigate Trotsky's literary tastes. Sometimes, he referred to young writers, like Malraux, whose novels he later discussed,[7] or the author of Le Paysan de Paris,[8] from which he had got nothing, or Céline, whose Journey to the End of the Night[9] had gripped him and greatly intrigued him. But that gave the impression of a need for distraction. At first I thought that he was refusing to envisage literature – and above all poetry – outside of the revolutionary context which was the touchstone for him... I was quite willing to credit him with such a refusal. But as he didn't stint from praising Anatole France, and especially the Lys Rouge,[10] I couldn't confine myself to such a criterion. A certain kind of French trifling sometimes attracted him, as it still charms so many Russians who mistake verbal froth for emotional analysis.

But Stendhal or Proust, I established, mainly suggested dilettantism to him. The Romantics were not his line either. He kept symbolism at arm's length... Amongst the naturalists, he preferred Zola and Maupassant. As far as Zola was concerned, it goes without saying that the social spectrum analysed in his works, and the transfiguration of characters by style made an impression on him – even more so than in the case of Tolstoy. As far as the symbolists were concerned, many things escaped him in their use of language. But rather than dwell on the difficulty, he dwelt on the obscurity of intention, as it is attributed to Mallarmé, to Rimbaud and many others. As for surrealism... But it was precisely on this point that I in my turn became unable to enlighten him. For him, obviously, it was only in any case an oddity, a curiosity. From this point of view, he wanted to understand it, which led him simply to ask questions... which I had too many reasons for evading. The transition was a quite dangerous one, and it was enough for me to succeed in making it for myself...

One day, in some book or other, I came across an account of Blanqui: this irreproachable revolutionary had nothing but distaste for Romantic bric-à-brac; he admired the classics of the ages of Louis XIV and Voltaire –

7.   See 'The Strangled Revolution' in Leon Trotsky on Literature and Art, New York, 1970, pp179-90.
8.   A surrealist poetic narrative describing Paris, written in 1926 by Louis Aragon (1897-1982).
9.   Louis-Ferdinand Céline (1894-1961) was a French novelist; Voyage au bout de la nuit (1932) appeared in an English translation, Journey to the End of the Night (London, 1934); see 'Céline and Poincaré' in Leon Trotsky on Literature and Art, op cit, pp191-203.
10. Anatole France (1844-1924) was a novelist, and a sympathiser of the French Communist Party (PCF) in his last years. He was the author of Le Lys rouge (1894), translated as The Red Lily (London, 1908), a story of sexual jealousy in Florence.

as can easily be understood – but, surprisingly, he had a high view of the tragedies of Népomucène Lemercier.[11] This was a strange attraction when one thinks of the marvellously brisk writing and speech of the 'prisoner',[12] equal and perhaps superior to those of Diderot, Saint-Just and Rimbaud. I speculated about this futile, paradoxical taste of great revolutionaries for a literary art which has only a degraded appearance of nobility and order, where architectural affectation passes itself off as majesty. Is it the price that has to be paid for the discipline that is imposed and demanded by a life that is tense in the face of events, commanding, the study of the ebb and flow of society, the spectacle of failure and self-satisfaction. Perhaps it was also a sort of indulgence for a form of expression that may be perceived as secondary? I called that the *Blanqui paradox*. I thought I had discovered it in LD. I can't yet attempt to explain it fully. To tell the truth, I never managed to question him at all seriously about his taste for Anatole France, or his indifference towards Baudelaire...

❖   ❖   ❖

Really it's only a storm in a teacup. Breton relates that for our part, we did nothing to assist his visit to Trotsky; that I almost prevented him from speaking at the meeting held by *La Vérité* against the Moscow Trials, etc. All that is false. I heard in Paris that Breton was due to go to Mexico, but at that time I had not seen him for eight or nine years. I got a message from Coyoacan, asking me what attitude they should have to Breton, and whether he should be received. I can no longer remember exactly what I replied, except for this: that amongst writers of his sort, he had, on occasion, given proof of his courage. In any case, he was not in the remotest way infected with Stalinism. So why not see him, all the more so since LD had met so many others?

And if I still remember this detail, it's that Breton himself told me about it on his return (for then he met me). Trotsky said to him (it's Breton speaking): 'Yes, Naville has written to me about you.' – 'Oh, that won't be up to much...' – 'Oh yes, he writes that you are a courageous man.' Breton breathed a sigh of relief. And at once this good report, which on my part was wholly relative to Breton's intentions, immediately led him to regret some mean tricks in the past[13] which didn't worry me in the slightest. As for Breton's statement to the meeting referred to, it was in fact through my intervention that he was able to read it. He arrived at

11. Népomucène Lemercier (1771-1840) was an author of historical comedies and tragedies; his tragedy *Agamemnon* (1797) was highly regarded at the time.
12. Blanqui was known as 'l'enfermé' because of the many years he spent in jail.
13. Breton had written a sharp attack on Naville in the *Second Surrealist Manifesto* (1930), notably for using his 'very rich' father's money to finance revolutionary publications!

the beginning of the meeting, and asked me if I would object if he read a text which he had prepared. I simply replied that if the other comrades on the committee did not object, then neither did I. Nobody objected...

Later, when he came back from Mexico, it was at my invitation that he read his *Visit to Trotsky*[14] to our meeting for the anniversary of the October Revolution. As soon as he had finished reading it, I asked him for the text and permission to publish it, which was done. It seemed that Breton was upset at having too few people to hear and read his text – which was nothing to do with me.

❖   ❖   ❖

I have already said that Trotsky had a view of art which I was far from sharing. When he contributed to the manifesto prepared by Breton and Rivera, *Towards a Free Revolutionary Art*, on the eve of the Second World War, I don't think he had any intention other than to affirm the freedom of the creative artist, denied in the USSR as in many other places. It would be going too far to deduce from this that he had rallied to the spirit of surrealism, or for that matter to that of any other literary school. I cite in proof of this what he wrote to us at the time (letter to Gérard Rosenthal of 27 October 1938):

'A few words on Breton. I don't think we can, as a party, demand that he should make his literary review into a review of the bloc. He represents the surrealist school. We don't bear the slightest responsibility for him; in the sphere of art, which for him comes before everything else, he naturally has the absolute right to dispose of himself. It is not for us to mix together artistic tendencies, but to regroup them as they are for a common struggle against the totalitarian attacks on art. Any attempt on our part to subordinate artistic tendencies as such to a political interest could only compromise us in the eyes of true artists.'[15]

It couldn't be put better. *Complete freedom for art.* But art in its turn must not lend itself to the manoeuvres of politics, and must not claim to dictate to it, either in the name of poetry or of morals. And yet: *complete freedom*... even in opposition to any politics at all? It would be futile to conceal the incompatibilities which result from such an invitation, for which the boldest manifesto will still for a long time to come have to make allowances, at least until the time when the words *art* and *politics* are both merely relics of a past age.

14.   Breton's speech 'Visite à Léon Trotsky' was delivered to a meeting organised by the POI at the Mutualité in Paris on 11 November 1938. It appears in his book *La Clé des Champs* (Paris, 1953), pp42-54; English translation, *Free Rein* (Lincoln, Nebraska, 1995).

15.   A different translation of this extract from this letter appears in *Writings of Leon Trotsky 1938-39*, New York, 1974, p93.

❖   ❖   ❖

[Naville describes an afternoon fishing with Trotsky in the Sea of Marmara.] All at once LD asks me, quietly: 'You've seen those pictures in the surrealist review? What are they?' I remained silent. 'Explain them to me!' I didn't sense the slightest criticism in his voice, scarcely even curiosity. He had taken advantage of a moment when we were alone, and was trying to understand *me* better, that was all. I didn't know what to say. At that particular moment, I wouldn't have known what to say about surrealism, especially about what had been printed over there, long ago... I would have given all the pictures in the world for one moment of that *surreal* fishing trip. I managed a few rather evasive words: first of all, what is painting? I should have had to express ideas about art – and besides I thought the functions of art and struggle were always diametrically opposed... Trotsky didn't pursue the point, and left me where I was. I know he had been sent some old publications, in order to turn him against me, but he never spoke to me about it, for he had a low view of that kind of behaviour. And in his look, in his questions, I sensed something like: well then, can that also be defended? Is that also a form of enquiry? Something like that. But then I myself was too tense to be able to reply as simply as I should have done. I was not sufficiently at my ease.

Richard Greeman

Did Trotsky Read Serge?

Ignorait-il qu'il s'agissait d'un romancier?

THROUGHOUT the 1920s and 1930s, Victor Serge, the Belgo-Soviet writer and revolutionary, was popularly identified as the principle literary representative of Trotskyism in the French language. During the early period of the isolation of the Soviet Union, Serge was the first to popularise Trotsky's ideas through articles in magazines like *Clarté*, and Serge later translated many works of Trotsky including *Leur Morale et la Nôtre* and *La Révolution Trahie* into French.[16] Mainstream French critics and reviewers of Serge's novels were in the habit of situating Serge for their readers as Trotsky's 'friend' or Trotsky's 'disciple', and even as late as the 1970s, a hostile British reviewer dismissed my translation of Serge's novel, *S'il est minuit dans le siècle*, under the heading of 'Trotskyite Disdain'.

16. For some reason Serge's name as translator was omitted from the 1963, 1971 and 1973 Éditions de Minuit edition of *La Révolution trahie*.

Serge's personal relationship with Trotsky went back at least as far as 1925, when Victor left a safe Comintern assignment in Vienna to return to Russia and participate in the Left Opposition's struggles, and despite the political differences that developed between the two men after 1937 over the rôle of the POUM in the Spanish Republic and the significance of the Kronstadt affair of 1921, Serge remained passionately loyal to Trotsky. One recalls that one of Serge's last books was an uncritical biography, *Vie et Mort de Trotsky*, written in collaboration with Natalia Sedova.[17]

Yet although Trotsky was passionately interested in French literature and professed a special tolerance for works of the imagination, one looks in vain for any allusions to Serge's novels or other creative work in his voluminous writings. Indeed, one wonders if Trotsky ever read any of Serge's literary works.

Serge certainly devoured Trotsky's. In 1936, after re-reading Trotsky's *My Life*, Serge recounted the following moving anecdote to its author:

'I recall that by some miracle, soon after its publication, a dozen copies of *My Life* appeared in the International Bookshop in Moscow!!! No doubt somebody got deported very far off for that mistake. A copy of it was then passed from hand to hand, completely dismantled so that each page could be read and hidden separately. But *all* the pages, creased and soiled, were there! Someone lent me that copy *for one night*. Later on it must have landed up with the GPU.'[18]

Later, Serge developed this incident into an extremely moving scene in his novel about the resistance of the Left Oppositionist in exile, *S'il est minuit dans le siècle*. The heroes, Elkin and Ryzhik, become intoxicated reading aloud from a book of Trotsky's found by chance on an illiterate woman's market-stall. The men become exalted by their vision of Trotsky's heroic intellectual figure: 'Nothing is lost if one man remains erect. Everything is saved if he is the greatest.' The scene climaxes when Elkin gently pushes Galia, his beautiful peasant lover, back out onto the night steppe to make room for other 'visitors'. 'Nothing to fear', he explains, 'They are ideas...'[19] Alas, when this exalting literary tribute to Trotsky's

17. V Serge and N Sedova, *Vie et Mort de Trotsky*, Amiot-Dumont, 1951; Maspero, 1973; English edition, *The Life and Death of Leon Trotsky*, London, 1975. Again, for reasons unknown, this pioneering work of collaboration, rich in original material, is barely mentioned by Trotsky's standard biographers, Pierre Broué and Isaac Deutscher, who must have relied on it to some extent. Deutscher, in fact, refers to Serge misleadingly as 'a French ex-Communist writer', although his nationality was Russian, and he was an outstanding Left Oppositionist.
18. Letter from Serge to Trotsky, 16 June 1936, in D Cotterill (ed), *The Serge-Trotsky Papers*, London, 1994, p73.
19. V Serge, *Les Révolutionnaires: cinq romans*, Seiul, 1967, pp543-4.

character and stature appeared in 1939, Trotsky was busy fustigating Serge as a renegade; moreover, although Serge's novel was widely reviewed and even mentioned for the Goncourt Prize, there is no evidence that the Old Man ever read it.

Indeed, there is no evidence that Trotsky ever read any of Serge's literary works. The closest we get is a pathetic incident in 1936, just after Serge's liberation from the Gulag. The two exiled Oppositionist were at the height of their politico-literary collaboration and warm personal relations, exchanging letters almost daily between Belgium and Norway, and Serge sent Trotsky a copy of his magnificent short story, *Mer blanche*, which had just been published in Paris. Natalia Sedova apparently appreciated the story, but Trotsky himself seems not to have read it. He gives the excuse of 'eye strain' in one letter, and there the matter drops.[20]

Nonetheless, it is impossible to imagine that Trotsky was not aware of Serge's literary merits and reputation as a 'Trotskyist novelist' much earlier. To begin with, we recall that Serge's first three novels were published between 1929 and 1932 by Reider, who also published Trotsky's *My Life* in 1930. Serge's brilliant Civil War novel, *Ville conquise*, was serialised in the French review, *Europe*, to which Trotsky also contributed, and was then published by Reider in 1932, when Trotsky was in Constantinople. A veritable paean to the founder of the Red Army, it features a wonderful portrait of Trotsky in intimate dialogue with Lenin (their names discreetly omitted to pass the censorship), and climaxes in the heroic defence of Petrograd, Trotsky's most famous victory.

Earlier still, Serge had dedicated his *L'An I de la Révolution russe* to a murdered Oppositionist comrade, Chadaev, and to '*a great living man*' ('*un grand vivant*') – obviously the unmentionable exile, Trotsky. Written in the Soviet Union based on original documents and interviews, Serge's *Les Débuts de la dictature du prolétariat* represented the first book-length documented history of the Russian Revolution. It was published by the Librairie du Travail in Paris in 1930, just when Trotsky was preparing his own *History*, and could not have failed to provoke his interest.

Moreover, Trotsky was living in France during 1933-35 when the Victor Serge affair created a major scandal for the Communists, and mobilised literary stars like Romain Rolland, André Gide and André Malraux over the imprisonment of this Oppositionist writer. Nor was Trotsky too busy to pay attention to French literature at this time. His celebrated essays on Malraux and Céline attest to that. On the contrary, during part of this French period, he was straining under house arrest with little to do but read for distraction. Moreover, Trotsky had followed French fiction closely from his days in Tsarist prisons and, even during the Civil War, he read the latest French novels on his famous armoured train. In

20. See Trotsky's letter to Serge, 24 June 1936, in Cotterill, op cit, p76.

his Turkish exile, he accumulated 'a whole little library of contemporary French works'.[21]

Moreover, both in Constantinople and during his semi-legal years in France, Trotsky's main contacts with the outside world were his close supporters, Pierre Naville and Gérard Rosenthal, two Frenchmen with strong literary backgrounds who had been introduced to Trotsky by none other than Serge. Indeed, it was Serge, through his voluminous correspondence with the *Clarté* group in Paris, who first weaned these French surrealists away from Stalinist orthodoxy, organised their trip to the Soviet Union in 1927, and introduced them to Oppositionist circles in Moscow and Leningrad. They were later involved in every aspect of Trotsky's literary work in exile, and supplied his constant hunger for books and reviews.[22] It is hard to imagine them not discussing Serge's writings.

Trotsky thus had every inducement and opportunity to read Serge's fiction prior to 1936, but did he? When their correspondence resumes after Serge's liberation in the spring of 1936, Trotsky courteously pays homage to Serge's 'literary talent' and reputation as a writer, but never once does he refer to a specific title. Nor does he acknowledge Serge's dedication of *L'An I* to him or Serge's literary recreation of his legend in *Ville conquise*. Trotsky's letters show him altogether eager, however, to advance Serge's literary and financial prospects; for example, he proposes to promote Serge's forthcoming book in the USA by quoting it in articles in mass media. Yet it never seems to have occurred to him promote Serge's published novels with a critical article about, say, *Ville conquise* and much less his 1939 Trotskyist epic, *S'il est minuit dans le siècle*, as he did for Malraux's *Les Conquérants* and works by Marcel Martinet, Jean Malaquais and Ignazio Silone. Nor did he recognise Serge's literary works in any other way. As Régis Debray so wryly said of Serge: 'This potential Malraux did not find his de Gaulle. Trotsky didn't play the game.'[23]

The only plausible explanation for this paradox is the bizarre hypothesis that Trotsky simply never bothered to read Serge's stories and

21. Pierre Broué, *Trotsky*, Fayard, 1988, p897.
22. Interviews with Gérard Rosenthal, August 1969, and Pierre Naville, March 1991. Naville could not specifically recall bringing any books by Serge to Trotsky, but he gave me the impression that as early as 1927 Trotsky was uncomfortable with Serge as a man who was difficult to define politically — a freelance, a writer. The word 'flou' — vague — came up several times in our conversation with reference to Serge, although nothing specific was alleged against him. One wonders if Naville, Rosenthal and the other young French disciples in awe of the Man of October did not unconsciously distance themselves from the independent Serge on the basis of their impression that Trotsky was distrustful of him. How else to explain their inactivity during the 'Free Victor Serge' campaign in Paris, which provided a ready-made opportunity for French Trotskyists to rally public opinion in defence of an imprisoned Oppositionist who had done so much for them?
23. Régis Debray, 'Preface' to Victor Serge, *Carnets*, Actes Sud, 1985, p11.

books. If he had, he would certainly have proclaimed in them precisely those Marxist values he found missing in the novels of Malraux, and celebrated in him the bard of the revolution. Trotsky was certainly never less than generous in recognising new literary talent. For example, in 1939 he hailed Jean Malaquais as 'a new great writer' on the occasion of the publication of his first novel, *Les Javanais*.[24] He also wasted precious hours flirting with André Breton, whose books he sent for, but probably never read.

Even granting the unlikely hypothesis that Trotsky found Serge wanting as a novelist, he could easily have penned an article contrasting Serge's truthfulness and sincerity with the 'written-to-order' productions of Socialist Realism without actually praising his style. In any case, the utter frankness of their private correspondence left ample room for critical comments if Trotsky had read anything that displeased him. But there is no evidence that he read anything by Serge, and the sad irony is that when Trotsky finally decided to break with Serge, it was on the basis of a text by Serge, 'Marxism in Our Time' ('Puissance et limites du marxisme'), which, according to Serge's protests and internal evidence, Trotsky had never actually read!

This bizarre paradox leads us to another puzzling aspect of the Serge-Trotsky relationship. For if we set aside the bitter final quarrel, which was 'final' only because an assassin's axe precluded any reconciliation (much as if Trotsky had disappeared in the midst of his violent altercation with Lenin), we discover an extraordinary concordance of commitments and views between the two men. Indeed, there are so many remarkable coincidences in the timing and subjects of the books they published that concepts like 'affinity of ideas', 'spirit of the times', and 'emulation' are barely sufficient to account for the following concurrences:

★ Trotsky: *Lenin* (1924)
★ Serge: *Lenin 1917* (1925)

★ Serge: *Soviets 1929* (published under the name of Panaït Istrati), 1929
★ Trotsky: *La Révolution défigurée* (1929)

★ Trotsky: *Literature and Revolution* (1923)
★ Serge: *Literature and Revolution* (1932)

★ Serge: *Year One of the Russian Revolution* (1930)
★ Trotsky: *History of the Russian Revolution* (1932-33)

★ Serge: *From Lenin to Stalin* (1936) and *Destiny of a Revolution: USSR 1917-1937* (US title *Russia Twenty Years After*) (1937)
★ Trotsky: *The Revolution Betrayed* (1937, French translation by Serge)

24. LD Trotsky, 'A Masterly First Novel: Jean Malaquais', *Leon Trotsky on Literature and Art*, New York, 1977, pp225-34.

★ Serge; *Portrait de Staline* (1940)
★ Trotsky: *Stalin* (1941, Serge partially completed a translation of this work)

★ Trotsky: *My Life* (1930); *Diary in Exile* (1935)
★ Serge: *Life and Death of Leon Trotsky* (in collaboration with Trotsky's widow, Natalia Sedova; completed 1947, published 1951)

The concordance of subjects and dates becomes even more striking when one includes not just books but journalism and the important series of essays (later collected as books or pamphlets) by both authors, for example on the German crisis of 1923 and the Chinese Revolution of 1927-28. Moreover, the harmony of ideas amongst these works is striking, notwithstanding inevitable differences of emphasis, style, and appreciation of detail. This is not really surprising, given two authors representing a well-defined current of ideas more or less simultaneously elaborating their responses to continuing events. Sometimes it is Trotsky who treats a subject first, sometimes Serge. Typically, they are elaborating a subject more or less at the same time, as during 1936-37, when Serge is simultaneously writing his own analyses of Stalin's betrayal of the Russian Revolution whilst translating Trotsky's *The Revolution Betrayed*. Indeed, to some extent, Serge can be seen from the outset as amplifying his rôle as Trotsky's French 'translator', beginning in 1921, into that of unofficial spokesman for Trotsky's ideas to the French-speaking public.

It is thus all the more remarkable to note that whilst all of Serge's writings pay homage to Trotsky, quote him and acknowledge his ideas, I have not been able to locate a single acknowledgement of Serge's work in any of Trotsky's writings — excluding their final public debate where Trotsky refers to Serge's 'history' of the revolution (not by title) in a sarcastic jibe, and alludes to his 'poems' about the revolution only in order to portray him as a dilettante.

One is tempted to speculate that if only Trotsky had read Serge's writings, especially the novels, he might have respected his independence and exploited his talents as a fellow-travelling ally. Would Trotsky have treated Serge any differently had he appreciated him as an artist? If Trotsky's behaviour toward the great Mexican painter, Diego Rivera, is any indication, the answer is probably not. Trotsky certainly appreciated Rivera, who was his host and protector in Mexico and the principle financial supporter of the Mexican Trotskyist movement — divided, naturally, into two rival factions — of which he had long been an active and influential member. Rivera admired and respected Trotsky, and there were no serious political differences between them. Yet according to Broué's description, Trotsky could not refrain from interfering in the internal affairs of the Mexican section, and succeeded in totally alienating Rivera through a bureaucratic manoeuvre designed to undermine his influence. Trotsky thus lost the friendship and support of Mexico's greatest artist (not to mention the home and protection Rivera provided him) over a trivial local organisational matter in which the only issue involved was control.[25] Rivera eventually returned to the Stalinist fold. Serge, on the other hand, continued to defend Trotsky and his ideas, albeit from a heterodox viewpoint, long after their break.

An interesting light is thrown on this curious relationship when one recalls that both men, the President of the 1905 Petrograd Soviet and the Anarchist turned Civil War Communist, considered themselves revolutionaries, men of action, as well as writers. Writers for whom in any case the pen — Trotsky's youthful *nom de guerre* — was an instrument for the preparation or amplification of political action. Both were cosmopolitans, and had agitated in many countries. Trotsky was older by a decade, a full 'revolutionary generation', a brilliant orator, agitator, administrator and military genius. Serge's pretensions and accomplishments were more modest: to be a rank-and-file militant, and to bear witness to the truth through his writings.

After Lenin's death, and especially in exile, Trotsky towered over his associates like a colossus. Yet Serge, representing the younger generation, was also an experienced agitator, had experienced his share of revolutions, prisons, exiles, polemics and organisational battles, and had a following as a writer in France and Spain.

By the time Serge was expelled from Russia in 1936, he had lived nearly 18 years in the Soviet Union to Trotsky's 12, including the critical years of clandestine opposition, famine, industrialisation and full-blown Stalinist repression. To be sure, Serge had consciously eschewed positions of power in Russia, and had no pretensions to Trotsky's superior brilliance and leadership experience. Yet after 1936, with the entire Bolshevik leadership effectively crushed under Stalin, Serge was the closest thing to a peer — or rival perhaps? — to Trotsky left at large, indeed the only member of the original Left Opposition in a position to unite with him. Trotsky's reaction to the report on the condition of the deported and imprisoned Russian Opposition which Serge prepared for him in May 1936 shows the degree to which Trotsky, after years in exile, was cut off from the Russian Opposition of which he was the titular leader.

Serge's untiring devotion to the cause is unquestionable, as his correspondence with Trotsky's son, Leon Sedov, who himself sacrificed his every hour, and indeed his health itself, to carrying out his father's tasks, amply illustrates. What then prevented the Trotskyist movement from making better use of Serge's undeniable talents and moral stature, much less recognising his stature as a creative writer? Could uncon-

25. See Broué, op cit, pp903-5.

scious rivalry or jealousy, if not on Trotsky's part, then amongst his European followers, themselves divided by bitter sectarian rivalries, have been the cause?

As Serge's biographer, I would like to leave these questions open, and appeal to the readers of *Revolutionary History* to help me clarify them by communicating to me any documents, memories or opinions that might shed light on them. On the other hand, since we are on the subject of whether or not Trotsky actually read Serge, I would like to take this opportunity to clarify two incidents that in my opinion have muddied the waters for over half a century, and perhaps prevented the Trotskyist movement from properly appreciating Serge as its foremost literary representative, for the continuing prejudice against Serge in this milieu is based on Trotsky's attack on two 'Sergean' texts: one which Trotsky didn't read, and the other which Serge didn't write.

In the summer of 1938, Serge published an essay in New York in the *Partisan Review* entitled 'Marxism in Our Time'.[26] He might well have called it 'In Defence of Marxism', for it is one of the best argued and succinct answers to Marxism's critics ever penned. After outlining the powerful achievements of Marxist thought, crowned by the 'prodigious success of the Bolshevik party in 1917 (Lenin-Trotsky)', Serge points out that even in defeat Marxism alone finds nourishment and provides explanations:

'Marxism showed itself impotent in Germany before the Nazi counter-revolution; but it is the only theory that explains the victory of a party of the déclassé, paid for and supported during an insoluble economic crisis by the chiefs of the big bourgeoisie... It is the same with the terrible degeneration of the dictatorship of the proletariat in Russia. There, too, the punishment of the Old Bolsheviks, exterminated by the regime which they have created, is no more than a phenomenon of the class struggle. The proletariat, deposed from power by a caste of parvenus entrenched in the new state, can take an accounting of the basic reasons for its defeat and can prepare itself for the struggles of tomorrow only by means of the Marxist analysis.'

So far, Serge stood on common ground with Trotsky. Where he differed was in fixing the date when the degeneration of the revolution was first a visible threat. Citing Rosa Luxemburg's early critique of Bolshevik authoritarianism, Serge showed how, after a brief libertarian period, the Bolsheviks systematically built up a strong state machine beginning in 1918. This policy might have been justified by the mortal dangers of the Civil War, but it later led to the defeat of the workers at the hands of the bureaucracy.

26. *Partisan Review*, Volume 5, no 3, August-September 1938, pp26-32.

After victory had been won in the Civil War, the Socialist solution of the problems of the new society should have been sought in workers' democracy, the stimulation of initiative, freedom of thought, freedom for working-class groups – and not, as it was, in centralisation of power, repression of heresies, the monolithic single-party system, the narrow orthodoxy of an official school of thought... By the time Lenin and Trotsky realised the danger and wished to retrace their steps – timidly enough, at first; the greatest reach of boldness of the Left Opposition in the Bolshevik party was to demand the restoration of inner-party democracy, and it never dared dispute the theory of a single-party government – by this time, it was too late.

For Serge, the decline in the prestige of Marxist thought was a direct result of its degeneration in Russia. Naturally, the 'confused and bloody Marxism of the gunmen of Moscow is not Marxism', but Stalin had succeeded in usurping its banner, and it would be some time before the workers would be able to recover a genuine Marxist consciousness (as became all too clear after the opening of glasnost). The lesson in all of this was that Socialism is essentially democratic. For Marxism to regain its prestige and revitalise itself, it must return to the spirit of liberty, 'as necessary to Marxism as oxygen to living beings'. After completing his panoramic view of nearly 100 years of Marxism's political and intellectual fortunes, Serge concluded by affirming:

'Scientific thought cannot regress below the Marxist level, nor can the working class do without this intellectual weapon... Marxism will go through many vicissitudes of fortune, perhaps even eclipses. Its power, conditioned by the course of history, nonetheless appears to be inexhaustible. For its base is knowledge integrated with the necessity for revolution.'

Serge's essay was a classic reformulation of the essential Marxist perspective aimed at reaffirming its intellectual power in the face of defeat, deformation, doubt and declining prestige. We can only imagine its author's shock and surprise when, a few months after its publication, Trotsky singled him out for vituperation in a blast entitled 'Ex-Revolutionary Intellectuals and World Reaction', with the subtitle 'The Crisis of Bolshevism's Disappointed Fellow-Travellers is not the Crisis of Marxism'.[27] In it, Trotsky asserted that Serge was proclaiming 'the crisis of Marxism' and had joined the ranks of the disenchanted who, in aban-

27. Trotsky's text, dated 7 February 1939, appeared in the Belgian Trotskyist Review *La Lutte ouvrière*, 11 March 1939, in *Biulleten Oppozitsii*, no 74, and in *Quatrième Internationale*, no 16, April 1939. It appeared in the USA under the title of 'Intellectual Ex-Radicals and World Reaction', *Socialist Appeal*, 17 February 1939. See *Writings of Leon Trotsky 1938-39*, New York, 1974, pp194-6.

doning Stalinism, were also abandoning a Marxism which they had 'never known'. He explained: 'A gunner may miss his target; this does not invalidate ballistics, that is the science of artillery. If the army of the proletariat suffers a defeat, this does not invalidate Marxism, which is the science of revolution.' This, minus the obtrusive military metaphors, was exactly Serge's point! But Trotsky's next sentence added: 'That Victor Serge himself is going through a "a crisis", that his ideas are desperately confused is clear. But the crisis of Victor Serge is not the crisis of Marxism.'

Serge immediately penned a reply to the Belgian Trotskyist review which had printed Trotsky's attack, but the editors did not publish his letter. Meanwhile, other Trotskyist publications took up the charges. In his response, [28] Serge pointed out that Trotsky had evidently not bothered to read his *Partisan Review* essay before attacking it:

'This is deplorable. As it was so often done to Trotsky in Russia in the days when I was defending him to my utmost, he imputes to me ideas which I have not expressed and don't hold, whilst at the same time ignoring those I do express. This is a senseless method of discussion which belongs to the Bolshevism of decadence and to all sectarianisms...'

Comparing passages of Trotsky's text to his own, Serge showed that they were in complete agreement – indeed almost identical in their formulations – on the question of Marxism. Where they differed, Serge noted, was on the historical problem of when and how Bolshevism had begun to degenerate – the problem of freedom in the revolution. He repeated his earlier argument on the error of instituting the Cheka, which Trotsky had failed to answer, and added:

'I want to underscore only one point: that is that a large number of the last fighters of the Left Opposition of the Communist Party of the USSR (later known as Trotskyists) – if they still survive in Stalin's jails – agree with me on these essential questions; and that from this I have the inner certainty of remaining in complete unity of ideas with them, faithful to the liberating goals of the 1923 Opposition which certainly was not fighting to replace the stranglehold of the bureaucracy with a stifling sectarianism.' [29]

28. 'Lettre de Victor Serge à *Masses*', published in *Juin '36*, organ of the Parti socialiste ouvrier et paysan, on 21 April 1939. Reprinted in Michel Dreyfus, *La Lutte contre le Stalinisme*, Maspero, 1977, p230.
29. Note that here, as elsewhere in his quarrels with Trotsky, Serge's orientation flows from his identification with currents in the Russian Left Opposition. Dreyfus (op cit, pp 42-5) tries to explain their differences by alluding to Serge's 'isolation' from the Left Opposition during his years of deportation in Central Asia. Dreyfus apparently

Despite Trotsky's attack, Serge retained his deep respect for the man, and tried to avoid a rift. A few days after he penned his reply to Trotsky's blast, Serge wrote a warm personal letter to his old comrade in an attempt to clarify their political relations. He began 'Dear and Most Esteemed Lev Davidovich', and closed: 'I send you and Natalia Ivanova my most cordial greetings, and beg you to remember that I will always be — despite our arguments — happy to be useful to you.' In the letter, Serge explained that he had refrained from replying to the offensive note on him that had appeared in the *Bulletin of the Opposition*, and that he had no desire to engage in polemics with him: 'Your activity is much too precious to me, despite these divergences.' Far from 'intriguing against the Fourth International', Serge explained that he had done his best to patch over the many splits and quarrels that divided the movement.

During this same period, Serge had translated Trotsky's *Leur Morale et la nôtre*, the controversial pamphlet in which the leader of the October Revolution defended the historical principles of revolutionary action against those who would condemn them in the name of a timeless abstract morality. In it, Trotsky defended the idea that the end justifies the means, but maintained that certain means were incompatible with the Socialist goal of human liberation. Serge's translation was published in Paris in March 1939 by Les Editions du Sagittaire and accompanied by a 'Prière d'insérrer', a 'blurb' or press release, which Trotsky found extremely offensive.[30] This blurb was a vulgar sensationalistic resumé of Trotsky's subtle and complex argument, and contained such gems as the following: 'Shooting hostages takes on different meanings depending on whether the order is given by Stalin or by Trotsky or by the bourgeoisie.'

Without bothering to check with the publisher, Trotsky jumped to the conclusion that the blurb had been written by Serge, or under his inspiration, and assumed that Serge was out to sabotage his book.[31]

confuses the inner squabbles of the various European sects formed by Trotsky in the 1930s with the historical Left Opposition, which was Russian. In fact, it was Trotsky who, through no fault of his own, was 'isolated' from the latter. Dreyfus also attempts to assimilate Serge's outlook to the various European left-wing currents known, somewhat derisively, as the Two-and-a-Half International. This again is inaccurate. Serge was always hostile to this tendency (see his letter to Angelica Balabanova dated 23 October 1941, in Cotterill, op cit, pp187-9), although he collaborated with some of its representatives during the Spanish Civil War. The divergences between Serge and Trotsky are far better understood as an expression of antagonistic tendencies *within* the Russian Left Opposition than by reference to currents in the European left.

30. The text is available in English as 'Appendix C' in Trotsky, *Their Morals and Ours* (Merit Publishers, 1969), and in French in Dreyfus, op cit, pp240-1.

31. He later noted that 'the supposition that the prospectus was written by Victor Serge occurred to various comrades, independently of one another'. We can only wonder if Étienne, the agent provocateur, was behind these 'suppositions'. See Trotsky, 'An-

Summoning up all his trenchant wit and vituperative verve as a polemicist, Trotsky penned a furious protest under the title *Moralists and Sycophants Against Marxism*, and subtitled *Peddlers of Indulgences and their Socialist Allies, or the Cuckoo is in a Strange Nest*.[32] Resorting once again to the technique of amalgamation, Trotsky lumped Serge with the hypocritical Philistines (including Catholic apologists for Franco) who had attacked his book in the press.

He then advanced the supposition that Serge, his 'severest critic', had assumed the deceitful guise of a 'friend of the author' and smuggled his attack into the book's prospectus, like a cuckoo who deposits her eggs in other birds' nests. This, he claimed, was because Serge had 'no considered point of view', and was incapable of arguing openly. Ignoring Serge's three decades of revolutionary activity and the scores of books and articles in which Serge had defended Lenin, Trotsky and the Bolsheviks, Trotsky caricatured Serge as 'a disillusioned petit-bourgeois intellectual', a dilettante who 'plays with the concept of revolution, writes poems about it, but is incapable of understanding it as it is'. He went on to create a straw man out of what he supposed were Serge's 'moralistic' opinions, and then proceeded to flail this dummy in a half-dozen pages of bitter polemic.

It is the nature of insult and false argumentation to sully the best-earned reputations, as Trotsky knew from bitter personal experience. Serge wrote out an indignant refutation, and then, not wishing to engage in further mud-slinging with a man he still deeply respected, decided to refrain from public protest.[33] He did, however, write privately to Trotsky on 9 August 1939 denying any connection with the offensive blurb, and protesting against Trotsky's slanderous and unjust imputations. Trotsky's only reaction was to publish a short note to the effect that he had voiced only the 'supposition' not the 'assertion' that Serge was responsible for

other Refutation by Victor Serge', *Biulleten Oppozitsii*, no 79-80, reprinted as 'Appendix B' in the Merit edition of Trotsky's *Their Morals and Ours*, but omitted by Dreyfus in his defective edition of the Serge-Trotsky correspondence.

32. Included in the Merit edition of *Their Morals and Ours* and in Dreyfus.

33. Serge's self-censored refutation was discovered by Peter Sedgwick amongst Serge's posthumous papers, and published, in Sedgwick's English translation, under the title 'Secrecy and Revolution – A Reply to Trotsky', in *Peace News*, 27 December 1966. The text exists in the form of corrected galley-proofs whose format is identical to the typography of *La Révolution prolétarienne*. Serge explained in a letter to Balabanova dated 23 October 1941: 'But, in all this painful argument with the Old Man, I kept such esteem and affection for him that, even though he wrote a long polemical attack accusing me of writing an article which was never mine and of advocating ideas which were never mine, I first sent a powerful rebuttal to the printers of *La Révolution prolétarienne* (Paris) and then took it back from them, preferring to suffer this unjust attack in silence. And I still think I was quite right: truth can work its way out in different ways than by offensive polemics.' (Cotterill, op cit, p189) It has taken 50 years...

the 'cuckoo's egg'.[34] He 'willingly' accepted Serge's declaration of innocence, but in the same breath he dismissed Serge's protest that 'all the "arguments" which you ascribe to me are at great variance with everything which I have written on the Civil War and Socialist ethics in my books and articles'.[35]

Trotsky's acknowledgement has not prevented a whole generation of commentators from attributing to Serge both the authorship of the prospectus and the ideas Trotsky had put in his mouth during the polemic.[36] This method of analysis is rather like reconstructing the views of the Epicureans on the basis of the denunciations of the Church Fathers. It creates a totally false impression – an impression all the more unjust considering Serge's gallant decision to suppress his own refutation out of respect for his adversary. Nonetheless, Serge's reputation, particularly in circles influenced by Trotskyism, never quite recovered.

Let us end this unpleasant excursion on a positive note. The unfortunate quarrel between Serge and Trotsky took place during history's darkest hour – the triumph of Stalinism and Nazi Fascism – when both men were tracked by assassins and surrounded by agents provocateurs, and when even first-rate Marxists were facing an uncertain future without a compass, as it were. Today, with the centenary anniversary of Serge's birth only just behind us, we can see that both men, whatever their divergences, were deeply devoted to the same cause and have left us an incomparable heritage – Trotsky in politics and Serge in literature. Whether or not Trotsky read or appreciated Serge's novels, they remain as a monument to the victories and defeats of an outstanding generation of militants. If our goal is to help create a new generation capable of continuing

34. Trotsky, 'Another Refutation...', op cit.
35. Serge to Trotsky, 9 August 1939, in Cotterill, op cit, p111.
36. Thus Deutscher (*The Prophet Outcast*, Oxford, 1979, p437) substitutes Trotsky's straw man for the real Serge, depicts Serge 'blaming' Trotsky for the shooting of hostages by the Bolsheviks during the Civil War, and wonders why Serge did not 'see the moral and political difference between Trotsky's use of violence in the Civil War and Stalin's present terror' [sic!]. The French Trotskyist, Pierre Frank, in his 'Introduction' to the second French edition of *Leur Morale et la Nôtre* in 1966, asserts that the prospectus was 'probably drawn up by Victor Serge', whom he accused of 'making Siamese twins of Stalin and Trotsky at a time when Stalin was hunting Trotsky down' [sic!]. To their credit, the US Trotskyists did append a fragment of Serge's 'Denial and Protest' to the 1969 Merit edition of *Their Morals and Ours*. Finally, Dreyfus, in his collection of exchanges between Serge and Trotsky, lists Serge as the author of the prospectus in his table of contents and as its 'probable author' in a footnote. He makes no reference either to Serge's refutation or to Trotsky's acknowledgement. This collection, replete with 46 pages of scholarly introduction and endless footnotes, appears to be 'scientific' and exhaustive, yet it leaves the reader with a totally erroneous impression at the end. Dreyfus' errors and omissions are all the more blameworthy in that he rebuffed the offers of the French representative of the Serge estate, Jean Ribre, to check his edition and to supply additional texts where necessary.

the struggle, what better way of touching the souls of young people than to encourage them to read Serge's books?

Esther Leslie
Elective Affinities
The Hunched Man, the Old Man and BB[37]

Meshwork

THE relationship between Benjamin and Brecht has often been assessed, including, most notoriously, the charge from both Adorno and Scholem that Brecht's 'exotic' influence was 'disastrous' or 'catastrophic' for Benjamin's theorising.[38] Trotsky and Benjamin have been brought together somewhat more rarely. Victor Serge, in his *Memoirs of a Revolutionary*, written in Mexico in 1942-43, connects the two names, suggesting the connection between Trotsky and Benjamin to be something more than coincidence, and rather more epochal:

'... the poets Walter Hasenclever and Walter Benjamin commit suicide. Rudolf Hilferding and Breitscheid are carried off out of our midst and handed to the Nazis... In the newspapers: suicide or murder of Krivitsky in Washington. Trotsky murdered in Mexico. Yes this is just the moment for the Old Man to die, the blackest hour for the working classes: just as their keenest hour saw his highest ascendancy.'[39]

In a modern context, Terry Eagleton's *Walter Benjamin or Towards a Revolutionary Criticism* draws some analogies between the two men's theoretical, literary and historiographical method.[40] Similarly, Cliff Slaughter contends that of all the major writers on literature and art who have adhered to Marxism, only Walter Benjamin and Leon Trotsky have remained true to the fundamental legacy of Marx.[41] Over the last decade,

---

37. A version of this paper was delivered in November 1992 to the London Socialist Forum discussion group at Conway Hall in London.
38. See, for example, Adorno's letter to Benjamin, dated 18 March 1936, translated in F Jameson (ed), *Aesthetics and Politics*, London, 1977, and G Scholem, *Walter Benjamin und sein Engel*, Frankfurt/Main, 1983, p26.
39. V Serge, *Memoirs of a Revolutionary 1901-1941*, London, 1980, pp364-5.
40. See T Eagleton, *Walter Benjamin or Towards a Revolutionary Criticism*, London, 1981, pp173-9.
41. See C Slaughter, *Marxism, Ideology and Literature*, London, 1980.

European Trotskyists — Daniel Bensaïd, Enzo Traverso, Michael Löwy — have published work on Benjamin, reconstructing an alternative Marxist tradition that disentangles Marxism from the atrocities of Stalinism.[42]

Some of these political reconstructions of Benjamin's ideas formed a response to developments in Benjamin studies. In their bibliographic survey of Benjamin scholarship, Reinhard Markner and Thomas Weber argue that a 'depoliticisation' of Benjamin's work took place in the 1980s.[43] Depoliticisation is a troublesome concept, but it is evident that there has been a powerful wave in Benjamin studies that detracts from his interest in Marxism and radical politics, substituting instead a dalliance with Judaic motifs or a fusion of the very different projects of Heidegger and Benjamin. Such studies refuse to place Benjamin's work historically, and filch motives from here, there and everywhere, in order to derive a philosophy, whilst side-stepping the task of situating Benjamin's writing within the context of his dialogue with left-wing politics. The large corpus of work written by post-structuralists treats the political as a black hole at the centre of Benjamin's work, in which can be found only contending, conflicting and contradictory energies. In a backlash against these developments, it is necessary to go back in time, so as to witness affinities between Benjamin and Trotsky. That black hole may be illuminated with the glare of political and historical light.

Building upon the importance of the motif of constellation in Benjamin's own theory, the following words consider some relationships of biography and thought between Benjamin and Trotsky. Brecht, too, is called upon.[44] To rip things from their resting places, bring them together, match this one against that, noted Benjamin, is the method of the allegorist. Out of this practice dialectical syntheses may be fashioned. What follows is an allegory of a dangerous political history of the first half of the twentieth century.

42. See D Bensaïd, *Walter Benjamin; sentinelle messianique. A la gauche du possible*, Paris, 1990; E Traverso, *Les Marxistes et la question juive: histoire d'un débat (1843-1943)*, Montreuil, 1990 (in English, *The Marxists and the Jewish Question*, New Jersey, 1994); M Löwy, *On Changing the World: Essays in Political Philosophy from Karl Marx to Walter Benjamin*, New Jersey, 1993.

43. See R Markner and T Weber (ed), *Literatur über Walter Benjamin*, Hamburg, 1993. For one pertinent example — when Gary Smith translated Benjamin's *Moscow Diary*, he noted in the afterword that the diary contained no political judgements. This essay hopes to show otherwise.

44. There is no poem by the politically prudent Brecht relating to the death of Trotsky. But, in his third volume of Trotsky's life, Isaac Deutscher writes that Brecht's *Life of Galileo*, written in 1938, is an allegory of the battle between the Trotskyists and the Stalinists. Galileo is Bukharin, Rakovsky or Zinoviev. The character Bruno, who is sacrificed as a warning example, claims Deutscher, represents Trotsky. The play depicts the tragedy of a people too immature in a land unhappy enough to need such hero-victims as these (I Deutscher, *The Prophet Outcast: Trotsky 1929-40*, Oxford, 1979, p370).

Origin of a German and Russian Tragedy: To Begin At The End — 1940

'It is certainly victims that move humanity forwards.' — Leon Trotsky

Within a month of each other, two exiled Jewish revolutionaries met their deaths in Spanish-speaking lands. On 20 August 1940, Leon Trotsky was murdered by a Stalinist agent whilst he was halfway through reading the book *Hitler Speaks*. Benjamin died in the shadow of Fascism, committing suicide on the Franco-Spanish border on 26 September 1940. He was in the process of escaping from Vichy France and Nazi-occupied France, through Spain, to America. He was refused right of passage and threatened with deliverance to the Gestapo. The Gestapo had his number, for his German nationality had already been revoked. It appears that suicide was preferable to certain murder by the enemy.

Contrary to an oft-voiced view that sees Benjamin as embracing death willingly, a tragic figure, an ill-fated man of letters, whose work is interpreted only in the light of the author's self-termination, Benjamin's suicide has to be placed within the context of the historical defeat of the progressive revolutionary forces.[45] His fate was not the unique destiny of an unlucky and hapless victim. It was arguably the typical fate of certain groups of people at a definite period of history. Indeed, the factors involved in Benjamin's death are not disconnected from factors that played a rôle in Trotsky's death. The double death of Benjamin and Trotsky stands as a marker of the lethal complicity between their murderers. This complicity was the odd affinity of interests underwritten in the Ribbentrop-Molotov non-aggression pact of 1939 that allied Germany with the Soviet Union.

Trotsky was a Marxist, a non-practising Jew, a brilliant writer, and a perceptive critic of the two murderous ideologies of the twentieth century: Stalinism and Fascism. He was a victim of Stalinism. Benjamin was a Marxist, a non-practising Jew, a brilliant if somewhat gnomic writer, a perceptive critic of Stalinism and Fascism, and a victim of Fascism. Actual connections between the two men, of course, go in only one direction. I do not know whether Trotsky read Benjamin — he may have done, for Benjamin did publish articles in some Communist journals. But certainly Benjamin read Trotsky. His bibliographies record several books by Trotsky. After his visit to Moscow in 1927, Benjamin wrote a series of literary-political articles on the situation in the post-revolutionary Soviet Union. His essay, *New Poetry in Russia*, contains a concise summary of

45. For just one example of the melancholic mythologisation of Benjamin, see Z Baumann, 'Walter Benjamin, the Intellectual', *New Formations*, no 20, Summer 1993, p47. There are many others, for contemporary intellectuals seem very attracted to the poetics of failure.

Trotsky's literary pronouncements.[46] In 1933, Benjamin read *The Fourth International and the USSR*. He read Trotsky eagerly. He thought highly of *Where is Britain Going?*.[47] He 'breathlessly' devoured *My Life* and *The History of the Russian Revolution*.[48] Lukács, regarded by many as one of the greatest Marxist cultural critics, rarely referred to Trotsky's literary studies, and then only disfavourably. Lukács' preferred literary-critical mentors were Plekhanov and Mehring. Unlike Benjamin and Trotsky, he had no time whatsoever for avant-gardist experiments with art. Benjamin, however, was one of the few leftists who continued to refer to Trotsky through the 1920s and 1930s, in both literary-critical contexts and in political discussions. Benjamin continued to refer to Trotsky because his detachment from the Communist Party allowed him to avoid the *Diktat* that stated that Trotsky was politically suspect, petit-bourgeois and 'faschoid'.

There is a difficulty in comparing Benjamin, the cultural critic, with an engaged revolutionary. Although they were contemporaries, Trotsky had been centrally active in a revolution, and he lived in the shadow of that event, as it was slowly receding in time, and as its gains were reversed by the Stalinist bureaucracy. By the time of Benjamin's concrete political formation, the German workers' movement had already suffered major defeats, and Nazism was increasingly in the foreground of events. Benjamin was, in some ways, the embodiment of 'pessimism of the intellect, optimism of the will', or, in his own words, an adherent of the concept of the 'organisation of pessimism', in what Brecht calls 'darkened times'. However, theoretical affinities are plenty, and to uncover them is to lay bare aspects of the politics and aesthetics that are influenced by discussions amongst the Russian modernist avant-gardists who called themselves variously futurists, productivists, and constructivists.

Benjamin and Trotsky were both critically opposed to reformism. Both suspected Stalinism. Both formulated versions of historical materialism that refused to accept that human activity was an inert reflection of the economy, or an embodiment of the Will of the Party, or the inevitable and natural by-product of mechanistic developments. For both, historical development was not a one-way street of progressive linear evolution, but the succession of disparate epochs. In *The History of the Russian Revolution*, Trotsky's account of this world-historical event placed massive emphasis on subjective as well as objective factors. Benjamin was interested in the composition of consciousness in capitalism. He focused on moments of change and potential change in consciousness through

46. See W Benjamin, *Gesammelte Schriften*, Volume 2/2, Frankfurt, 1991, p758. Some translations in this essay are not identical with the translations cited in the footnotes.
47. W Benjamin, *Briefe*, Volume 1, edited by G Scholem and TW Adorno, Frankfurt/Main, 1978, p409.
48. Op cit, p553.

activity. A phrase from one of Benjamin's final pieces of writing, *Theses on the Philosophy of History*, with an emphasis on the self-activity of the proletariat, found an echo in Trotsky: 'The subject of historical knowledge is the struggling, oppressed class itself.' Both Benjamin and Trotsky coincided, in many senses, in their critique of Popular Frontism, as well as in their cautioning analyses of Stalinism. Both men were interested in Freud. Both investigated the relationship of Marxism and psychoanalysis. And both had dealings with the Surrealists. Benjamin saw Surrealism as a practical critique of official Marxism and of 'metaphysical materialism', which, he argued, had consistently neglected the unconscious and libidinal side of human experience. Trotsky formed a literary alliance with the Surrealists Breton and Rivera in 1938. The three collaborated in the autumn of 1938 on *Towards a Free Revolutionary Art*, a manifesto that called on artists and writers to turn to 'those who with unshaken fidelity bear witness to the revolution ... [and] who, for this reason, are alone able to bring it to fruition, and along with it the ultimate free expression of all forms of human genius'. They insisted on one condition. There must be complete opposition to any restriction on artistic creation, let alone commands from above, whether from the Communist Party or from capital. In their discussions of art, both Trotsky and Benjamin salvaged elements of traditional inherited culture whilst remaining open to avant-garde movements. In the preface to *Literature and Revolution*, Trotsky assumed a sort of art-into-life stance, close to Benjamin's productivism. Trotsky elided art and social life, positing an active appropriation of culture – and called for a self-conscious art that was 'active, vitally collectivist, and filled with limitless creative faith in the future'. Culture formed an essential part of political debate for these men. Both scrutinised the connection between intellectual culture and the development of the productive forces. Both were interested in the affinities between art's own laws of development and the incitements and demands of the class struggle.

The two men lived through turbulent times. Rapid industrialisation in Germany, culminating in the imperialist First World War, shattered the relations between capitalism, culture and morality. This splintering demanded analysis and reaction, and it politicised a whole layer of German intellectuals. The October Revolution gave further cause to question these relationships, both for intellectuals and activists within the Soviet Union and outside of it. And the attempted and yet failed German Revolution had an impact on questions of culture and on intellectual formations in the Weimar Republic, having created an immensely politicised situation in which revolutionary and reformist politicians battled seriously against each other – and the right – for hegemony. Benjamin followed events in the Soviet Union closely. Trotsky was no less alert to German developments.

In order to view these matters in close-up, let us review Benjamin's journey to Moscow in December 1926. Trotsky was still there, but clinging on by the skin of his teeth.

1926-27: Left Wing Melancholy; The New Angel in the Land of the Bolsheviks

In 1926, Trotsky and the Left Opposition were expelled from the Politbureau. At the end of this year, Benjamin travelled to Moscow. It was the year following Stalin's final consolidation of the doctrine of 'Socialism in One Country', first formulated in November 1924. The programme of 'Socialism in One Country' announced nine months after Lenin's death and four months after the appearance of *Literature and Revolution*, was a terse expression of the political outlook of the bureaucracy. Bolshevik revolutionaries had upheld the necessity of internationalism. A revolution, especially one that had broken out in an economically underdeveloped country, could be no more than a holding operation. Its success was tied up with the spread of revolution into other countries. Lenin stated the case precisely in his 'World Revolution or Perish' argument at the Third Congress of the Comintern in 1921. The programme of 'Socialism in One Country' ignored Lenin's argument, and set about consolidating a political-national order.[49]

Arriving at the end of 1926, Benjamin stayed in Moscow until February 1927. The year of 1927 saw the beginning of the period of Thermidor, according to Trotsky's analysis from the late 1920s. Trotsky defined Thermidor as the first stage of the counter-revolution. It represented bourgeois restoration, 'the direct transfer of power from the hands of one class into the hands of another'.[50] The years of 1926 and 1927 were the time in which Benjamin first began to consider seriously whether or not to join the Communist Party.[51] The visit to Moscow was to be a testing out of the party, and an experiment in life under the party's control. Benjamin's toying with the idea of entering the party was not entirely new. He had been considering it since the mid-1920s, when he read Lukács' *History and Class Consciousness*. At the same time, he had fallen in love with a Latvian Bolshevik called Asja Lacis. His love for Lacis, who was based in Moscow, was another reason for visiting the Soviet Union.

In actual fact, his time there led him to distance himself from the

49. For documents pertaining to Bolshevik internationalism, see A Richardson (ed), *In Defence of the Russian Revolution: A Selection of Bolshevik Writings 1917-1923*, London, 1995, especially pp119-82.
50. Cited in T Cliff, *Trotsky: The Darker the Night the Brighter the Star 1927-1940*, London, 1993, p62.
51. See, for example, a letter written to Scholem on 29 May 1926, Benjamin, *Briefe*, Volume 1, op cit, pp425-30.

Communist Party. Benjamin had travelled to Moscow with an open mind, and yet he was already suspicious of the way things were developing. Throughout his visit he kept a diary, the *Moskauer Tagebuch*, recording conversations with intellectuals and meetings with the left literary oppositionists who still remained in Moscow.[52] The diary also noted observations about life in the capital, and was drawn on for the production in 1927 of a city portrait entitled *Moskau*.[53] The sojourn in Moscow gave Benjamin the opportunity to study post-revolutionary culture. It was an interesting time, for as Benjamin noted in his diary, the Left Opposition was being fervently debated.

Developments in the Soviet Union at the end of the 1920s gave rise to ferocious struggles over official economic, social, political and cultural positions. At the time of Benjamin's visit to Moscow, the Opposition was experiencing its last vigorous gasps. The United Opposition of 1926-27 attempted to encourage workers' resistance to the political decline that was occurring under the government's New Economic Policy.[54] Hopes were raised in some quarters for a change in party leadership at the Fifteenth Party Congress in 1927.[55] At the end of 1927, the Stalinists finally began to clamp down hard on the Opposition. Thousands of industrial militants were imprisoned. Trotsky was arrested, charged with counter-revolutionary activity, and exiled to Alma-Ata, near the Chinese frontier, on 17 January 1928.

Benjamin recorded that events in the Soviet Union at the time of his visit were working to the disadvantage of the left and were impairing cultural politics, but he was also aware of a vibrancy still present in Soviet society.[56] He wrote: 'Life here is so extraordinarily meaningful. The entire scheme of existence of the Western European intelligentsia is utterly impoverished in comparison to the countless constellations that offer themselves here to the individual in the space of a month.' He noticed that everything was still in flux a decade after the revolution – from the determining of laws to regulations on the positioning of bus stops. On a cultural level, he argued that the proletariat had genuinely begun to take possession of bourgeois culture, a stage demanded by Trotsky, and he was

52. See W Benjamin, 'Moskauer Tagebuch', *Gesammelte Schriften*, Volume 6, Frankfurt, 1991, pp292-409. In English, *Moscow Diary*, Cambridge and London, 1986. Whilst still a young man, Benjamin decided that the journal was the completion of the journey. Writing a journal was a frequent task, for Benjamin travelled much in his life – from the north of Finland to the south of Spain – as tourism turned into exile.

53. See W Benjamin, 'Moskau', *Gesammelte Schriften*, Volume 4/1, Frankfurt, 1991, pp316-48; 'Moscow', *One Way Street and Other Writings*, London, 1979, p177-208.

54. For information on industrial struggle and the opposition see I Deutscher, *The Prophet Unarmed: Trotsky 1921-1929*, Oxford, 1959, pp275-8.

55. See op cit, p356.

56. See, for example, Benjamin, 'Moskau', op cit, pp325, 337-9; 'Moscow', op cit, pp185-6, 197-9.

struck by how confidently the proletariat moved in Soviet museums and galleries. In Germany, he remarked, if the working classes happened to be in galleries, they looked as if they had broken in in order to steal something.[57] One of the starkest impressions in Benjamin's diary was the sense of a momentous mood in the Soviet Union. For example, early on in his visit, a man he met reported to him that Trotsky was speaking before the Comintern in defence of Zinoviev, whom Stalin had defeated in 1925 and had removed from the presidency of the Comintern in October 1926. The man informed Benjamin that the party was possibly set to make an about-turn. This refers perhaps to the renewed zest pervading the Opposition at the very time Benjamin was in Moscow. On the whole, though, the frailty of the Opposition in the face of Stalinism was rather more apparent in the diary. Any renewed activity around the Left Opposition would seem to be the last gasp. One of the first things Benjamin recorded on arrival was the pessimism of his friend Bernd Reich, who was based there and got by making a living as a writer, involved with the theatre. As soon as Benjamin arrived in Moscow, he discussed with Reich the issue of joining the party. Reich's main problem with the party, given that he was a cultural producer, was its stance on cultural matters. Reich told Benjamin of the party's reactionary turn. Reich, reported Benjamin, feared that the left-wing movements in art that were state-approved and employed at the time of War Communism would be totally dropped. Proletarian writers, noted Benjamin, had become, against Trotsky's wishes, state recognised, although they were given no actual state support.[58] This new 'proletarian culture' was a component of a narrow pragmatic vision of a culture based on the foundations of the perceived characteristics of the working class and its revolution. It was not a utopian-idealist rejection of bourgeois culture, along the lines of *proletcult*, but rather a bureaucratic artistic policy that determined the value of culture according to the class origins of the cultural producers. It was soon to become an instrument of policy for Stalin, from 1928 onwards, at around the same time as the First Five Year Plan. The promotion of 'proletarian culture', primarily through the organisation called the Association of Artists of the Revolution, was consistent with an indifference to the absence of the cultural and productive conditions for Communism. Instead of a new culture emerging, the bureaucratic concept required a culture called up by order of state in order to corroborate the lie that Communism could be forced through from above. Through this 'proletarian culture', declared Benjamin, the state, in fact, championed the artistic production of reactionary peasant art.

57. See Benjamin, 'Moskauer Tagebuch', op cit, p363; *Moscow Diary*, op cit, pp76-7. See also 'Moskau', op cit, p323; 'Moscow', op cit, p183.
58. See Benjamin, 'Moskauer Tagebuch', op cit, p294; *Moscow Diary*, op cit, pp11-12.

Trotsky believed in giving complete freedom of form to those artists who were on the side of the revolution. This was a position he maintained from *Literature and Revolution* to the *Manifesto* that he issued with Breton and Rivera. The revolution in the Soviet Union was understood to be a transitional phase – hence the impossibility of 'proletarian culture'. He asked how a class in dissolution could be blessed with a culture all of its own. From 1923 to 1926, Trotsky wrote a number of articles on art and literature. These articles formed a part of a many-headed struggle against Stalinism and, as Trotsky termed it, its 'theoretical corrosion' of the Bolshevik party. In his most detailed study of culture and literature, *Literature and Revolution*, written at the time of the first phase of the rise of the Left Opposition, he pointed out that the proletariat was not creating a culture that conformed to its needs as a proletariat. The proletariat, in its revolutionary phase, was engaged in a struggle to abolish itself. On these grounds, the idea of 'proletarian culture' as promoted by the state was misguided. Art had its own laws, noted Trotsky. In *Literature and Revolution*, Trotsky bound culture to its material roots, adamant that whilst the 'class criteria' were vital in art, art must be 'judged according to its own laws'. Trotsky's point found some sort of echo in Benjamin's cultural analysis of artistic production on the part of a disaffected bourgeoisie. Benjamin insisted that the character of the artwork itself was of decisive importance, and not just the class origins of the author. Questions raised in *Literature and Revolution* echoed Benjamin's concerns, particularly as they surfaced in his critical reviews of the late 1920s: how would a social revolution affect literature? What types of literature and what types of writers would express the revolutionary process? Should revolutionaries encourage particular artistic schools? What is the literature of the post-revolutionary future? For Trotsky, art was not a mirror that reflected society, nor a hammer that shaped society according to its own desires. The proletariat must take control of the old culture as well as forging the new. In doing this, they would create new forms, as well as enlivening old ones.[59] In *Literature and Revolution*, he expressed an interest in the futurist and productivist groupings and the artists associated with *LEF* (the journal of the Left Front of the Arts), although he admitted that his understanding of its tenets was not fully comprehensive. He wrote: 'Though remaining, in some respects, a Bohemian revolutionary offshoot of the old art, futurism contributes to a greater degree and more directly and actively than all the other tendencies in forming the new art.' Trotsky's conception of art can be aligned with that of the left formalists. For them, artistic experimentation aimed to prefigure changes that could take place in the real world. They assumed that subjectivity could be reformed – and the type of 'new man' who was the citizen of the post-revo-

59. See LD Trotsky, *Literature and Revolution*, Ann Arbor, 1960, p323.

lutionary society had a prototype in the spectator of modern art. Trotsky insisted that art is not an autonomous realm, but nor is it an unmediated expression of socio-political needs. Art is not propaganda. Speaking of the party in a way that was indubitably to become wishful thinking, Trotsky wrote:

'The party understands the episodic character of the literary groups of a transition period and estimates them, not from the point of view of the class passports of the individual gentlemen literati, but from the point of view of the place these groups occupy and can occupy in preparing a Socialist culture.'[60]

Similarly, in his contention in *The Author as Producer* that the artist is a producer but not a proletarian, Benjamin drafted the Marxist debate on art in terms of the category of agency, an active category, and not in terms of the passive sociologistic fact of class. Official Communist art theory, he charged, could not advance beyond a listless paradigm of the reflection of class interests in artworks, asking only whether artworks are reactionary or revolutionary in their subject matter.[61]

Benjamin had experienced first-hand the distortions of a literary analysis that based itself solely, contrary to Trotsky's advice, on the class origins of writers. Whilst in Moscow, Benjamin was allowed to submit an entry on Goethe for the *Great Soviet Encyclopaedia*, but his submission was rejected.[62] The authorities desired a sociological treatment of Goethe's life, concentrating on his class origins. Benjamin wrote an analysis of the afterlife of Goethe's works. He was certain that it is only the history of a poet's influence that can be fruitfully analysed in materialist terms, and not his or her life. Karl Radek rejected Benjamin's article, citing as reason Benjamin's overuse of the words 'class struggle'.[63] Benjamin complained to his friend Scholem that the abstract submitted turned out to be too radical for the authorities. His bid to submit a materialist analysis had fallen foul of the perplexing aims of the editorial board: 'They are shaken by good old Aristotelian fear and pity when it comes to the European intelligentsia; they want a standard work of Marxist science, at the same time, however, they want to create something that will awaken vain admiration in Europe.'[64]

Insisting on the centrality of the class origins of cultural producers, the Soviet authorities inherited a bourgeois-derived obsession with per-

---

60. Op cit, p19.
61. See W Benjamin, 'Der Autor als Produzent' [1934], *Gesammelte Schriften*, Volume 2/2, op cit, p685; *Reflections*, New York, 1986, p222.
62. See Benjamin 'Moskauer Tagebuch', op cit, p321; *Moscow Diary*, op cit, p39.
63. See op cit, p366; p81.
64. See Benjamin's letter to Scholem, 23 February 1927, *Briefe*, Volume 1, op cit, p442.

sonalities, rather than a materialist interest in the work and its afterlife. At the same time, the desire to secure recognition for scholarship in Europe compelled them to defuse the political resonances of the analyses that they put out. This conundrum was typical of the contradictions that struck Benjamin in Moscow. Benjamin's diary recorded how confused political life was in the Soviet Union in this period. For example, he observed how:

'Externally the government seeks peace in order to undertake trade agreements with imperialist states; but, above all, internally it attempts to suspend militant Communism. It strives to institute a harmony between classes, to depoliticise bourgeois life in as far as that is possible. On the other hand, in the pioneer groups, in the Komsomol, youth are being educated as *revolutionaries*. That means that the idea of revolution comes to them not as an experience, but as a slogan. The attempt is made to disconnect the dynamic of revolutionary processes in state life — whether one likes it or not, the restoration has begun — but in spite of that, the attempt is made to store up revolutionary energy in youth like electric power in a battery. That just is not possible.'[65]

Benjamin continued on the theme of the ignorance of Soviet youth in respect of bourgeois culture, a point also made by Trotsky. But he also noted that bourgeois values were being officially popularised by the party. 'The party officially recommends the popularisation of these values. Now it is possible to see in Soviet Russia how these values are being popularised in just that distorted and desolate form, which owes its existence to imperialism.'[66] Benjamin caught all the shock-waves of an experiment in revolution in decline or, even, in reverse.

On his return from Moscow, Benjamin wrote a piece about Moscow for a left-wing journal. He distilled images and annotations from his Moscow diary, and presented a picture of the city that fuses excitement, and a caution about burgeoning forms of oppression and cult. He specifically described the Lenin cult, noting how little babies were called October or Wolf from the moment they could point to Lenin's picture. He reported how Lenin's picture was sold on icon stalls, with pictures of saints flanking it like a police guard.[67] He told of how in the Red Army Club there was a map of Europe. Turn the handle and all the places where Lenin went in his life lit up one after another. Other cities were not marked at all, as if they had no significance without the charmed presence of Lenin. With heavy traces of irony, Benjamin wrote: 'On it Lenin's life appears like a colonialist conquering of Europe.'[68] Benjamin

65. Benjamin, 'Moskauer Tagebuch', op cit, p338; *Moscow Diary*, op cit, p53.
66. See op cit, pp338-9, p54.
67. See Benjamin, 'Moskau', op cit, pp321-2; 'Moscow', op cit, p182.
68. Op cit, p336; p196. See also 'Moskauer Tagebuch', op cit, p350; *Moscow Diary*, op cit,

also concentrated on how life had become increasingly collectivised. Any deviation from the bureaucratic norm slammed up against an enormous apparatus and immeasurable costs. It was a country of 24-hour mobilisation, where specialists were fetishised. Benjamin related that at the Red Military Academy, there was an old general who had been given a teaching post. He had been notorious in the Civil War. Every Bolshevik imprisoned by him had been hung. Now he had a post. Benjamin saw that in this case ideology was sacrificed to objective skills. Intellectual specialists were also returning to posts that they sabotaged during the Civil War. Neither the Opposition nor an independent intelligentsia which opposed the Bolsheviks existed in any particularly meaningful sense any more. Either it had been destroyed, or it had called a truce, wrote Benjamin.[69] A new bourgeoisie had emerged.

Trotsky's Thermidor analysis contended that the various forces – the NEP capitalists, sections of the party, and also the wealthy peasants – were interested in some sort of bourgeois restoration. This generated a number of confusions a decade after the revolution. The ebbing of the revolutionary wave in 1921 and the stabilisation of the world capitalist system meant that, to sustain itself, the post-revolutionary society had to introduce temporary measures in the form of the NEP. This was supposed to be a temporary measure until capitalist crisis was reasserted and class struggle internationally was on the rise again. But the NEP turned away from this perspective, and, from the mid-1920s, began to reconsolidate the Soviet economy along capitalist lines. By the time of the onset of capitalist crisis in the late 1920s, the central plan of Bolshevik policy was to build up an independent industrial state, initially within the scope of the mixed, unplanned economy of the NEP, and later within the rigidly planned economy of the 'Third Period'. According to Benjamin, the contradictory nature of the situation in the Soviet Union was expressed precisely in the misalignment between money and power, two forces that were aligned in the West.[70] In the Soviet Union, social status was determined by the relationship between an individual and the party. The party or the bureaucracy retained the power, and the NEP men had the money. Benjamin commented: 'If the European correlation of money and power were to emerge here, the country would not be lost, not even perhaps the party, but Communism in Russia would be.'[71]

Trotsky, of course, argued that the two forces, the new capitalists and sections of the party, as well as the wealthy peasants, were interested in some sort of bourgeois restoration. Economic realignments were the re-

pp63-4.
69. Benjamin, 'Moskau', op cit, p327; 'Moscow', p187.
70. Op cit, pp333-4; pp193-4.
71. Op cit, p336; pp195-6.

sults of political struggle. They brought their own political and cultural concomitant. On a visit to the theatre in December 1926, Benjamin noted in his diary:

'As soon as I entered the auditorium I was met by the smell of perfume. I could not see a single Communist in a blue tunic, but there were a few types who would not have been out of place in any of George Grosz's albums. The performance had absolutely the style of a completely dusty royal theatre.'[72]

The ideals of the revolutionary avant-garde were definitely on the retreat, and this, to a certain extent, went hand-in-hand with the forced retreat of the Left Opposition. The revolutionary avant-garde had been opposed to the social stratification that the NEP brought in its wake, and to the reactionary turn in cultural policy to which it also seemed to give succour. It should not of course be forgotten that Dziga Vertov and Osip Brik, both partisans on the side of the avant-garde and therefore not disinterested, noted that the proletariat had responded positively to new cultural techniques in art. They contended that it was the NEP-men who were antipathetic to experimentation, preferring conventional notions of art as a luxury item, emotive and separate from life. NEP culture thus contravened the central core of the avant-garde project of production art. It appeared undeniable that a new class with its cultural shibboleths was in the ascendant. This re-emergence of the bourgeoisie was further promoted by Stalinist entrenchment. There was little to choose between the aesthetic preferences of NEP culture and Stalinist-approved 'proletarian culture'. Both discouraged experimentation. The new ground-rules of Soviet art encouraged figurative easel-painting and monumental sculpture in order to depict an 'heroic realism'. Trotsky had warned about the fetishism of the style of great realism in *Literature and Revolution*. Benjamin disclosed the cultural perspectives of the bureaucracy:

'Political affiliation and content are deemed most important. Formal controversies had played a not inconsiderable rôle right up until the Civil War. Now they have been silenced. And today, the position is official. Content and not form is decisive for the revolutionary or counter-revolutionary attitude of a work. Today banal clarity is demanded.'[73]

The sad consequences for both art and artists of this policy, and the fact of its successful enforcement can be assessed by its effect on the old revolutionary avant-garde. Trotsky, in an article on the suicide of the futurist-revolutionary poet Mayakovsky in 1930, made a poignant point

72. Benjamin, 'Moskauer Tagebuch', op cit, p328; *Moscow Diary*, op cit, p44.
73. Op cit, pp338-9; pp53-4. See also 'Moskau', op cit, p339; 'Moscow', op cit, p199.

about the effects of bureaucratisation on art. He wrote of the arrival in Stalin's Soviet Union of a system of bureaucratic command over art. Such bureaucratism would lead to the impoverishment of art, and to its devastation.[74]

In February 1929, in an essay on Surrealism, Benjamin brought together Trotsky's analysis from *Literature and Revolution* and his vision of the rôle of the revolutionary intelligentsia:

'If it is the double task of the revolutionary intelligentsia to topple the intellectual predominance of the bourgeoisie and to gain contact with the proletarian masses, it has virtually failed in the second half of this task, because the masses are no longer to be won over contemplatively. But that has not stopped them from acting as if they could be and calling for proletarian poets, thinkers and artists. Trotsky had taken up this idea in *Literature and Revolution*, pointing out that they would only emerge in a successful revolution. In reality, it has less to do with trying to turn an artist of bourgeois origin into a master of *proletarian art*, than of placing him in a functional capacity, even if it is at the cost of his artistic effectivity, at important points of the image-space. Perhaps the interruption of his *artistic career* might be an essential part of this function.'[75]

Intellectuals could be deployed differently in the modern age, argued Benjamin, side-swiping at the old guardians of cultural heritage, as well as at the proletarian novel-writers. The pivotal task of the Marxist critic was to engage actively in directing the cultural emancipation of the masses — not by serving up proletarian-bred culture, but by interrogating forms. Revolutionary images proposed a certain structure of appropriation which related to questions of function, rather than to content. Benjamin's essay on Surrealism summoned up a realm in which creative contact could be made with the proletarian masses. A new collective body needed new image forms to represent its new reality to itself. This would become a reality, for Benjamin, in the organisation of writers' workshops and the presentation of popular theatre, as well as the active engagement of revolutionary intellectuals and worker-intellectuals in literacy programmes and journalism. Benjamin called for the transformation — '*Umfunktionierung*[76] — of the cultural and educational apparatus. He saw the artistic producer rôle transformed in Brecht's artistic practice, as well as in the work of Sergei Tretyakov and the experimental wing of Soviet cinematographers.

74. See LD Trotsky, 'The Suicide of Mayakovsky', *On Literature and Art*, New York, 1970, pp174-8.
75. W Benjamin, 'Der Surrealismus', *Gesammelte Schriften*, Volume 2/1, Frankfurt, 1991, p309; *One Way Street and Other Writings*, op cit, p238.
76. A term borrowed from Brecht.

1934: First Call at Brecht's

Benjamin's experiences in exile – always framed by persisting social and financial insecurity – led him to seek relief at Brecht's fugitive home in Scandinavia in 1934. Benjamin remarked of his relationship to Brecht that it was an 'ever-recurring constellation in his life'. The relationship between Benjamin and Brecht has often been viewed according to the prejudices of Benjamin's friends, Adorno and Scholem, who remonstrated about Brecht's crude and catastrophic influence, and saw Benjamin as a hapless victim of the callous Brecht. A more sympathetic study might reveal that the support provided was mutual: social exchange, literary and political discussion, attempts by Brecht to get Benjamin published in Moscow in the mid-1930s, and efforts by Benjamin to secure Brecht a good reputation in Paris. But most importantly, Brecht was instrumental in directing Benjamin to a closer engagement with the possibility of a revolutionary art practice, for he offered an operative model of this sort of practice. Benjamin found this model to be contemporary and appropriate for the needs of class struggle in culture in Germany. Brecht's influence found its most vivid expression in the two essays *The Author as Producer* (1934) and *The Work of Art in the Age of its Technical Reproducibility* (1935-39).

The *Author as Producer* was written in the spring of 1934. It was designed as a lecture to be delivered to the Paris-based Institute for the Study of Fascism, a Communist Party operation. Benjamin's lecture stressed the necessity for theorising relations of production in art, in order to suggest ways to bring them into line with the forces of production. In *The Author as Producer*, Benjamin aimed to provide some guidelines for artistic practice in non-revolutionary Europe, through a seemingly empirical study of events in the Soviet Union. Initially, the paper included a quotation from Trotsky. This was dropped. Benjamin checked himself, bowed to pressure, and subjected himself to self-censorship, the order of the day. The quotation from Trotsky had been included to attack the intellectuals who claimed to be above the messiness of material political struggle, but who thought they could somehow challenge Fascism with the power of rational thought. The doomed mock internationalism of the League of Nations was promoted by just such a group of enlightened pacifists who insisted on the ability of reason to counter the propulsion towards war, and were unable to recognise the futility of such appeals in the context of capitalist imperialism.[77] Originally Benjamin had written:

77. For the communist critique of the 'insincerity and hypocrisy of social-pacifism' of the League of Nations, see the 'Twenty-One Conditions' for affiliation to the Third International, presented at the Second World Congress of the Comintern in 1920, in B Hessel (ed), *Theses, Resolutions and Manifestos of the First Four Congresses of the Third International*, London, 1980, pp92-7.

'Or to use Trotsky's words: "When enlightened pacifists undertake to abolish war by means of rationalist arguments, they are simply ridiculous. When the armed masses start to take up the arguments of reason against war, however, this signifies the end of war.""[78]

And, in a very real sense, war was not about to disappear suddenly because the intellectuals were pointing out its irrationality. Preparations for war were in high gear. Kurt Hiller's activism, typified as an idealist 'Conscience Communism' for intellectuals, was rejected by Benjamin because it opposed the designing of cultural models that prioritised authors as producers and producers as audiences. Conscience Communism relied on the moral guidance of the polity by the intellectual élite.[79] Benjamin's argument in *The Author as Producer* insisted that political art is predominantly concerned with reception effects, generated by modes of production that provide conditions for consumers to become the producers or authors of the meaning of a work of art. Artistic production must have the character of a model that introduces other producers to production, by placing an 'improved apparatus' at the disposal of authors and audience, bringing audiences into contact with the production process, and turning readers or spectators into collaborators.[80] Intellectuals who claim to identify with the encouragement of the class struggle must be forced to consider their place as producers in the clash between the forces and relations of production.

In *The Author as Producer*, Benjamin analysed the politics of the artistic representation of the 'real'. Representation of the real in art should not rely for its progressiveness on a mirroring of surface appearances, whether it be the bald photographic realism of new objectivity, or the reflection theory aesthetic recommended by policy makers in the Communist parties. Such passive reflection disempowers viewers, denying their intelligence and participation in making meaning. Reflection art seems to do all the work for the viewer, and does not prioritise art as the place of a struggle over making meanings. It does not introduce elements that break the framing devices or make the artifice obvious, in order to make the constructed nature a basis for discussion and critique. Benjamin was opposed to any aesthetic theory founded on an ontological materialism, as in the *Widerspiegelungsästhetik* of Socialist Realism, an aesthetic standpoint state-sanctioned in 1934, and transmitted through the Comintern to the international sections. This aesthetic decreed that art should relate in a simple reflective relationship to social reality. In promoting

78. *Gesammelte Schriften*, Volume 2/3, Frankfurt, 1991, p1464. Benjamin also quotes this passage in 'Der Irrtum des Aktivismus: Zu Kurt Hillers Essaybuch Der Sprung ins Helle' [1932], *Gesammelte Schriften*, Volume 3, Frankfurt, 1991, p351.
79. See W Benjamin, 'Der Autor als Produzent', *Gesammelte Schriften*, Volume 2/2, op cit, pp690-1, 701; *Reflections*, op cit, pp226-7, 237-8.
80. Benjamin, 'Der Autor als Produzent', op cit, p696; *Reflections*, op cit, p233.

reflectionism, Benjamin perceived a restorative bias in the *Kulturpolitik* of the Stalinised Soviet Union. In one passage in *The Author as Producer*, Benjamin insinuated that it was indeed Fascist aesthetic recommendations that most closely approximated the Comintern's directives to writers to imitate the nineteenth century realists.[81]

At the same time as Benjamin planned to offer his paper to the Institute for the Study of Fascism, street demonstrations broke out in Paris. Benjamin had been living here in exile for a year, after rapidly leaving Nazi Germany. The loudest protests on the streets emerged from the right wing. These street commotions were responses to the intensification of the world economic depression. Battles on the Place de la Concorde on 6 February 1934 left 15 dead and well over 1000 wounded.[82] The French parliament argued that a Fascist putsch was looming. When not at Brecht's Svendborg home, Benjamin watched the events from his hotel room on the Boulevard St Germain, which lay in the thick of the disturbances.

1935-36: Benjamin, Trotsky and the Unpopular Front

The riotous events on the streets and the growing power of the right unified the left in France. The Communists and the Socialists came together in a Popular Front against Fascism. Previously, the official Communist Party policy had been one adapted to the Third Period. The concept of the Third Period was the offshoot of an ultra-left lunacy. In the Third Period, Social Democrats were dismissed as 'Social Fascists', representing the 'moderate wing of Fascism'.[83] Social Fascists, promoting the lie of reformism, were viewed as the main enemy, disseminating illusions, and blocking the revolutionary development of the proletariat. Communist Party doctrine had insisted that the Third Period registered the imminence of economic catastrophe, the precondition for revolution. The concepts of the Third Period and Social Fascism had been first mooted in 1924 at the Fifth Congress of the Comintern. They became part of official doctrine after 1928, once Stalin was firmly in control of the Comintern. Trotsky was immensely critical of these divisive concepts. He insisted that such divisions acted to split the working-class movement.[84] Party policy began to change during the frenzied early months of 1934. In France, the call for a general strike in February brought the Communist Party-controlled trade union federation, the CGTU, together with

81. Op cit, pp695-6; pp232-3.
82. See Cliff, op cit, p187.
83. Reference to this quotation from Stalin can be found in op cit, p111.
84. See, for example, Trotsky's article 'The Turn in the Communist International and the Situation in Germany', written 26 September 1930, *The Struggle Against Fascism in Germany*, New York, 1971, pp55-74.

the main trade union federation, the CGT. The Socialist Party and the Communist Party joined forces on a huge demonstration.[85] New alliances were forming in response to Fascism's European victories. Though few would admit it, Trotsky's advice was – belatedly – taken.

In May 1934, Benjamin wrote a difficult letter to his friend Scholem. Quite contemptuously, Scholem had challenged Benjamin's commitment to the 'credo' of Communism. Benjamin felt compelled to defend his position by referring to his Communist affiliation as being deeply rooted in his historical experience. He added that his Communist sympathies were distant from orthodox conceptions.[86] He described Communism as a 'lesser evil', in comparison to everything else that surrounded them, and it was to be supported in its 'practical, fruitful form', but not in its dogmatic 'impractical and sterile form'.[87] Such a statement might suggest that Benjamin was impressed by the practical activity on the streets of Paris – the *de facto* alliance between Socialist and Communist trade unionists and militants, as yet unsanctioned by the dogma from Moscow.

In June 1934, there was a United Front agreement between Socialists and Communists in France. In October 1934, it was expanded to include radicals, and in 1935 the policy was made official. According to Dimitrov's and Togliatti's definition, like a vanishing target, the conglomeration of capitalist interests that Fascism was seen to represent was diminishing. This enabled the making of a very broad coalition of anti-Fascist elements. The Popular Front had an elastic concept of who allies might be, and an excessively concentrated idea of the enemy. Two hundred families of finance capitalists, it was argued, had enacted the Nazi obscenity. The Popular Front's programme combined worker's demands with patriotic loyalty to the state. Class politics were out, national defence was in. In this analysis, as in its mirror-reflection, the ultra-left Third Period analysis, the specific conjunctures of class struggle and the nature of the mass labour movement were overlooked. Trotsky denounced the Popular Front in France as a betrayal of the French working class to imperialism. Benjamin, too, saw various dangers in the left's political response. The Popular Front slate won the elections in 1936. Shortly afterwards, strikes began in the city. Communist and Socialist trade union officials and the Communist Party leadership refused to join the strikes, and decided to make accords with the frightened business leaders. By June, 1.5 million workers were on strike. Trotsky stated that the French revolution had begun.[88]

85. See J Danos and M Gibelin, *June '36: Class Struggle and the People's Front in France*, London, 1986, pp33-4.
86. See W Benjamin, *Briefe*, Volume 2, edited by G Scholem and TW Adorno, Frankfurt/Main, 1978, p604; *The Correspondence of Walter Benjamin and Gershom Scholem 1932-1940*, New York, 1989, p109.
87. See op cit, p605; p110.
88. See Cliff, op cit, p204.

Léon Blum's government seized the Trotskyist newspaper that had carried Trotsky's call for the establishment of revolutionary French soviets. The government put the *gardes mobiles* on red alert. Communist, Socialist and radical leaders denounced the strikes and factory occupations as illegal actions. The wave of militancy gradually subsided, as employers plotted their own offensive, bolstered by the government's initiatives against a combative working class.

Both Trotsky and Benjamin opposed the ultra-left lunacy of the Third Period. The adherents of the Third Period thesis proclaimed the imminence of economic catastrophe, and, on the back of that, they insisted, would follow a revolutionary situation. Such a catastrophe was assumed to benefit the organised proletariat. To criticise this concept was not necessarily to fall in line with the politics of the broad alliance. Both Trotsky and Benjamin rebuffed the illusional promises of Social Democracy and the alliance of the forces of Communism and Social Democracy with the liberals which served only to double-cross supporters of both Communism and Social Democracy. Trotsky's polemics against the Popular Front conception of anti-Fascist struggle were matched by Benjamin's scorn for simple alliances with traditional culture and its representatives. In a letter to Alfred Cohn, written in July 1935, Benjamin alluded to the Congress for the Defence of Culture, the great Popular Front effort to bring together respectable, liberal bourgeois writers and Communist Party members. Depressingly, Benjamin considered his encounter with Brecht there as the only positive feature of a conference that had been designed to bring together anti-Fascist intellectuals. In a letter to Alfred Cohn at the close of June 1936, Benjamin described the opposition to his essay *The Work of Art in the Age of its Technical Reproducibility* that had been expressed by emigré writers who were members of the Communist Party. Or rather, he described their silence when he presented his paper to them, and that spoke volumes to him. The recent founding of the journal *Das Wort* in Moscow led to fears on Benjamin's part that the Communist Party's literary policy had become the patronage of *belles-lettres*. In a keynote article, the German Communist Johannes Becher introduced the phrase 'the great turning point' to describe the new party platform in cultural affairs – the policy of literary Popular Frontism. The turning point in question was the turn towards realism, which was also known in conjunction with that popular Stalinist adjective 'great' – 'Great Realism'. Writers were to become in Stalin's words 'engineers of the soul', a cadre at the service of the 'people'. This appeal to Great Realism marked a return to the cultural heritage of the nineteenth century with its classical values of harmony and heroism. It was accompanied not just by the restoration of a bourgeois past, but also by the traditional division between author and public. Culture became a booty that the people expected the artists to rescue. Great Realism and great artists went hand in hand, wrote the realist Romain Rolland. All of this countered Benjamin's ideas of self-organisation, of workers' participation in art, and of the reformulation of artistic practice.

Benjamin followed the political developments in France, and noted his observations in correspondence, often in letters sent to his Christian Communist friend Fritz Lieb. Benjamin was highly critical of developments. In a letter written in July 1937, he stated: 'They all cling solely to the fetish of the "left" majority, and they are not concerned that this majority executes a kind of politics which, if it was being done by the right, would lead to an insurrection.'[89]

Strikes in the following December, led by Doriot's Fascist movement, were further evidence of all sorts of confusions in French class politics. Benjamin attributed the confusion to the activities of the leadership of the working-class movement who had devoted their energies to stifling all potential for escalation. A letter to Fritz Lieb, written in San Remo at the end of December 1937, concluded that the leadership had succeeded in robbing the workers of their elementary sense of instinctive action over the preceding two years. It had destroyed their infallible sense of when and under what conditions a legal action must give way to an illegal one, and when an illegal action must become violent.[90]

In July 1936, a fortnight after the election of the Popular Front government in France, the Spanish Civil War began. By 2 August, Blum had spawned a plan for a non-intervention pact, despite the Spanish republican government's urgent request for aeroplanes and *matériel*. In Spain, the Popular Front policy translated into a subordination of the proletariat to the Spanish bourgeoisie. It eventually led to the liquidation of the militants.[91] The war finished with the final victory of Franco's Fascist troops in 1939. Victor Serge, in his *Memoirs of a Revolutionary*, related how the effect of the Spanish collapse was to provoke a catastrophic moral breakdown in France, as the state and its organs rejected and abused the dispossessed Spanish refugees and interned many in concentration camps, whilst the tattered, confused adherents of the left did little to help.[92] On the other side of Europe, the Nazis were annexing Austria. Hitler triumphantly entered Vienna on 14 March. It was an invasion that met with no resistance, and was the first episode of *Gleichschaltung*. The subsequent

89. Benjamin, *Briefe*, Volume 2, op cit, p732.
90. See Chryssoula Kambas, 'Politische Aktualität: Walter Benjamin's Concept of History and the Failure of the French Popular Front', *New German Critique*, no 39, Fall 1986, pp93-4.
91. For Trotsky's account of events in Spain, see his *The Spanish Revolution 1931-1939*, New York, 1973. See also the collected articles in 'The Spanish Civil War: The View From the Left', *Revolutionary History*, Volume 4, no 1/2, 1992.
92. See Serge, op cit, pp345-6.

plebiscite in Germany and Austria gave the Nazis more than 99 per cent of the vote. Foreign governments voiced little opposition.[93] In a letter to Karl Thieme in March 1938, taking note of events in Austria and Spain, Benjamin alluded to his sense of despair. He wrote:

'As far as I am concerned, I can hardly conceive any longer of suffering or death still making sense. What seems terrible to me, in the case of both Austria and Spain, is that the martyrdom is endured not for the actual cause itself, but rather for a compromise proposal, be it the compromise of Austria's precious ethnic culture with a despicable economy and state, or that of revolutionary thought in Spain with the Machiavellianism of the Russian leadership and the mammonism of the local leadership.'[94]

Leadership in these dark European days was corrupt and compromising. It is as if Benjamin foresaw the possibility of the Ribbentrop-Molotov pact between the Soviet Union and Nazi Germany, sealed in August 1939. There were no alliances that could not be forged — except for the right ones.

1938: Eavesdroppings from Brecht's House

Benjamin's conversations with Brecht recorded their shared interest in Trotsky and the degeneration of the Soviet workers' state. Brecht, on one occasion, showed a poem to Benjamin, *The Peasant to his Ox*. The poem was a death ode to Stalin, but Stalin was not yet dead. Benjamin wrote:

'Brecht, by the way, is not prepared to offer a more enthusiastic form of honour; he is sitting in exile and waiting for the Red Army. He follows the Russian developments, and Trotsky's writings as well. They prove that there is cause for suspicion; a justifiable suspicion, which demands a sceptical consideration of Russian affairs. Such a scepticism stands in the tradition of the classical writers. Should it be proven one day, one would have to fight the regime — publicly. But "unfortunately or thank God, as you will", this suspicion is today not yet a certainty. To derive such a politics from this situation, as the Trotskyists do, is not founded. That, on the other hand, in Russia itself, certain criminal cliques are at work, is not to be doubted.'[95]

Suspicion was the watchword of this purge period. The cliques were forming, but what did they represent? Benjamin and Brecht were keen to

93. See J Joll, *Europe Since 1870; An International History*, London, 1990, pp369-70.
94. Benjamin, *Briefe*, Volume 2, op cit, p747.
95. 'Tagebuchnotizen 1938', *Gesammelte Schriften*, Volume 6, op cit, pp536-7; 'Conversations with Brecht', *Reflections*, op cit, pp215-6.

monitor the Marxist cultural theory emerging from the Soviet Union and its sympathisers. But discussions of literary theory and aesthetics quickly veered into a discussion of cultural policy, and then turned into discussions of politics in a broader sense. Brecht's formulation echoed the Trotskyist assertion that, contrary to Stalin's doctrine, there could be no Socialism in one country. In late July 1938, Benjamin recorded:

'The publications of Lukács, Kurella, *et al*, are giving Brecht a good deal of trouble. He thinks, however, that one ought not to oppose them at the theoretical level. I then put the question on the political level. He does not pull his punches: "A Socialist economy does not need war, and that is why it is opposed to war." The "peace-loving nature of the Russian people" is an expression of this, and nothing else. There cannot be a Socialist economy in one country. Rearmament has inevitably set the proletariat back a lot, back to stages of historical development which have long since been overtaken – amongst others the monarchic stage. Russia is now under personal rule. Only blockheads can deny this.'[96]

And, a few days later, he said again of Lukács, Gabor and Kurella, the leading Communist literary critics. 'With these people', commented Benjamin, 'no state can be formed.' Benjamin recorded Brecht's reply:

'Or only a state, but no communality. They are simply enemies of production. Production gives them the creeps. It cannot be trusted. It is unpredictable. One never knows what will come out of it. And they themselves do not want to produce. They want to play apparatchiks and control others. Each of their criticisms contains a threat.'[97]

Brecht reached the essence of the matter, indicating the bureaucratic mind-casts of the Stalinist-friendly hacks who defended the centralised control of industrial production in the same way as they dictated the terms of cultural production. Self-activity would scare them. Self-activity would mean workers' activity. Autonomy would unbalance the hoped-for sureties of the Five Year Plans, and disrupt the top-heavy recasting of class society. Questions of culture and politics were intertwined. In a conversation about new novels in the Soviet Union, Benjamin admitted that they did not follow what was produced any longer because of the deterioration in literary quality. Cultural work had gone to seed in the Soviet Union. In revolutionary times, revolution bit into the heart of literature. Now there was nothing of aesthetic-technical interest anymore. Bourgeois models were imitated; bureaucratic control insisted the only legitimate subject for art was hero-worshipping. Cultural production

96. Op cit, pp535-6; pp214-5.
97. Op cit, p537; p216.

twisted on a pinhead: 'Then we talk about poetry and the translations of
Soviet Russian poetry from various languages with which *Das Wort* is
flooded. Brecht thinks that the authors over there have a hard time. "It is
seen as a deliberate provocation if the name of Stalin does not appear in
a poem."'

A realisation was dawning on Benjamin and Brecht, but it was such a
cautious admission, and a contradictory one that twisted and turned in
order to disavow the magnitude of the defeat. This reluctance to acknowledge defeat was more perceptible on Brecht's part. It was simply
too catastrophic. Benjamin transcribed Brecht's ambiguous position:

'In Russia, a dictatorship rules over the proletariat. We should avoid dis-
sociating ourselves from this dictatorship for as long as it still does useful
work for the proletariat – that is to say, so long as it contributes towards
a reconciliation between the proletariat and the peasantry, giving prime
recognition to proletarian interests.'

A few days later Brecht spoke of a 'workers' monarchy', and Benjamin
'compared this creature with certain grotesque sorts of nature dredged up
from the depths of the sea in the form of horned fish, or other mon-
sters'.[98]

In a letter to Gretel Adorno, written in July 1938, Benjamin criticised
the intellectual poverty of Johannes Becher's party-line journal *Internationale Literatur*. He was offended by the journal's equation of his work
with Heidegger's philosophy, on the basis of an extract from an early
piece of writing.[99] In the letter, Benjamin confirmed Brecht's view that
the theoretical line imposed by Russian cultural politics spelt catastrophe
for everything that they had been defending for the last 20 years.[100]

Finally, the evidence was incontrovertible: 'There can't be any doubt
about it any longer: the struggle against ideology has become a new ideology.'[101]

Back To the End Again: 1940 And Death

I am told that you raised your hand against yourself
Anticipating the butcher.
After eight years of exile, observing the rise of the enemy
Then at last, brought up against an impassable frontier
You passed, they say, a passable one.

98. Op cit, p539; p219.
99. See Benjamin, *Briefe*, Volume 2, op cit, p771.
100. See op cit, p772.
101. Benjamin, 'Tagebuchnotizen 1938', op cit, p538; 'Conversations with Brecht', op cit,
p217.

Empires collapse. Gang leaders
are strutting about like statesmen. The peoples
Can no longer be seen under all those armaments.

So the future lies in darkness and the forces of right
Are weak. All this was plain to you
When you destroyed a torturable body.

Brecht, *On the Suicide of the Refugee WB*

Exhaustion tactics were what pleased you,
Sitting at the chess table in the shadow of the pear tree.
The enemy, who chased you from your books
Does not allow himself to be exhausted by our kind.

Brecht, *Walter Benjamin, Who Took His Life While Fleeing Hitler*

In 1939 and 1940, Benjamin worked on one of his last pieces, a series of gnomic vignettes known in English as *Theses on the Philosophy of History*. One of the theses divulged the significance of this short final fragment:

'At a moment when the politicians in whom the opponents of Fascism had placed their hopes are prostrate, and confirm their defeat by betraying their own cause, these observations are intended to disentangle the political worldlings from the snares in which the traitors have entrapped them.'[102]

The political worldlings were the European proletarians, and the identities of the betrayers were the politicians who failed to mobilise effectively against Fascism. This failure resulted in the French Communist Party (PCF) and the German Communist Party (KPD) exiles in France welcoming Hitler as Stalin's ally. With their non-aggression pact in August 1939, Hitler and Stalin divided Poland, and the pact gave the German army a free hand on the Western front. The leadership of the PCF called for capitulation, and justified this 'theoretically' by positing Fascism as a necessary historical phase. Just like the Social Democrats in the late nineteenth century, the Communist Party 'was happy to play for the working class the rôle of a saviour of *future* generations'. Benjamin's reaction was a refusal to side with those on the left who underestimated the destructiveness and violence of Fascism for the specific forces in history at *that* moment. This was the basis of Benjamin's attack on a belief in progress. Benjamin disputed the crass, undialectical idea of progress, which he saw perpetrated both philosophically and historiographically by political

102. Benjamin, *Gesammelte Schriften*, Volume 1/2, Frankfurt, 1991, p698; *Illuminations*, op cit, pp249-50.

creeds across the spectrum. He depicted catastrophic progress in the image of a storm that blows humanity off any just course. Progress as concept, he insists, needs to be broken down and specified. Progress for whom, and at what cost? Benjamin was unable to participate in any Marxist account that saw history as moving inexorably, automatically and progressively towards Socialism. Such thinking had resulted in disaster:

'Our consideration proceeds from the insight that the politicians' stubborn faith in progress, their confidence in their "mass base" and finally their servile integration into an uncontrollable apparatus have been three aspects of the same thing. It seeks to formulate a concept of how dear our usual thinking is when it tries to cast an image of history that avoids every complicity with that to which these politicians remain wedded.'[103]

Benjamin identified a dual carriageway of Social Democratic and Stalinist thought in the years before and after the Nazi *Machtergreifung*. Comintern orthodoxy had defined Fascism as the final stage of capitalism on the road to collapse. The Stalinist road was undeniably zigzagged, as alliances were forged and broken *en route*. But always, Communism was just around the next corner. Onwards and upwards! The Social Democrats' underlying dogma held faith with the permanently progressive nature of history, the ever-developing forces of production and technical progress, and an automatic mass base. A central contention of the KPD was that Nazism represented a bourgeois counter-revolutionary movement, a purely defensive step against an insurgent working class, close to revolutionary victory. In his *Theses on the Philosophy of History*, Benjamin challenged this notion of an insurgent proletariat. He made reference to the conformism of the working class. The working class had been corrupted by the notion that they were 'swimming with the current' of history. Organised elements of the class were shocked by what seemed to be a sudden turning of the tide. Trotsky likewise admitted the dismal state of the German organised working class, much shaken by the mistakes of its leadership.

In his unparalleled commentaries on Germany in the 1930s, Trotsky considered the impact of Fascism on all classes. Fascism, he declared, expressed the interests of finance capital at the time of a crisis of profitability and difficulties in the realisation of surplus value in monopoly capitalism. He accounted for the swelling ranks of the National German Socialist Workers Party by pointing to the deep social crisis of capitalism that threw the petit-bourgeois masses into disarray. He noted that the working class was on the defensive by the time Fascism dug in, and not,

103. Op cit.

as the KPD would have it, on the offensive. But neither Trotsky nor Benjamin assumed that this defeat was irreversible. The final victory of the proletariat was not written in the stars. But the possibility remained of a renewed offensive on the part of the working class. Trotsky recognised that there was a split between Fascism as a movement, resting on a petit-bourgeois base, and Fascism as a regime, organised around an economic restructuring in favour of certain sections of capital. That split was a crack of light. Benjamin translated this hope into a messianic hope for redemption. He called for an intervention into history. It demanded actors, those who were 'man enough to explode the continuum of history open'.[104] Who was man enough? The angel blown in by the storm of progress was incapable of reassembling the debris of a world gone awry. Such restitution became the job of the 'historical materialist' who remembered past dismemberments, and it was the task of the 'subject of historical knowledge', the 'fighting, oppressed class itself', which was Marx's revenging class.[105]

In his introduction to the Pathfinder edition of Trotsky's writings on German Fascism, Ernest Mandel discusses the historiographical relevance of Fascism in terms that are remarkably close to Benjamin's. Mandel calls Fascism a 'new phenomenon' which appeared suddenly and 'seemed sharply to reverse a long-term historical trend of progress'. He continues:

'The shock experienced by attentive observers was all the greater because this historical reversal was accompanied by the even more direct brutality of physical violence against individuals. Historical and individual fate suddenly became identical for thousands of human beings, and later, for millions. Not only were social classes defeated and not only did political parties succumb, but the existence, the physical survival, of broad human groups suddenly became problematical.'[106]

Mandel's words evoke Benjamin. As a Marxist, as a Jew and as a critical intellectual, Benjamin partook of the same tragic fate as thousands of others. He was forced into exile, interned and persecuted. Mandel uses the word 'shock' to describe the arrival of Fascism. One of Benjamin's central concepts was the notion of shock, and the designation of shock experience as a way of life in capitalism itself. Shock is at the core of the experience of industrial modernity. Mandel speaks of reversal, the interruption of a complacent belief in progress. Benjamin took this idea further, debunking historical progress, and also unmasking it as a compelling myth in capitalism. Within capitalism, argued Benjamin, progress is

104. Op cit, p702; p254.
105. Op cit, p700; p251.
106. E Mandel, 'Introduction' to Trotsky, *The Struggle Against Fascism in Germany*, op cit, p9.

illusory and ideological. For every inch of progress on a technological level under these relations of production, the oppressed suffer regression on a social level, like Marx's understanding of machinery as potential liberator, which at *this* moment, under *this* organisation of relations of production, only intensifies our exploitation and often our discomfort.

Benjamin cut apart history and 'tradition', the tales of the dispossessed and oppressed. Tradition includes the rite of revolutionary remembrance, the command to recollect the history of the oppressed, and never to forget it. Terry Eagleton reminds us that Trotsky said: 'We Marxists have always lived in tradition.' There are always battles over the content of tradition. The struggle is to yank the power of tradition clear of the ruling class lineages in which it is constrained, and to slice sideways into time, dashing the endless continuum of ruling class propagandism, in which the oppressed are encouraged to empathise with the rulers. Tear through this, combining a moment of the crisis-rocked present with a redeemed fragment of the tradition of the oppressed; in other words, to disrupt ruling-class history without spilling tradition. In his theses on the philosophy of history, Benjamin relayed a phrase now much quoted: 'There is not one document of culture which is not at the same time a document of barbarism.' Its sentiment reverberates in Trotsky's perceptive warning against an indiscriminate celebration of tradition. The cultural legacy must be viewed from a dialectical perspective. Culture's contradictions are historically formed. Civilisation's achievements supply knowledge of humanity and nature, but they also conserve social cleavage. Only social struggle illuminates the textured surfaces of progress.

And so the purpose of this essay is revealed — as a contribution to a social struggle over the progress of a legacy. For, whilst Trotsky has been sold short here, in ridiculously brief readings of his cultural theory and political judgements, at least we have pulled Benjamin out of the political black hole into which he has been cast by contemporary academics.

James T Farrell

A Memoir of Leon Trotsky

I MET Leon Trotsky in Mexico in 1937. He seemed different from what might have been expected. He gave the impression of extraordinary simplicity. Alice Rühle – wife of Otto Rühle, one-time left-wing Socialist member of the German Reichstag and biographer of Karl Marx – said of Trotsky that he had changed from his younger days: he had, she said, become more simple, more like Lenin.[107] Many who knew him earlier said that he was cold. He did not seem so in Mexico. He was easy to talk to, and one felt less distance between him and oneself than is sometimes the case when one meets a man prominent in political life. But this comparison is perhaps not a good one. Trotsky was then a defeated leader, and a man in exile. He was seeking to rebuild a political movement, and was engaged in the most dramatic fight of his life. Accused of betraying the revolution he helped to lead and the society he did so much in helping to found, he was defending his revolutionary honour. He lived behind guarded walls, and followers and secretaries of his carried guns inside his home. He was preparing to answer the charges Stalin launched against him in the Moscow Trials.

Elsewhere I have described the Coyoacan hearings held by the Commission of Inquiry of which Dr John Dewey was chairman.[108] I shall not repeat this here, but shall merely offer a few personal impressions and anecdotes about him.

One could not separate Trotsky the man from Trotsky the historical figure. When you saw him and spoke with him, you were aware that he was the man who organised the practical details of the Bolshevik revolution in 1917, and also that he was the organiser of the Red Army. You were aware that you were speaking with one of the greatest revolutionaries in history. He himself had a deep sense of history and of his own historic rôle. The intense drama of his life was known to me. There he was in that home on Avenida Londres in Coyoacan, pitting his brain against an empire. It was because he was Trotsky that his simplicity was so striking when he was grey and living like a hunted man in Mexico. His followers spoke of him in worshipful tones. For them, he made life more

---

107. Otto Rühle (1874-1943) was subsequently a founder of the German Communist Party, and went with those who split away in 1919 to form the ultra-left Communist Workers Party of Germany. He later came to consider that parties constituted a barrier to the success of the class struggle.

108. See 'John Dewey in Mexico' in my book, *Reflections At Fifty and Other Essays*, New York, 1954. [Farrell's note]

important. He permitted them to believe that they, too, were entering history. They called him 'the Old Man', and they acted like disciples. Constantly, they would pose questions to ascertain what one thought of him, and when John Dewey remarked on Trotsky's brilliance, they immediately began thinking and hoping that Trotsky would convert Dewey to Trotskyism.

There was an exactness about Trotsky. Even in English, his choice of words revealed this. He seemed to know how far he wanted to go with each person, and his choice of words conveyed or suggested this. There was not, however, much spontaneity in him — or, rather, his spontaneity was kept in check. He, himself, had given his life to an Idea. This Idea — the Revolution — and his personality were as though fused together. A brave man, he was always ready to make any sacrifice to the Idea, and he dealt with people in terms of their relationship to and their acceptance of the Idea. What use would they be to this Idea, this cause? He was working for and living for the cause.

Thus, whilst he was easy to talk to, it yet remained that there was a distance between him and others. You did not come into contact with his full personality as you did with, say, John Dewey. This seemed most clear to me the last time I spoke with him. We sat by the long table on which he worked in the home of the painter, Diego Rivera, on Avenida Londres in Coyoacan. He asked me what I was going to do when I returned to America.

'I'm going to write novels.'

He said he knew that, but again asked me what I was going to do. The service to the cause was more important to him than your personality. Max Eastman, who knew him much better than I did, has often said that he was cold. This I believe is what Eastman means, this seeing individuals as servants to an aim and an idea rather than as personalities in their own right.[109] And this was a trait in his character which marked him off as so different from John Dewey.

He was a witty, graceful, and gallant man. There was something deeply touching and inspiring in his relationship with his wife, Natalia. She was very small and elegant. One could see that she had once been a beautiful woman. The tragedies of her life, the loss of her children in particular, had saddened her. Hers was one of the saddest faces I have ever seen, and she is one of the bravest and noblest of women. Whenever you saw them together, you could not but sense how there was a current of tenderness between them. A gentleness and depth of feeling was apparent in the way he looked at her or touched her hand.

109. Max Eastman (1883-1969) helped to publish Trotsky's writings in the USA, and continued to translate his works into English after he had broken from him politically in the mid-1930s.

We went on a picnic with him after the ending of the Coyoacan hearings. Waiting to leave and standing on the porch of the patio of the Rivera home, there was Trotsky bustling about, making sure that there was enough food for everyone, that there was beer for me, that nothing would be forgotten or overlooked. My wife said to me teasingly that Trotsky took an interest in his home and that if he could, why couldn't I? He came up to me a moment later. I remarked: 'LD, you have ruined my life.' I explained what I meant, and told him what my wife had said.

'It is very simple', he answered, speaking with a strong accent. 'Once' – pronouncing it like *vunce* – 'I had to feed five million men. It is a little more complicated than feeding five.' Often there was a point, a political reference, a moral in his wit.

We left for a nearby wood in two cars. My wife and I got into the back seat of a roadster. All was in readiness for our departure. Suddenly, Trotsky appeared at the side of the car and said: 'Jim, I will' – the *w* pronounced like a *v* – 'ride in the open car, and Hortense will ride in the closed car.'

There was gallantry here. For Trotsky to ride in an open car meant a possible risk to his life. Along with his gallantry, there was in his nature a deep respect for women. I have met many Europeans of the left and of the revolution, and I have read much of their lives and been told many anecdotes about them. Many of these men, without being quite aware of it, have given the best years of their lives to an effort to emancipate mankind. But with a good proportion of them, emancipation stops at the door of their own homes. Their wives are not completely included in this emancipation; they do all of the housework and serve their revolutionary husbands, sometimes slavishly. In one place in his recent biography *The Prophet Armed: Trotsky 1879-1921*, Isaac Deutscher mentions how Trotsky, busy as he was, would in a very un-European fashion, help Natalia with the housework and the care of the children. Trotsky's gallantry was, I believe, real, and it was based on a sense of the dignity of women and of respect for them.

At the picnic, Trotsky and Natalia went off to walk in the woods in opposite directions. This was undoubtedly a solace to him. He lived a guarded life of confinement with little freedom of movement. His secretaries constantly guarded him, with guns in holsters at their side. A contingent of Mexican police stood outside the Rivera home to protect him. He fretted and balked in this confinement, and he was fatalistic about the danger of his being assassinated. He believed that when Stalin wanted really and finally to have him murdered, Stalin would undoubtedly succeed. And as is known, this happened.

After taking the walk, he returned to the group. One of the Americans present was building a fire. He was an ex-follower of Trotsky's who had left the Trotsky movement, but who had come to Coyoacan to help the work of the Dewey hearings. Trotsky watched him for a moment and became impatient. He didn't like the way the American friend was going about making the fire. He took over and made his own fire, accompanying it with raillery that was friendly but also sharp. And there was a political point to this. Trotsky was teasing a one-time follower for having broken ideologically with the Trotskyite movement. Trotsky always liked to tease Americans, especially about so-called American efficiency, and he also teased his American ex-follower in this vein.

We ate and talked and sang. One of Trotsky's police guards was a tall, young, and good-looking Mexican cop. Trotsky liked and trusted him. This policeman sang 'El Rancho Grande', and everyone liked it so much that he was asked to sing it again. After Trotsky was murdered, I was told that this policeman had been bought by enemies of Trotsky's.

I had several talks with him. Having been an American in the 1920s, and having read my HL Mencken, I sometimes took a relish in telling stories which recounted stupidity.[110] I told a story of this kind. The subject was a famous European writer with whom Trotsky had had controversies. This writer is not stupid, but he appeared this way because he had been evading questions concerning Stalin that would have pinned him down. Trotsky became quickly impatient and didn't want to hear the end of the story. It bored him. He interrupted and said: 'X should learn how to write better novels.'

He asked questions about American literature and spoke of having read *Babbitt*, but his admiration for Lewis' book was qualified. The character of Babbitt seemed unintelligent to him.[111] I spoke of Dreiser whom I praised as a great writer but whose philosophical and general ideas I thought sometimes banal.[112] Trotsky asked how could a man be a great writer if his ideas were stupid. 'What American writers need', he said, 'is a new perspective.'

He meant a Marxian perspective. He believed that America would one day have a great Marxist renaissance. Actually, he hadn't read enough of American literature to know whether American writers did or did not need a new perspective. His statement was a consequence of the confidence of faith. Marxism was a science to him, and it permitted him to predict in faith.

Speaking of how Americans viewed him, I said that many saw him as a romantic figure, in fact as a romantic hero. He said that he knew this,

---

110. HL Mencken (1880-1956) was an editor and satirist.
111. Harry Sinclair Lewis (1885-1951) was a novelist who satirised the small-town complacency of American life. His book *Babbitt*, published in 1922, described a businessman completely drained of all his individuality.
112. Theodore Dreiser (1871-1945) was an American radical writer who became a fellow-traveller of Stalinism in the 1930s. He joined the Communist Party, and converted to Christianity in 1945.

and disliked being so regarded. He wasn't interested in my explanation of how it happened that he seemed to some Americans a romantic figure.

Just before the beginning of the first of the hearings of the Dewey Commission, Trotsky was standing on the porch outside his workroom. The divorced wife of a famous American writer crashed the gate, and, inside the home, she went up to Trotsky. She told him that he didn't know who she was and then identified herself by giving her former husband's name.

'I am sure', responded Trotsky, 'that if I did know, I should be most impressed.'

Another time, I asked him if he thought that Stalin and Hitler would get together. This was in 1937, and some of us who had engaged in the bitter fight against the Moscow Trials had come to believe that a Nazi-Soviet alliance was going to be made. Trotsky answered by remarking that if this happened, it would be a great catastrophe. Around that time, he predicted the Stalin-Hitler Pact.

My publisher, James Henle, an old newspaper man, had worked on the *New York World* in 1917. He had been sent to interview Trotsky, then in New York, and they had met in a bakery on the East Side. Trotsky had struck Henle as an intelligent man. He had predicted the Russian Revolution. But as Henle tells the story, he heard endless predictions in those days. A month later, the February Revolution in Russia happened. Trotsky did not remember this interview.

The last time I saw him, I went to his home on the day before I left Mexico. When I arrived he was talking with Otto Rühle in his office. Rühle had stood with Karl Liebknecht during the First World War. When the Bolshevik Revolution succeeded, Rühle had characterised it as a 'pacifist putsch'. He and Trotsky had almost never agreed, it seemed. There they were, two old revolutionaries in exile in Mexico. They still disagreed, and speaking in German, their voices rose. I heard Trotsky talking loudly, in fact shouting. I couldn't understand a word of German, but I could guess what they were arguing about. Rühle was still, in Mexico, determined to press his disagreement with the Bolsheviks of 1917. I was told that soon after this Otto Rühle and Trotsky stopped seeing each other.

The lunch was simple, but less so than normal. Trotsky was a most gracious host. There was not much talk and then we said goodbye. He went to take an afternoon siesta.

His was one of the fastest working minds I have ever encountered. And just to see and talk to him, one had a sense of a great will. His body, his habits were bent to that will. In many ways, he was Spartan. There were times in fact during his days of power when he spoke like a man of a modern Sparta, and Isaac Deutscher uses the word Spartan in reference to Trotsky at one point in his biography.

This memoir is passing and random. It does not treat of Trotsky's theories and ideas. This I shall try to discuss on another occasion. Here, I merely wished to set down passing impressions of Trotsky. His personality was not only strong but highly attractive. He was very gracious. There was a mocking look in his bright eyes, and I had the feeling that he looked out on life with a kind of mockery and irrepressible sense of irony. He had committed himself to an Idea, and he had risen to heights of power that few men know. And then, there he was, back in exile. Most of his life was spent in exile. In Siberia, Turkey, England, France, Italy, Germany, Switzerland, Austria, Norway, he had been an exile – writing, talking, urging, serving a burning idea with total conviction.

He was strikingly different from many exiles. Revolutionary exiles frequently decay and disintegrate. Trotsky didn't. No man could have known a defeat more total than he. It was amazing how little it damaged him. Writing, fighting the same battle, he didn't seem like an embittered or unhappy man. I thought of this, and how different are the stories of Napoleon's exile. Trotsky was a man who might be compared to Napoleon. But in exile, Napoleon bore the strains and the isolation less well than Trotsky. With Napoleon, power was all. To Trotsky, power was the means of making his ideas possible. It was the means whereby man achieved his historic destiny. Power was the arm of a faith. That faith served him in exile.

I was in the hospital, weak and worn, following an operation for a carbuncle. It was night. A radio was on at the head of my bed. I was not listening to it. There was a news broadcast. About half of the words penetrated my mind. 'Leon Trotsky... assassin... not expected to live.'

I was shocked. I couldn't sleep and was given a pill. The next morning, I woke up with a feeling of guilt. I had had some dream. Then the news vendor came, and there was the story of the murder. His life was like a Greek tragedy. He was a great hero and a great martyr. But the tragic character of Trotsky's death only focuses on great and terrible tragedy of our century. Such burning conviction, such brilliance, such Spartan sacrifice as his – and it went to create a state that evolved into the most terrible tyranny in history. Today, the state which he helped to create stands threatening the freedom of all of us. The values we cherish, the hopes of man for a more decent world, these are now threatened by that powerful state.[113] Trotsky and Lenin were amongst the great men of this century. But has it ever been that the work, the life of two great men has ended in such brutal and inhuman tyranny? The ironies of their stories are written

113. It should be remembered that by the time Farrell wrote this memoir, he had broken from the Trotskyist left, and was chairing the Committee for Cultural Freedom, which was discreetly bankrolled by the CIA. He subsequently joined the Social Democrats USA.

in blood and suffering. It is now almost 37 years since they were the leaders of the October Revolution. And as we can look back, it seems from this particular vantage point that we could be no worse off if their work and their achievement had never been. The horrors of Tsardom are as nothing to those which succeeded it.

Trotsky walked in his garden. The sun was shining. The afternoon was at the point of beginning to wane. He went into his work room and sat down with the manuscript his assassin had brought him. The Alpine stock was driven into his brain. His blood fell on a page of the manuscript of his biography of Stalin. The last words he had written were 'the idea'. His own blood spilled on that page.

Leon Trotsky

Marcel Martinet

This tribute to Marcel Martinet was written by Trotsky for the special issue on Martinet of *Les Humbles*, Volume 21 no 1-2-3, January-March 1936, pp81-3, and republished in *Le Pont de l'Épée*, no 6-7, May 1959, pp13-15. Martinet (1887-1944), a poet, novelist and dramatist, was aligned with the revolutionary Syndicalists before 1914, and opposed the First World War from the outset. He was literary editor of *L'Humanité* in 1921; later, despite poor health, he was consistently aligned with the anti-Stalinist left. In November 1936, Martinet wrote to André Gide offering his support after Gide was attacked by the Stalinists for his criticisms of the Soviet regime, see A Gide, *Afterthoughts on the USSR* (London, nd [1937]), pp140-1. His play *La Nuit*[114] was discussed by Trotsky in the article 'A Drama of the French Working Class' in *Leon Trotsky on Literature and Art*, New York, 1970, pp148-61.

OUR personal connection did not last long; we met on several occasions at the beginning of the Great War. We were both 20 years younger than we are now, and what years they were! I knew Marcel Martinet first of all as a revolutionary, and only later as a poet. At the meetings of the handful of internationalists, on the quai Jemmapes, in what were the premises of the *Vie Ouvrière*[115] of those days, Marcel Martinet was perhaps the most silent of all. He would take his place at the very end of the table, not only, perhaps, out of modesty, but so as to

114. There is an English translation by Eden and Cedar Paul, *Night*, London, 1927.
115. The revolutionary Syndicalist journal founded in 1909 by Pierre Monatte. It later became the official CGT organ.

have a better position from which to observe: in him the artist lived side by side with the revolutionary, and they both knew how to act in harmony. A magnificent silky beard seemed to have no other function than to bring out the childlike clarity of his eyes. The artist's contemplative look was warmed to life by the hidden flame of the rebel. Beneath his gentle gaze you could detect depth and fidelity. His whole being breathed simplicity, intelligence, and nobility of mind. Automatically you wanted to come closer to this man, to deserve his trust and his friendship. But events separated us before friendship had time to take shape.

How and when did I first receive Martinet's poetry and his play? Possibly it was through Rosmer.[116] In any case, it was after the October Revolution, during the years of the Civil War. Martinet's works burst into the stormy atmosphere in which I was then living, like a ray of light from a Paris that was distant and yet close. All the problems of the French revolutionary movement were brought back to life for me in a creative transposition. I read Martinet in the military train in which I was living during those years; I read with great pleasure and passionate sympathy for the author, and my article on his play was dictated to my dear and faithful assistant, Glasmann, whom, later on, Stalin hounded down to his death.[117]

The publication of the article in *Pravda*[118] must have coincided with one of my appearances in Moscow, since I have a very clear memory of Lenin's expression of amused astonishment when we met in the morning: 'A whole article on some play! What's all this about?' And he pointed in a reproachful fashion to the newly appeared paper. And it was true that at the time our life seemed to be moving along paths that were far removed from poetry and theatre. In order to justify myself, I spoke about Martinet, my relations with him at the beginning of the war, and the meetings on the quai Jemmapes. I don't know if it was on this occasion or another that Lenin unexpectedly asked me: 'But couldn't we advise the French Communists to throw out those corrupt parliamentarians Cachin[119] and Frossard,[120] and replace them with the *Vie Ouvrière* group?' Unfortunately, it was a solution that it was impossible to apply...

116. Alfred Rosmer (1877-1964) was a revolutionary Syndicalist and a leading figure in the early Comintern, and was expelled from the PCF in 1924.
117. Warning to M Romain Rolland: This remarkable young man, a wholly untarnished character, a true hero, killed himself with a revolver shot in 1924, being unwilling to bear the infamy of the deliberately lying accusations made against him. He was persecuted solely because he didn't want to be either a traitor or a false witness. [Note by Trotsky]
118. In fact, it appeared in *Izvestia*, 16 May 1922. An English translation appeared in *Labour Monthly*, August 1922.
119. Marcel Cachin (1869-1958) was a Socialist deputy before 1914, a fervent nationalist during the war, a founder member of the PCF, and subsequently a loyal Stalinist.
120. Ludovic-Oscar Frossard (1889-1946) was Secretary of the PCF during 1921-23; he later rejoined the SFIO, and then became a minister in Pétain's first government.

During my recent stay in France, I followed closely what Martinet was writing, and I was still as always won over by the freshness of his perception of people and things, by his style which is both cautious and confident, and above all by the organic combination in him of the poet and the revolutionary...

How splendid it is that Marcel Martinet has nothing in common with those gentlemen who express their devotion to the Soviets all the more noisily because they have been very late in discovering their revolutionary soul! Martinet is too honest, he can't play a rôle, he can't dress himself up in someone else's coat. He hasn't *become* a friend of the October Revolution through some sudden revelation, he was one even before it happened. And at present, he still has an indestructible fidelity towards it which is far deeper and more certain than anything that could be felt by all the 'friends' of the bureaucratic Kremlin and of... the Moscow State Publishing House.

The situation in France is confused, tense and alarming. But however bewildered the working masses may be at the moment by the cowardly lies of the Cachins and Blums,[121] the Jouhauxes[122] and Monmousseaus,[123] the French proletariat will emerge from 'the night', and find its road to victory. And in the list of those who have prepared the way for this victory, it will strike out many arrogant and redundant names, but in a place of honour it will inscribe the name of Marcel Martinet.

From a snow-covered Norwegian village, I send him my fraternal greetings.

Leon Trotsky

The Attitude of Men of Letters[124]

Dear Comrade Pfemfert

Thank you very much for the newspaper cuttings you sent me. To avoid any misunderstanding, I should like to draw your attention, and that of our other friends, to the fact that M Puntervold is *only* my lawyer; politically, he is a long way from me, so that our relations are confined to the

121. Léon Blum (1872-1950) was the leader of the Socialist Party, and was Prime Minister of the Popular Front government in 1936.
122. Léon Jouhaux (1879-1954) was the Secretary General of the CGT during 1909-40. He supported the First World War, and led the Force Ouvrière split in 1947.
123. Gaston Monmousseau (1883-1960) was a former Anarchist trade unionist, and later a loyal Stalinist.
124. Letter dated 9 October 1936 to Franz Pfemfert. Translated from the French version of the German original.

trial.[125] For general political questions, write via the passport office. The great Heinrich Mann,[126] as far as I can see, is invoking his 'imagination' to justify his grovelling servility. Which 'imagination', precisely, are we dealing with? That which opens up the possibility of actively foreseeing great events? Or that which allows one to adapt comfortably to facts that are established and already fossilised? This second sense of the term is very much the style of French academicians who, thanks to their senile 'imagination', discover extraordinary virtues even in the Prince of Monaco. Marx, Engels and Lenin showed magnificent contempt for adulators and sycophants, even if they were very much 'on the left', if they invoked their aristocratic privileges as poets or whatever else to hide under the table when times were difficult. You can even find in Marx's correspondence some sarcastic phrases about a man like Freiligrath with his 'poet on a higher tower'.[127]

I think I'm going to embark on a lawsuit in Czechoslovakia if we can come to a complete agreement on this matter with Doctor B Bill.[128] I've already sent him a power of attorney. We ought to have a meeting. But is it possible?

My best wishes to AI[129] and yourself.

Of course, you can make whatever use you see fit of this letter, or of any part of it.

---

125. Michael Puntervold had left the Norwegian Labour Party to the right, and had later returned to it, but no longer played any political rôle.
126. Heinrich Mann (1871-1950), a German dramatist and novelist, had left Germany as an anti-Fascist, but was giving support to the first Moscow Trial.
127. Ferdinand Freiligrath (1810-1876), a republican and Socialist poet, had been a passionate supporter of Marx. However, the latter in a letter to Engels of 7 June 1859 directed a stream of insults at him (K Marx and F Engels, *Collected Works*, Volume 40, p458). In 1841, in a poem entitled 'Aus Spanien' ('From Spain'), Freiligrath had written:

> Der Dichter steht auf einer höheren Warte
> Als auf den Zinnen der Partei.
> (The poet stands on a higher watch-tower
> Than on the battlements of the party.)

A polemic ensued which was provoked by the reply to Freiligrath from the poet Georg Herwegh (1817-1875) in his *Poems of a Living Man* (1842). In a letter to Weydemeyer of 16 January 1852, Marx was brimming over with praise for Freiligrath (*Collected Works*, Volume 39, p8).
128. Friedrich Bill had been in contact with the Trotskyists since at least 1933. In August, he had signed the appeal of the Committee for Justice and Truth, and had taken the necessary procedures for a legal action against several Stalinist papers appearing in Czechoslovakia — *Meztikor* (the Czech edition of *Inprekorr*), *Rudé Pravo*, the central organ of the Czech Communist Party, and *Die Rote Fahne*. A hearing to examine the possibility of conciliation had been fixed for 21 December.
129. Alexandra Ivanovna Ramm, Franz Pfemfert's wife.

An Interview with Jean Malaquais

In 1939, Trotsky wrote an article in praise of Jean Malaquais' first novel, *Les Javanais*, a 'proletarian novel' describing the life of immigrant workers in the lead and silver mines of Provence. It was published in English as *The Men from Java* (London, 1941). This article is reproduced in *Leon Trotsky on Literature and Art*, New York, 1970, pp225-34. There are also a couple of brief letters[130] commending Malaquais. This interview with Malaquais, conducted by François de Massot, appeared in *Informations Ouvrières*, no 220, 28 February-5 March 1996. Malaquais maintained his integrity and his revolutionary principles to the day of his death on 22 December 1998 (see James Kirkup, 'Jean Malaquais', *Independent*, 6 January 1999; Michel Lequenne, 'Jean Malaquais, réedite au crepuscule de sa vie: *Les Chef* – ouvre d'une littérature de sous-prolétaire', *Rouge*, 11 February 1999; Fabienne, 'Jean Malaquais', *World Revolution*, March 1999).

IO: Your first novel, *Les Javanais*, is set in France. What was your first contact with France?

JM: When I had taken my school-leaving exams, at the age of 17, I left Poland and my family. However, paradoxical it may seem today, my intention of seeing the world was also a determination to move outside the world of books. My father taught Latin and Greek, and I grew up surrounded by books. I wanted to know something different. I travelled across Romania, Poland, Palestine...

But my real aim was to get to Paris. For me, as for many people, France was the homeland of the Rights of Man, of freedom and the Commune. I was in Paris on 14 July. What else was there to do but go to the Place de la Bastille? Just before dawn, I went to get some sleep under the awning of a roundabout. I was – in brutal fashion – dragged out by two policemen, who took me to the police station. As my papers were in order, they had to let me go again. I was unwise enough to ask one of the policemen why he had hurt me. In reply I got a smack across the face that knocked me right off my feet... It left an indelible mark on me. Of course, cops are the same all over the world, but France has a particular 'aura' about it.

IO: And how, after this experience and the rejection of your books, was it possible to become a writer?

JM: I survived by working at night in the Paris food market. I spent my

130. Letters dated 19 June 1939 and 9 August 1939, *Oeuvres*, Volume 21, p226, p380.

days in the Sainte-Geneviève library. One day, in October 1935, I found by accident an extract from Gide's *Journal*, an extract dated March 1935. Gide regretted the fact that he had never had to 'work for his living'; he had thus been deprived of an essential experience. These remarks threw me into a terrible rage.

I wrote to tell him that he didn't know what he was talking about, that if he had had his hands in the grease of the factory, there would have been one proletarian more, but one writer less... He replied to me. We met. He told me: 'You must write.' He encouraged me and helped me. We remained friends until he died...

IO: Your novel *Les Javanais* appeared in 1939. You won the Théophraste Renaudot prize. Leon Trotsky wrote to you very enthusiastically...

JM: Yes. I only found out about the letter and his article later on, as I had been called up. I think also that Trotsky was impressed by the fact that in the book Stalin appears as the incarnation of evil.

On this point, let me tell you an anecdote. My book has been translated into Hungarian. In the text, Trotsky's name appears repeatedly. Now the name of Trotsky does not appear in my novel: it had been brought in to replace Stalin by the publishers who were under the Stalinists' thumb. I have never been a member of a Trotskyist organisation. But there is one point on which I will take no argument. For me, Stalinism is the supreme form of counter-revolution, the vomit of the earth.

IO: If you didn't receive the letter Leon Trotsky sent you, there was another point of contact. You wrote a book called *Planet Without a Visa*,[131] which dealt with the fate of refugees stuck in Marseilles in 1941 waiting for a visa. Now 'The Planet Without a Visa' is the title of the final chapter of Trotsky's autobiography, *My Life*.

JM: Of course. And I lived this experience. It was at the very last moment that I was able to get to Mexico, by way of Venezuela. There, I became a friend of Natalia Trotsky, who was a remarkable woman.

IO: When you returned to France, in 1947, when *Planet Without a Visa* appeared, the Éditions Spartacus also published a pamphlet by you called *Louis Aragon, Professional Patriot*. You were not very kind towards the official poet of the French Communist Party. Many things have happened since then. Do you still stand by your position?

JM: Absolutely. The Stalinists, who hadn't hesitated to get into bed with the Nazis at the time of the Hitler-Stalin Pact (which Aragon supported), wanted to present themselves as the only 'anti-Fascists'. Aragon went so far as to demand Gide's head. I repeat, the crimes of Stalinism are

131. *Planète sans visa*, Paris, 1947; translated as *World Without a Visa*, London, 1949.

abominable. The worst thing is that it has discredited for a long time – perhaps for a century – the very idea of a classless society.

IO: So, after all these experiences, what would you say in particular to the youth of today?

JM: That under no circumstances, despite everything, should they accept this society, this society which, in the name of money, crushes and mutilates. They must rebel – I don't mean by that breaking windows, but refusing this system which is worse than slavery, and what goes with it, xenophobia, something which makes my book completely contemporary. That is why, after having lived through this century, I can say: 'I'm a dirty foreigner, it's my main claim to fame.'

Books Wanted

Please write to us if you can provide us with any of these

Belfort Bax, *The Legal Subjection of Men*
Elspeth Cameron, *Earle Birney: A Life*
Contre le Courant, Facsimile Reprint
Mika Etchebehere, *Ma Guerre D'Espagne a Moi*
Peter Kropotkin, *Memoirs*
VI Lenin, *Collected Works*, part ii of index
James Malloy, *Bolivia: The Uncompleted Revolution*
Ivan Maistrenko, *Borotbism: A Chapter in the History of Ukrainian Communism*
Karl Marx, *Ethnological Notebooks*
J Moneta, *La Politique coloniale du PCF (1921-1965)*
Peter Petrov, *The Secrets of Hitler's Victory*
John Reed, *The War in Eastern Europe*
Arthur Rosenberg, *The History of the Weimar Republic*
David Rousset, *The Other Kingdom*
Jorge Semprun, *The Second Death of Ramón Mercader*
The Balmain Trotskyists: Reminiscences 1930s and 1940s, Militant Publications (Australia)
Léon Trotsky, *Oeuvres* (French), first series, volumes 22 to end; new series covering 1928 onwards, all volumes.

Fritz Keller

Stalinism versus Hedonism

The (Non-) Publication of Paul Lafargue's Works in the So-Called 'Socialist' Countries

SHORTLY after the October Revolution, a German group of the Russian Communist Party in Petrograd published a pamphlet for the German soldiers and workers by Paul Lafargue (1842-1911) in which he writes:

'By that time [after the workers have seized power], not only the means of production but also luxury articles will be common property. And since the forces of production have developed to such a degree that everyone's day-to-day needs can be satisfied, poverty will be eradicated, and wealth will be held in common, despite all the prophesies made by the moralists from the privileged and ruling classes.'[132]

It was no coincidence that the Bolsheviks used a pamphlet by Karl Marx's deceased son-in-law for their agitational work, because the Frenchman Lafargue, who was born in Cuba, represented internationalism like no other Socialist before the First World War by his descent from Africans, Jews and Caribbean natives. His *magnum opus*, which was really a thinly-disguised satire, *La Droit à la paresse* (*The Right To Be Lazy*), had already been translated into Russian before the *Communist Manifesto*.[133]

Lafargue's personal contacts with the Russian revolutionary movement went back to 1870 when he contacted Herman Lopatin,[134] the popular ideologist of the Narodniks, with the help of the member of the International Workers Association, AW Korvin-Krukovskaia. Since the early 1870s, he corresponded with the Narodnik Nikolai Utin,[135] the central figure in the negotiations with the First International, especially in

132. P Lafargue, *Zum Reich des Sozialismus! – Die ökonomische Revolution und der Kommunismus*, Petrograd, 1918, p26. At the same time, the worker's and soldier's deputies publishing house published *Mir o neprotsnam zatsatii*.
133. LE Derfler, *Paul Lafargue and the Founding of French Marxism 1842-1882*, Cambridge, 1991, p183.
134. Herman Alexandrovich Lopatin (1845-1918) was a follower of Chernyshevsky and was on the General Council of the First International. He helped translate *Capital* into Russian.
135. Nikolai Utin (1845-1883) was a Russian exile and a supporter of Marx in the First International.

the context of the fight against the Bakuninists. During 1881-90, he corresponded with the Russian economist and Narodnik Nikolai Danielson.[136] Towards the end of the 1880s, the relationship between Lafargue and the founder of the first Marxist organisation in Russia, the Emancipation of Labour Group, Georgi Plekhanov, grew stronger. Lafargue also had friendly relations with the Russian Marxists Pavel Axelrod and Vera Zasulich.[137] The leading men and women of the Bolsheviks were regular guests of the Lafargues. Lenin visited Laura and Paul as early as 1895 on his travels through Western Europe.[138] In 1909, Nadezhda Krupskaya cycled with her husband from Paris to the suburb of Draveil, just because Lenin needed to discuss with him his book *Materialism and Empiriocriticism*.[139] Alexandra Kollontai also frequently visited the Lafargues in 1911.[140] David Riazanov, subsequently the director of the Marx-Engels Institute in Moscow, stayed with them in Draveil for some weeks.[141] The memoirs of Ossip Piatnitsky[142] and Victor Serge[143] show that they felt close to Paul...

But the 'Empire of Socialism' in Russia stood in distinct contrast to the conceptions spread by Lafargue. What good could his dreams of the 'destruction of the state' and of a 'society without a ruling class' be for authoritarian apparatchiks? Wasn't it plain subversion in the face of the omnipotent NKVD to continue writing about 'the freedom... to travel, to change one's place of residence and occupation at one's own discretion'?[144] What could 'the right to be lazy' mean to officials who have founded a 'League for Time' to fight 'loitering, idleness, unpunctuality and loquaciousness',[145] who emulated Taylor and Ford, the capitalist technicians of rationalisation; what could it mean to a state which embodied the obligation to work and the slogan 'Those who don't work, shall not eat!' in its constitution? Moreover, Lafargue's impetuous commitment to the liberation of women[146] combined with the conception of a matriarchal society without classes, in which 'a different morality will oblige people... to be unfaithful',[147] could not exist alongside the

136. Nikolai Frantsevich Danielson (1844-1918) was a Narodnik economist and writer, and helped translate *Capital* into Russian.
137. IA Bolyrev, *Lafarg*, Moscow, 1984, p56ff.
138. WI Lenin, *Unbekannte Briefe*, Zürich-Köln, 1967, p6; E Zetkin-Milowodowa, *WI Lenin – Die Jugendjahre*, Berlin, 1953, p91; Bolyrev, op cit, p68.
139. N Krupskaya, *Memories of Lenin*, London, 1970, p177-8.
140. AM Kollontai, *Iz mooi zizni i raboty*, Moscow, 1974, p119.
141. D Riazanov, *Karl Marx: Man, Thinker and Revolutionist*, London, 1927, p268.
142. O Piatnitsky, *Memoirs of a Bolshevik*, Westport, 1973, p19.
143. V Serge, *Memoirs of a Revolutionary 1901-1941*, Oxford, 1978, p33.
144. Lafargue, *Zum Reich des Sozialismus!*, op cit, pp5, 27-9.
145. F Jung, *Nach Rußland! – Schriften zur russischen Revolution*, Hamburg, 1991, p344.
146. P Lafargue, *Geschlechter-Verhältnisse*, Hamburg, 1995.
147. *Le Socialiste*, 30 Juni 1901; Lafargue, *Geschlechter-Verhältnisse*, op cit, p277.

'revolutionary restoration' (as Antonio Gramsci put it) of bourgeois family norms and sexual morality.

Accordingly, the Stalinist nomenklatura slowly restricted the circulation of Lafargue's 'hedonistic Marxism'[148] by publishing it only in his collected works[149] and in non-committal collections[150] – and not for the use of Stakhanovites. The members of the Russian Communist Party who were in opposition to the general line remembered him less for his theories than for the Lafargues' joint suicide, which resembled Epicurean stoicism,[151] when they planned and carried it out in the same way as Adolf Joffe[152] or Trotsky's son-in-law PI Volkov[153] because of the hopelessness of their struggle within the Communist Party. After 1937, the Trotskyist opposition in France embraced the ideas of his which were proscribed in Soviet Union.[154]

In 1950, Joseph Stalin – who claimed to be a linguist without knowing any foreign languages – declared publicly that Lafargue had not been justified in speaking of a 'sudden revolution in language between 1789 and 1794 in France'.[155] So Paul also became a non-person for the party in public. This fact was documented in the *Bolshaya Sovetskaya Entsiklopediya* (*Great Soviet Encyclopaedia*) which appeared in Moscow in 1953. It not only slavishly repeated Stalin's unfavourable verdict, but added an absurd reproach to it: 'Lafargue was incapable of recognising Kautskyism, and took a centrist position on a number of questions.'[156]

Neither Lafargue's writings nor historical papers about him could be published until the era of Nikita Khrushchev.[157] But there was no funda-

148. 'Dieser Begriff für die Theorien Lafargues wurde von Leszek Kolakowski geprägt', in *Hauptströmungen des Marxismus*, Volume 2, München, 1978, p163.
149. P Lafarg, *Sochineniya*, Volumes 1-3, Moscow-Leningrad, 1925-31.
150. P Lafarg, *Pamflety*, Moscow-Leningrad, 1931; *Literaturno-kriticheskie stati*, Moscow, 1936; *Religiia i kapital*, Moscow, 1937 .
151. 'Epicurus lay down to die in a bath filled with warm water, and drank strong wine.' (*Diogenes Laertius*, X, 15)
152. See Joffe's farewell letter to Trotsky at the time of his suicide on 16 November 1927, *Leon Trotsky, The Man and His Work*, New York, 1969, pp125-6.
153. P Broué, *Léon Trotsky-Alfred et Marguerite Rosmer Correspondance 1929-1939*, Harvard, 1982, p188.
154. Which legitimately criticises the incompatibility of Lafargue's views with the theory of the Popular Front (see the article presumably written by Pierre Naville, 'La vie et la mort de Paul Lafargue', *Quatrième Internationale*, no 2, February 1937).
155. J Stalin, 'Marxism and Problems of Linguistics', *Works*, Volume 16, London, 1986, p222; with reference to Lafargue's study *Die französische Sprache vor und nach der französischen Revolution*, Hamburg, 1988. In 1925, Stalin still placed great value on Lafargue's writings in his personal library (D Volkogonov, *Stalin: Triumph and Tragedy*, London, 1991, p101).
156. *Bolshaya Sovetskaya Entsiklopediya*, Volume 14, Moscow, 1953, p369. In his funeral oration, Lenin had called Lafargue 'one of the most gifted and profound disseminators of the ideas of Marxism' (VI Lenin, *Collected Works*, Volume 17, Moscow, 1977, p304).
157. KN Momdzhian, *Lafarg i nekotorye voprosy marksistskoi teorii*, Yerevan, 1954; P Lafarg,

mental change in assessment of hedonism: 'This bourgeois philosophy abstracted the theory of pleasure from the conditions of individual life, and turned it into a dissembling moral doctrine.'[158]

Because of the economic and social stagnation of the Soviet Union under Leonid Brezhnev, no special works on Lafargue appeared for some time. The revised edition of the *Bolshaya Sovetskaya Entsiklopediya* which appeared in 1973 in Moscow appreciated only his fight 'against any kind of opportunism', and managed to avoid mentioning *The Right To Be Lazy* at all.[159]

However, a number publications by and about Lafargue started to appear at the end of the 1970s, and more appeared shortly before Gorbachev came to power.[160]

The leaders of the official Communist movement, under the spell of the Soviet Union, simply implemented Moscow's ideological decisions, especially in respect of the ban upon *The Right To Be Lazy*. This satire, which greatly annoyed the rulers in Moscow and their vassals, was only published in new editions in Tito's Yugoslavia,[161] Gomulka's Poland[162] and Castro's Cuba.[163] It is surely no coincidence that in all these countries the political hegemony of the Communist Party of the Soviet Union was broken or at least questioned, and revolutionary mass movements appeared that were committed, like the Bolsheviks long before, to fighting for the interests of the masses.

The German Democratic Republic took its task of suppression and restriction very seriously. Since the Socialist Unity Party tried its hardest to ignore the decisions of the Twentieth Congress of the CPSU in 1956, the associates of Walter Ulbricht behind the Berlin Wall did not at first see any necessity for any ideological change. Lafargue remained an 'unperson', because Stalin had so pronounced. When Iring Fetscher cited

Za i protiv kommunizma – Sobstvennost i ec proishchozdenie, Moscow, 1959; V Goffenshelfer, *Iz istorii marksistskoi kritiki: P Lafarg borba za realizm*, Moscow, 1967; VM Dalin, 'Bylo li gedistkoe napravelnie edinym', *Liudi i idei*, Moscow, 1970. During the Khrushchev period, there also appeared historical essays about Lafargue's correspondence with Baliki, Engels and Guesde (cited in detail in Bolyrev, op cit, pp170ff), and official atheist propaganda made use of many of his writings (see *Korotky nauchnniateisticheski slovar*, Moscow, 1964).

158. FV Konstantinov (ed), *Entsiklopediya Filosofskaia*, Volume 3, Moscow, 1960, p339.

159. *Bolshaya Sovetskaya Entsiklopediya*, Volume 14, Moscow, 1973, pp645-6.

160. KN Momdzian, *Pol Lafarg i filosofiya marksizma*, Moscow, 1978; 'Lafarg P-Bruss P Ende April 1881', *Voprosoy istorii*, no 11, 1978; 'Lafarg P – Mesa Ch 26 Oktober 1881', *Voprosoy istorii*, no 11, 1978; 'Lafarg P-Marks K v Ramsget', *Voprosoy istorii*, no 5, 1978; *Sovremenniki o Markse* (P Lafarg, V Libknecht, F Lessner), Moscow 1982; *Kritik idealizma i religii soratnikami K Marksa i F Engelsa*, Minsk, 1984; Bolyrev, op cit.

161. P Lafargue, *Krjizevne kritike*, Belgrade, 1949; *Poceci romantizma*, Zagreb, 1950; Mile Joka (ed), *Polzbor iz djela*, Zagreb, 1957.

162. P Lafargue, *Pisma wybrane*, Warsaw, 1961.

163. P Lafargue, *Textos escogidos*, edited by Salvador Morales, La Habana, 1976.

a few sentences from *The Right To Be Lazy* in a speech in the DDR, he was immediately accused in public 'of having undermined the work ethic'.[164] The DDR's regime could not and would not tolerate idleness, particularly in the period of the economic reforms which had started in 1963. Not until the period of the seventh and eighth party congresses in 1971 did the SED's leaders decide to adopt a more liberal ideological position.[165] The limited span of that liberalisation was shown in two volumes by and about Lafargue; *The Right To Be Lazy* and his writings on women's liberation were still beyond the pale. The regime only accepted non-committal writings, critiques like 'The Greatness and the Limitations of Lafargue',[166] or else Lafargue's rôle was reduced to that of Marx's biographer and physician[167] – and this was not even changed by glasnost and the breakdown of the entire DDR.[168] Hedonism 'always represented the moral tendencies of certain privileged classes'[169] to the ideologists of the SED, but these 'certain privileged classes' of course did not under any circumstances include the regime's ruling Stalinists.

❖   ❖   ❖

Rudolf Bahro wrote: 'From the standpoint of political economy, under actually existing Socialism the workers have a far greater opportunity to blackmail "the entire society" than do the trade unions under capitalism, and they do actually use this, against all surface appearance, even if they can do so only in an unfruitful way, that is, by holding back on their output.'[170] He continued: '... exploitation, which was the original lever of a remarkable level of expanded reproduction, is "ashamed" of itself under actually existing Socialism. It must make use of a complicated and inhibitary façade.'[171] The (non) publication of Lafargue's writings – especially *The Right To Be Lazy* – is further evidence for the accuracy of both theses.

164. Iring Fetscher, *Das Recht auf Faulheit & Persönliche Erinnerungen an Karl Marx*, Vienna, 1966, p9.
165. 'Zu den Hintergründen vgl Werner Wohlau: Die Kulturpolitik der DDR nach dem VIII Parteitag (1971)', *die Internationale*, no 5, October 1974.
166. P Lafargue, *Vom Ursprung der Ideen*, Dresden, 1970.
167. Karl Dessler (ed), *Ärzte um Karl Marx*, Berlin, 1970.
168. The book *Ärzte um Karl Marx* was republished in 1985. See Eva Kratzer's article 'Marx Mitarbeit an Paul Lafargues Manifest der Parti Ouvrier Français', *Beiträgen zur Marx-Engels-Forschung*, no 16, 1984, pp219ff. *Das Philosophenlexikon*, edited by Erhard Lange und Dietrich Alexander, Berlin, 1984, managed to avoid any mention of *The Right To Be Lazy* in a three-page assessment (pp510ff).
169. Georg Klaus and Manfred Buhr (eds), *Marxistisch-leninistisches Wörterbuch der Philosophie*, Reinbek, 1972, Volume 2, p471. Likewise, the *Kleine Wörterbuch der marxistisch-leninistischen Philosophie*, edited by Manfred Buhr and Alfred Kosing, for the sake of simplicity, did not contain any entry for 'hedonism'.
170. R Bahro, *The Alternative in Eastern Europe*, London, 1978, p207.
171. Op cit, p211.

V: The International Federation of Independent Revolutionary Artists

All the articles in this section have been translated for us from the French and annotated by Ian Birchall. To gain a full appreciation of this material, the Federation's manifesto should first be read ('Towards a Free Revolutionary Art', 25 July 1938, *Leon Trotsky on Literature and Art*, New York, 1977, pp115-21), along with Trotsky's subsequent letter to Breton (22 December 1938; op cit, pp122-4). Philippe Geneste reproduces and discusses the French text of the *Manifesto* giving the draft and contributions by Breton and Trotsky in *Critique Communiste* (nos 116-117, February-March 1992). Trotsky's involvement with the FIARI caused a quite stir at the time (cf Harry Ratner's remarks in *Reluctant Revolutionary* (London, 1994), p25) and inevitably led to an extensive discussion, which shows no signs of abating (for recent examples, cf Peter Fryer, 'Trotsky and Artistic Freedom', and Charlie Pottins, 'Artists' Rôle', *Workers Press*, 11 May and 24 September 1996; Mike Driver, 'Towards a Free Revolutionary Art: Leon Trotsky on Culture, the Class Struggle and Socialism', *Marxist Review*, Volume 12, no 4, April 1997, pp13-15, no 5, May 1997, pp16-20, and no 6, June 1997, pp16-20).

A good description of the setting of Breton's visit to Mexico is Alain Dugrand, *Trotsky in Mexico 1937-1940* (Manchester, 1992, pp9-55; cf the reviews by Julian Symons, 'The Ice-Pick Man Cometh', *Times Literary Supplement*, 29 May 1992; and Al Richardson, *Revolutionary History*, Volume 5, no 1, Autumn 1993, p120). From amongst the major treatments the most concrete and useful is Mark Polizotti's description of Breton's visit to Trotsky and the formation of the FIARI in his biography of Breton (*Revolution of the Mind*, London, 1995, pp441-72; cf the reviews by Peter Conrad, *Observer*, 15 October 1995, and Lachlan MacKinnon, *Times Literary Supplement*, 3 May 1996). To it should be added Jean van Heijenoort's account of the same event along with his remarks on Trotsky's literary tastes (*With Trotsky in Exile*, Harvard University Press, 1978, pp121-41; cf 'Seven Years with Trotsky', *InterContinental Press*, 1 May 1978, pp518-9), and Breton's own recollections in *Free Rein* (Lincoln, Nebraska, 1995) and *Entretiens* (Paris, 1969). Arturo Schwartz's *André*

Breton, Trotsky et l'anarchie (Paris, 1977) also contains Jacqueline Lamba's recollections of the Mexico visit (pp64ff; cf 'La rencontre Trotsky-Breton', *Les Lettres nouvelles*, no 4, 1975, pp99-111). Gérard Roche draws together most of the sources in 'La Rencontre de l'aigle et du lion: Trotsky, Breton et le manifeste de México', *Cahiers Léon Trotsky*, no 25, March 1986, pp23-46. A more hostile view is expressed by Otto Karl Werckmeister in 'The Summit Meeting of Revolutionary Art: Trotsky, Rivera and Breton at Coyoacan, 1938', *L'Art et des révolutions: Acts of the 27th International Congress on the History of Art, 1-7 September 1989* (Strasbourg, 1992), pp157-70.

Trotsky's association with Breton has exercised the imagination of many, to the extent that surrealism has come to be regarded almost as a 'Trotskyist' art form. A broad outline of the relationship between the two is provided by Marguerite Bonnet, 'André Breton and the Surrealist Movement', *International Socialist Review*, Volume 35, no 3, March 1975, pp26-35; 'Trotsky et Breton', *Cahiers Léon Trotsky*, no 25, March 1986, pp5-17; 'Trotsky, La Littérature et les écrivains', *Cahiers Léon Trotsky*, no 47, January 1992, pp5-10; and Etiemble, 'The Tibetan Dog', *Yale French Studies*, no 31, May 1964, pp127-34. Helena Lewis' *Dada Turns Red: The Politics of Surrealism* (Edinburgh UP, 1990) devotes a chapter to the FIARI and Trotsky's relationship with the surrealists, and also discusses their response in Paris to Trotsky's expulsion from the Soviet Union in 1929. A full analysis of the relationship between surrealism and French politics at this time can be followed in Ian Birchall's 'Des Marteaux matériels', *French Studies*, Volume 44, no 3, July 1990, pp300-18. Shorter introductions include Serge Obreon, 'André Breton sur l'Honneur des Poètes', *La Vérité*, no 535, December 1966-January 1967, pp20-2; and Alexis Violet, 'Surréalisme et politique: Les vastes communicants', *Rouge*, 1 May 1991. Breton was, of course, more deeply politically involved than most of the others. He had reviewed Trotsky's *Lenin* as far back as 1925 (reprinted in the *Cahiers Léon Trotsky*, no 25, March 1986, pp19-22). He organised prominent literary figures in opposition to the Moscow Trials (Marguerite Leuven, 'Il y a un siècle naissait André Breton', *La Vérité*, new series, no 18 [624], September 1996, pp143-7, which reprints the Appeal of the Intellectuals against the Moscow Trials of 3 September 1936 and a speech by Breton on the same subject on 26 January 1937; Jean Boyer, 'André Breton et les procès de Moscou', *Informations ouvrières*, 18-24 September 1996). But he made it clear that he still cherished the memory of the Russian Revolution ('La Révolution d'Octobre', fraternal message to the PCI rally to commemorate the Russian Revolution held on 19 November 1937, reprinted in *La Vérité*, no 535, December 1966-January 1967, p23).

Surrealism is in general a vast subject, and only the thinnest of documentation can be provided here. Breton himself wrote the *Position politique du surréalisme* and the *Manifeste du surréalisme*, and Maurice Nadeau the *Histoire du surréalisme*. *What is Surrealism?: Selected Writings of André Breton* can be consulted in English, along with the companion volume provided by Franklin Rosemark, *André Breton and the First Principles of Surrealism* (London, 1978).

Our Italian sister organisation published a facsimile of the first two issues of *Clé* as no 35 in the series *Studi e Ricerche* of the Quaderni del Centro Studi Pietro Tresso in May 1995. Valuable background to the surrealists in 1939 is provided by Pierre Naville, 'Que sont les intellectuels?', *Rouge*, 30 May 1991.

Our final piece can be followed up in Rachel Stella's anthology of Benjamin Péret's writings, *Death to the Pigs* (London, 1988), which was reviewed by Jon E Lewis in *Revolutionary History*, Volume 2, no 1, Spring 1989, pp45-6. It should be read along with Henri Langlois, 'Benjamin Péret', *La Vérité*, no 519, May-June 1960, pp24-5; Franklin Rosemont, 'Benjamin Péret', *Radical America*, Volume 4, no 6, August 1970; Fulvio Abramo and Dainis Karepovs, 'Artiste et révolutionnaire: B Péret au Brésil', *Cahiers Léon Trotsky*, no 25, March 1986, pp65-80; cf Karepovs' later article, 'Benjamin Péret et la Ligue communiste du Brésil', *Cahiers Léon Trotsky*, no 47, January 1992; and Antoine Rigal, 'Benjamin Péret', *Rouge*, 8 May 1991. Unlike other signatories to the FIARI Manifesto, Péret had always played an active part in the Trotskyist movement (cf the correspondence with the Brazilian Trotskyists from as far back as 1932 reprinted in *Cahiers Léon Trotsky*, no 47, January 1992, pp97-100), and he shared the disquiet of Natalia Trotsky and Grandizo Munis about its disorientation after the Second World War (cf 'The Fourth International in Danger', *Internal Bulletin* of the International Secretariat, December 1947). He later developed ideas of the type generally described as 'ultra-left' (Ian Birchall, 'Some Comments', *Revolutionary History*, Volume 2, no 3, Autumn 1989, pp51-2).

Trotsky's association with Diego Rivera and Frida Kahlo in Coyoacan continues to exercise the imagination of gifted and mediocre alike, and has lately given rise to a certain amount of speculation. Amongst recent discussions we might notice those by Roger Spencer, 'Mexican Murals', *Socialist Outlook*, no 3, September-October 1987, pp36-7; Peter Waymark, 'Messages on the Walls', *The Times*, 20 November 1987; Franklin Balch, 'Has the Legacy of Rivera's Murals Been Forgotten?', *Socialist Action* [USA], April and May 1993; JMG Le Clézio, *Diego et Frida* (reviewed in *Lutte ouvrière*, 7 January 1994); Richard Gott, 'Two Houses in Coyoacan', *Guardian*, 11 November 1998; and two unattributed articles, 'Diego Rivera, Artist and Revolutionary', *Fighting Worker*, 1986; and 'Diego Rivera: Art and Politics', *Workers Press*, 24 October 1987. The latest full length work is Patrick Marnham, *Dreaming with his Eyes Open: A*

Life of Diego Rivera (London, 1998; cf the reviews by Amanda Hopkinson, *Independent*, 28 October 1998, and Liz Jobey, *Guardian*, 31 October 1998). The life of Rivera's companion is dealt with in Hayden Herrera's *Frida: A Biography of Frida Kahlo* (reviewed in the *Independent*, 22 November 1998). Most outrageous of all is the assertion by Phil Davison that Rivera was all the while informing to the FBI, a smear in which he seeks to implicate Trotsky as well ('Diego Rivera's Dirty Little Secret', *Independent*, 25 November, 1993; cf the reply by Alex Mitchell, 'Truth about Trotsky, Rivera and the FBI', *Independent*, 30 November 1993).

Maurice Nadeau

Trotsky and Breton

Maurice Nadeau (born 1911) was expelled from the French Communist Party (PCF) in 1932. He contributed to *La Vérité* and *La Lutte des classes*, worked with Léon Sedov on contacts with the Russian Trotskyists, and was a founder member of the Parti ouvrier internationaliste in 1936. Later, he became well-known as a journalist, critic and publisher. He helped to organise the *Manifesto of the 121* against the Algerian War in 1960. The following extract is taken from his autobiography, *Grâces leur soient rendues* (Albin Michel, Paris, 1990), pp33-6.

ONE day, it must have been late 1938, Naville said to me: 'I've talked to Breton about you; go and see him, you're going to give him a hand with this alliance which the Old Man wants him to set up.' Breton had been to visit Trotsky in Mexico. He had brought back with him a manifesto – *Towards a Free Revolutionary Art* – signed by him and Diego Rivera. 'In fact', Naville told me, 'it was mainly the Old Man who drew it up.' They wanted to bring together 'honest' artists and writers, which in our language meant those who were not subservient to either money or Moscow. 'Breton needs material assistance, inasmuch as we can give him some.'

I had been to listen to Breton at the meeting we had organised against the Moscow Trials when he came back from Mexico. I was struck by the marble whiteness of his face. His luxuriant hair, brushed back, gave him an 'artistic' appearance which, in the circumstances, seemed to me a little inappropriate. He read his speech with a sonorous, even theatrical voice, but in ringing tones. He denounced Stalin's crimes, and spoke up in defence of Trotsky. His speech stood out in contrast to the others we had heard. The atmosphere in the hall was electric, and the temperature went up a few degrees. We comrades who were listening looked at each other, smiling with delight; we had the feeling that we had won over poetry in person to our cause. He arranged to see me at the Deux-Magots where the surrealists normally gathered.

I saw him arrive, in a midnight blue camel-hair overcoat, accompanied by Jacqueline, who had a scaffolding of birds and flowers in her hair. I was flabbergasted. I was encountering a world that was unknown to me. Until then, I had known — writers apart — only the pariahs of the revolution: workers at the Gnome and Rhône factory, the destitute from the Jeanne d'Arc estate, and my party comrades. I reasoned with myself: why shouldn't the revolution have its great lords?

The surrealists who were present — Brauner, Seligman and Nicolas Calas — looked at me sympathetically. I had an appointment with Breton, and Breton, who could see that I was stiff with embarrassment, tried to put me at my ease. I was the representative of the Trotskyists, and he was not only addressing me.

'The FIARI (International Federation of Independent Revolutionary Artists) must have a newsletter, and it would be good if you took responsibility for the practical organisation. You won't be on your own, you'll have your friend Benjamin Péret to work with you.' I was happy to accept. I knew about printing, for years I'd been helping Naville put *La Vérité* together every week.

I immediately felt close to Benjamin Péret, who shared our political ideas. He was a 'comrade', and we called each other *tu*. He had fought in Spain with the POUM forces and the Durutti column. It was said that when he was on guard outside the POUM premises in Barcelona, conscious of his duty and respectful of his orders, not even a gunshot could have made him change his position. For the time being, he was a proofreader on the *Journal officiel*. Marthe[1] and I visited him, hauling ourselves up the rope which served as a hand-rail on the staircase up to his studio in the rue Froidevaux, with an unobstructed view of the Montparnasse cemetery. On the wall was a large canvas by Picabia, which he was unsuccessfully trying to sell, a cast-iron stove, burning wood, for the winter days, and cats. His partner, Remedios, designed the title of the FIARI newsletter, *Clé*. She gave Marthe a little black kitten, Panchita, which was to share our life (and our occasional steaks) during the Occupation.

Breton came to observe the production of the first issue of *Clé*. We were in the printshop, with the workers. Breton bowed to Marthe, whom he didn't yet know, and raised her hand to his lips. Marthe giggled, thinking it was a joke. The printers just gaped. We weren't used to such aristocratic manners. Marthe admitted to me that she found Breton fascinating.

1. Marthe Forni, who married Nadeau in 1934.

For the FIARI, we met at Breton's home in the rue Fontaine. The place has frequently been described, and photographs have been published. In this luxury flea market which Breton had transformed into a den of wonders, there were canvasses by Tanguy and Chirico, African masks, Hopi statuettes, precious objects of all sorts. I didn't know where to look. I felt somewhat uncomfortable. Through the big bay window that looked out onto the boulevard, I could see the flickering neon signs of the night-clubs. A muffled sound came up from the place Blanche.

Which writers and painters were we going to invite to join? The 'proletarian' writers, those of Henry Poulaille's literary 'New Age',[2] and those who published with Rieder and in the review *Europe*? 'If they want', said Breton, 'there must be no sectarianism.' 'Why shouldn't we ask Valéry?' The question came from Breton. There was silence. Péret, who supported all Breton's proposals, said nothing. Valéry, of the Académie Française and the Collège de France,[3] it was a bit much, after all, despite the admiration which the young Breton had had for him. The conversation began to drift. Pierre Mabille talked about psychoanalysis, and about secret societies, of which there were said to be many in Lyons. Accustomed as I was to cell meetings obsessed with 'concrete' decisions and practical activity, I was floating in an empyrean presided over by a Jupiter whose muffled laughter sometimes brought him down amongst us, a Jupiter who ceremonially accompanied us to the door of his flat amid a torrent of 'goodbye, my dear friend'.

Was it still 1938 or was it already 1939? Breton asked me to attend a meeting which was to be held at Yves Allégret's home in the rue de Grenelle. I did not know what was planned. I thought it must have something to do with the FIARI. In fact, from the outset Breton was accusing Eluard.[4] Eluard had made some scandalous statements about the Moscow Trials, which he supported. He had moved closer to Aragon, whom earlier he had abused, and had moved so far it was said that he had joined the Communist Party.[5] Breton said that we must denounce the 'unspeakable' attitude of Eluard. Georges Hugnet ('you can't suspect me of Stalinist sympathies', he said to Breton, 'I was an anti-Stalinist before you were') defended his friend. 'Eluard is a poet, the greatest of them all. His political attitudes have nothing to do with poetry.' 'They have to do with surrealism', responded Breton. 'I insist that Eluard shall no longer be considered a surrealist, that he be considered officially and publicly as an enemy.' Referring to Hugnet, he added: 'I observe that he has some

2. Henry Poulaille (1896-1980) was the leading French advocate of 'proletarian literature'; *Nouvel âge littéraire* was the title of a book published in 1930 and a review launched in 1931.
3. The oldest of French institutions of higher education.
4. Paul Eluard (Eugène Grindel, 1895-1952) was a surrealist poet, and a Stalinist from the late 1930s.
5. Eluard did in fact join the French Communist Party, but only in 1942.

strange defenders here.' Hugnet got angry, Yves Allégret spinelessly supported Breton, Maurice Heine, biographer of the Marquis de Sade, wearing a long black cape that went down to his feet, obstinately remained silent. As for me, I had been brought into a settling of scores between surrealists without having wished it, and whilst I agreed with Breton, I didn't feel I had the right to intervene. Nonetheless, the alliance which the FIARI was aiming to create seemed to me to have been compromised. Certainly, Eluard had to be repudiated, but no approach had been made to get him to join. He himself had asked for nothing. The argument seemed to me to be futile. By getting me to be present, hadn't Breton simply intended to make me a witness?

In the first issue of *Clé*, in February 1939,[6] there was no denunciation of Eluard, but there was a reference to 'dissident' activity on the part of unnamed 'surrealists'. They were, apparently, liable to 'present themselves in the form of an alliance which, however labelled, would be, whether apolitical or pro-Stalinist, the enemy of our revolutionary objectives'. This mysterious statement, aimed at very different 'enemies', was signed by, amongst others, Georges Hugnet and Maurice Heine. So Eluard was not part of it? Before its birth, the FIARI seemed to me to be involved in quarrels harmful to the proposed alliance. Since Breton was controlling it in a high-handed manner, I should have suspected this would happen.

After Daladier's return from Munich,[7] war had not yet been declared, but already the Trotskyists faced repression. I offered Péret should write an article for *Clé*. He made it into the manifesto 'Against the Grey Terror'.[8] We had time to print it in the second issue of *Clé*. There was not to be a third one. Just as there would not be an aggregate meeting of FIARI supporters. Events had moved too quickly for us.

Leon Trotsky

You Must Not Whisper[9]

Dear Comrade Breton

We've just received your letter from Portugal (I think it's the first letter

---

6. In fact, issue number 1 is dated January 1939, number 2 is dated February 1939.
7. In fact, the Munich agreements were in September 1938.
8. No such article appears in *Clé*, no 2; there was an article on Munich by Maurice Heine in *Clé*, no 1.
9. Letter to André Breton dated 31 August 1938, dictated in French, from *Oeuvres*, Volume 18, pp269-70.

from Portugal I've ever had in my life) and the little note from Jacqueline. We were very happy to have news of you both.

I was sincerely touched by the very warm and friendly tone of your letter, dear friend, and, I must say, a little embarrassed. In all sincerity, your praise seems to me so exaggerated that I am a little anxious about the future of our relations. As for the danger of being spoilt by my friends' praise, I am, thank Heaven, well protected by the far more numerous insults of my enemies.

As for the *Manifesto*, it seems to be moving very slowly here in Mexico. The reason is that until now there has been nobody to take practical responsibility for it. In the United States, things seem to be going much better. I am sending you a copy of the letter I received about it from Dwight Macdonald.[10] I'm also sending you copies of all my correspondence with *Partisan Review*, which may interest you and your collaborators, in view of your plans for a journal. The editorial board of *Partisan Review* has moved towards us in quite a visible fashion. Dwight Macdonald is even writing regularly in *New International*. But their own journal remains too neutral, too insipid, and too contemplative on the political level. In my opinion, that is why they were obliged to give up the monthly in favour of a quarterly. I think there is a major lesson to be learnt from this fact. If you want to be heard in our age, you must speak aloud and not whisper. I hope you will find a way of collaborating with our friends over there, without crossing swords or confusing your responsibilities.

I am still completely absorbed in my book, and I am still surprised every day by the avalanche of official falsifications. Here life goes on more or less normally. Natalia had the chance to go to Acapulco with friends from Chicago. Van will tell you himself about his trip to the tropics. We work in the garden every day. We are waiting for news of the international conference. And that is about all.

We hope that you and Jacqueline found your little girl[11] in the best of health. Give dear Jacqueline a kiss from us.

10. Dwight G Macdonald (born 1906) was from a bourgeois family. He studied at Yale and then worked as a journalist on *Fortune*, then left it because he had been censored; close to the Communist Party, he broke with it at the time of the Moscow Trials, and joined the *Partisan Review* group, on whose behalf he made contact with Trotsky. Trotsky had written to him on 29 August, noting their determination to struggle for the FIARI and regretting that the magazine had become quarterly, whilst urging on him 'implacable aggression' against *The Nation*, *The New Republic* and *The Modern Monthly*.
11. Aube Solange (born 1935), the daughter of Breton and Jacqueline Lamba, was left in France during their visit to Mexico.

Leon Trotsky

Difficulties With Diego[12]

My Dear Friends[13]

I really am very embarrassed. Diego's silence has absolutely nothing to do
with any indifference or dissatisfaction towards the two of you, as you
suggest in your last letter. I know, too, that Frida was very pleased with
your preface, which she received the day before she left for the United
States.[14] Diego's refusal to write letters is a constant aspect of his character. He has also had many weeks of weariness, sickness and nervous tension. I myself had great difficulties in meeting him during those weeks.
He was tending to avoid everybody, including the FIARI. Now he's much
better physically. He left an hour ago, to go and paint in Patzcuaro. Before leaving, he got Van to pass to me your last letter, André Gide's letter
and the cutting about Malacki.[15] Unfortunately the Malacki affair came
up just as Diego was leaving and he won't be able to deal with it until
after he returns, in a week's time. Let's hope this week won't be too long.
In any case, Diego will do what is required to sort out the affair.

On the FIARI, Van will give you the information, which is not exactly a great deal because of the circumstances outlined above. I assure
you, my dear friend, that there have been plenty of attempts to set the
ball rolling. But they have come up against an inert destiny, as insuperable as during the period when the FIARI was being conceived (you remember). I'm also writing today to *Partisan Review*. Perhaps you know
that the magazine has become a quarterly instead of a monthly. This failure is the obvious result, in my view, of the willingness to adapt, the ma-
noeuvring, the lack of daring in going onto the offensive, and similar
original sins of petit-bourgeois intellectuals, even if they call themselves
revolutionaries. You will certainly have received the most recent issue of
the magazine containing the *Manifesto*[16] and a short statement prefaced to

12. Letter to André Breton dated 6 December 1938, dictated in French, from *Oeuvres*,
Volume 19, pp230-1.
13. The letter was addressed to André Breton, but also to his partner Jacqueline Lamba
(born 1910), whom Trotsky held in high regard.
14. Frida Kahlo de Rivera (1910-1954), a very talented painter, was Diego's wife. She had
left for the United States, then for Europe.
15. André Gide (1869-1951) was considered at the time as one of the greatest French
writers. For a long time he was a fellow-traveller of Stalinism, but he had broken with
it with the publication of his *Back From the USSR*. Trotsky had hoped to get him to
join the Commission of Inquiry or to come and visit him. We do not know to which
letter he refers. Vladimir Malacki, known as Jean Malaquais (born 1908) was a young
writer, one of Gide's protégés, of whom Trotsky had a very high opinion.
16. The manifesto *Towards a Free Revolutionary Art* appeared in the Autumn 1938 issue of

it. I'm going to ask them to give the most precise information on the organisational side.

Don't take what I have written as being a complaint against Diego. He must be taken as he is, and despite his distaste for letter-writing, he is magnificent.

I am very moved by your proposal to find a publisher for my book on literature, which now seems to me to belong to an almost prehistoric period.[17] From your letter I can't make out if the potential publishers are asking for a *French* version in order to make up their minds. If so, that would be an insuperable problem for me. But there is an English translation, and Van assures me that there are also German and Spanish translations. Could the publishers not form an opinion on the basis of the foreign editions, including the Russian?

As far as everything else is concerned, we carry on. From a physical point of view, Natalia and I are not quite so well as when you were here. The whole household (except perhaps Van, who is still in the diplomatic service[18]) is now busy with cacti; we are seeking the rarest and most magnificent specimens for the garden. You certainly wouldn't recognise it now.

Clé

Clé was the organ of the French section of the FIARI. Only two issues appeared – for January and February 1939 – but they do contain evidence that the FIARI was an authentic organisation which had genuine support. We publish below a selection of articles from the first two issues.

I: No Homeland!

This was the editorial on the front page of the first issue. It shows clearly the FIARI's internationalism and its involvement with political as well as aesthetic matters.

THE filthy campaigns conducted under the slogans 'France awake' and 'France for the French' are beginning to bear their poisoned fruit. M Sarraut's May decrees and certain terms in the appendix of the November statutory orders have brought into force, a disgraceful procedure inspired by that of Fascist countries, to the detriment of for-

Partisan Review.
17. The reference is to *Literature and Revolution*, first published in 1924.
18. A euphemism to indicate that Van Heijenoort had responsibility for all external relations, that is, with the authorities, press, etc, which did not allow him much leisure time.

eigners resident in France and especially of political refugees. Measures of exclusion already taken, and the preparations for internment which we are currently observing mark the accentuation of a politics based on panic and force which is tending to establish in France a regime which is 'authoritarian', and will soon become totalitarian... They bear witness to the rapid contagion affecting 'democratic' countries which are already being dragged, in contempt of the most elementary considerations of humanity, to repudiate the right of asylum, long considered *sacred* by us. The FIARI considers it as its prime duty to denounce this new degradation of bourgeois 'conscience', and to expose these xenophobic manoeuvres as one of the main dangers of the present time. Just as we have full confidence that the working class will demand the repeal of statutory orders aimed at it alone, we support with all our strength the protests and appeals for resistance issued by the revolutionary organisations SIA, PSOP[19] and POI[20] against the mass expulsions and the creation of concentration camps already in peace time.

In the more specific sphere of our own activity, we will take good care not to forget that if Paris has long been in the artistic vanguard, that is essentially a result of the hospitable welcome which artists coming from all countries have found there, and that if some of the great spiritual trends which the world has taken account of have been born in this city, it is because it has constituted a truly international laboratory of ideas. Art has no country, just as the workers have none. To advocate today a return to a 'French' art, as not only the Fascists but also the Stalinists are doing, means opposing the maintenance of this close link which is necessary to art; it means working for division and misunderstanding between peoples; it means acting deliberately in favour of historical regression. Our comrades who are foreign artists are today threatened in the same way as our comrades who are foreign workers. Both are now in a position to recognise who will support them, who will attack them, who will betray them. However depleted our forces may be at present, as a result of successive betrayals, it must not be said that they looked in vain for the protection of the working class.

We denounce in the statutory orders aimed at foreigners – called 'undesirables' by the reactionary bourgeoisie – an attempt to degrade the human personality in this country by creating *a first* category of men deprived of legal rights and dignity, and condemned to perpetual persecution by the very fact that, having resisted oppression or fled from inhuman dictatorships, they no longer have a legal 'homeland'.

The National Committee of the FIARI

19. The Parti socialiste ouvrier et paysan was founded by the *pivertiste* left of the SFIO after its exclusion in 1938.
20. Parti ouvrier internationaliste, the Trotskyist organisation founded in 1936.

II: From Our Friend Victor Serge

The first issue contained a number of replies from writers and artists approached to join the FIARI.

My dear André Breton
I have no objections to your manifesto *For an Independent Revolutionary Art*; the logic and the main line of thought in it seem to me correct. Basically, these have been my positions for a long time, and I set them out in 1931 or 1932 in *Literature and Revolution*.[21] I am therefore joining you.

To give our organisation the best chance of coming to life and surviving, we must, it seems to me, conceive of it broadly and freely, and not demand from those who join us the clarity of ideas we ourselves possess; we should demand from them only a sincere commitment to revolution, which may be conceived other than in Marxist terms. Minds formed in an anarchistic or eclectic fashion are the most numerous, and there are some excellent, healthy ones amongst them. The present crisis of Bolshevism will undoubtedly lead to a crisis of Marxism which we shall have to face up to. We shall not succeed in this by claiming – even in a surreptitious fashion – to impose a Marxist hegemony which at other times also I should have considered as oppressive.
Victor Serge

III: Amongst Those Who Have Joined up to Today

The first issue also contained a substantial list of those who had joined the FIARI.

ADOLPHE Acker, Yves Allégret, Géa Augsbourg, Renée Ballon, Charles Baron, Paul Bénichou, Pierre Berger, Roger Blin,[22] Jean de Bouchère, André Breton, J-B Brunius, Claude Cahun, Nicolas Calas, Carrouges, André Chenal, Michel Collinet,[23] Gaston Criel, G-A Dassonville, Luc Daurat, Frédéric Delanglade, Gisèle Dubouille, Marcel Duhamel, H Spinoza, Gaston Ferdière, Roger Gilbert-Lecomte, Michel-Marie Godard, Jean Giono,[24] Maurice Heine, Georges Henein, Maurice Henry, Lucien Hérard, Madeleine Hérard, Henri Horne, Georges Hugnet, Sylvain Itkine, Marcel Jean, Simone Kahn, René Lefeuvre,[25] Jean Lévy,

21. Serge's *Littérature et révolution* was first published in Paris in 1932; a new edition appeared in 1976.
22. Roger Blin (1907-1984) was an actor and producer, and staged work of Beckett and Genet.
23. Michel Collinet (1904-1977) was a member of the *pivertiste* left of the SFIO and of the POUM.
24. Jean Giono (1895-1970) was a novelist of peasant life and a pacifist.
25. René Lefeuvre (1902-1988) was a *pivertiste* in the 1930s, and was later the publisher of

Maurice Lime, Pierre Mabille, Léo Malet, André Marchand, Victor Margueritte, André Masson,[26] Jean-Daniel Martinet, Marcel Martinet, Gaston Modot, Maurice Nadeau, Albert Paraz, Henri Pastoureau, Magdeleine Paz,[27] Benjamin Péret,[28] Marceau Pivert,[29] Jean Poilvé-Leguen, Henry Poulaille,[30] Charles Ratton, Jean Rémy, Robert Rius, Gérard Rosenthal, Léo Sabas, Victor Serge, Ignazio Silone,[31] Yves Tanguy,[32] André Thirion,[33] Charles Vincent, Francis Vian, Maurice Wullens.[34]

IV: An Avowed Enemy

The second, February, issue contained this piece on Spain by the surrealist poet Benjamin Péret.

'THE final victory of republican Spain must be considered as certain': such is the conclusion of M Emile Hambresin's article on 'the crushing of Spanish Anarchism and the resurrection of Spain' (*Esprit*, 1 February 1938).

Who is M Emile Hambresin? The editorial introduction to the aforesaid article indicates that the author has written noteworthy studies of corporatism and property, and that he had wanted to visit Fascist Spain. He was refused permission by Franco's representative, since the latter considered that the Catholic conservative Belgian paper he represented was too lukewarm. But M Hambresin wanted to go to Spain, and so he went to the other side of the barricades where they were less fussy about the quality of journalists. He came back delighted, singing the praises of Negrín and the Spanish Communist Party, and pouring out insults over the Anarchists, the POUM and the Trotskyists. In zoology, therefore, our journalist can be placed between the pig and the hyena.

The revolution of July 1936, responding to the military coup, is, for

Cahiers Spartacus.

26. André Masson (1896-1987) was a surrealist painter, and an important influence on Jackson Pollock and abstract expressionists.

27. Magdeleine Paz (1889-1973) was an early member of the Left Opposition and an anti-Stalinist in the 1930s.

28. Benjamin Péret (1899-1959) was a surrealist poet and a Trotskyist who fought in Spain, and in his last years collaborated with G Munis.

29. Marceau Pivert (1895-1958) was the leader of the SFIO left.

30. Henry Poulaille (1896-1980) was a novelist and an advocate of proletarian literature.

31. Ignazio Silone (1900-1978) was an Italian Socialist and novelist, and the author of *Fontamara*.

32. Yves Tanguy (1900-1955) was a French surrealist painter who lived in the USA after 1939.

33. André Thirion (born 1907) was a surrealist in 1920s and 1930s, was expelled from the PCF in 1931, and was a Gaullist in 1950.

34. Maurice Wullens (1894-1945) was an Anarchist and pacifist who published review *Les Humbles* during 1916-40.

our author, merely a shameful episode, for 'Spain is making its bourgeois democratic revolution a century and a half later than we did'. In other words, the Paris Commune, the Russian revolutions of 1905 and 1917, and the proletarian risings which have taken place in various countries have no meaning, and are merely the acts of bandits. He refuses to see that we are no longer in 1789, that there is no longer any room anywhere for a bourgeois democratic revolution, and that only the proletarian revolution is on the agenda. M Hambresin is an avowed reactionary, and as such he esteems the work of the Negrín government: restoring bourgeois power by winning back the working-class gains of July 1936.

The Anarchists and the POUM, who had been in the vanguard of the revolutionary struggles at the beginning of the civil war, and who struggled for the slogan 'make the revolution to defeat Fascism', are the object of a quite particular hatred on the part of M Hambresin, who recognises in them enemies of the bourgeoisie, his own personal enemies, and happily identifies himself with the foul crimes of Stalinism. The 1937 May Days in Barcelona are in his eyes simply the work of provocateurs from the POUM. We can see that he has been sharply lectured on his responsibilities by the GPU.

The results of the Stalinist policies so highly rated by M Hambresin are now obvious. The final blow struck against the proletarian revolution in May 1937 has been followed by an uninterrupted series of defeats. The Basque provinces were lost at the same time that Nin was murdered. Aragon and Catalonia followed inevitably. Negrín's policy, which ever more revealed its counter-revolutionary character, has brought about a progressive demoralisation, not only of the revolutionary vanguard, but of the entire working class. Since the latter has lost sight of its own objectives, it no longer perceives any urgent reason for getting itself killed to defend the bourgeois democratic clique against the Fascist clique; that is, in the last resort, to defend Anglo-French capital against Italo-German imperialism. The civil war has increasingly become an imperialist war.

Of course, M Hambresin hasn't breathed a word about all that. For him, the enemy is not Franco, but the working class. If he wanted to go to Fascist Spain in the first place, it was because he saw it as an undying enemy of proletarian revolution, and if later he went over to Negrín it is because he saw him and his Stalinist allies as the more intelligent opponents of the working class, whose methods seem to him to be the better way of re-establishing and consolidating the power of the bourgeoisie. In that case, what does it matter who wins! Whether Franco or Negrín, it is still capitalist domination that is continuing. Today M Hambresin can be pleased with himself: if he was wrong in his predictions about Negrín's victory, in any case the revolution has suffered a bloody defeat which has strengthened its enemies; and amongst those enemies must be numbered M Emile Hambresin, despite the liberal mask he hides behind.

V: Disappearances in the USSR

The February issue also included an extract from an article by Victor Serge which appeared in the Liège paper La Wallonie on 21 January.

THIS week I have received the two following items of news from Moscow. Zenzl Mühsam has disappeared. She lived in the headquarters of International Red Aid; she had tried everything to get a passport to travel abroad. Nobody knows what has happened to her, whether she has been imprisoned or deported for the second time. Already in 1936-37, she had spent several months in prison, without any reason being given. The approaches and protests of her friends abroad had got her released... Zenzl Mühsam bears a beautiful tragic name, that of the Anarchist poet Erich Mühsam who was loved throughout Germany for the zest, human warmth and thought expressed in the work of a great artist and this great fighter. As a fighter for the 1919 Soviet republic in Munich, Mühsam suffered eight years in a military prison after the repression. Then he recommenced writing and political activity. In 1933, the Nazis put him in a concentration camp, tortured him and finally killed him. The official version of his death is that he was found hanged in his cell. His widow was then invited by International Red Aid to take refuge in Moscow. They even promised her that Mühsam's books and letter would be published there. How could she have foreseen that her place of refuge would soon turn into a prison?

The other news item is similar, and yet completely different in nature: Mikhail Koltsov and his brother, Boris Efimov, both disappeared some weeks ago... Since the advent of Stalin, Mikhail Koltsov was the official journalist who was the best known, the most influential, and in short, the most official. He ran several publishing houses, sponsored aviation, edited *Krokodil*, the governmental weekly humorous magazine, carried out important missions abroad, and attended congresses for the defence of culture...

(So he had many friends amongst progressive intellectuals in the West. Will they now defend him? Will they even notice his disappearance?) At one time, he had the job of welcoming M Pierre Cot,[35] then Minister of Aviation; he was one of the architects, so they say, of the Franco-Soviet rapprochement. His most recent missions have taken him

---

35. Pierre Cot (1895-1977) was a Radical deputy in the 1930s, Minister of Aviation in the Popular Front government, and after 1945 was deputy for the *Union progressiste*, close to the PCF. He won the Stalin Peace Prize in 1954.

to Spain, where he did some pretty obnoxious work in spreading the most poisonous slanders against the anti-Stalinist groupings, and to Prague, during the Czech mobilisation... I remembered finding in one of his articles about the Rykov-Bukharin trial a sentence along the following lines: 'These infamous traitors are not men, but beasts with human faces: when I see them I am seized with such rage that I should like to cast myself on them and bite them in the throat...' I am quoting from memory, but that was it, form and content. I and another comrade were terribly sad as we read it, but all the same we could not help bursting out laughing at this journalist who thought he was preserving a human face by proclaiming his desire to 'bite in the throat' men condemned to die a terrible death within a few days... His brother did the same job with cartoons. Few people in our day have committed more outrages in the world than those two characters, who were completely flexible, obedient, orthodox, etc, etc. Now they are both in a prison cell themselves, and in the very cells that were occupied by so many of the victims they insulted.

Obituaries

Tom Cowan (1929-1998)

I WAS shocked and saddened to hear of the death of Tom Cowan last year at the age of 69. In 1945, at the age of 16, he left the Communist Party and joined the Oehlerite Socialist Workers League, in whose journal, *Workers Review*, from January to March 1948, he published articles stating a position on trade unions which he reiterated in his review of the pamphlet *The Struggle for an Independent Trade Union in Merseyside and Hull, 1954-55*, in *Revolutionary History*, Volume 6, no 2-3. In 1958, as a member of the Electrical Trades Union, Tom was tried by the Stalinist controllers of the union for opposing their conduct. He opposed John Byrne and Les Cannon, the right-wing candidates, in the union elections.

For me, Tom was a living connection with a bygone period and with comrades who have long since gone. My condolences to his family, friends and comrades.

Ernie Rogers

Cornelius Castoriadis (1922-1997)

CORNELIUS Castoriadis, who died in Paris on 26 December 1997, was born in 1922 in what was then called Constantinople. Inspired by his family, he developed a very early interest in philosophy from the age of 13. At the same period, he was drawn to Communist politics and the works of Marx, joining the underground Communist Youth in 1935 on the eve of the Metaxas dictatorship. After several months, he had an early contact with political oppression when his comrades were arrested, and his cell was dissolved. However, he escaped arrest as he was never denounced, in spite of his colleagues being severely tortured, as he recounted in a 1993 radio interview.

He resumed political activity with the Greek Communist Party at the beginning of the German occupation in 1941, co-founding a journal with a view to influencing the policies of the party, an attempt he later described as absurd and an illusion. By 1942, he had left the Communist Party and joined the most left-wing of the Trotskyist groups, led by Spiros Stinas. However, the attempted Communist coup in Athens in 1944 clarified his criticism of the Trotskyist political position. For Castoriadis, it was clear that the Communist Party was not a reformist party, as the Trotskyists would have it, but an organisation attempting to install a regime similar to the one in Russia, namely, 'totalitarian bureaucratic capitalism' as he came to call it in the extensive analyses he developed in his writings of the 1950s.

Castoriadis spent this period in Greece avoiding both Stalinist and Gestapo agents. He went to France at the end of 1945, joining the French Trotskyist party, and continued his critique by founding a tendency within it. The final break came at the end of 1948 when the Trotskyists proposed forming a front with Tito after the latter's break with Moscow. Castoriadis and other comrades left the Trotskyists, and founded the group Socialisme ou Barbarie, publishing its first review in March 1949.

The group was founded at the onset of the Cold War, and as the left was dominated by the Communists during the period of the Korean War, up until the death of Stalin, this first period was one of isolation for the group, which counted fewer than a dozen members. Nevertheless, the critique of Trotskyism was developing, with Castoriadis abandoning the residual elements of the Leninist conception of the party in 1950. Some in the group rejected the very concept of organisation, on the grounds that it was simply an intellectual group which published a review, whilst Castoriadis and others argued for an organisation based on collective self-government in order to coordinate general activities. Thus the critique of Marxism-Leninism was inextricably bound up with the development of autonomy.

With the death of Stalin and the growing unrest in Eastern Europe, the East German workers' uprising in 1953 and the Czechoslovakian strikes of 1954, culminating in the Polish revolt and the Hungarian Revolution in 1956, the political climate started changing, and the review was selling about 1000 copies. The Algerian War and the opposition to it in 1958-59 saw the group grow to about 100 members, with meetings of between 300 and 400 people in the early 1960s.

It was during this period that Castoriadis' ideas influenced a group of ex-Trotskyists in England, which led to the formation of Solidarity in 1960, and a fruitful collaboration over a number of years during which his writings were translated into English in pamphlet form under the name of Paul Cardan. This period also saw his analysis of Marxism-Leninism culminate in the critique of Marxism itself in 'Marxism and Revolutionary Theory', published over the five final editions of *Socialisme ou Barbarie* in 1964-65. Ironically, the group itself was dissolved in 1966 as the members felt that although the review had been selling well, and more people were coming to meetings, they were merely passive consumers of ideas and not active participants. Furthermore, it was these very ideas that were the initial influence of the social explosion of May 1968, openly and freely borrowed by Daniel Cohn-Bendit.

As Castoriadis gained French citizenship, the threat of instant expulsion to the Colonels' Greece for political activity was lifted, and he was able to publish his writings in *Socialisme ou Barbarie* under his own name, having written under the pseudonyms of Paul Cardan and Pierre Chaulieu. These writings were now collected into an eight-volume paperback edition between 1973 and 1979. In addition, 'Marxism and Revolutionary Theory' became the first part of his major work, *The Imaginary Institution of Society*, published in 1975, with an English edition in 1987, which is now considered to be a modern philosophical classic in France, having undergone several reprints.

Castoriadis worked as an economist for the OECD between 1948 and 1970, later becoming Director of Studies at the École des Hautes Études en Sciences Sociales at the University of Paris in 1980.

As Castoriadis developed his critique of Marxism into that of Western thought as a whole with his key concepts of social-historical creation and social imagination, he simultaneously became a psychoanalyst integrating the concepts from that field into those above, from all of which he developed the principles of the autonomous society and the autonomous individual. These ideas are expounded in the five-volume collection of essays under the collective title of *The Crossroads in the Labyrinth*, published between 1978 and 1997 in France, with English selections under varying titles in 1984, 1991 and 1997. His academic fame was such that a multi-lingual festschrift of 30 essays in his honour was published in 1989 by the Librairie Droz, *Autonomie et autotransformation de la societe*.

In France, Castoriadis was seen as one of the major thinkers of the second half of the twentieth century. His writings, although demanding, have a distinct clarity of thought which he uniquely developed away from the rather ponderous Marxist-Leninist writings of the early 1950s. He is survived by his wife Zoe and his daughter Sparta (by an earlier relationship with Rilka Walter), both of whom actively collaborated with the production of his writings, and a younger daughter from his marriage with Zoe.

Alex Economou

Morris Lewit (1903-1998)

MORRIS Lewit, known in the Socialist Workers Party of the USA as Morris Stein, died recently at the age of 95. He joined the Communist League of America in 1930, and became a National Committee member of the Workers Party of the USA in 1934. After the SWP was founded in 1938, he continued to serve on the National Committee. He was an active member of the Plumbers Union in New York City. During the 1940s, whilst the Minneapolis Eighteen were in prison, Lewit served

as National Organisational Secretary of the SWP, and he continued in this position into the postwar period. He withdrew from the SWP in the early 1960s, but remained a revolutionary.
Alan Wald

Gentle Trotskyist: Sal Santen (1915-1998)

IN his hometown of Amsterdam, the town where he came into this world on 5 August 1915, the writer and mild-mannered Trotskyist Sal Santen passed away on Saturday, 25 July. He was still full of life, recovering from a serious hip operation when he unexpectedly died from a heart attack.

The last years of his life, which he spent in the Beth Shalom Old People's Home, were hard. However many heart-wrenching novels he devoted to the subject, the sorrow over the extermination of his family in the war never subsided, and became worse as his physical condition deteriorated. The death of his wife Beb five years ago was difficult to bear. Nevertheless, he continued to fight, as he had done all his life. With his typical whispering voice, he told those close to him: 'Life is always worth living, however difficult the circumstances are.'

'Brave because it is good' was the life-long motto of Sal Santen, who described himself as someone who in his heart was always a 'scared little Jewish boy'. He had borrowed this motto, which was also the title of one of his books, from the farewell letter of his father-in-law, the resistance hero Henk Sneevliet, written just before his death in front of a German firing squad. Through Sneevliet, Sal Santen, himself coming from the poverty-stricken family of a shoemaker who supported the SDAP,[1] landed in the revolutionary movement during the 1930s. When Santen decided for Trotsky and his Fourth International, their ways parted.

After the traumatic occupation years, Santen became even more convinced of his militant standpoint. Together with the Greek Michel Raptis, he became one of the leaders of the Fourth International. In 1953, he left for Latin America to stimulate the revolution amongst peasants and workers. Back in the Netherlands in 1960, he was arrested for his support for the Algerian Liberation Front (FLN). He had assisted with a clandestine arms factory in Morocco, and by forging identity documents and providing false money for Algerian nationalists. With Raptis, he was held in custody for a year, and after an infamous political trial was sentenced to 15 months. The long period on remand led to worldwide protests, and led to Santen receiving messages of sympathy from, amongst others, Jean Paul Sartre, Simone de Beauvoir and Salvador Allende. In the celebrated documentary *Sal Santen Rebel*, a reference to Santen's book *Sneevliet Rebel*,

---

1. The SDAP (Social Democratic Labour Party) was the predecessor of Dutch Labour Party.

made by the film director Rudolf van den Berg in 1982, Sal Santen recalled how he had defended forging identity papers to the judge: 'From my experience, I knew that such a scrap of paper could mean life or death.'

At the end of the 1960s, Santen broke with the International Secretariat of the Fourth International, not for political reasons – he continued to call himself a Trotskyist until his death – but because he couldn't cope personally. He was too soft, too human and too emotional to be a professional revolutionary. His political commitment came from his humanity. Those who knew him or saw his bushy hair and soft brown eyes could see that fanaticism was alien to him.

At the end of the 1960s, Santen began to suffer increasingly from the effects of his traumatic war experiences which expressed themselves in unbearable physical pain. He came to be treated by the psychiatrist Coen van Emde Boas, who encouraged him to write about the deportation of his parents and his brother Maurits. That resulted in novels such as *You People are Jewish People* (*Jullie is jodenvolk*), his first novel, from 1969, and *Saartje Baked Bones* (1983), dedicated to his sister who died at a young age from tuberculosis. The tangible mourning for Saartje, in book after book, was linked by Santen in an unparalleled way with the almost incomprehensible enormity of the destruction of the rest of his family and all the other Jews of Amsterdam. Only in this way could he verbally express his loss.

When he already had 10 well-received books to his name, including his impressive political memoirs *Adios Companeros!*, he told me that he wrote exclusively in order to give his three children their murdered family back. Politics finally turned out not to be the centre of his life. A few years ago, I asked him to draw a balance of his life. 'The most important thing is my family', he answered, 'That as a Jew I could still build a family is very important. And beyond that... I became a writer.'

Elspeth Etty
Translated by Colin O'Driscoll

Bob Wilsker (1919-1998)

BOB Wilsker died on 24 November, and it was the sad duty of the representatives of this magazine to attend our old friend's funeral just before Christmas. The respect in which he was held by all who knew him can be gauged by the attendance of over a hundred other people. His modesty, kindness and humane values did not fit easily into the caricature so beloved by the media when speaking of professional revolutionaries. He witnessed and survived the worst years of the European working class, whose virtues and courage were reflected in his personality.

Bob was born in Vienna on 13 January 1919, in the very turmoil of the central European revolution, the son of a Jewish refugee from Russia who had retained his sympathy with the Socialist movement when he moved into his adopted country. He thus grew up in a very political atmosphere. He even remembered how the workers burned down the Viennese Palace of Justice when Heimwehr thugs who had ambushed and murdered their comrades had been acquitted, which happened when he was only eight years old. Street battles involving deaths on both sides went on for two days when Seipel's clerical regime authorised the use of mounted police against the demonstrators. Bob's father was the printer and binder of the Communist Party's illegal edition of Lenin's *State and Revolution*, brought out at the height of the mid-1930s repression in Austria, and he often supplied the Trotskyists with the paper needed for their own publications. Bob himself began his political career as a Socialist Zionist, a member of Hashomer Hatzair, but then moved over with his group to the Trotskyist movement. By this time there were only about 50 of them in Austria, and their activities were totally clandestine. His memories of Dollfuss' suppression of the Austrian workers in February 1934, of which he later wrote an article in *Fourth International* over the pseudonym of P Berger (Volume 5, no 7, July 1944, pp211-3) were particularly vivid. The government had been carrying on repeated searches for months to seize the arms caches of the Schutzbund. There was some resistance to this in Linz, and the fighting spread to Vienna. The government turned the heavy guns on the Karl Marx Hof and a few other places where they were barricaded in. Bob was at work when the electrical workers replied with a defensive strike, immobilising the trams and some of the factories. The lights suddenly went out, and a rolling growl came from the heights around Vienna where the artillery was firing on the blocks of flats where the workers lived.

If this were not enough, Hitler himself rode triumphantly into the city four years later. A wave of anti-Semitism came with him, and Bob had buckets of water emptied all over him. By the time of the smashing of the houses and synagogues in the Kristallnacht he had served his apprenticeship, and his father told him: 'It is time for you to go.' This was several years before the 'Final Solution' of the Jewish question, and the Nazis were glad enough to allow Jews to leave. Bob's sister had already placed an advertisement for 'a young toolmaker' in the journal *Machinery*, and since by this time all Europe was rearming, he obtained a job and a work permit. He crossed Germany and Belgium, and made it safely here, where he went to work in a toolroom behind the Army & Navy Stores in Portchester Road, and joined the AEU.

Rita Dewar had met Austrian Trotskyists in Prague before she came to England, and although her new husband's group was the least favoured of the three existing British organisations by the International Secretariat, theirs was the only address Bob had been given. So his first contact over here was with Harry Wicks and Hugo Dewar, but being a skilled engineering worker he rapidly moved over to the Workers International League, which had an effective fraction operating within the arms industry and the AEU during the war. He was also a member of the German Trotskyist group in London, their only Austrian member, as the rest of the German speakers were either from Czechoslovakia or Germany itself. By the end of the war they were producing *Solidarität*, and several of them lived in Nora Saxe's house in Gayton Crescent in Hampstead (*Revolutionary History*, Volume 7, no 1, 1998, p79). They were not only watched by Scotland Yard, but spied on by the Stalinists as well.

Bob's impeccable anti-Nazi credentials had not prevented him from being arrested and interned on the Isle of Man after war broke out. Fortunately, he was not there for too long, and he remembers his stay as being one of the most intellectually stimulating times in his life (cf *War and the International*, pp82-5). After his release he got a job in Smiths Industries in Cricklewood, which allowed him a certain amount of leeway for his political activities. Along with English comrades such as Sid Bidwell, he took copies of *Solidarität* to fraternise with the German prisoners in Wormwood Scrubs. By this time the army authorities made no attempt to stop them, sensing that whatever influence they wielded there was obviously going to be firmly anti-Nazi (cf *Revolutionary History*, Volume 7, no 1, p145). Bob wrote for the paper under the pseudonym of 'Binder', amongst others.

The debates amongst the German Trotskyists over here towards the end of the war were very lively, and Laufer and the IKD tended to look down upon the British comrades of the WIL and the Revolutionary Communist Party as being theoretically somewhat underdeveloped. The main point at issue was over the *Three Theses*, the argument that the experience of Fascism, Nazism and Stalinism had such a retrograde effect on Europe that the only feasible policy by the end of the war was agitation for a return to the freedoms of bourgeois democracy (cf *Revolutionary History*, Volume 1, no 3, Autumn 1988, pp23-4; David North, *The Heritage We Defend*, Detroit, 1988, pp101-7; French translation of the full text in Rodolphe Prager [ed], *Les Congrès de la quatrième internationale*, Volume 2, Paris, 1981, pp102-7). Bob belonged to the London group allied with the WIL/RCP who opposed this view, although it had much more support amongst the scattering of German exiles elsewhere who supported the AK of the IKD. He remembers Laufer himself as being the only German Trotskyist in the London who fully supported it, and this only after some months, since he had first been in Coventry on his arrival.

Having settled in England after the war, Bob finally came round to something like this point of view many years later, and his political activity up to his death mainly revolved around the Labour Party, the Fabian Society and CND in the Oxford area. Apart from his wider horizons, this central European revolutionary, a fugitive from the worst storms of our century, could easily have been taken for an archetypal English gentleman. But his sympathy, his friendship and his regard remained with us.

Al Richardson

We are especially grateful to Karl Thierl for correcting our mistakes and providing us with much of the context for our memories of Bob, whom he first met in Vienna and later in London. We have incorporated most of the information he has supplied into the text, but we are sure that our readers will also find the following remarks very useful. We also take this opportunity to publish Karl's correction to our short summary of his own views in our previous vignette of Nora Saxe (*Revolutionary History*, Volume 7, no 1, p79).

Solidarität was written and produced by our group of Austrian and German Trotskyists... The group was formed on the initiative of Pierre Frank with a long polemic I drafted against the *Three Theses*, as a platform published in July 1944, signed by 'a group of European comrades' as our first publication. It first appeared in the *Fourth International* (Volume 5, no 11, November 1944, pp331-5), and later in an abridged version in *Quatrième Internationale* (new series, no 25-26, December 1945-January 1946, pp26-31). The article also dealt with the so-called Military Policy of the British and American parties, etc. The RCP allowed us to give their address as publishers for legal reasons. They had, however, no editorial control. *Solidarität* was mainly distributed by members of the RCP in the various POW camps... I was the only one of our group to keep in contact with Laufer – we were personal friends since Belgium, but after the *Three Theses* affair I was no longer welcome at their meetings. We were also members of the RCP, participating in their activities, whilst the members of their group completely isolated themselves...

I should like to add a few remarks concerning the vignette on Nora, mainly for your information. In the information on Nora I supplied you with I wrote that Nora joined the Trotskyist movement in 1934. I was mistaken, it was 1932.

The fourth paragraph speaks of the ferocious repression in '*Eastern Europe*'. The period in question is the 1930s, so the repression was in *central Europe* (Germany, etc).

I wrote back to you, among other things, that 'about 1948, or shortly after... I came to consider the Marxist theory mistaken and – insofar as scientific – as refuted by events quite some time ago, this very much along the line of K Popper, with whose writing I acquainted myself a few years later...'

You, however, wrote in the final version regarding myself... 'He later came to the view that the ideas of Marxism had become scientifically refuted by the writing of Karl Popper... ' I had, of course, said nothing like this. It is also factually wrong. In 1948 I had not even heard of Popper, or his ideas. The two works of Popper I read first were *The Poverty of Historicism* and *The Open Society and its Enemies*, editions of 1961 and 1966 respectively. I could not have read them before these dates, and other works of his I read even later.

To say that a theory like Marxism, that is, a theory about the development of society and the course of History is refuted by 'scientific writings' does not even make sense to me. This can only happen in non-empirical sciences, like mathematics or logic. Marxism is about society, History, and their laws of development. Actual events have proved the theory wrong. Engels used to say that 'the proof of the pudding is in the eating' — an empirical test — quite in accordance with the science of the time he regarded a tested and confirmed theory as certain knowledge. Although Popper does not regard a 'confirmed' theory — corroborated, as he would say — as certain knowledge, but only 'hypothetical', for him, too, it is the empirical test that is decisive. Events proved Marxism's predictions wrong.

There is, however, another aspect. The Marxist theory is also historicist, that is, it claims to predict the future of history. Historicism is, of course, a general term referring to all theories purporting to predict the future. This Popper claims to have refuted, or shown for strictly logical reasons to be impossible. The argument rests on the consideration that human history is strongly influenced by the growth of human knowledge, which of course cannot be known today, that is, before it has happened. Therefore, there cannot be any theoretical history or a historical social science that could correspond to theoretical physics. Of course, not all social predictions are refuted, all sorts of social predictions are possible — economic theories, for instance — but only the possibility to predict the historical developments that are influenced by the growth of our knowledge is ruled out.

Marxists of today, to save their beliefs, ignore Marx's life's work and search in forgotten or unpublished early writings of Marx. They remind me of augurs or suchlike, delving in the entrails of animals, or of fortune tellers examining tea leaves.

Marx has made many valuable contributions to our understanding of society and History. He deserves better than to be treated as an oracle whose obscure pronouncements need to be interpreted.
Best regards
Karl

Work in Progress

Argentine Trotsky Study Centre

THE Leon Trotsky Centre for Study, Research and Publication of Argentina was set up last year. It is devoted in particular to the work of Trotsky, and more generally to key events in the international class struggle. It aims to carry out in Argentina the work that is carried out in Europe by the Leon Trotsky Foundation (*Cahiers Léon Trotsky*) in France, the Centro Pietro Tresso in Italy, and *Revolutionary History* in Britain. It hopes to involve in its work a wide range of people in and around the Trotskyist movement. The first activity by the Centre was a declaration repudiating the slanders against Trotsky repeated by Gennadi Zyuganov, the leader of the Russian Communist Party, on his visit to Argentina.

The CEIP has recently published *Escritos Latinoamericanos de León Trotsky*, a compilation of Trotsky's writings on Latin America in Spanish. It contains articles, letters, discussions and interviews from the period of Trotsky's exile in Mexico from January 1937 until his assassination in August 1940, including the series of articles from the magazine *Clave*. Some of the material has appeared before in Spanish, although much of it has not been available for decades. Several articles have been translated from the French from the *Cahiers Léon Trotsky*, and are published here in Spanish for the first time. The book has 335 pages, including 16 pages of photographs, and costs £10.00 plus p+p.

Contact the Centre at CEIP, Calle Pasteur 460, 4ª piso, depto 'G', Capital Federal, Argentina (telephone 00 541 14 952 2302, e-mail: ceiplt@usanet). It is open from 17.00 to 21.00 Monday to Friday, and from 14.00 to 19.00 on Saturday.

Marxism on the Internet

THE Marx-Engels site <http://www.marx.org> is being reorganised, and is now quite distinct from the 'Marxists' site <http://www.marxists.org> where Lenin Trotsky, Luxemburg and so forth can be found. There does not appear to be, or did not at the time of writing, a link from Marx to the Marxists, though there is one going the other way. A happy development is that four comrades have taken the responsibility of scanning in and putting on line all 45 volumes of Lenin's *Collected Works*.

It has only just started, and it is estimated that the task will take at least two years. We will owe these comrades a great debt. As far as Trotsky is concerned, the problem of copyright has meant that such an approach is not possible, though about 45 articles appear, and the *History of the Russian Revolution* is nearly finished. However, one member of the Board of *Revolutionary History* has undertaken to scan in all the articles by Trotsky on Britain where there is no copyright problem, and *Where Is Britain Going?* is now on-line.

The ETOL (Encyclopaedia of Trotskyism On Line) site has a wide range of articles from the first three volumes, nos 1-12, of *Revolutionary History*. These issues are now out of print, and so this material is available once more to readers.

Ted Crawford

Other Websites

THE Victor Serge network has been set up on <http://users.sky net.be/johneden>. Amongst general material on Serge, it will also be including John Manson's translations of Serge's *Carnets*.

Material by and about the US Socialists Albert and Vera Weisbord can be found on <www.weisbord.org>.

Marx and Engels on CD-ROM

THE major works of Marx and Engels have been produced on a CD-ROM as part of the *Essential Classics in Politics* series. It is available from The Electric Book Company, 20 Cambridge Drive, London SE12 8AJ, £24.95 + £1.95 p+p.

Spanish Anarchist Shenanigans

BALANCE, no 18, the journal of labour and revolutionary history published in Barcelona, has reprinted a secret report to the congress of the Anarchist international, the International Workers Association, in Paris in December 1937. Curiously, the secret report, *El Anarcosindicalismo en la Revolucion Española*, by Helmut Rüdiger, a Swedish Anarchist who was the liaison officer with the Spanish movement, was published by the CNT some months later.

The document sheds new light on the Spanish libertarian movement, and Agustín Guillamón, the Editor of *Balance*, is to be congratulated on reprinting it. However, it is unlikely to be translated into English as few people, Anarchist or otherwise, will identify with it. Rüdiger is as scathing about the utopianism and immaturity of Spanish Anarchism prior to

1936 as he is admiring about its moderation and political judgement a year and a half later. The author provides a theoretical justification for the collaboration with the Stalinists and bourgeois republicans which the CNT leaders did not themselves make.

The argument is simple and familiar. Libertarian principles had to be shelved for the duration of the war and replaced by anti-Fascist unity, as it was essential not to annoy the Russians or the Western powers. Rüdiger constantly warns of the danger of 'totalitarian' action, by which he meant collaboration with left-wing forces such as the POUM. The CNT's traditional objective of a workers' revolution also becomes totalitarian. The Friend of Durruti are seen as playing into the enemy's hands. Foreign Anarchists are asked to exercise restraint on what they report. Rüdiger is alarmed at the prospect of too close an association with foreign parties, such as the Independent Labour Party and its cunning Marxist leaders.

The many CNT prisoners in the Republic's jails saw a more concrete version of 'totalitarianism' than that feared by Rüdiger. The report is a curiosity, as CNT activists in prison and exile took a more left-wing stance, and would probably prefer not to be reminded of it. No wonder the report was secret, but why was it published soon afterwards? Guillamón thinks that in December 1937 the CNT leaders did not want their allies to know that they were prepared to submit to any demand, but that a few months later that fact was self-evident.
John Sullivan

Publications from CERMTRI

THE third issue of the *Cahiers du Mouvement Ouvrier* contains an excellent collection of documents on the Soviet purges, the Kirov assassination and the fate of Riazanov, plus Daniel Guèrin on the Popular Front and the colonies, and much more. The fourth issue of the magazine has appeared, despite the untimely death of Vadim Rogovin, the joint editor. It features four articles by Rogovin, plus an interview he conducted with Ogan Yakovlevich Dogard, a survivor of the Soviet Left Opposition, material on the CNT in the Spanish Civil War, and a translation of John McNair's essay on Orwell. They each cost 50 francs plus p+p. *Cahiers du CERMTRI*, no 90 (September 1998) includes material on Trotskyist and Anarchist interventions in the class struggle; no 91 (December 1998) is devoted to the German Revolution of 1918-19, with contemporary articles by Luxemburg, Liebknecht and Radek, and historical pieces by Volkmann, Centizon and Prudhommeaux. They each cost 25 francs plus p+p. Write to CERMTRI, 28 rue des Petites-Ecuries, 75010 Paris, France.

Cahiers Léon Trotsky

THE latest issue of the *Cahiers Léon Trotsky* (November 1998) covers Stalin's policies in China, early Communism in Egypt, Saccho and Vanzetti, and the wartime revolutionary left in Italy, including a translation of Arturo Peregalli's article in *Revolutionary History*, Volume 5, no 4. The May 1998 issue contains a translation of Udo Winkel's article on Paul Levi from *Revolutionary History* Volume 5, no 2. They each cost 90 francs plus p+p. Write to Institut Léon Trotsky, 477 Chemin du Puits, 69210 Fleurieux sur l'Arbresle, France.

Russian Archive Collections

COLLECTIONS of documents from the Russian archives concerning vital episodes in the history of the Russian Revolution and the USSR – from Kronstadt to the Soviet repression of the 1956 Hungarian Uprising – are rolling off the presses. These Russian-language collections are mainly the work of publishing projects headed by academics, some Russian, and some in joint initiatives with Western universities. A journal devoted to publishing items newly uncovered in the archives has outlived the perestroika period when such material fascinated a wide audience. If the archivists and historians don't believe that dictatorship could return and the archives be closed again, they are certainly working as if they do.

This year, three volumes have been published by the Russian Political Encyclopaedia project (Rossiskaya Politicheskaya Entsiklopedia or Rosspen). *Letters to the Power 1917-1927* (*Pisma vo vlast 1917-1927*, Rosspen, 1998, pp664) is subtitled *Declarations, Complaints, Informers' Statements and Letters to the State Structures and Bolshevik Leaders*, and includes 360 items. It was edited jointly by historians from the Moscow State University, the Italian Institute for Philosophical Studies and two French institutions, the School for Advanced Study of Social Science and the Humanities Institute.

The Soviet Countryside As Seen By The Secret Police, Documents and Materials 1918-1922 (*Sovetskaya Derevnya Glazami BChK-OGPU 1918-1922, Dokumenty i materialy*, Rosspen, 1998, pp864) is billed as the first of four volumes that will continue the theme up to 1939. The team of editors is headed by A Berelovitch (France) and V Danilov (Russia), working with the support of the same French institutions and of both the police and army archives.

The Soviet Union and the Hungarian Crisis of 1956: Documents (*Sovetsky Soyuz i Vengersky krisis 1956 goda: Dokumenty*, Rosspen 1998, pp864) is the result of collaboration between Russian and Hungarian academics, and includes documents relating to the interaction of Soviet and Hungarian party machines and the process by which the Soviet invasion was decided upon.

The International Democracy Foundation (Mezhdunarodny Fond Demokratia), with which the Gorbachev-era historian Aleksandr N Yakovlev is associated, has begun a major publishing programme of documentary collections. The foundation is well-regarded by the American establishment, and has found funds for an ambitious publishing programme.

In 1997, the foundation published four volumes. *Kronstadt 1921* (*Kronshtadt 1921*; Fond Demokratia, 1997, pp432) should hopefully provide the means to advance a dispute amongst revolutionaries that has long been going around in circles. A contemporaneous story, less well-known outside Russia – of Filip Mironov, the Don Cossack leader who first sided with the Bolsheviks, then fell out with them, and was killed by the Cheka in early 1922 – is dealt with in *Filip Mironov: The Quiet Don 1917-1922* (*Filip Mironov: Tikhy Don v 1917-1922 gg*; Fond Demokratia 1997, pp780). A third collection on the killing of Polish officers at Katyn is entitled *Katyn: Prisoners of an Undeclared War* (*Katyn: plenniki neobyavlennoy voiny*); a fourth, *Lubyanka: VChK-KGB 1917-1960*, covers the history of the secret police more in outline than in the detail of the other volumes.

The foundation promises literally dozens of further volumes. A series of Stenogramme Reports of the Plenums of the CPSU Central Committee and other documents 1953-64 has begun, with a volume on Beria's fall (*Lavrenty Beria 1953*). Other volumes on Stalin, Malenkov, Zhukov and Khrushchev are promised; Molotov, Malenkov and Kaganovich will come as a one-volume package. Other subjects the foundation promises to cover include 1941, the Gulag Archipelago, the Siberian uprisings against the Soviet power in 1920-21, the transition from the NEP to forced collectivisation, the Soviet power and ecology, Czechoslovakia 1968, and the Soviet rôle in the Middle East. A monster eight-volume series on Russian-American relations is envisaged.

A team of historians of rural Russia, headed by Viktor Danilov and Teodor Shanin, has begun another publishing project, which has so far put out documents on another key clash between Lenin's government and the peasantry, *The Antonovshchina: The Peasant Uprising in the Tambov Region 1919-1921* (*Antonovshchina: Krestyanskoe Vosstanie v Tambovskoi gubernii v 1919-1921 gg*, Intertsentr, Tambov, 1994 pp325, large-format), as well as an oral history collection, *Peasant Voices: Twentieth Century Rural Russia in the Peasant Memory* (*Golosa Krestyan: Selskaya Rossiya XX veka v Krestaynskikh Memuarakh*, Aspekt Press, Moscow, 1996, pp414). Another Canadian-Russian team of academics has recently published a special document collection on the impact of forced collectivisation in Saratov.

The journal *Istochnik* (*Source*), which consists mainly of documents from the archives and commentaries on them, also deserves mention. It recently celebrated its fifth birthday, having survived a turbulent and financially difficult period in which paper prices have soared and demand for specialist literature has fallen with purchasing power. *Istochnik* covers all Russian history, but consistently turns out new documents from the Soviet period. The first number for 1998, for example, included a lengthy letter written from prison in 1937 by the veteran Left Social Revolutionary leader, Maria Spiridonova, and a letter to the Bolshevik Central Committee written in September 1920 by Anton Vlasov, a Red Army commander, protesting at the privileges enjoyed by state bureaucrats behind the lines during the Civil War. *Istochnik* is a sister publication of the more popular historical journal *Rodina*.

As for the archives themselves, comprehensive information on them is available in English on the Internet, at <http://www.iisg.nl/~abb/>, a site maintained by the International Institute of Social History in Amsterdam; the information is provided by Patricia Kennedy Grimsted and the Federal Archive Service of Russia. For those sufficiently robust to withstand gusts of right-wing sensationalism, there is also the Revelations from the Russian Archives page of the US Library of Congress at <http://lcweb.loc.gov/exhibits/archives/intro.html>.

For revolutionaries who see the Russian revolution as 'ours', it is blindingly obvious that the volume of new material now becoming available on the social order that ensued from that revolution is as vast as our resources to study it are meagre. There may be few sensational revelations left to emerge from the archives, and we may not share the priorities and prejudices of those now editing the document collections – but there is plenty of material here for the reconsideration of our history. Those with an interest in this work and/or information to add to the above are invited to get in touch via *Revolutionary History*.
Simon Pirani

Paul Flewers

'I Know How, But I Don't Know Why'

George Orwell's Conception of Totalitarianism

A *New Interventions* Pamphlet

£2.50 UK, £3.00 Europe, £3.50 rest of the world

Write to *New Interventions*, PO Box 485, Coventry CV5 6ZP, United Kingdom

---

Reviews

André Liebich, *From the Other Shore: Russian Social Democracy After 1921*, Harvard University Press, Cambridge, 1997, pp476, £29.95

THIS book is a real labour of love. There can be very few people who would spend a great deal of time and effort chronicling the fate of the exiled remnants of a defeated and persecuted party, but that is what Professor Liebich has done with this most valuable account of the Mensheviks after their enforced exile in 1921.

Readers will probably be familiar with the approach elaborated by the Mensheviks' leader Yuli Martov, which condemned post-1917 Bolshevism as an authoritarian utopian Socialist leadership coming to power in a backward country in which Socialism was impossible to construct, whilst refusing to side with right-wing attempts to overthrow the Soviet regime; and with the subsequent development of the post-Martov Menshevik leaders, with Rafael Abramovich becoming a Cold War anti-Communist, and Fedor Dan becoming a virtual apologist for Stalinism. However, readers may well be unaware of many of the other factors that Liebich outlines, such as the fact that the Mensheviks' internal regime was fairly authoritarian and at times intolerant, and that their recruitment regulations did not permit people from outwith the Soviet Union or their own offspring to join, which effectively doomed the party to extinction.

One important issue which Liebich brings to the fore is the way in which the Mensheviks revised *post festum* their history and analyses in order to present the development of their party as distinct and divorced from the dread influence of Bolshevism from the start, a mirror image of official Soviet historiography. Hence, the fuzzy differentiation between the two halves of Russian Social Democracy, the policy concurrences and personnel interchanges, prior to 1917 were subsequently reinterpreted as an irreconcilable and unbridgeable gulf from 1903. Similarly, the Mensheviks' hesitant and inconclusive analyses of the great changes in the Soviet Union in 1927-30 were forgotten as the Stalinist socio-economic formation was subsequently seen — either positively or negatively — as the inevitable product of Bolshevism.

The Mensheviks maintained a sustained appraisal of Soviet affairs, and Liebich outlines their critique of the New Economic Policy, their following of the leadership struggle in the Soviet Communist Party, their critique of Stalin's collectivisation and industrialisation schemes, and their accounts of the Menshevik Trial of 1931, the Moscow Trials, the 1936 constitution, and so on. He describes the Mensheviks' relations with other Socialist parties, comparing their lack of success with the insular and indifferent British Labour Party leaders with the support they received in France and Germany. He also shows how the Mensheviks participated in the theoretical debates in the Socialist movement, and how the split between Dan and Abramovich was influenced and exacerbated by the rise of pro-Soviet tendencies, especially around Otto Bauer, and the emergence of theories of totalitarianism in the 1930s. Liebich also investigates the fate of the Mensheviks in exile in the USA. Dan's minority wing, which split away in 1941, worked for pro-Soviet publications, whilst Abramovich's majority aligned themselves with the predominant anti-Communist forces within the US labour movement, and subsequently concentrated upon academic work on the Soviet Union; not, it is worth noting, that this prevented them from being investigated as potential subversives by the FBI into the 1950s.

Noting that some Mensheviks considered that by 1930 their position on the Soviet Union was quite close to Trotsky's, Liebich touches briefly upon the possibility of some sort of radical anti-Stalinist unity emerging in the 1930s. Nonetheless, this unity could not be forged. It was not so much that Trotsky, as Liebich correctly notes, refused to cooperate with them (although his programmatic call by the late 1930s for the legalisation in the Soviet Union of all parties accepting the soviet system implied the retrospective rehabilitation of all but the most right-wing Mensheviks, and the possibility of some sort of cooperation with them, at least with those who still adhered to Martov's line), but the fact that many Mensheviks changed as the 1930s drew by. Liebich shows how the evolution of Dan and Abramovich drew them away from Martov's line (although, rather confusingly, he also says that Dan kept to it, compare pages 84 and 198). Yet surely the great changes in the Soviet Union, with the creation in the 1930s of a huge working class through the building of a massive industrial base and the collectivisation of the peasantry, meant that the objective preconditions for a move towards Socialism now existed in the Soviet Union, and that Martov's line could then have been updated to coincide with the programmes of various dissident Communists, Trotsky included, rather than rejected.

More perhaps could have been said about the relationship between the general trends within Social Democracy and the Mensheviks' political evolution. The latter was most clearly exemplified by the repudiation of Martov's line by both wings of the party. Dan's pro-Soviet faction paralleled the left-wing Social Democrats who were willing to overlook or even justify the unpleasant nature of Stalin's regime in their admiration of Soviet economic growth and in their quest to build a broad front against Hitlerite Germany, and whom after 1945 sailed too close to Stalinism in their desire to find a counterweight to capitalism and its apologists in the labour movement. Abramovich's anti-Communist faction paralleled the mainstream Social Democrats who concluded that the revolutionary overthrow of capitalism would only end in tears, and that the sole way forward was through modifying capitalism, refining bourgeois society, rather than abolishing it.

Abramovich and his comrades were not *sui generis* in this respect. Many left-wingers fell into despair in the 1930s and especially after 1945, giving up on any transformative concept of Socialism, substituting for it at the most piecemeal reformism, and jumping with almost indecent haste into the clutches of the Campaign for Cultural Freedom and Cold War hysteria. Cold War Social Democracy did not need the Mensheviks to kick it off, it had long been hostile to the Soviet Union to the extent that it would line up with its own capitalist class against it, rather than take an independent class approach. As for the influence of the Mensheviks upon Western and especially US Sovietology in the postwar period, although their empirical and interpretative analyses were and remain eminently valuable, their political approach tended merely to add grist to the Cold War mill, and we had to await for a new generation of scholars to arise in the late 1960s before a more objective approach to the Soviet experience emerged.

In conclusion, one can only repeat what Isaac Deutscher said about 'the long melancholy story' of the Mensheviks in exile:

'Thus Menshevism has ended its long career, driven into two ideological impasses: in one we saw the conscience-stricken Dan humbling himself before Stalinism; in the other we heard Abramovich praying for the world's salvation by the Pentagon. What an epilogue this is to the story of Martov's party; and how Martov's ghost must be weeping over it.' (*Ironies of History*, p225)

Minor points apart, this is an excellent book, and anyone interested in the history of the Socialist movement, the Russian Revolution and the Soviet Union should make the effort to read it.
Paul Flewers

Noreen Branson, *History of the Communist Party of Great Britain 1941-1951*, Lawrence and Wishart, London, 1997, pp262

THE Communist Party of Great Britain was formed in 1920 for the explicit purpose of overthrowing capitalism and instituting Socialism. Even of late, when its political programme was openly reformist, it still called for the Socialist transformation of Britain. So it is an irony of history that the CPGB considered its finest hour to be during the Second World War, or at least the period after the Soviet Union joined the fighting in June 1941. This was the time when it stood closest to the ruling class, opposing working-class militancy, and supporting a coalition government led by the arch-Tory Winston Churchill. This book, the fourth volume of the history of the CPGB, covers the period when Stalin became a national hero in Britain, and the party bathed in his reflected glory. It also covers the gloomy years of the Cold War, when Stalin became the devil incarnate, and the CPGB was obliged to operate in the shadow of his infamy.

Noreen Branson presents a superficial and sanitised account. She is economical with the truth. It's not that she tells porkies *à la* the *History of the CPSU(b) (Short Course)* or James Klugmann's *From Trotsky to Tito*, but many issues are only lightly touched upon or are glossed over altogether.

We cannot find in this volume any evidence of the CPGB's vindictiveness towards left-wingers who refused to obey the strictures of the wartime *union sacrée*. Perhaps Branson feels that others have given sufficient publicity to, say, William Wainwright's *Clear Out Hitler's Agents* that she need not raise the matter. It's not a minor issue, as the CPGB spent a lot of effort harassing recalcitrant Socialists, and in other parts of Europe this sort of mentality actually led to the Stalinists killing their left-wing rivals.

As for another embarrassing episode during the war, Branson does rather sheepishly admit that the *Daily Worker* 'went so far as to suggest' that the atomic bombing of Hiroshima 'would expedite Japanese surrender and thus save "valuable lives"' (pp99-100). The actual words of the *Daily Worker* on 7 August 1945 were: 'The employment of the new weapon on a substantial scale should expedite the surrender of Japan.' Not one or two, but their 'substantial' use; which represents a substantial distortion on the part of Branson.

The unsuspecting reader will not gather from this account that the CPGB maintained its hostility to working-class militancy for two whole years after the Second World War finished. It's interesting what a little research will reveal. Coming up against a few contrary delegates, General Secretary Harry Pollitt warned the party's 1945 congress:

'You are either in favour or not of the line that has been expounded here of mass strikes as the only way to realise the workers' demands, and if you are, I warn you you are playing with fire that can help to lose the peace and reduce this country to ashes... You can get a strike in the coalfields tomorrow if you want it. Will it advance the working-class movement of this country, or the perspective of our nation being a first-rate nation in the family of united nations?' (*World News and Views*, 8 December 1945)

True to their leader's proclamation, the Stalinists who ran the Scottish region of the miners' union made no protest when the Minister of Fuel and Power shut down Fauldhouse pit in April 1946 after an unofficial strike, putting 370 miners on the dole. A strike in Grimethorpe led to the whole of Yorkshire coming out in the summer of 1947. Arthur Horner, a CPGB Executive Committee member and the miners' union General Secretary, said that the strikers were 'holding the country to ransom' (*The Times*, 9 September 1947). Shortly before, on 7 May, the *Daily Worker* delicately referred to 'substitute winders' during a winders' strike in Durham and Lancashire. Such was the spirit of cooperation of the Stalinists in the miners' union leadership that they continued to work closely with the National Coal Board and the government after the CPGB belatedly turned to support workers' militancy when Moscow called for a harder line in late 1947.

Branson takes many of the party's contemporary rationalisations at face value, betraying either naiveté or disguised disingenuousness. Are we really to assume that Pollitt did not recognise the reactionary nature of Clement Attlee's government until 1948 (p157), or was it Moscow's harder stance in late 1947 that made him think again? And as with the CPGB at the time, Branson makes much of the voting figures at the TUC and Labour Party conferences, as if these block votes wielded by union bureaucrats are anything but the vaguest reflections of working-class sentiments. She talks of the 'hundreds of millions' of people who signed the Stalinists' international peace appeal during 1950, forgetting to add that every adult in the Soviet bloc was a signatory, showing, as Fernando Claudín put it, 'the same impressive efficiency and unanimity with which they voted for the single lists at elections' (*The Communist Movement*, p578).

Branson devotes a few pages to the CPGB's anti-racist work, but she refrains from mentioning her party's attitude to the German people, who, in an imitation of Hitlerite racial stereotyping, were held *en bloc* responsible for the Nazis. The *Daily Worker* said on 3 August 1945 that reparations, which hit the German workers more than any other class, were fair: 'The German people have to pay for their support of the Nazi plunderers.' Nor does Branson mention her party's campaign against Poles in Britain. Horner's pamphlet *The Communist Party and the Coal Crisis* warned: 'We will not allow the importation of foreign – Polish, Italian or even Irish – labour to stifle the demands of the British people to have decent conditions in British mines.' And as he fulminated against his members' legitimate – and necessarily unofficial – action over pay and conditions, he threatened the government with a strike over foreigners, saying that it 'might get Poles or displaced persons but not coal' (*The Times*, 24 February 1947). The Stalinist-controlled Civil Service Clerical Association barred Poles from membership.

This chauvinism was accompanied by increasingly fierce manifestations of British nationalism as the 1940s drew to a close. Britain was seen as a mere colony of the USA, and the CPGB's main gripe against the British bourgeoisie and the labour movement leaders was that they were unpatriotic. On 12 September 1949, the *Daily Worker* howled: 'Britain and the Empire is to be sold piecemeal to the American money-lenders.' In his subtly-titled pamphlet *Get Out!*, party historian Leslie Morton complained that US troops were spreading 'corruption and moral degradation among our young people'. He condemned the influence of American comics and films, he demanded policies that would 'put Britain first', and called for the defence of 'our cultural heritage' and for 'the protection of our children from the spread of these alien and disgusting attacks on their moral welfare'.

The CPGB's aggrieved patriotism, of course, could not prevent it from coming under heavy fire during the Cold War, and Branson spends a fair amount of space describing the witch-hunts of the late 1940s, which ranged from party members being sacked from jobs and removed from union posts to the Cabinet discussions over whether to try the *Daily Worker* for treason – a capital offence – during the Korean War. This, it should be remembered, was under a Labour government! Whilst condemning these attacks, we should not forget that the Stalinists pulled the roof down on their own heads by defending the appalling conduct of the Stalinist regimes in the Soviet Union and Eastern Europe. Branson's halfhearted efforts at explaining her party's apologies for Stalin's actions add nothing to what her colleagues have said elsewhere.

Branson makes much of the attempts by the CPGB to appear as a British party rather than a British section of an international conglomerate, a task that was formally made more easy by the dissolution of the Communist International in 1943. I say 'formally', as few observers were fooled. It made no real difference, and the CPGB continued dutifully to follow Moscow's twists and turns until at least the mid-1950s.

The CPGB was a product of the great wave of working-class radicalism that erupted at the end of the First World War. Formed in the wake of the Russian Revolution, it failed to recognise that the Bolshevik experience was to go sour, and that the regime they supported in Moscow was a cruel caricature of Socialism, ruled by an anti-working-class élite. British Stalinism's 'finest hour', when its membership topped 50 000 for the only time and when its influence was at its zenith, was also when it most clearly failed in the fundamental duty of any Socialist organisation – the promotion of the independent interests of the working class – and this failure was rooted in its fealty to Moscow. Whilst it is a caricature to see British Stalinists purely as 'agents of Moscow', the CPGB nonetheless followed the Moscow line on all the major issues. Its most fondly remembered time was when the Soviet bureaucracy was aligned with the British ruling class, which is why the CPGB considered that the interests of the working class were synonymous with those of the bourgeoisie. The Stalinists did not understand this at the time, and, judging by this book, they are still unable to do so.

Paul Flewers

David King, *The Commissar Vanishes: The Falsification of Photographs and Art in Stalin's Russia*, Canongate, Edinburgh, 1997, pp192

READERS will know how 'unpersons' vanished from Soviet pictures during the Stalin era, and will recall that infamous example where Trotsky and Kamenev became a set of steps up to the podium from which Lenin was speaking. Indeed, a few years ago, a graphics software advert reproduced that picture with a caption which went something like: 'We could make Trotsky disappear better than Stalin.' Certainly, there was often something incompetent about the hatchetmen's scissor-work in Stalin's time and afterwards. I remember seeing a pamphlet recounting Brezhnev's wartime career illustrated with a picture of the man not only in which his head was twice as big as it actually was, but you could also see the join under his chin.

The Commissar Vanishes is a striking and chilling insight into the insane proportions of Stalin's regime. The vivid style that we have come to expect from David King is used to brilliant effect, showing how people who had fallen from grace literally disappeared from official photographs, and the continual purges meant that each revision had to be replaced by a further one, often until only Stalin remained. Moreover, people would mutilate their own copies of books to ensure that 'unpersons' did not disgrace their shelves, and thus leave them open to accusations of sympathy towards them.

Oppositionists from the 1920s disappeared from photographs, airbrushed out or cropped. In one example here, Mr and Mrs Trotsky vanish behind two nonentities who have been crudely pasted over them. Later on, it's Stalin's cronies who disappear. Yagoda's fall meant that Dmitri Nalbandyan's group portrait was revised, with the disgraced secret police chief's image being replaced by a coat draped over a handrail 'as if he had neither the time nor the need to take it with him' (p156). It wasn't just political rivals who went. Some editing jobs were pointless, like the ordinary worker who vanishes from Stalin's side, or just bizarre, like the telescope pointing at Krupskaya's head in a family shot by Lenin's sister Maria, which gradually disappears over three revisions.

Although all governments lie about their activities and try to suppress unpleasant facts, and although much history is written to serve the paymasters, and even in the most open parliamentary democracies much is withheld from the probing historian, let alone the general public, official falsification under Stalinism was peculiarly intense and far-reaching. How did the Soviet regime get into this appalling position? Why did it feel obliged continually to rewrite its history? Although this is not touched on in this book, it's worth making an analytical aside.

The Bolsheviks took power in October 1917 at the head of a militant working class, with which it had a dynamic and close relationship. However, that relationship soon started to disintegrate as the more militant workers took up posts in the party-state apparatus, and many others returned to the countryside or became disenchanted with the Bolsheviks as conditions deteriorated during the Civil War. Rather than gradually dissolving itself within the working class, as a revolutionary party should do under the dictatorship of the proletariat, the party started to substitute itself for the disintegrated working class, representing it in spirit, as it were. Instead of a dynamic relationship between party and class, the party-state apparatus started to see itself as the incarnation of the interests of the working class, and in its insecure position in the Soviet republic, it then began to see itself as the indispensable core of society.

Although the Bolsheviks looked to this mystical image of the party in order to legitimise their rule, it should not be thought that this was necessarily cynical or even conscious on their part, at least at first. As the 1920s drew on, however, and as the party-state apparatus developed into a discrete social stratum with interests that diverged from those of the working class, the myth of the party took on an increasingly cynical tone as the party's leadership battled against the sharp criticisms of its revolutionary opponents, and used it as a device to discipline and expel them. Under these conditions, the sense of indispensability became mutated into a quasi-religious sense of infallibility – from having a monopoly over power to having a monopoly over the truth.

The cult of the mystified infallible party reached a peak under Stalin with the transformation of the Soviet bureaucracy into a self-conscious ruling élite. This coincided with the hypertrophied state control that was imposed during the massive industrialisation and collectivisation schemes of the First Five Year Plan. Lacking the coherence that genuine planning or even the market would provide, the Stalinist system was chaotic, with the centre attempting to control all aspects of social life. This proved an impossible task, and rule of the omniscient and infallible centre was necessarily convulsive and subject to sudden and dramatic shifts. Infallibility cannot coexist happily with drastic changes. In a situation in which what was correct yesterday may be totally wrong today, those responsible for the blunders of the past must not only be punished if the myth of infallibility is to survive, but their very presence and their actions must be struck from the record as well, in order to enable the current version to be seen as the only possible historical truth. This, of course, runs into problems as today's truth may well be tomorrow's blunders, thus leading to another round of record expunging and new historical truths. And so it goes on.

Faced with the rewriting of history, Trotsky told the Stalinist regime:

'You can juggle quotations, hide the stenographic reports of your own speeches, forbid the circulation of Lenin's letters and articles, fabricate yards of dishonestly selected quotations. You can suppress, conceal and burn up historic documents. You can extend your censorship even to photographic and moving-picture records of revolutionary events. All these things Stalin is doing. But the results do not and will not justify his expectations. Only a limited mind like Stalin's could imagine that these pitiful machinations will make men forget the gigantic events of modern history.' (*The Stalin School of Falsification*, p69)

Although the re-emergence and discovery of hidden Soviet photographs, documents, etc, occurred in circumstances that Socialists did not particularly desire, at least they are now in the open, as are the 'pitiful machinations' of those who usurped and destroyed the Russian Revolution.

Paul Flewers

Aindrias Ó Cathasaigh (ed), *James Connolly: The Lost Writings*, Pluto, London, 1997, pp265, £45/£13.99

> 'The evil that men do lives after them,
> The good is oft interred with their bones.'
>
> Shakespeare, *Julius Caesar*

IT is the unfortunate fate of great political and religious leaders that when they die, their message frequently falls into the hands of their principal followers, who proceed to use it for their own purposes in ways with which the leaders would have disagreed had they remained alive. As Aindrias Ó Cathasaigh's excellent introduction demonstrates, Connolly's writings have suffered from this process with a vengeance. Following his judicial murder by the British authorities in Ireland in 1916, James Connolly's literary and political legacy passed into the hands of his son-in-law William O'Brien, who became leader of the Irish Transport and General Workers Union and also one of the principal 'labour lieutenants of capital' (in the time-honoured phrase) in Ireland. As a result, the main collection of Connolly's writings, which appeared between 1948 and 1951, is an abbreviated version which creates difficulties for anybody trying to attain an overall picture of Connolly's political development.

We have reason, therefore, to be immensely grateful to Ó Cathasaigh for assembling this collection of some 65 additional writings. Instead of dividing the material according to subject matter, as the 'official' collection does, the editor has arranged the pieces in more or less chronological order. As a result, it becomes easier to see how Connolly included in his vision of Socialism the conception of a free united Ireland under working class leadership — a goal which remains to be fought for.

It is by no means only Irish Socialists for whom these writings are of interest. Connolly had first-hand knowledge of the British labour movement, and parts of the collection deal with the deficiencies of HM Hyndman's Social Democratic Federation. The article 'Parliamentary Democracy' (*The Workers' Republic*, 22 September 1900) gives a critique of the British Constitution. One of Connolly's criticisms is:

'The powers of parliament are... somewhat arbitrary and ill-defined. Every general election is fought on one or two main issues, and on these alone. It may be the franchise, it may be temperance, it may be Home Rule, or any other question, but when parliament has received from the electors its mandate on that one question it arrogates to itself the right to rule and decide on every other question without the slightest reference to the wishes of the electorate.' (p48)

This point was originally made by Rousseau in *The Social Contract*:

'The English people imagines that it is free: it is gravely mistaken. It is only so during the election of members of parliament: as soon as they are elected, it becomes a slave, it is nothing. The English people makes such use of the brief moments of its liberty that it deserves to lose it.'

Connolly, however, goes on to deepen our understanding of this lack of freedom:

'The democracy of parliament is in short the democracy of capitalism. Capitalism gives to the worker the right to choose his master, but insists that the fact of mastership shall remain unquestioned; parliamentary democracy gives to the worker the right to a voice in the selection of his rulers, but insists that he shall bend as a subject to be ruled.'

Capitalist democracy is, in other words, a contradiction in terms: the people do not rule, the capitalists do.

Not surprisingly, in view of the above, we find in the *Platform of the Socialist Labour Party* of 1903 that Connolly includes a section as follows:

'Public Ownership: 1. Right of all national and municipal employees to elect their immediate superiors and to be represented upon all public departments directing their industry. 2. Nationalisation and municipalisation of all industries upon the above basis.'

As can be seen from writings by Connolly reproduced up to now, it is the style which he employs that marks him out as a publicist. He constantly grasps the essential feature of a given situation, describes it graphically, and then finishes by drawing the necessary conclusion and ramming it home in an uncompromising fashion – and all this not without a spark of humour if possible. In this way, he contrives to follow his own advice to the Irish TUC:

'We need to feel in every fibre of our consciousness that all the offices and positions through which civilisation performs its every function are manned, equipped and sentinelled by alert and implacable enemies of our class, and so feeling we must labour to create a public opinion that shall eventually supersede and destroy the public opinion of the master class as the standard by which our patriotism and the value and efficiency of our institutions are to be judged.' (p136)

The more adverse the conditions, the more Connolly seems to be able to rise to the occasion. Most of the second half of the volume, to whit, pages 138-218, covers the period of the First World War. Absolutely typical of Connolly's response is an article written for *The Workers' Republic*, in which he begins by quoting the results of a survey of housing conditions in Dublin as reported in the *Irish Times*. This revealed that nearly 28 000 of Dublin's citizens were living in accommodation deemed by the Corporation to be unfit for human habitation. This news reinforces Connolly's basic Marxist conviction that the main enemy is at home:

'Therefore we cry aloud that all might hear: War or no war, those slums must be swept out of existence; war or no war, those slum landlords are greater enemies than all the "Huns" of Europe; war or no war, our children must have decent homes to grow up in, decently equipped schools to attend, decent food whilst at school; streets, courts and hallways decently lighted at nights; war or no war, the workers of Dublin should exert themselves first for the conquest of Dublin by those whose toil makes Dublin possible; war or no war, the most sacred duty of the working class of Ireland is to seize every available opportunity to free itself from the ravenous maw of the capitalist system and to lay the foundations for the Co-operative Commonwealth – the Working Class Republic.' (p153)

It is vintage Connolly. The Ulster poet John Hewitt was wrong when he said that Ireland had no equivalent of the Levellers and Diggers. They were there all right, right in front of his nose in his own century: Padraic Pearse was the Irish Lilburne, and James Connolly was the Irish Gerard Winstanley. Of course, the differences are also considerable between these Irish democrats and their English predecessors, but the part played in each national tradition is roughly the same.

Aindrias Ó Cathasaigh indicates in the introduction that there remains a great deal more of Connolly's writings still uncollected, plus all his letters. We look forward to their appearance in print, and, I must say, it is our duty to do all we can to ensure this can be achieved. In conclusion, let me add, for any readers conversant with the Irish language, that Ó Cathasaigh has written a study of Connolly entitled *An Modh Conghaileach*, which, if this selection and its introduction is anything to go by, should be worth reading.

Chris Gray

FA Ridley, *Socialism and Religion*, Rationalist Socialist League, Amersham, 1997, pp39, £1.50

FRANK Ridley (1897-1994) was well qualified to write this short pamphlet, which serves as an introduction to a fascinating subject. Ridley was the author of a number of books on the place of religion in history, such as, for example, *The Assassins* (1938, republished by Socialist Platform in 1988), *The Evolution of the Papacy* (1938), *The Jesuits* (1938) and *The Papacy and Fascism* (1937). These have not, in my opinion, received the attention they deserve; if this pamphlet tempts readers to explore these writings, so much the better.

As Ridley says, religion involves a belief in a god or gods, from whom humans may derive benefits. He traces its roots back at least as far as the neolithic period of human history, if not earlier. In primitive societies, the gods appear either as personifications of mysterious natural forces, such as the sun, moon, thunder and so on, or else as the ghosts of great ancestors whose memory lives on. Later, with the growth of the division of labour and the emergence of 'civilisation', religion develops in the direction of greater abstraction. Hence Ridley draws a (useful) distinction between 'natural' and 'supernatural' religion (under which heading we may find Buddhism, Judaism, Christianity, Islam and presumably also Hinduism, although the latter supposedly retains many features of the prior form of religion). He then goes on to outline ways in which established religion has served to support the status quo in numerous class-divided societies, from ancient Egypt onwards. Understandably, most of the remainder of the pamphlet deals with Christianity, most space being taken up by observations on Roman Catholicism, although there is some mention of the Church of England and of the 'special case' of the Russian Orthodox Church, which Stalin reestablished in the Second World War. (The pamphlet was originally published in 1948.) Ridley's conclusion is that established religion in all its forms is irreconcilably opposed to Marxian Socialism: were the latter to triumph on a scale sufficient to realise its programme, it would inevitably undermine the social bases of religion – namely, ignorance and fear. Hence 'the gods form a united front against the revolution, for the revolution digs a common grave for all the gods'.

Despite this, however, Socialist regimes will, if they remain true to the ideals of the revolution, refrain from religious persecution, 'which would be offensive to the humanitarian ethic that is an integral part of international Socialism'. Even so, Ridley regards 'scientific Socialist propaganda' as being inevitably directed against religion, and sees the revolutionary party as obliged to combat 'all manifestations of capitalism, including those which belong to the sphere of religion' (p34).

Ridley indeed includes a brief note in which he sets out some arguments against the notion of the existence of a god:

'Historically, in the pre-capitalist days of such sects as the Lollards and the Anabaptists, there were undoubtedly heretical churches that can accurately be called revolutionary, having regard for the circumstances of the time, but this is all ancient history. It is a far cry from the revolutionary Anabaptists of the sixteenth century to the smug Baptists of the twentieth; from Jan of Leiden to Spurgeon's Tabernacle.' (p30)

Most of this analysis seems to me sound, but Ridley could perhaps have allowed himself a little more space in which to develop certain points. For example, he could have mentioned the early Greek philosopher Xenophanes in connection with his 'natural-supernatural' distinction. Xenophanes criticised the ancient Greek polytheism of his day in the name of a single non-anthropomorphic deity; in the course of this criticism he advances propositions which are not inconsistent with the view that it is humans who make the gods in their own image, and not vice versa:

'Mortals consider that the gods are born, and that they have clothes and speech and bodies like their own. The Ethiopians say that their gods are snub-nosed and black, the Thracians that theirs have light blue eyes and red hair. But if cattle and horses or lions had hands, or were able to draw with their hands and do the works that men can do, horses would draw the forms of gods like horses, and cattle like cattle, and they would make their bodies such as they each had themselves.' (See GS Kirk and JE Raven, *The Pre-Socratic Philosophers*, Cambridge University Press, 1957, pp168-9)

Similarly, Ridley's discussion of religious movements opposed to the status quo could well have been extended. True, he does acknowledge the possibility that 'as is not at all unlikely, Christianity itself started as a revolutionary mass-movement against Roman society', but adds that 'it was soon effectively captured by the ruling classes of the day' (p24).

Here it would appear that the key rôle was played by St Paul, the Hellenistic Jew of Tarsus in Asia Minor, who correctly saw that any movement marked by Jewish revolutionary nationalism stood no chance of gaining mass support among the gentile populations of the Roman Empire (see Hyam Maccoby, *The Myth Maker: Paul and the Invention of Christianity*, Weidenfeld and Nicholson, 1986). In this connection, Ridley praises Karl Kautsky's *Foundations of Christianity* as 'probably the best single book ever written by a Marxist on a religious theme' (p9), but Kautsky's book was written in 1908, and there has been a wealth of scholarly commentary since then on the topic. Kautsky found it hard to accept the existence of Jesus of Nazareth as a historical person – see Part One of his book – but the alternative, that the Christians invented some fictitious Messiah, raises even greater difficulties, and must be discarded. The most important recent development has been the discovery and publication of the Dead Sea Scrolls, writings which contain in places concepts that find their parallels in the so-called 'synoptic' gospels (Mark, Matthew and Luke), and which require consideration in any complete analysis of early Jewish Christianity. Here the work of Geza Vermes – *Jesus the Jew*, *Jesus and the World of Judaism* and *The Religion of Jesus the Jew*, plus his edition of the Scrolls in English translation, is of paramount importance. Robert Eisenman and Michael Wise's book *The Dead Sea Scrolls Uncovered* (Element Books, 1992) is also worth consulting. Kautsky's work of 1908 is indeed of high quality, but it is certainly not the final word on the subject.

It is perhaps also regrettable that when Frank Ridley and Ellis Hillman were preparing the pamphlet for republication in 1986, they did not include anything on the so-called 'Liberation Theology', which appeared amongst supporters of the Catholic Church in Latin America. This was a movement which tried to incorporate certain elements of Marxism into Christian thought, and which exerted an influence in, for example, the Brazilian labour movement, with the Partido dos Trabalhadores. Ridley would no doubt have been able to make some interesting observations on this.

Ridley's anti-theological arguments are also somewhat unsatisfactory. Epicurus' contention that God must be either all-powerful or all-good or neither is open to the objection that the 'gift' of free will for humans is of supreme importance, enabling them to establish themselves as co-workers in God's scheme of things; also if the soul has a beginning, there is no *a priori* reason why it should have an end – although on materialist grounds this seems an acceptable conclusion to draw. Finally, by the term 'cause' we do not necessarily understand something that is also an effect of a previous cause; hence a 'first cause' is a distinct possibility. However, this first cause does not have to be 'God' or 'the gods'; it might just as possibly be matter in some form. In the European middle ages, David of Dinant proposed something of this kind when he argued that God was in fact 'prima materia'. He was roundly condemned for this by St Thomas Aquinas, but Aquinas' difficulty sprang here from the prevalent notion that matter was essentially passive and inert. According to modern physics, this is by no means the case, and accordingly active matter can play the rôle of a non-theological first cause, if necessary.

So much for the criticism of religious metaphysics, which is, of course, not the sole possible criticism of organised religion. Space prevents any further remarks on this: I would only like to mention in this respect the entertaining and (hopefully) thought-provoking observations on the subject made by the comedian Dave Allen.

One final cavil: Ridley quotes Marx's dictum 'Religion is the opium of the people' without giving the full quotation, which runs:

'Religious distress is at the same time the *expression* of real distress and the *protest* against real distress. Religion is the sigh of the oppressed creature, the heart of a heartless world, just as it is the spirit of a spiritless situation. It is the *opium* of the people.' ('Introduction' to *Contribution to the Critique of Hegel's Philosophy of Right*)

Ridley quotes only part of the next paragraph of Marx's text on page 8 of his pamphlet; the paragraph in full runs:

'The abolition of religion as the *illusory* happiness of the people is required for their real happiness. The demand to give up the illusions about its condition is *the demand to give up a condition which needs illusions*. The criticism of religion is therefore *in embryo the criticism of the vale of woe*, the *halo* of which is religion.'

The passage is worth quoting in full, I think, because it shows amongst other things that Marx was more aware of the appeal of religion than many religious people are of the appeal of Marxism, and also that Marx did not demand that religious believers should simply give up their past beliefs, merely that they should work for real happiness achievable on earth.

I have indicated where I think Ridley could have expanded his analysis, but, in conclusion, I wish to stress one of the points he makes. He writes on page 21:

'Under capitalism, and in particular under monopoly capital, the most advanced form of capitalism which brings all its contradictions to a head, the first natural root of religion – man's awe of natural phenomena – becomes extremely weak, and indeed, in the most advanced countries, almost disappears with these societies' growing mastery of natural forces due to the machine age. However, the second, social root in insecurity and in social disharmony acquires a terrible and altogether unprecedented power due to the previously unheard-of intensity of prevailing social contradictions, expressed in war, crisis, and universal instability. Hence, in our dealing with current religion, it is its second, *social* root that almost exclusively concerns us, as Lenin specifically insisted.'

The tasks for Socialists is to identify the insecurities and social disharmonies, and outline measures for their elimination.

The pamphlet includes an introduction by Terry Liddle, who also contributes a useful list of books. *Socialism and Religion* can be obtained from the publishers at 70 Chestnut Lane, Amersham, Buckinghamshire HP6 6EH, for £1.50 plus postage, cheques payable to Colin Mills.

Chris Gray

Richard Brenner, *Trotsky: An Introduction*, LRCI publications, London, 1997, pp51, £1.50

THIS handy pamphlet aims at being a young people's introduction to the life and contribution of Leon Trotsky, and as such should be welcomed. It is organised around a number of well-chosen sections, followed by short but useful bibliographies. It touches upon most of the main aspects of Trotsky's contribution to Marxism. Unfortunately, it has been written with less care than it should have been. Because a publication aims at an elementary explanation, that does not mean that it has to be cavalier with the facts.

Apart from sloppy formulations that can easily give the wrong impression – such as that 'the Left Opposition was based on the revolutionary working class' but 'the Bukharinites' class basis was amongst the richest peasants' (p24), there are a large number of straight factual bloomers. Orwell's *Animal Farm*, for example, takes the form of an animal fable, not a 'fairy story' (p24); Trotsky was not the only former Bolshevik leader not to capitulate to Stalin (p25); it is not true that the Chinese Communist Party made no attempt to win over soldiers in the Guomindang army (p31) – several of its future generals came from there; the Freikorps were set up in December 1918, not '1919' (p33); it was impossible for Stalin to negotiate with the Nazis in 1924 (p37). (Even if this is a misprint for 1934, the Treaty of Berlin had been signed the year before, in May 1933.) The well-known quotation originating in Mexico claiming to come from *Pravda* describing the GPU's activity in Spain (p39) was proved to be apocryphal some years ago. And if Comrade Brenner has been told 'little of the great slave rebellion led by Spartacus' (p1), then perhaps he should apply himself again to his books, for on this topic there have been enough of them. Similarly, he might be 'left ignorant' (p1) of the strikes of the tomb workmen of ancient Egypt (so ignorant, indeed, that he seems to think that they were paid in gold), but they have been known to modern scholarship for over a century (the best more recent account for those who do not read in Late Egyptian is in the *Journal of Near Eastern Studies*, Volume 10, no 3, July 1951, pp137-45).

Moreover, some of the particular positions of *Workers Power* have been fathered upon Trotsky without any attempt to distinguish between them. Now Marxism is a creative methodology, and there is, of course, nothing at all wrong in principle for the theorists of our own day to disagree, alter or revise the points of view of the giants of the past, though in this case it has to be admitted that Mr Brenner is rather full of himself. But if this is to take place, the least we should require is that it be recognised in the text. For example, Trotsky resolutely refused to side with any one national group struggling against the others in his reportage of the Balkan wars, whilst *Workers Power* on the whole sides with the Bosnians; this deep difference is covered up with the seemingly innocuous remark that 'he distinguished at all times between reactionary wars fought for profit and the justified resistance of nations whose fundamental freedoms were being denied' (p7). Similarly, whatever the reasons for forming the Fourth International in 1938, the argument that each national party should operate 'as an integral part of a democratic centralist international movement' (p45) was hardly one of them, for the International Communist League had never operated on any other basis until then. And readers of such statements as 'Trotskyists are not disillusioned by Stalinism's collapse because we have been proved right' (p21) might be forgiven for assuming that *Workers Power* had foreseen this outcome, which is certainly not the case.

It is a great shame that this carelessness should have marred so excellent an undertaking, for there is a deep need for such a basic introduction. Let us hope that such *Workers Power* veterans as Dave Stocking or Keith Hassell are allowed to correct the text before it is reissued in a second edition.

Al Richardson

International Communist Union, *Hungary 1956: When the Workers' Councils Raised the Banner of the Proletarian Revolution*, Workers Fight, London, 1996, pp28, £1.00

THIS pamphlet, no 30 in the Internationalist Communist Forum series, commemorates the fortieth anniversary of the Hungarian uprising, as well as placing it within the framework of the analysis developed by the ICU's parent organisation, *Lutte ouvrière*. It makes the claim that the objective of the Hungarian insurgents was to create 'the dictatorship of the proletariat' (p1) by overthrowing an 'artificial bourgeois regime' (p4), further defined as a 'bourgeois regime... prone to nationalist tendencies' (p6). This is in line with *Lutte ouvrière*'s theory that the Soviet Union alone was a workers' state, and that in spite of the parallel social, economic and political structures, all the 'peoples' democracies', as well as China, Cuba, etc, remained bourgeois. This is not as illogical as it sounds, for it is undeniable that the USSR alone was founded by a true workers' revolution, and so must retain more of a working-class character than states created by peasant insurrection or imposed by Russian conquest.

But there are obvious problems with this analysis, which surface from time to time in the text. It is early on admitted that it was Hitler's conquest, rather than the Soviet occupation, which destroyed the embryonic bourgeoisies of Eastern Europe, and that 'to all intents and purposes, the Eastern European bourgeoisies were therefore virtually expropriated by German capital' (p2). Yet within a year or so these seemingly dead bourgeoisies come to life, apparently without any injection of capital, and Stalin is then said to have 'filled the political vacuum with these artificial bourgeois regimes' (p4), so that 'because the Eastern European state bureaucracies remained intact, representing the same privileged classes, these regimes retained their original fundamental constitution' (p6).

But for a state to retain a bourgeois character, a bourgeoisie has to wield power within it. The bourgeois parties in the Eastern European governments were transparent fictions, and real power lay in the hands of the local Stalinist bureaucrats, installed in office by a several million-strong Russian army in 1945. Whatever happened to the Marxist analysis of the state as 'armed men standing in defence of property'? Wasn't the Red Army the instrument of a workers' state? Doesn't the victor in a war between states of a different class character impose his property forms upon the vanquished? Even this text has to admit that 'the Soviet bureaucracy was already in control of the state machineries' (p6). So the only way out of the contradiction is to argue that Stalin's puppets administering these states somehow represented the bourgeoisie there as well, so, for example, Imre Nagy is described as 'a responsible politician of the bourgeoisie, and at the same time an entrenched Stalinist' (p12).

It has to be said that the demands of the Hungarian insurgents as summarised in this pamphlet in no way prove that they were facing a bourgeois state. They are no different from the programme of a workers' insurrection against Stalinism in the USSR as defined by the *Transitional Programme*. Khrushchev's regime had already degenerated far from the norms of a workers' republic, whereas regimes such as that of Rákosi and Gerö had never even approached them. By 1956, the distance was about the same, so that taking on one regime meant taking on the other.

Al Richardson

Jane Rowlandson (ed), *Women and Society in Greek and Roman Egypt: A Sourcebook*, Cambridge University Press, Cambridge, 1998, pp406, £16.95

AS far as the ancient world is concerned, the present reviewer would be the last to accept cheap jibes about 'dead white males', but it is still true that university courses in the history of political ideas have led Marxists to concentrate on Aristotle, Plato and other great thinkers, to the total neglect of how the system might have worked in practice. Anyone who wishes to take a real look at ancient society would do far better to study this book. However, it should be done in the knowledge that it is dangerous to use it for generalisations to apply to the rest of the Mediterranean world. Egypt was certainly not typical, and it is only the wealth of documentation provided by its hot dry climate that justifies so close an examination.

One of the reasons for Egypt's anomalous position is that Graeco-Roman civilisation was largely imposed upon the older society without displacing it, leaving the original social and economic system intact in the countryside for some centuries. In fact, no less than three legal systems operated at different levels, Roman law at the top, Greek in the middle, and Egyptian custom at the bottom. Since this book draws largely upon Greek documents to illustrate the manners, mores and legal position of the upper classes, and upon Demotic documents for the native population, Marxists are able to compare them and draw important conclusions. For example, those who accept the contention that the position of women is a measure of the advance of any society, and uphold the schema of Engels' *Origins of the Family, Private Property and the State*, will be disturbed to learn that although Greek society was considerably more advanced and dynamic than ancient Egyptian, women had an infinitely lower status within it. Legal documents show that the native Egyptian woman had far greater property rights and autonomous standing than her hellenised upper-class sister (pp156ff), and 'there is considerable evidence in Egyptian literature to suggest that the Egyptians took a much more relaxed attitude towards the sexual activity of unmarried women than the Greeks' (p156). This was clearly part of Graeco-Roman Egypt's legacy from Pharaonic times, and whilst the status of women in ancient Egypt was exceptional, other pre-classical civilisations also gave them more rights than did the Greek polis (cf JN Postgate, *Early Mesopotamia*, p105).

Once we are on our guard against drawing sweeping conclusions, and ignore stock feminist anachronisms such as 'weaklings or viragos: the ambiguities of womanhood' (p354), this fascinating and well-illustrated book contains a wealth of material from an incredible spread of sources. Its other great strength is its careful organisation into well-ordered themes with informative introductions, such as 'royalty and religion', 'family matters', 'economic activities', 'being female', and, most interestingly, 'status and law'. But because women's studies do not have a clear methodology of their own, other disciplines have to be drawn upon, in this case making it very difficult for the editor to create a coherent picture, as well as to exercise complete control over her material. Few people can possibly combine a knowledge of Egyptian archaeology, papyrology, Hellenistic Greek, Patristics and Roman and Byzantine history, and even fewer (no more than a hundred in the entire world) can read Demotic documents.

This comes out in the lack of balance in this collection between pedantry and ignorance. On the one hand is the insistence upon such spellings as 'Boubastos' (p19), 'Horos' (pp49, 51, 54), 'Anoubis' (pp64, 69) and 'Kleopatra', and on the other we are told that Clemens Alexandrinus was not only a 'bishop' (p21), but even 'bishop of Alexandria' (p72). The 'prophetess of Jeme' named on the London Demotic papyrus not only lived in the 'area around the temple of Ramesses III at Medinet Habu' (p59), but was obviously attached to the small temple alongside it, by then known for centuries as 'the mound of Djeme'. Contrary to what we are told on page 72, the cult of Longinus was far more popular in Cappadocia than in Egypt. And whilst it might be the case in the Late Period that 'the Egyptian priestly caste was a closed one' whose 'wives and daughters served within the temple communities' (p55), this was certainly not so earlier. During the New Kingdom, there was no more common title for upper-class ladies than 'Chantress of Amun', whatever the religious status of their husbands. Not only is there 'no evidence in ancient Egypt for the widespread use of cotton' (p247), there is no evidence for its use at all before the third century BC. And if Procopius' description of Theodora's party turns before she assumed the purple are anything to go by, describing her as 'of non-aristocratic origin' (p45) must rank amongst the understatements of the last two millennia. Continuing in the same vein, the gentleman who asks his wife to be 'subject to me in all ways that it befits women of nobility to display to their well-endowed and most beloved husbands' (p210) can hardly be saying to the translator what he appears to be saying to the general reader.

Nonetheless, there is a great deal of life, interest and solid scholarship in this book. It cannot be ignored by anyone who aspires to understand the broader rhythms of history.

Al Richardson

Marilyn Vogt-Downey (ed), *The Ideological Legacy of LD Trotsky: History and Contemporary Times*, International Committee for the Study of Trotsky's Legacy, New York, 1998, pp179, $11

THIS book contains papers submitted to the International Conference on Leon Trotsky held in Moscow on 10-12 November 1994. Since the organisers seem to have taken their subject more seriously than previous gatherings held there, the result is a very satisfactory publication. Most of the contributors have something to say, and some of the Russian ones are very stimulating indeed, cut off as they were for so long from Trotskyism's stale orthodoxies abroad. Only rarely does this cease to be an advantage, such as when Dubrovsky discusses Trotsky's policy on the Ukraine without betraying any knowledge whatsoever of the position of Hugo Oehler, against whom he was polemicising at the time (pp167-72; cf *Revolutionary History*, Volume 3, no 2, Autumn 1990, pp1-8).

Although Voyeikov's initial formulation of the problem of the Russian state ('bureaucratic Socialism', p5) is not a happy one, he gives a brilliant demonstration of the accuracy of Trotsky's predictions about the further development of the counter-revolution in the USSR (pp17-8). It is also of note that he supports the position of the majority of the Greek Trotskyists, that the revolution cannot be completely reversed (p25), a view later endorsed by Chris Edwards (p157), although how the latter could have got it into his head that the capital required to create a national bourgeoisie there can only come from Eastern Europe itself remains a mystery to me (p158). Mamutov, on the other hand, calls the Russian model 'Asiatic in character', and points out that 'it is fully legitimate to contrast the contemporary European model to "Asiatic Socialism"' (p51). He also refers to the link between the existence of the USSR and social welfare in the West. 'If there had not been a Soviet Union', he notes, 'there would neither have been present-day Western society' (p52), a view we saw confirmed when moves to dismantle the welfare state took on added momentum after the collapse of the USSR. Mil Nikolaevich Gretsky provides a fascinating treatment of the thought of Bruno Rizzi (pp126-33), whose theories of the part that could be played by the market, producer cooperatives, etc, in the transition to Socialism have influenced such Socialist thinkers as our own Walter Kendall. Since Shachtmanites have for so long dishonestly denied Rizzi's influence upon them (cf *Revolutionary History*, Volume 2, no 2, Summer 1989, p7, and Volume 4, no 4, Spring 1993, p169), restoring him to his rightful place in the development of thought is most welcome, and Gretsky also directs our attention in passing to another Italian thinker, Umberto Melotti (p129), whose *Marx and the Third World* must be one of Marxism's most neglected classics.

But perhaps the most exciting Russian article as far as this reviewer is concerned is that by Vladimir Borisovich Volodin (pp54-60), since it approaches from a different angle the reasoning in the preface to *In Defence of the Russian Revolution* and the article 'The Russian Revolution: A Twentieth Century Enigma' (*Lanka Guardian* and *What Next?*, 1997). 'Insofar as the means of production belong to the state', he points out, 'the bureaucracy emerges as a substitute for the bourgeoisie. Lenin had even contemplated the problem when he wrote about a bourgeois state without a bourgeoisie. According to Trotsky, the bureaucracy is a bourgeois organ of the workers' state.' (p55) After thus defining the nature of the state, Volodin goes on to place it in its historic context: 'Normal primitive accumulation which was necessary for the transition from a patriarchal to an industrial society is the function of the bourgeoisie, which fulfils the task by means of uninterrupted violence against the workers', he argues, 'but the bureaucracy replaced the bourgeoisie.' (p56) Now this in turn was itself only a stage in the development of the counter-revolution: 'The bureaucracy's total supremacy was the prelude to the restoration of capitalism, when state property had not yet been privatised but the workers had already been driven from state power.' (p59) Jim Miles approaches the problem in like mind, describing the Stalinist bureaucracy as 'the consummate expression of the bourgeois tendency within the Soviet workers' state', whilst noting that 'it is the bourgeois side of the workers' state that has to "wither away" in order to make the transition to Communism; if this does not occur, the capitalist restoration is inevitable' (p61).

Other Western contributions are less exciting, not necessarily because they have less to say. For example, Ticktin's address (pp105-13) has already appeared in *The Ideas of Leon Trotsky* (pp65-85). Much the same can be said for Simon Pirani's compact essay on the Chinese and Vietnamese revolutions, which goes over ground already familiar to readers of *Revolutionary History* (Volume 2, no 4, Spring 1990, and Volume 3, no 2, Autumn 1990), Ngo Van's *Revolutionaries They Could Not Break*, and the various books translated and written by Greg Benton. Geoff Barr, on the other hand, appears to believe that the united front could only be posed in Britain in 1926 in trade union terms – by the Anglo-Russian Committee and the National Minority Movement (pp157-8), and not at all at the level of state power by means of the Labour Party tactic. Since the remarkably obtuse British Communist Party had already been groping towards this with the National Left Wing Movement, and entire chapters in Trotsky's *Where is Britain Going?* hinge upon it, we can hardly conclude that the Workers Revolutionary Party and its successors have advanced the Marxist understanding of these islands very much.

A further defect of the Western contributions is to limit themselves to arguments of the 'Trotsky woz right' variety, but an additional disappointing feature that emerges in some of them (and not only those from the West) is an attempt to smuggle into the conference the sterile factional conflicts we have to endure over here. Chris Edwards, described as 'a worker and an activist in the workers' and Socialist movements in the United Kingdom' (p177), uses most of his space (pp157-66) for an attack upon Sean Matgamna. The hapless Matgamna himself was not, of course, present to reply, though he would have found himself broadly in agreement with the thesis of Butenko (pp117-21; the coincidence in names is unfortunate) as opposed to the following article by Kuryonyshev (pp122-5).

In this context, it cannot be said that the work of the English language editor has at all added to the value of what is here. Spellings like 'Dzhilas' have been left as they were. The first article by Voyeikov has two sets of footnotes, one on the bottom of the pages and the other at the end, which makes following the text very confusing. The reason for this appears to be that the editor wished to abuse her position by 'amplifying and clarifying some points' (p v), which on several occasions (for example, p14, n8; p22, n10; p23, n11) amounts to polemicising with the writer's point of view. This is all the more impudent when we discover that she has seen fit to place her own contribution immediately after his, and subjects a later article by Gusev to the same treatment (for example, p83, nn2 and 3; p88, n5; p98, n7; p99, nn8 and 9). Her own article 'setting the record straight' includes the old story about Cannon, 'one individual' who 'by chance learned about Trotsky's positions' and so 'began' the Trotskyist movement in the United States (p31). Such fairy tales do not gain in credibility the more they are repeated, and should have been abandoned long ago (cf *Revolutionary History*, Volume 5, no 1, Autumn 1993, pp106-7; *Journal of Trotsky Studies*, no 2, 1994, pp226-7).

However, it would be small-minded to allow such things to get in the way of the instruction to be gained from this splendid book. And how exciting it is to discover that the great theorist of the revolution should again be so well understood in the land of his birth!

Al Richardson

Hall Greenland, *Red Hot: The Life and Times of Nick Origlass*, Wellington Lane Press, 1998, pp336, £10

THE author of this biography, who was for a short time the organising secretary of the Vietnam Solidarity Campaign in Britain, has given us a well-sketched-out picture of one of international Trotskyism's most endearing characters, as well the authentic flavour of the Australian labour movement, so like our own, and yet so unlike. Let us hope that we do not have wait for the death of his old comrade Issy Wyner before we get a similar biography of him.

After leaving the Communist Party in 1931, at the height of the 'Third Period' lunacy orchestrated there by the double agent HM Wicks (p25), Nick Origlass was for many years the leading Australian Trotskyist. His infectious activism left a permanent stamp upon his movement, which has always carried on a high level of political activity on both local and international issues, and never spawned such contemplative sects as we trip over in Europe and North America. So the great value of this book lies in its detailed descriptions of Jack Sylvester's work amongst the unemployed (pp15ff, 34ff) and the industrial conflicts in which Origlass himself invariably played a courageous and honourable rôle (pp7-13, 48-54, 105-9, 122-35), culminating in the historic Balmain strike of 1945 that put an end to the onward march of Stalinism within the Australian trade unions (chapter 15, pp137-48). This heroic wartime activity is by far the most exciting part of the book, even if its context is hampered by the author's inability to grasp Trotsky's politics at the time. For it is very dubious to argue that Trotsky 'spoke out in favour of the entry of the United States into the war, principally because it would give Stalin courage to break his alliance with Hitler' (p99; cf *Revolutionary History*, Volume 1, no 3, Autumn 1988, pp39-40; Volume 3, no 4, Autumn 1991, p14), and it is simply not true to say that Trotskyists 'would not sabotage production for the war effort in countries allied to the Soviet Union' (p100).

However deeply involved he was in his own movement, Origlass never forgot the international dimension of all true working-class politics. His first contribution to the American *Militant* was as early as October 1935 (p65), and for many years it was he who sat painfully translating Pablo's manifestos and theses, word for word from a French dictionary (p viii). It was on his insistence that the Australian group continued to support Pablo after Frank, Maitan and Mandel had decided to remove him from the leadership of the International Secretariat of the Fourth International. The description of this unseemly operation, which was carried on after Pablo's imprisonment over the Algerian currency affair, so that the Troika could end its divorce with the Americans, occupies several pages (pp227-35). 'When the Secretary was released after being captured by the enemy', complained Origlass, 'resumption of his position should have been automatic.' (p231) The full toy-box of factionalism's petty tricks is poured onto the floor for us to look at, including a notable contribution from Livio Maitan (p230). (Maitan seems to have been even better at this sort of thing than Frank, for he once allowed one of our comrades to go all the way to northern Italy to appeal to a world congress, and then had him ordered home on the station platform.)

But it is interesting (and enigmatic) to note that whilst Origlass insisted upon international democratic centralism, it appears to have been purely on the level of programmes and manifestos, for he does not seem to have applied it to himself. The mid-1930s was the first period of Trotskyism's entry into Social Democracy, and the author admits 'the absolute centrality of the Labour Party for anybody interested in working-class politics' in Australia (p199). Yet Origlass himself was for many years the main opponent of entry into the Australian Labour Party on a thoroughly Oehlerite basis, it was only undertaken by the group as late as 1941, and he only applied to join himself in 1950! So having refused to accept Trotsky's policy, when he did finally get in, it was in order to carry out the *sui generis* tactic of Michel Pablo instead (pp202ff).

For all its value (and it is considerable), the book still cannot escape history's curse, which comes from its very nature, that it is always written with the advantage (?) of hindsight. Origlass himself rose to the leadership of the Australian group at its 1937 congress (pp73-7) by opposing the revision of Trotskyist theory and practice undertaken by John Anderson, described as a 'precursor of the New Left ideas of the 1960s and 1970s' (p74). 'It seems ironical when we consider the later Nick Origlass, the pioneer of participatory democracy, that he should have been such an uncritical Bolshevik at this time', comments the author; 'later, of course, he would come to agree with much of Anderson's thesis. Experience, social change, Balmain and Michel Pablo would ring that change.' (pp77-8)

This is therefore very much a book written from an ex-Trotskyist point of view, so we get the obligatory references to the New Left, along with Gramsci, 'the great Italian reformer [!]' (p5). And whilst we can agree with its description of the War/Revolution thesis of the Third World Congress of the Fourth International as 'apocalyptic' (p193), the same label is also applied to the *Transitional Programme*, along with 'messianic', 'dreaming', 'sectarian certainties' and 'a strong whiff of determinism' (pp90-3). The author evidently shares Origlass' final break with Trotskyism, repeatedly describing his politics as 'maximum democracy – in the factory, in the office, in the union, in the neighbourhood – anywhere and everywhere' (pp vii-ix, 137, etc), 'the urban environment being important' (p viii).

So from the mid-1960s onwards, Origlass became increasingly involved in the sort of green and community politics that we associate with crusties and Young Liberals, with the inevitable result of emptying them of all class content. Since the focus of the last five chapters is limited to Balmain, an area not much larger than Stepney, the book from then on loses all its international appeal, and I suspect that it must leave many Australians themselves mystified. How did a man who set out so bravely to change the world end up in his own backyard?

Al Richardson

Enquiries for this book in Britain should be addressed to 11 Temple Fortune Lane, London NW11 7UB.

Ralph Darlington, *The Political Trajectory of JT Murphy*, Liverpool University Press, Liverpool, 1998, pp316, £32.00/£12.99

Molly Murphy, *Molly Murphy: Suffragette and Socialist*, introduced by Ralph Darlington, Institute of Social Research, University of Salford, Salford, 1998, pp164, £7.99

JT MURPHY was a significant figure on the British left between 1917 and 1936. He was a leading activist in the shop stewards movement of the First World War, and subsequently the Socialist Labour Party, the Communist Party of Great Britain, and finally the Socialist League in the 1930s. Sadly, Murphy's career demonstrates how a fierce fighter for revolution, workers' democracy and Socialism from below became a passionate advocate of Stalinism and Popular Frontism. Murphy is of particular interest to readers of this journal for, as a functionary of the Communist International, he was directly instrumental in the consolidation of Stalinism and its imposition on the national Communist parties. It was Murphy who moved the expulsion of Boris Souvarine, the French defender of Trotsky, from the Comintern in 1926, and the resolution which removed Trotsky himself from the Comintern Executive in 1927.

Murphy was born into the Sheffield working class in 1888. He was strongly influenced by reading Marx and by the Syndicalist ideas of the 'Great Unrest' of the early years of the twentieth century. As an activist in the Amalgamated Society of Engineers, he became involved in the shop stewards movement which from 1915 fought against wartime dilution, the undermining of craft skills, and the conscription of skilled engineers. The strongholds of the agitation were on Clydeside, where the workers' committee was led by members of the SLP, the small, intransigent dual unionist organisation influenced by the ideas of Daniel DeLeon, and in Sheffield.

The Shop Stewards and Workers Committee Movement was formally established in early 1917. Its suspicion of leadership was incarnated in the designation of its leading body as the National Administrative Council. It stood in theory for the overthrow of capitalism. Its practice was defensive struggle to maintain trade union controls in the workshops which spilled over into opposition to the state's prosecution of the war, but never properly confronted the issue of ending it. The movement was largely limited to the skilled workers, and to the large engineering centres.

As a member of the NAC from August 1917, and of the SLP shortly thereafter, Murphy wrote the SSWCM's credo, *The Workers' Committee*, which analysed the weakness of union organisation and officialdom. It urged the creation of rank-and-file bodies, elected in the workshops but linking up across the industry, as a means of overcoming the lack of democracy and centralisation of the union leadership. For all its virtues, the statement remained within a Syndicalist problematic, circumventing the issues of political power and the capitalist state.

Perceiving the soviets as the realisation of their aspirations, the SSWCM leaders played a key rôle in the creation of the CPGB in 1920-21. After returning from Moscow, where he attended the first Comintern congress in 1920 and eagerly embraced Lenin's prescriptions for Britain, Murphy was involved in the formation of the British Bureau of the Red International of Labour Unions, which absorbed an SSWCM now severely weakened by the postwar downturn. He headed the party's industrial departments, and became the British correspondent of *Pravda*. Although he joined his former SLP comrades, Arthur McManus and Tom Bell, in criticising the implementation of the Dutt-Pollitt report dedicated to the 'Bolshevisation' of the CPGB, Murphy was to be a loyal advocate of the party's twists and turns throughout the decade, with only the occasional deviation. He was in the forefront of the campaign against Trotskyism in 1925-26.

After the General Strike, Murphy spent two years in Moscow as the CPGB's representative on the Comintern's Executive. His final transformation into a Stalinist functionary was confirmed by the attack on the CPGB he co-authored with Robin Page Arnot at the behest of the Comintern dignitary Otto Kuusinen. They rubbished the party's failure to criticise the union lefts in the aftermath of the General Strike. Murphy's assault on a policy in which he had been deeply involved in creating provoked severe, perhaps fatal, strains on his relationship with other British leaders. He came in for further excoriation in 1927 when he suggested that the National Left-Wing Movement, a coalition of CPGB and Labour Party members fighting Labour's exclusion of Communists, should be transformed into a 'third party'.

After intensive experience in key Comintern bodies as they underwent assimilation into the apparatus of the Soviet state, Murphy returned to Britain in 1928 a fanatical supporter of the 'Third Period' with its disastrous 'class against class' policy, and its denunciation of the Labour leaders as 'Social Fascists'. Sensing Soviet disapproval — for reasons that finally remain obscure — Murphy became embroiled in a dispute with the CPGB over his call for a campaign for British government credits to facilitate the Soviet Union's purchase of British goods. Somewhat mysteriously — although the party was at its lowest ebb ever — he resigned, and was ritually expelled. The whirligig of time wreaks its revenge. From Prinkipo, Trotsky wrote to his British supporter Reg Groves: 'I have learned that Murphy is expelled as "a near Trotskyist". What does this wonderful story mean?'

Murphy speedily established himself in the 'Social Fascist' Labour Party and the Socialist League, which was formed in the summer of 1932 by those members of the Independent Labour Party who wished to remain in the Labour Party after the ILP disaffiliated, and Labour lefts. By 1934, he had become the League's National Secretary. His move to the right roughly paralleled the changing policies of the party he had deserted. By 1936, with the Soviet Union in the League of Nations, he was supporting military sanctions against Mussolini's invasion of Ethiopia, a minority voice on the right of the Socialist League. In the summer of that year, he quit both his secretaryship and the League itself to prosecute the Popular Front as the full-time organiser of the People's Front Propaganda Committee, recently set up by Liberals and 'progressive' capitalists. Murphy strongly supported the Second World War, and maintained his admiration of Stalin in a panegyric published in 1945. He renounced Marxism in the 1950s, and died in 1965 at the age of 76.

Ralph Darlington's book provides the first full-length account of Murphy's life. As such, it adds only a little to our existing knowledge of his formative years. Both his activities and their context – the Sheffield engineering industry, the ethos and policies of the ASE, the politics of that city's labour movement prior to 1917 – are explained in a cursory manner. It is intriguing that Murphy joined a political party only when he was almost 30 years of age. Most of the important shop steward leaders, and certainly those who went into the CPGB, were long-standing members of the SLP or the British Socialist Party, organisations which contributed so much to the political feeling of the Marxist left in the years preceding the Russian Revolution. It is inadequate to dismiss the complexities of the BSP's attitude towards trade unionism as 'contempt' (p12). It recruited leading shop stewards, such as Fred Shaw, Willie Gallacher, Harry Pollitt and Harry McShane, not to speak of John Maclean. Contrary to what is said here, Nellie Connole's *Leaven of Life: The Story of George Henry Fletcher* (1961) implies that Ted Lismer, the leading ASE steward in Sheffield and a close comrade of Murphy's, was a member of the BSP. So of course were the Sheffield union activists and later CPGB cadres Sam Elsbury and George Fletcher.

If the SLP had 'no real base' in Sheffield (p12), it had a branch after 1906 and again from 1912, whilst its paper, *The Socialist*, was readily available throughout this period. There is an interesting note on the Sheffield branch and the problems it faced in the issue of January 1915. According to Connole's account, it was an SLPer, Jimmy Bowns, who initially forged links between Sheffield and the leading Clydeside stewards McManus (SLP) and Gallacher (BSP). At least one Sheffield SLPer, Lawrence Smith, was jailed for his opposition to the war. There may be problems with the availability of the materials required to pursue these matters, and Connole's book certainly needs checking. But more attention to Murphy's activities in the years and the environment in which his ideas developed would have made for a richer narrative, and a deeper grasp of his emerging politics.

Of course, this was the great age of Socialist pedagogy, and many young workers immersed themselves almost completely in the activities of the Plebs League and the struggle for independent working-class education. It is plausible that Murphy, something of an autodictat, recoiled, like others, from the shadow that Henry Mayers Hyndman cast over the BSP, and from the sectarianism, doctrinal disputation and dual unionism of the SLP to devote himself to the Labour College movement. Despite its potential importance to the formation of somebody he terms 'an organic intellectual' and 'a worker intellectual polymath' (p xviii), the author does not pursue this avenue. He addresses the Labour Colleges only in passing in relation to their dispute with the CPGB in 1924. Yet together with his union, this movement was one of the few constants through Murphy's life. It was *Plebs*, the journal of the National Council of Labour Colleges, which first announced Murphy's ideas to a wider audience. It published his article *Industrial Organisation*, an early draft of *The Workers Committee*, in February 1917. In the very different world of 1959, the same journal recorded Murphy's lifelong allegiances: 'AEU Highgate with JT Murphy in the chair have started a class on automation.' (*Plebs*, January 1959, p24)

The personal and intellectual influences on Murphy excite minimal curiosity in this text. Recent work of some relevance, such as Logie Barrow and Ian Bullock's *Democratic Ideas and the British Labour Movement, 1880-1914* (1996), is not drawn on. There is little about the growth – across the political spectrum – of the idea of 'the servile state'. Hillaire Belloc's term was used in the SLP, and William Paul wrote a book about it. There is the suggestion in a footnote that Murphy's conceptions of the trade union bureaucracy may have been influenced by reading Sidney and Beatrice Webb's *The History of Trade Unionism* (1894). Another possible source was Roberto Michels, who ultimately presented in his 'iron law of oligarchy' a fatalistic account of the inevitability of bureaucratic control of the labour movement. Darlington mentions in a footnote a review by Murphy in 1920 of Michels' *Political Parties* (p308, n42). But the book had been available in a translation by the British socialists Eden and Cedar Paul since 1916 – a year before *The Workers' Committee* was published. And before he fell into despair, Michels had actively fought the bureaucratisation of the German Social Democratic Party, and wrote about it in *The Socialist* in 1905.

Rather than following these trails, Darlington relies on occasional conjecture as to Murphy's activities before 1916, and on *New Horizons*, the autobiography Murphy published in 1941. Such retrospective accounts should be used, but – particularly in the case of a man who went underwent such drastic political reinvention – with circumspection and in conjunction with other sources. A mendacious statement of Murphy's from 1956 makes the point succinctly: 'When I resigned from the ranks of Communism at the introduction of Stalinist methods into the leadership of the British party...' (p256)

When Darlington's text moves on to 1917 and the climax of the shop stewards movement, it is derivative. It follows closely, sometimes too closely for comfort, James Hinton's *The First Shop Stewards Movement* (1973), as well as the same author's introduction to reprints of Murphy's *The Workers' Committee* and *Preparing for Power*, both republished in 1972. Following Tony Cliff and Donny Gluckstein's *Marxism and the Trade Union Struggle: The General Strike of 1926* (1986), only one significant revision of Hinton's work is offered. The shop stewards are criticised for failing to provide leadership in mobilising industrial action to halt the war as the movement against conscription developed in early 1918. Hinton sensitively analysed the interaction of the attitudes of the NAC – with their responsive conceptions and critique of leadership in terms of manipulation and substitutionism – and the consciousness of their members. He carefully contextualised these problems in the traditions of engineering trade unionism and craft consciousness. He concluded that the decision to retreat from calls for a strike against the war after they had consulted their members was understandable and realistic on the part of *these* stewards with *these* members in *these* conditions.

That judgement remains persuasive. It is rejected here, not on the basis of any detailed re-examination of the episode and elaboration of a rigorously documented and argued alternative course of action, but in terms of abstract, timeless rhetoric. Hinton, it is asserted, lets Murphy and his comrades off the hook for their failure actively to oppose the war, because 'the only hope lay in trying to harness the strength of an engineers' craft-based workshop organisation to the wider interests of the working-class movement, a class-wide agitation for militant trade unionism, fusing immediate economic issues with politics in a struggle against the war' (p46). This is somewhat easier on the page than in the workshops. When Murphy was victimised at this time, it proved impossible to secure sympathy action, a fact which Darlington glosses over (p50). Nor could the NAC win wider support for the Midlands strikes in the autumn of 1918. What price then a national stoppage to secure peace? As Bernard Waite's *A Class Society at War: England 1914-18* (1983) demonstrated with a wealth of detail, there was a lack of support amongst workers for an anti-war movement. Posing alternatives is fruitful, but only so long as we have evidence to justify their serious consideration, and only so long as we operate with proper conceptions of historical possibility, related to a careful examination of what actions could have been realistically conceived by the protagonists at the time, as well as both the potential and the constraints within the prevailing situation. In the case under scrutiny, the social forces for the realisation of an alternative history were simply not present.

Much of Darlington's material on the events leading to the formation of the CPGB flows directly from secondary sources, primarily Ray Challinor's *The Origins of British Bolshevism* (1977). Perhaps understandably, Darlington tends to overemphasise Murphy's rôle in the development of the SLP towards Bolshevism. The *party* was moving in that direction before Murphy became a member. As with *The Workers' Committee*, we must recognise the dialectic between individual and collective in the generation of ideas. The rôle, amongst others, of McManus, Bell and Paul, stalwarts of the party from the start of the century, deserves more emphasis than it receives in statements such as 'Murphy and the other SLP shop stewards' and 'Murphy and his comrades' (pp58-9). The enmity that Murphy's individualist stance on the BSP-SLP unity talks engendered amongst his comrades was longstanding (see Tom Bell, *The British Communist Party: A Short History*, p57).

The best section of this book examines Murphy's involvement in the problems of the CPGB through the 1920s. Darlington has examined the documents of the CPGB in Moscow, and tracked down Murphy's papers in Canada. The result is an account which adds significantly to earlier work such as Walter Kendall's *The Revolutionary Movement in Britain 1900-21* (1969), and LJ McFarlane's *The British Communist Party: Its Origins and Development Until 1929* (1966). Darlington's research vindicates Kendall on the extent of Russian influence and subsidy to the CPGB. He estimates that around £1 million was expended on launching the party, although he emphasises the ideological confluence of the British Marxists and the Bolsheviks. The impact of the Soviet funds – some would argue they played a disorganising rôle rather than simply lubricating both the passage of alien conceptions of organisation and politics from the USSR to Britain and the CPGB's subordination to Moscow – requires further assessment.

As against the recent tendency to detect and celebrate the CPGB's autonomy from the Russians, Darlington is clear and emphatic; allowing for the need for tactical realisation of broad policy on the national terrain, political subservience was the norm. Any autonomy, he concludes, was 'strictly circumscribed and limited mainly to day-to-day operational issues. All the major strategic issues were laid down by the Comintern in Moscow, and adhered to by the various national sectors.' (p293) Whilst no good judge would disagree, the author occasionally minimises the space available for opposition. Discussing the lack of dissent in the CPGB over the excommunication of Trotsky in 1924-25, he argues a stark either... or: 'The problem for the CPGB leadership was that it had to accept the situation or break with the Comintern.' (p141) Why then was there initial and sometimes extensive and sustained opposition in other national parties? As with much recent work on British Communism, the absence of international comparison limits the analysis. The history of the French party or, more dramatically, the similarly small and weak Belgian party demonstrates that before the ultimate interdiction of the International descended, there was room for manoeuvre. The specific weaknesses of the CPGB in relation to other parties, particularly the range of concrete factors which saw the British workers' leaders of 1920 reduced by Stalinism, requires further exploration.

Darlington's book is valuable in at least beginning to look in more detail at the precise processes by which the Comintern was subordinated to the emerging Stalinist state, and the national parties to the Comintern. One essential mediating factor was the reconstruction and absorption of national leaders such as Murphy. The rôle the International Control Commission played in hunting out heresy in individual parties, and the activities of the Comintern's Commission on Internal Relations, touched on here, will bear further scrutiny. Murphy sat on both, and his activities on the Special Commission on the French party will be of particular interest to *Revolutionary History* readers.

Murphy's resignation from the party is not even mentioned in Noreen Branson's quasi-official *History of the Communist Party of Great Britain 1927-41* (1985). Darlington provides the first detailed account. The incident remains difficult to understand in purely political terms. And quite why he terms Murphy's subsequent expulsion 'unjustified' (p214) is unclear. Against the background of the CPGB's practice and regime, Murphy's baffling resignation and subsequent refusal to attend the Political Bureau to explain himself left the leadership with no alternative but to administer the *coup de grâce* to somebody most of them had very little time for anyway. This volume is of less interest in its treatment of the Socialist League, whilst Murphy's speedy political evolution in the 1930s from ultra-leftism to Popular Frontism is explained only very broadly in terms of his acute awareness of the Fascist threat. Whether Murphy still remained in intellectual thrall to the party to which he had given so much of his life is not discussed. Darlington's round-up of Murphy's life in the 1940s and 1950s means we have a fuller picture of a life which for many on the left appeared hitherto to have ended in the 1920s.

At least some of the problems with this text lie in the framework in which the author has chosen to cast his story. Darlington is explicit, saying 'this book derives from the theoretical tradition of the Socialist Workers Party' (p xxi). Many of the weaknesses of the evaluations made in the text of people and events flow from the debility of that tradition and the use of its preoccupations as a sometimes intrusive and ahistorical yardstick. One example will suffice: the Labour Party is portrayed in a one-sided, inflexible, unstrategic fashion in the chapters dealing with the 1920s and 1930s, as it has been by the International Socialists and the SWP over the last 30 years. It is to be avoided at all costs; it is as destructive to revolutionaries as kryptonite is to Superman. Thus Murphy is taken to school: 'His notion that Socialists in the circumstances of the early 1930s should remain inside the Labour Party merely helped to provide a left cover and breed false expectations in such leaders.' (p229) A few lines later, we are given a specific example: 'As the German revolution of 1918-19 had demonstrated, the consequences of Socialists staying inside a reformist party in a revolutionary period led inevitably to catastrophe.' (p229) The yawning gulf that separated the problems of British revolutionaries in 1932 and their German counterparts in 1918-19 is simply excised. The question also arises as to whether Tony Cliff has proved uniquely immune to kryptonite; did the sojourn of his followers in the Labour Party from 1950 to around 1965 merely help to provide a left cover and breed expectations in Attlee, Gaitskell and Wilson? Sensing the difficulties, Darlington provides a rather evasive footnote stating that entrism *is* permissible, but only when revolutionaries are very weak, and so long as it is not long term. Most people would judge that revolutionaries were very weak in 'the circumstances of the early 1930s'. So why is Murphy criticised for joining the Labour Party? Moreover, the Socialist Review Group's decade-and-a-half visit was something more than the quick raid that its successor insists Trotsky envisaged.

Murphy, of course, was as isolated in 1932 as the SRG was in the 1950s. To criticise him for joining the Labour Party is ludicrous. But the Socialist League, 2000 to 3000-strong, is also taken to task for remaining in the Labour Party. Those who had any thoughts of leaving would have looked to the ILP, of which they had been members. The League is compared unfavourably with the CPGB, 'despite its increasing Stalinism and the adoption of the Popular Front policy... the Communist Party still rejected Labour's parliamentary cretinism and had an orientation on the struggles of the working class' (p231). That word 'despite', how small but how mighty in banishing little things like Stalinism and Popular Frontism and the ultimately integrated nature of Communist Party politics. It is unclear whether Darlington is suggesting that revolutionaries of the early 1930s should have stayed within the CPGB as on his judgement that it was healthier than the Socialist League — that is certainly the drift of his analysis. If so, the aspiration is utopian, as the expulsion of the Trotskyists in 1932-33 graphically demonstrated. It is interesting that these flesh-and-blood revolutionary activists of the early 1930s — Reg Groves, Henry Sara, Harry Wicks and their comrades, the difficulties they confronted, the decisions they took — are not mentioned in the text, still less used as a yardstick to measure Murphy's activities. And there are only brief references to 'the Trotskyists' in the footnotes. After all, Groves was on the League's Executive when Murphy was its Secretary. Instead of examining the concrete problems and alternatives that the revolutionary left faced in the 1930s in deciding whether to join the Labour Party or ILP or build an open organisation, that distant world and its struggles are refracted through the prism of the contemporary SWP. This is not the way to write history.

A second problem lies in Darlington's eschewal of 'standard biographical narrative (with irrelevant details of personal idiosyncrasies)' (pp xxiv-v). But life and logic teach us the importance of the 'personal' in understanding an individual's political trajectory. The biographical form, still frowned upon in the academic world, is a useful weapon in the armoury of historians, its vices and virtues recently illustrated by Patricia Hollis' *Jennie Lee: A Life* (1997). More intensive engagement with Murphy's values, motivations and 'personal idiosyncrasies' just might have helped explain key incidents in his political trajectory which remain vague. Various personal details about Murphy and his wife Molly, whose autobiography has been published to coincide with Darlington's book, are scattered through these texts. They are never brought together to frame his political trajectory, and thus deepen our understanding of it. Murphy, for example, demonstrated early aspirations to upward social mobility. But he was forced to abandon early plans to enter the civil service. Study, self-improvement, the shop stewards movement, the SLP and CPGB provided an alternative path to emancipation. Yet Murphy's ambition remained intact. A recent article suggests that he attracted the patronage of 'a prominent individual' at the highest level of the Comintern. He saw criticism of the CPGB as a sure road to an internationally-assisted passage to its leadership (Andrew Thorpe, 'Comintern "Control" of the Communist Party of Great Britain 1920-43', *English Historical Review*, Volume 113, June 1998, pp646, 653-4).

If ambition and its thwarting was one possible factor in his evolution, the bourgeois family was another. What appears to have been a very conventional marriage to a woman who described herself as 'lower middle-class' and took little interest in politics saw both parents' ambitions transferred to their son. As Molly Murphy wrote: 'From his earliest years, both his father and I had determined that he should have the kind of education which we wish had been ours.' (*Molly Murphy*, pp159-60) These working-class revolutionaries were determined to send their son to a fee-paying public school, in Britain the pathway to the élite, and an important litmus test of class consciousness. Perceived as scandalous behaviour on the part of a leading Communist, this stimulated sharp criticism within the CPGB. It became an additional tension in a situation where personal differences inevitably play some rôle in political conflicts. It drew the Murphies into the domestic economy and life of the middle class. It imposed on the couple a financial burden beyond the reach of a working-class family, and most political activists, intensified by the need periodically to hire domestic help. The salary Murphy received from *Pravda* became essential to pay the fees.

By 1932, Murphy was relatively isolated in the CPGB leadership, and had lost the patronage of the Comintern. He was impressed by the resilience of the Labour Party. The CPGB had little more than 2000 members. Its prospects appeared grim, as did Murphy's when he lost his job. Harry Pollitt, admittedly a political antagonist, had little doubt that personal and material factors, as well as political issues, were involved in his resignation (p215). Thereafter, his desire to operate as a professional intellectual and continue his son's education produced a willingness to accept financial donations from rich friends. Taken out of their political context, emphasis on these factors may provide a distorted, one-sided portrait. If we want to understand the man and his politics better, they should be critically confronted and integrated within that context. Greater attention to the interpenetration of the personal and political might have produced a richer, more complex study. As it is, we get little sense of the man and the texture of his life. Murphy remains as inscrutable at the end of Darlington's book as at the beginning.

Written in the 1960s, *Molly Murphy: Suffragette and Socialist* is more revealing, although those expecting the story of a British Kollontai or Pasionaria will be disappointed. Molly comes across as very much a woman of her class and time. She saw herself as 'typical' of English lower middle-class respectability and conventionalism (p74). She felt out of her depth in the world of the Comintern, embarrassed when Kollontai responded to her enquiry after her husband: 'Which

one, my dear?' (p74) She played little part in political debates: 'That was my husband's job.' Though she joined the CPGB, she emphasised 'it meant simply that my husband's friends were my friends, his loyalties my loyalties' (p87). Intensely involved before 1914 in the suffragette movement, she seems to have been only briefly active in the CPGB, and not at all thereafter. Her main interests were children and nursing, although the quality of her commitments was demonstrated when she spent six months nursing in Spain in 1937. Very much the stereotypical supportive wife and mother, this record of her life surely deserves better than the Dave Spart-like comment: 'She provides no analysis of the degeneration of the Russian Revolution as a result of the combined impact of civil war and the revolution's isolation internationally...' (p v) Many women of that era, like Helen Crawford, Isabel Brown and Rose Smith, were Communist leaders. Others led overt or subterranean lives of great complexity and emotional intensity. There is no evidence of that here. And once again, the plot thickens; we are informed that according to her son, 'her account was actually ghost-written by JT Murphy' (p iv). The editor has faith: 'There is no question that the substantive nature of the account is Molly's.' (p iv) For the conscientious historian, this leaves matters unresolved. Are we listening to Molly's voice recapitulating what she thought, felt and did all these years earlier? Or are we listening to the voice of that inscrutable old Stalinist Jack Murphy, remembering, perhaps imperfectly, what he thought she ought to have thought and felt?
John McIlroy

Ben Watson, *Art, Class and Cleavage*, Quartet, London, 1998, pp431, £14.00

BEN Watson stands at the point of intersection of two traditions – a Marxist tradition running from Trotsky to the 'state capitalist' theories of CLR James and Tony Cliff, and a tradition of revolt in (or against) art that goes from surrealism via situationism to the music of Frank Zappa and the poetry of JH Prynne. The only problem is to know whether these traditions do in fact intersect; for if they don't, Watson has nowhere to stand, and is in free fall into the void – a conclusion supported by some of the more bewildering sections of this insightful but confusing book.

Watson's declared aim is to overcome the 'cleavage' between art and politics/class. In particular, he champions modernism in music and poetry, arguing that the 'refusal of exchange values gives Modern Art its relationship to revolutionary politics' (p222). The argument takes us through knowledgeable and perceptive expositions of Coleridge, Fourier, Josef Dietzgen, Walter Benjamin, James Joyce and Philip K Dick. Watson treats Stalinists and liberal academics with contempt, arguing that 'both contend that knowledge exists objectively, independent of the person who thinks and the society that funds the thinker' (p75). Post-modernism, Political Correctness and feminism all get their fair (and sometimes unfair) share of abuse.

I suspect that many readers of *Revolutionary History* will be profoundly irritated by Watson's writing. The assault on the art/politics cleavage takes his writing beyond the boundaries of most works on either politics or culture. The footnotes repeatedly alternate between Lenin's philosophical writings and Frank Zappa's lyrics. A taste for puns and the sheer range and obscurity of the references ensure that this is not an easy read.

But in his insistence that music, poetry, sex, schizophrenia and death deserve discussion by Marxists, Watson is firmly in the tradition of Trotsky's writings on culture and everyday life. He claims, convincingly, that the art/politics cleavage has produced 'a marginalised and unimaginative revolutionary left and an effete, ornamental avant-garde' (p341). Watson has done his best to provoke a dialogue, though he will get few thanks from either side.

The back cover promises a 'rediscovery of Trotsky'. Watson skilfully deploys Trotsky against current academic trends, makes some useful comments on Trotsky and Freud, and claims that 'Trotsky is the most appropriate political complement to the revolt of Modern Art' (p185).

But he does not avoid a certain romanticisation of his hero. He dismisses as Stalinist misrepresentation (p10) the claim that Trotsky's alliance with the surrealist Breton was primarily tactical rather than political or aesthetic, although there is impeccably Trotskyist confirmation from Naville and van Heijenoort that Trotsky knew little of surrealism, and didn't much like what he knew. Likewise he claims that Trotsky 'carried a book of Mallarmé's poetry in his pocket when leading the Red Army' (p10). We know from Alfred Rosmer that Trotsky had Mallarmé on his bookshelves in his military train, but to infer that he was declaiming 'Le vierge, le vivace et le bel aujourd'hui' as the bullets whistled through his hair is unsubstantiated wish-fulfilment. It is also unfortunate that Watson, an enthusiast for poodles, does not note Jacqueline Lamba's recollection that Trotsky, in argument with Breton, 'attributed an almost human soul to dogs...' (Arturo Schwarz, *André Breton, Trotsky et l'anarchie*, Paris, 1977, p210).

The last third of the book is devoted to Voloshinov's work on Marxism and linguistics. Again, there is much that is valuable here, but some of the claims are dubious. Watson counterposes 'concrete utterance' to 'abstract systems' (p373), and thus dismisses Saussure's work, identifying it with the traditional grammar of the schoolroom. But his stress on utterance forgets that language cannot function unless it has a grammatical structure that makes it possible for one speaker to understand another; the English language exists independently of particular speakers, just as the solar system exists independently of human beings. In rejecting the 'abstract', he forgets that science requires abstraction; Marx's *Capital* moves between the concrete and the abstract. Far from reinforcing traditional grammar after the manner of a Labour education minister, Saussure's affirmation of the arbitrariness of language undermines any claim that one grammar is 'better' than another. And in his stress on ambiguity, Watson focuses excessively on literature. Ambiguity is a virtue in poetry, but a distinct disadvantage in Health and Safety regulations.

James Thurber once drew a cartoon of a bewildered man in an art gallery, captioned 'he knows all about art but he doesn't know what he likes'. Watson knows only too well what he likes, and the book sometimes turns into a catalogue of his personal tastes. Watson calls his method Materialist Esthetix; the eccentric spelling abbreviates as ME! (The conventional spelling would have given the acronym Ma, to the hilarity of amateur Freudians; or perhaps MA, symbolising the academics for whom he feels such searing hatred.) At one point, he lists 10 names (all unknown to the present reviewer) and describes their work as 'the only poetry worth reading in England' (p325). Anyone who disagrees with Watson's tastes is damned, not only aesthetically, but politically and morally. This style of intellectual terrorism is much closer to Matthew Arnold and FR Leavis than Watson would like to think. Before attempting to establish a single revolutionary canon in music and literature, he should ponder the passage in Trotsky's *Literature and Revolution* which promises that under Socialism political parties will be replaced by 'parties' advocating different tendencies in theatre, music and sport.

As Watson acknowledges, to overcome the art/politics cleavage requires, not the best efforts of the best intellectuals, but social revolution (p341). Without that revolution, Materialist Esthetix, like surrealism and situationism, must be a judged a failure. Yet an interesting failure is sometimes preferable to a boring success.

Ian Birchall

Pierre Broué, *Histoire de l'Internationale Communiste*, Fayard, Paris, 1997, pp1120, FF295

PIERRE Broué's history of the Communist International is an impressive achievement. As well as over 800 pages of scrupulously documented text, it contains a detailed chronology, an extensive bibliography, and an index with biographical sketches of virtually every individual who plays a part in the story. In addition, there is a list of some 8000 pseudonyms used by those active in the Communist movement. (I was slightly less impressed when the first entry I checked – Tony Cliff – turned out to be inaccurate.) Doubtless there are errors and omissions, but it would require a whole team of specialists to locate where they are. Broué has provided not only an enthralling narrative, but a work of reference which will be indispensable to anyone working in the field.

Whilst the account centres on the key states of Central and Western Europe which decided the fate of the post-1917 revolutionary wave, Broué includes much material from other parts of the world, and there are full accounts of the development of revolutionary Communism, and then Stalinism, in both Asia and Latin America. Whilst some sections rely heavily on established accounts – Isaacs on the Chinese Revolution, Renshaw on the British General Strike – Broué also makes substantial use of recently discovered archive material. An important example is the use of material from the work of Bernhard Bayerlein, showing the divergences within the Comintern leadership at the time of the German events of 1923 and after. Amongst other material, he quotes a letter from Stalin in August 1923, urging that the Germans be held back and not stimulated; Zinoviev's draft theses on Germany from August 1923; details of the dispute between Trotsky and Zinoviev in the autumn of 1923; and Rákosi's report to Zinoviev of October 1923.

The latter part of the book, dealing with the Stalinised Comintern, is perhaps the less interesting. The broad outline of the crimes of the Third Period and the betrayals of the Popular Front are a well-known story, and although Broué adds much detail, he does not revise the general picture. Certainly he provides sufficient documentation to belabour any surviving admirers of Stalinism. Whilst the catastrophic outcome of the Third Period in Germany is all too familiar, the story of the massacres in Colombia and El Salvador, also produced by Third Period policies, will be less so. Broué also details the leadership changes carried out during the Third Period; as he points out, it was the leaderships established during the Third Period who implemented the policies of the Popular Front. Chapter 32 provides an extensive roll-call of those murdered at the hands of the Stalinist apparatus.

Yet, as Broué shows, the Comintern was never altogether a 'monolith' (as some of us have perhaps too easily believed). The famous zigzags were neither unanimous nor executed without hesitation. Thus the Comintern opposed Duclos' attempt to get *L'Humanité* published legally under the Nazi occupation of France. Even when Stalin decided that the Comintern must be dissolved, there were divergent voices on the Executive. No-one defied Stalin, but there were several views as to *how* the strangulation should be carried out. Perhaps such differences should not surprise us in an organisation where fear and ambition had replaced principle. But individuals did make a difference, and Broué attempts to evaluate their rôles. Thus Dimitrov (whose direct involvement in the Sofia Cathedral episode Broué makes clear) emerges as a complete scoundrel, who drank too much and sexually harassed secretaries; André Marty, however, is said to have been a 'big-mouth', but not the butcher he is often accused of being.

Broué considers that by 1935 the Comintern was no more than a 'direct dependency of the political police of the [Soviet] state'. Undoubtedly there is a substantial degree of truth in this, and Broué provides much detailed material on the rôle of Russian agents within the various Communist parties. Nonetheless, a number of reservations should be noted. Firstly, the various Stalinist parties retained sufficient roots in their national labour movements for them subsequently to develop into variants of Social Democracy. Secondly, in the 1930s and during the Second World War, the Communist parties continued to attract many of the best class fighters of their generation. To dismiss militants of the quality of Harry McShane or Joe Jacobs as merely 'Stalinists' because they became embroiled in Communist parties at a time when Trotskyism was almost invisible would be sectarian folly. And thirdly, a theoretical question arises: if the counter-revolutionary Comintern was simply a projection of the Russian state machine, then what sort of state was it? Could it in any sense be a state that represented workers' class interests, in however degenerated a fashion? Wisely, Broué makes no attempt to pursue this point.

But it is the first half of the book which is much more illuminating and thought-provoking, and highly relevant to the education of a new generation of revolutionaries. For here we are dealing with a living movement, with all its richness and contradiction, its spontaneity and its mistakes. Anyone who believes there was a line of continuity between the early Comintern and the later monstrosity that bore the same name should read Broué's detailed account of the full debate and open argument that characterised the first congresses.

But Broué also undermines the romanticisation that has existed within the Trotskyist camp. I recall a faction in the International Socialists (led by Sean Matgamna) which included in its programme support for the 'first four congresses of the Communist International'. I was never sure what this might mean, and having read Broué I am finally convinced it was meaningless. Indeed, the real Comintern was something of a ramshackle affair, a hasty improvisation to deal with an urgent and unpredictable situation. We can learn at least as much from the early Comintern's mistakes – which were numerous – as from its programmatic declarations. But precisely these were the mistakes – and often dubious manoeuvres – of a living movement. The point was neatly summed by Georg Lukács, in a remark recorded by Victor Serge: 'Marxists know that dirty little tricks can be performed with impunity when great deeds are being achieved; the error of some comrades is to suppose that one can produce great results simply through the performance of dirty little tricks.' Here we have beautifully encapsulated the essential difference between Lenin and Zinoviev.

For many on the revolutionary left, even today, the Comintern is cited as though it provided a simple recipe book for the construction of revolutionary parties. But as Broué shows, the formation of the Comintern was a complex process, in which individuals, networks of personal contacts, the various 'foreign sections' based on ex-prisoners-of-war in Russia, small political groups and mass parties all interacted in the context of a unique revolutionary wave emerging from the war and the Russian October. Those who seek to reduce this to the *shibboleth* that all revolutionary parties come simply from splits within existing working-class institutions should study Broué and think again. Thus in the example of France, revolutionary Syndicalists like Rosmer, Monatte and Martinet played a key rôle in the formation of the Communist Party, even though they had never felt any inclination to 'enter' the SFIO. And if they had played an even larger rôle, whilst the corrupt parliamentarians like Cachin had been excluded, the PCF might have been better able to face up to the demands of the new period.

The real problem was, of course, that the overwhelming majority of the established leadership of the working class had sold out in 1914. The Comintern's task was therefore to forge a new leadership, at every level from Central Committee to shop steward, within the few brief years before the revolutionary wave began to subside. The amazing thing is not that there were mistakes and that bizarre short-cuts were pursued, but that so much was achieved. Some of us might draw the lesson, contrary to the advocates of 'entrism', that it is a great pity that the left in the Second International did not break away – or at least develop a much more solid factional organisation – before 1914.

Be that as it may, the Comintern leadership found themselves in a race against time. Paradoxically, the Russians had to try to teach other parties to rely more on their own concrete analysis of circumstances, and less on imitation of the Russian example. This is the message of Lenin's magnificent but despairing speech to the fourth Comintern congress, when he warned: 'We have not learnt how to present our Russian experience to foreigners.' Broué provides a neat example of the tendency to see the world through Russian eyes when he cites the repeated practice of the Italian Communists of referring to Mussolini's Blackshirts as 'White Guards' – something hardly calculated to clarify the issues for the average Italian worker.

It is also in this context that the question of ultra-leftism in the Comintern must be understood, and here Broué can be criticised for taking too superficial a view of matters. It is easy enough in retrospect to condemn the March Action and the 'theory of the offensive'. Of course, it is quite right to blame Béla Kun for his stupidities – as Lenin did one once occasion to such an extent that the congress record had to be altered to moderate his vituperation. But the fundamental questions are: firstly, why was there such a shortage of cadres that a man like Kun was given responsible positions? And secondly, why did the ultra-leftism of such leaders find a genuine 'resonance' (as our Pabloite friends used to call it) amongst the layers of newly radicalised young workers, militant, angry and impatient, but lacking experience and any real sense of tactics.

Lenin himself seems to have related to ultra-lefts of all types with understanding and patience. He realised that most ultra-lefts were genuine revolutionaries, and even amid the tremendous pressures of post-revolutionary Russia, he found time to argue and convince. Broué's account brings out the differences between the various Bolshevik leaders. Indeed, contrary to the popular image of 'Bolshevism', even the leading core of Bolsheviks was far from being homogeneous. Broué brings out the different rôles of Lenin, Trotsky, Zinoviev, Bukharin, Radek and others. Zinoviev, despite his talents as an orator, appears mainly in a negative light. It was Zinoviev (not Trotsky, as is often alleged) who threatened to shoot the Kronstadt insurgents 'like partridges'. It was above all Zinoviev's 'Bolshevisation' of the Comintern that paved the way for Stalin. Moreover, Zinoviev is shown to have been one of the very first proponents of the 'theory' that Social Democracy was a 'variety of Fascism'.

But most striking of all is the visible gap between Lenin and even his most gifted associates. Lenin understood that the art of party-building requires a knowledge of when to split and when to pull together. Of course, splitting is a lot easier than pulling together, and all too many of Lenin's would-be followers (including even, at times, Trotsky) have preferred to split rather than pull together.

Broué's sympathies tend to be with the right wing of the revolutionary movement. In particular Paul Levi, whom he had already presented in a relatively positive light in his 1971 book on the German Revolution, is here presented as a major figure in the Comintern leadership. Certainly Broué is quite right to endorse Levi's critique of the March Action; Levi was undoubtedly a shrewd analyst of the political situation. But it must also be said that he was an inept faction-fighter. One can scarcely imagine Lenin deciding to break party discipline, but then failing to follow through, and retreating from the debate. Within a more stable leadership team, Levi could certainly have played a very useful rôle, but in the near chaos of the German party he failed to live up to the demands upon him.

One review can only touch on a very few of the many issues raised in Broué's book, which will undoubtedly continue to provoke discussion and further research for years to come. In the last issue of *Revolutionary History*, Al Richardson described the book as 'magisterial'. Perhaps I am not quite so easily pleased, but there is no doubt that this is an important and valuable book. I would add the hope that an English translation will soon appear, but it might look as though I am volunteering for the job. Good luck to whoever has the stamina to undertake it.
Ian Birchall

Sean Matgamna (ed), *The Fate of the Russian Revolution: Lost Texts of Critical Marxism*, Volume 1, Phoenix Press, London, 1998, pp603, £16.99

We present two reviews of this important collection, the first by Barry Finger, the second by Jim Higgins.

T HE purpose of this ambitious volume is to acquaint the Socialist public with the living political legacy of the Workers Party/Independent Socialist League. A Marxist tendency which never amounted to more than a few hundred members, which endured for less than 20 years, and which led no revolutionary insurrections, the WP/ISL nevertheless bridged the gap between the epoch of the Bolshevik revolution and the retrogressive collectivist epoch which followed from its defeat. It germinated as a minority tendency within the Trotskyist movement, and came fully into its own by formulating an unabashed and full-throated defence of revolutionary Socialism, free of the fatuous and still fashionable insistence that Stalinism was the inevitable outcome of Leninism, and offered the struggle against Stalinism, in the words of Max Shachtman, the leading political personality of the movement, 'a theoretically unassailable basis and a political program that rested on international Socialism'. In an age in which the 'general idea of Socialism' is still invariably linked in the public mind with the fate of the Soviet Union, they stood alone in categorically rejecting the notion that what went awry was simply the results of 'mistakes', 'serious errors' or even 'crimes', and went on decisively to dismiss the notion that Stalinist Russia was any kind of workers' state, degenerated or otherwise.

That these remonstrations remain largely unheeded and unassimilated explains to no small extent why the pall of the lunatic asylum hangs over the remnants of the Socialist movement. The endless, unintentionally self-mocking pronunciations of the 'crisis of capitalism' issued in the teeth not only of Socialism's own unrelieved political failures, but against its own deepening moral and theoretical bankruptcies, is unwitting testimony to the continued relevance of the ground-breaking work of the 'Shachtmanites', for the larger failures of Socialism are attributable to issues other than that of mere inadequate reality contact. The heroic political failures of the oppressed and exploited are, after all, forgivable. The unbroken record of complicity of the non-Stalinist left in making alibis for, rationalising and defending totalitarian barbarism to the oppressed and the exploited – whilst coyly holding its nose, a project a bit less heroic – is not.

If Stalinism perverted the most liberating doctrines and noble instincts of humanity into a means of enslavement, and, for a while, marched relentlessly ahead on that basis, the erstwhile non-Stalinists of the left were reduced to wringing their hands and shaking their heads balefully at the dialectical way 'history' chose to march forward. And marching forward is exactly what history is said to have done when Stalinism advanced. So insisted not only the soothsayers of the Social Democratic left – the Coleses and Bauers and Dans; yet no more so, and certainly less flagrantly so, than the adepts of post-Trotsky Trotskyism – the Deutschers and Mandels and Cannons. The stormy spectacle of doctrinal hairsplitting and organisational reconfiguration with which official 'Trotskyism' greeted Stalinism's advance measured little beyond the geometrically precise degree of accommodation with which this or that orientation was willing to greet Stalinist imperialism or its national manifestations. Like the vaudevillian lament over the restaurant whose food was so atrocious, and, what's worse, served in such miserly portions, Trotsky's epigones distinguished themselves at length by bemoaning Stalinist atrocities, whilst castigating its irresolution whenever a supposed opportunity for expansion was eluded.

That remarkable ambiguity remains the principal impediment in translating non-Stalinist sentiments into something coherently approaching a viable anti-Stalinist theory. 'Orthodox' Trotskyism never truly outgrew the faction fights of the 1920s when Marxists considered Stalinism to be a legitimate – if errant and reactionary – faction within the broader Socialist and working-class movement. It never in practice assimilated the evolving dynamic of Stalinism, a dynamic from which was to crystallise a new social organisation of labour serving an historically new ruling class, and held fast instead to a static picture of Stalinism derived from its origins as a petit-bourgeois tendency within Bolshevism. This led the deans of Trotskyism to 'confirm' Trotsky's view that Stalinism was capitulating to capitalist restoration whenever a peasant in Siberia was found to have owned a cow. The initial lessons of the Stalinist Czech coup of 1948? Why, merely additional evidence, according to the American Socialist Workers Party, of Stalinism's capitulation to capitalism. Was it not after all the Cannonites – and not they alone – who blithely announced just days before the Chinese Stalinist armies were to defeat Chiang, that Mao's and Stalin's greatest desire was – appearances notwithstanding – to surrender to Chiang? Of course, after the fact all sorts of additionally fascinating and equally erroneous lessons were drawn.

Trotsky's analysis of Stalinism was necessarily in flux, and Matgamna's offers the analytically elegant suggestion that rereading *In Defence of Marxism* in chronological order demonstrates precisely how close Trotsky himself came just prior to his murder in recognising Stalinism's mutation into a new and hitherto unimagined social order. But it also true that these vague possibilities of historic alternatives other than Socialist revolution, once raised, were instantly dismissed or ridiculed. In the end, I think we are left with the conclusion that Shachtman and his comrades finally parted ways with Trotsky to a degree beyond which Matgamna is prepared to acknowledge. For if politics is the struggle for 'alternative programmes', the traditional conceptions of Marxism expressed in the theories and conclusions of Trotskyism were rejected in the search of a new programme within the broad framework of revolutionary Socialist principles. Trotsky distilled the problem of the day to that of the crisis of revolutionary leadership, and he sought its resolution on an international scale. He consistently insisted that the key to developing Russia on a Socialist basis and thereby breaking the stranglehold of the nationalist bureaucracy lay in ending Russia's enforced isolation. In this he faithfully reflected the perspective of the Bolshevik revolution. What Trotsky was unwilling to concede was not merely that the Stalinist bureaucracy might mutate into a new ruling class, but that it had already largely created a new type of international movement, a new type of imperialism, and a new type of party. Trotsky sought the salvation of the revolution in the defeat of capitalism. Shachtman and his comrades soberly faced the emerging programmatic implications of a new international force operating within the working class, claiming the trappings and traditions of the Socialist movement, which at the same time sought the destruction of world capitalism in terms of its own reactionary bureaucratic collectivist interests.

If history had, in any case, by the late 1930s proceeded beyond the limits of 'permissible' speculation, Trotsky's 'orthodox' following could not. Trotsky's inquiries were not received as the provisional propositions of an unfolding understanding, but as a series of eternally fixed, self-contained truths — the cornerstones of a 'finished' programme. Apparent internal inconsistencies and contradictions were ascribed to the subtlety of the historic dialectic. This was less a synthesis than a juggling act, a juggling act, to be precise, where the very foundation of Marxism — the foundation which imbued Bolshevism in its time with an integrated revolutionary content — was simply suspended in mid-air. Thus Stalinism was at once the bureaucratic guardian, or night watchman, of the gains of October, whose privileges were derived from the defence of state industry and the planned economy; the wavering capitulator to capitalism; and above all a bureaucratic growth in the labour movement bisymmetrical with other forms of reformist Socialism, differing only in that it emerged out of and leaned on a workers' state. All this contributed to the summary judgement of Stalinism as narrow, conservative and provincial — whose economic and social structures were incompatible with imperialist expansion, and whose internal frailties and limited life expectancy precluded its playing an independent historical rôle. Stalinism could only be understood and indeed it was, for Trotsky, the responsibility of Socialists to insist on an understanding of Stalinism solely within the traditional language and analysis of the bipolar world of classical Marxism.

So much the worse for Marxism. For wherever else Trotsky's investigations led him, he left unquestioned the theoretical viewpoint of the 1924 opposition: that the Soviet Union represented a 'degenerated workers' state', and that the responsibility of the revolutionary Socialists everywhere was to defend that state if threatened by war or intervention. But whereas the revolutionary movement could still make the case in 1924 that, despite draconian inroads against democracy, workers still tacitly exercised considerable control over the conditions of social life through elective bodies in the soviets, trade unions and cooperatives, the consolidation of bureaucratic power extinguished these remnants of revolutionary rule, and in so doing fundamentally transformed the revolutionary responsibilities of the left. The original programme of the left aimed to reform and thereby salvage the gains of the revolution by means of an invigoration, extension and deepening of workers' democracy; by reining in the bureaucracy, and subjecting it to decisive subordination under party authority. Yet the society that Trotsky fought to revive was simply a different order and conception of humanity than that which he ultimately confronted in Stalinist Russia. And so too did Trotsky tacitly acquiesce to this judgement by dropping the 'reformist' strategy — of labouring to redirect the Communist movement, invoking instead the need for a political revolution predicated on a new International.

In this acquiescence lay, tragically, a greater obfuscation. For it had been the inherited understanding of the revolutionary movement that a given class is the ruling class when the entire economic and social structure is in conformity with its mode of production and its social domination, and is not compatible with the rule of any other class. Because the working class is not a property-owning class, its social rule must be bound to its political rule, and therefore cannot exist – in contradistinction to the capitalist class – where it has no political rights. Trotsky, for whom revolutionary Socialism was also inseparable from workers' democracy, was forced into the untenable position of offering unconditional defence to a society where the political mechanisms of working-class social domination had been irrevocably obliterated and replaced by a socially autonomous bureaucracy. Thus the dilemma: to abandon the cause of revolutionary defencism, or to revise the criteria upon which the judgement of Soviet Russia as a workers' state had crucially rested. Trotsky – who, better than any contemporary, had demonstrated that Stalinist Russia by reason of its politics, policies and activities, by its internal structure and world strategies, was a mortal enemy of Socialism and the working class everywhere – stumbled disastrously towards the latter alternative.

That this was a provisional judgement is clear from Trotsky's final essays, as members of the Workers Party soberly pointed out. But for his followers in the SWP majority, the defence of the Soviet Union was now to rest on the existence of nationalised industry and state planning, on juridical forms rather than the (unexamined) exploitative property relations. Socialism was no longer immutably identified with democracy, a workers' state with workers' power. Russia was a workers' state in which the workers exercised their social dominance, as it were, from jail. When Stalinism at the end of the war expanded its domain, by dint of bayonet and coup, Trotsky's followers initially pronounced these satellites as reactionary police states, incapable of implementing progressive anti-capitalist measures. After their economies were taken under a bureaucratic wing, replicating Stalinist Russia in every essential detail, other, that is, than in having overthrown a workers' revolution, these same 'revolutionaries' demonstrated heretofore unknown abilities for innovative social theory. By this time a bankrupt clique thoroughly permeated by a bureaucratic mentality, Fourth Internationalists declared yesterday's reactionary Bonapartist police states to be workers' states of a new kind, deformed perhaps, but the genuine article nonetheless. If 'workers' states' could be fashioned entirely from above and maintained without the participation of the masses and even against their expressed desires – if such transformative measures were 'progressive' anti-capitalist actions – the gap between Trotskyism and Stalinism had become appreciably narrowed. Every venue of accommodation could now be thrown open.

The WP/ISL operated from an entirely different understanding. The rise of Stalinism was situated within the broader disintegrative tendencies of interwar society. Unable to resolve the once acute, now chronic problems of mass poverty and unemployment on a capitalist basis through accumulation, unable that is to rationalise the technological advances which capitalism itself engendered, a vacuum was created. The working class, which Marxists have always looked to as that force uniquely qualified to fill that vacuum, proved unable to mobilise its forces and emancipate society. But the imperative to hold society together in an epoch of rampant dissolution required some form of collectivisation, that is some third social force from outside the ranks of capital capable of substituting a new dynamic for the flagging mechanisms of capitalist expansion. That need was answered through the pervasive growth of the state bureaucracy, of bureaucratic controls and regulations supplanting the market as a method of allocating resources and distributing the social product. These tendencies necessarily operated on a world scale, though at different, uneven and hybrid stages of completion. Directed by technocratic and managerial élites – products of capitalism as is the working class, but unable to express their will through the fusion of political and economic democracy, these tendencies could only be realised in the form of minority domination from above. Whatever problems may have been rationalised by the exercise of bureaucratic collectivisation, the resulting social stabilisation was secured without the exercise of any new power or expanded participation of the working masses in the life of society. The means of production and exchange which fell to the disposal of the state under such circumstances could be collectivised, but not socialised.

The rise of the state bureaucracy as a social tendency necessarily operated through different social channels throughout the capitalist world. It had as its precondition, however, the partial paralysis of capital coupled with a pervasive sense of weakness on the part of the working class, a weakness wherein self-awareness – Socialist consciousness – was replaced by bureaucratic dependency. But where managerial elements in the West move in this direction, they are constrained by their direct ties with immediate capitalist interests. As soon as individual members of the bureaucracy acquire sufficient capital, they are reabsorbed into the existing network of class relations. By siphoning off promising members of the state bureaucracy and depositing its rejects therein, the private sector temporises the appetites of the state, and paralyses its effectiveness. The revolving door between the state and capitalist managerial functionaries, to the extent that it remains well lubricated, blunts the rise of an independent bureaucratic class consciousness, and thereby limits the scope of its social vision. Bureaucratic tendencies operating within an existing bourgeois context therefore necessarily operate in contradictory fashion. They bind capitalism together, and to that extent act as the implementors of capitalist interest, whilst bearing the as yet unrealised seeds of an alternative social formation.

The Stalinist revolution was the extrapolation of the existing disintegrative tendencies of interwar capitalism brought to fruition. Post-revolutionary Russia, though revived by the limited capitalist openings of the New Economic Policy, found itself unable to advance by capitalist methods, and yet equally unable to modernise on a Socialist basis due to the enforced isolation of the revolution. Those elements latent in Russian society, technical and professional personnel no longer able to vouchsafe their privileges through service to capital, coalesced to positions of bureaucratic power in a milieu virtually absent of external constraint beyond the enfeebled resistance of a war-weary working class. When these last vestiges of independent, organised working-class power and influence were broken with the bloody suppression of the Bukharinites and the Left Opposition, the bureaucracy was able to constitute itself as a ruling class in every significant sense of the term. This bureaucracy was 'no longer the controlled and revocable "managers and superintendents" employed by the workers' state in the party, the state apparatus, the industries, the army, the unions, the fields, but the owners and controllers of the state, which is in turn the repository of collectivised property and thereby the employer of all hired hands, the masses of the workers, above all, included'. The new ruling class administered the property forms created by the revolution, but by transforming them into a vast apparatus of bureaucratic power and exploitation, they drained them of their emancipatory purpose.

The new bureaucratic ruling class similarly wasted no time in modifying in kind the revolutionary world view it inherited. The teachings of Marx and Lenin were scoured and brutally purged of all their inconvenient and dysfunctional mass democratic, revolutionary and working-class features against which a monstrous state-worshipping, soul-crushing caricature was substituted. This new housebroken ideology became, in short order, a powerful ancillary instrument in the perpetual cleansing – and self-cleansing – from the ranks of the Stalintern of any who betrayed even the barest potential for independent thought or action.

Stalinism, which relentlessly waged its political war simultaneously on the national, international and ideological fronts, established itself as one of the most virulently class-conscious and expansive of all reactionary ruling classes. It had its mass movements everywhere, and successfully made a powerful appeal to the wretched and exploited of the underdeveloped capitalist world on the basis, not of its grotesque ideological formulations, but by virtue of its demonstrated commitment to an anti-capitalist programme. Stalinism fostered and distorted the revolt against capitalism, and for quite some time successfully rode its wake. Yet the economic 'freedom' that Stalinism offered was nothing but a cynical cover for the brutal reality of another form of oppression and domination. For Communist party leaders and bureaucrats abroad, service in the interests of the Stalinist bureaucracy was the unavoidable means of advancing their own aspirations to become a national ruling class in the image of their sponsors. That is why the WP/ISL held the resolute conviction that such parties were not merely the ideological agents of Stalinism, as Social Democrats are of capitalism. For they, unlike the Social Democrats with respect to capitalism, could not realistically be expected to preserve the organisational independence of working-class institutions under Stalinist conditions. And under capitalist conditions, they could only be expected to wage or participate in working-class struggles to the extent in which the conjunctural interests of the Kremlin were served by such actions. Where Stalinists were aligned with New Deal capitalism, as they were during the Second World War, or where they had limited potential for gaining control over revolutionary events such as in the Paris uprising of 1968, the Stalinist movement advanced or preserved its own interests by sabotaging working-class interests. The Stalinists were, in the oft-repeated phrase of the WP/ISL a 'reactionary, totalitarian, anti-bourgeois and anti-proletarian current *in* the labour movement, but not *of* the labour movement'.

But this already takes us far afield from the subject of Volume One of this compelling undertaking. It can only be hoped that this, amongst other aspects of the comprehensive reconstruction of the Socialist project that the 'Shachtmanites' pioneered, can be continued in forthcoming editions. In its time, the WP/ISL aspired to mobilise the third camp in its own name, and under its own political banner, completely independent of the two war camps. Freed of Stalinism as a menacing world force, the vestigial progressive community – there is no Socialist working class, no revolutionary movement as Trotsky or even Shachtman knew it

— is today so thoroughly infected by the patterns of bureaucratic thought and habit which are the legacy of Popular Front Stalinism that this volume cannot, of necessity, be directed to them. Its great strength and significance lies as a tool for educating those who aspire to something other than permanent sectarian status at the boundaries of politics; those who intend to engage this broader leftish public with the ideas and ideals of revolutionary Socialism, fully determined to avoid rerunning the last reel of history, and moving on to the next.

Finally, much has been made of Shachtman's moral and political collapse, as if the politics Shachtman came to adopt in support of the Democratic Party, of the labour bureaucracy and of American intervention in Vietnam were genetically programmed into his revolutionary critique of Trotsky and Trotskyism. This is an all-too-convenient, and equally dishonest, dodge on the part of those unwilling and unable to confront the WP/ISL analysis head on, and who continue to shirk responsibility for their own politics of disorientation. Matgamna deals with this issue pointedly, insisting that the true corpus of Shachtman's work constitutes a 'lineal defence, elaboration and continuation of Trotsky's ideas... as they really were developing at Trotsky's death'. Whether Matgamna overstates the case for continuity, it is even more true, as Matgamna suggests, that Trotsky's orthodox followers lived for decades in a fantasy-world existence of their own making. Pitiably clinging to all the tentative, semi-contradictory positions of their mentor, necessarily unable to integrate these positions into a coherent theory, and smugly content to expand upon the mistakes of the past, Trotsky's epigones became Stalinism's attorneys — an unbroken political consistency which, unlike Shachtman's, continues for that very reason to reverberate as their precise political legacy. If the gravitational pull of new class relations ultimately lured the majority of the Trotskyist movement into the camp of bureaucratic collectivism, 'Shachtman and his comrades kept alive Marxist method, culture, political memory and the aspiration to working-class liberty in the age of political barbarism'.

Barry Finger

❖   ❖   ❖

WHEN, in 1957, I became a Trotskyist, one of the great joys of this rather lonely allegiance was that a great treasure-house of quality political writing opened up for study. Although there was nothing like the sheer volume of material that appeared in the late 1960s and 1970s, there were, nevertheless, the key texts of Trotsky and the publications of American Trotskyism in both its Cannonite and Shachtmanite manifestations. One particularly valuable cache was the back issues of the American Trotskyists' *New International*. From 1934 to 1958, this excellent journal appeared, setting a standard for its rivals to aspire to but seldom to achieve. Much of the credit for the quality of the *New International* was due to Max Shachtman, who for most of those years was the main guiding hand behind the magazine. Shachtman was a revolutionary man for all seasons, a fine orator, witty, eloquent, penetrating and very funny, sometimes savagely so; all qualities that were equally in evidence in his writing. In the 1930s, he was, after Trotsky, held in the highest esteem in the international movement, where he helped in developing the sections and preparing the way for the foundation of the Fourth International. Trotsky certainly thought very highly of him, appointing him his literary executor, and making strenuous efforts to avoid the split in the US Socialist Workers Party in 1940.

There was, as one might assume, another side to all this, and, as Bob Pitt has observed in a recent issue of *What Next?*, Shachtman was, despite his manifest talents, a bit of a smart arse. In this, of course, his smart arsery was of the same character as your run-of-the-mill group gurus, where the leader's stranglehold on the dialectic enables him to pontificate on all questions, even if it does sound like piffle. With Shachtman, the piffle always sounded plausible, and often the speed of the pen deceived the unwary.

I met him only once, when, in pursuit of material for his never-written *magnum opus* on the Comintern, he visited these shores in the early 1960s. He was staying with Jock Haston, and several of us were invited to meet him. He was something of a patrician figure, given to making his statements as if in papal infallibility mode, and I gained the distinct impression that contact with the hem of his garment might prove efficacious for any troublesome skin conditions one might be enduring. He was, however, graciously pleased to relieve me of my incomplete file of *Labour Monthly*.

This is the Max Shachtman whose writing on the Russian question forms the overwhelming bulk of the volume here under review. In a way, this is unfortunate, because whilst bureaucratic collectivism might have been a useful defining theory for the Workers Party/Independent Socialist League, it was one of the least attractive or interesting parts of that organisation's life, and was certainly the main factor impelling, or allowing, Shachtman finally to make his peace with American imperialism.

The theory had its first outing in America in the SWP in 1937, propounded by James Burnham and Joe Carter. CLR James, whose opinion of bureaucratic collectivism was not high, referred to it as 'Carter's little liver pill'. There is some evidence to suggest that it was an adaptation of Bruno Rizzi's theory, and, despite strenuous denials by the WP/ISL, the jury is still out on this question. Shachtman, who was a co-factionalist with Burnham and Carter, did not adopt the theory himself until late in 1940, after they had all been expelled from the SWP. This makes it seem rather unfair that all subscribers to bureaucratic collectivism are now called 'Shachtmanites' rather than 'Burnham-Carterites'. This may be explained by the fact that Burnham defected to the right in 1940, whilst Shachtman spent nearly 20 years more or less attached to a revolutionary outlook before he, too, followed the well-worn path. Carter, probably the real originator, was not an easy read, and the few articles he did write have all the charm of a bare-faced fletton. So, Shachtmanism it is, and perhaps there is some justice in that, for they deserve one another.

As a theory, bureaucratic centralism tells us that Russian Stalinism represented a new ruling class based on the super-exploitation of slaves. The birth and evolution of this class is not charted, and seems to be based on anecdotal evidence, a fine and justified moral outrage at the crimes of Stalinism, and a desire to produce something to replace the inadequate 'workers' state' theory of Trotsky. It is also quite possibly the case that Shachtman's late conversion represented a need to have a central defining theory to set him apart from Cannon's SWP, which already had the franchise on Soviet defencism. Like all of these theories, it was a bit of a mix and match, and Shachtman spent years patching here and extending there, and gradually squeezing out any revolutionary content from the original.

One of the more bizarre aspects of Shachtmanism is the rôle it ascribes to the Communist parties. It suggests that, as capitalism grew up within the interstices of the feudal system, so the Communist parties were a bureaucratic collective class-in-waiting. In pursuit of this particular thesis, Shachtman engaged in a strange debate with Theodore Draper in the pages of the *New International* in which he claimed that the American Socialist Party left of 1912 was quite different from the left of 1917. If this sounds dangerously like the debates of the mediaeval schoolmen on whether the late JC of Bethlehem was of the same stuff or similar stuff to God, there is definitely a whiff of that kind of incense in the air. That left of 1917 was, of course the main element that went into the foundation of the American Communist Party. Within that party, amongst others, were Max Shachtman and his mentor James P Cannon, struggling manfully in one factional alignment or another to convince Zinoviev that they were the men to lead the American section of the Comintern. Between 1922 and 1928, in all his activity as a second-rank leader of the party, Shachtman managed to avoid turning into a new ruling class. We do not know, of course, what nocturnal anguish he endured in his struggles to resist this transformation, especially when the moon was full.

From 1940 to 1948, the Workers Party thought of itself as a Trotskyist organisation, dedicated to the Fourth International, and, apart from the Russian question, broadly adhering to the ideas of the movement. It was more open and tolerant than most Trotskyist groups, but until 1948 it followed the debates within the Fourth International, and attempted to contribute to the discussion. Whatever their differences with the SWP, they were as concerned with creating an international leadership for the coming struggles. Perhaps it is the case that because they were unorthodox they were more aware of the way that postwar reality invalidated so many of Trotsky's predictions. With the expansion of Stalinism into Eastern Europe, it was imperative, they thought, that the International rectify its mistaken line on Russia so that the workers could be given a clear and unequivocal lead. The condition of the Fourth International in the immediate post-1945 period, in the light of what it saw as its prospects, would have made a cat laugh, that is if the cat didn't have more pressing matters in mind. Shachtman attended the 1948 congress of the Fourth International, he found the rhetoric of Michel Pablo empty and dispiriting, and the International, at whose founding in 1938 he had presided, a shell whose past had been based on hopes, and whose future was nostalgia for the past. Not only that, Shachtman's own brand of Trotskyism made little impression on anyone. He returned to the US disappointed, and within a short time the Workers Party had not only broken with the Fourth International, but had changed its name to the Independent Socialist League, a recognition that a party of a couple of hundred people was a contradiction in terms.

Nevertheless, those first few years of the Workers Party were their best. In the 1940 split, they had taken slightly less than half the membership of the SWP, perhaps 400 people. They were, in the main, young and middle-class, but they were exceptionally dedicated. During the war, when engineering plants had many vacancies, they became factory workers, joining the union and fighting for leadership on the shop floor. Hal Draper, an archetypal intellectual, was one of those who became a factory worker. Unfortunately, when the war ended, the arms factories closed down and demobbed soldiers took the jobs that were available. Once again, they were commenting from the outside, and the slow but steady attrition of the members began.

For Shachtman, the non-revolutionary character of the postwar working class and the strength of Stalinism internationally inevitability impelled him to the right. If Stalinism was the barbaric antithesis of Socialism, and revolutionary Socialists just could not be heard, then Socialists should support those structures within capitalism that enabled workers to organise and better their conditions. By 1949, he was floating the idea of supporting trade union candidates in the Democratic Party.

By 1958, the ISL still had enough of its old spirit for there to be a faction fight when Hal Draper led the opposition to dissolving the ISL into the American Socialist Party. It was to no avail, the organisation had outlived its time, and having signed the humiliating dissolution statement demanded by the Socialist Party, Shachtman took his followers into the palsied embrace of Norman Thomas. One of the great paradoxes of all this is that the leaders of the Socialist Party were even more tired than the ISL, and within a short time Shachtman and his camarilla were in control of the organisation, and remorselessly driving it to the right. In the end, poor Shachtman was a caricature of his former self. Gradually he broke with his old comrades of many years' standing. He supported the Bay of Pigs landing, he backed Johnson over Vietnam, backed Humphries for US President, and then refused to back McGovern against Nixon, and finally, in 1972, he died some years after his demise as a Socialist.

The *Fate of the Russian Revolution* is subtitled *Lost Texts of Critical Marxism*, and, it has to be said, not all of it needed finding, but for those interested in the history of the Trotskyist movement, there is plenty to satisfy their appetite. Apart from the reprints from *Labour Action* and *New International*, there are Workers Party conference documents and internal bulletins, with contributions by such luminaries as CLR James and Hal Draper.

Sean Matgamna not only edited this volume, he also provides us with an introduction which aims to set the historical material in an overall context, both in relation to Trotsky and Trotskyism, and also to the Leninist tradition. The need for such an attempt rests in the fact that nobody in the ISL ever took the trouble to produce a coherent text on the theory of bureaucratic collectivism, not its origin, dynamic, political economy, or its laws of motion. Shachtman published a collection of his articles, under the title *The Bureaucratic Revolution*, in which he tinkered a little with the original texts to prove that from 1940 he had always been an opponent of the 'evil empire'. Hal Draper put out another collection of articles, *An Introduction to Independent Socialism*, but all his major works were devoted to other more valuable tasks. I regret to say that Sean has not rectified the omissions of more talented Shachtmanites. I did, however, notice in Sean's acknowledgements at the front of the volume, where he thanks Martin Thomas for help in editing the draft of part two of the Introduction to just a tenth of its original length. Now part two in the final text is 69 pages long, I counted them, and if you will just multiply that number by 10 you will realise that Martin deserves a heartfelt vote of thanks from all of us for his selfless endeavours. Now there's a man I would be happy to go to the barricades with any day.

The Russian question certainly has its place in any examination of the life of the WP/ISL, but it really was much more than that. For 20 years, against great odds, an organisation was maintained that vigorously preached the message that Socialism is an expansion of, not an alternative to, democracy. And from all the evidence, that idea also informed the practice of the organisation, which puts it one up on practically every other group extant today. If you asked Alan Thornett whether that spirit of fair play that characterised the ISL has somehow trickled down to the Alliance for Workers Liberty, I'll bet a modest sum that the enamel would fall off his teeth and steam come out of his ears before he was able to reply.

I believe that for young comrades coming into the movement, an altogether more valuable and entertaining book from the WP/ISL archive, a selection that would faithfully cover the whole of the Shachtmanite canon, would have yielded something of much greater interest. The point of this volume, I suspect, is not for the edification of the young, or indeed the not-so-young. Its purpose is to add a certain theoretical respectability to Sean's own organisational needs. He has attached himself to a tradition that had some good ideas, but not on the Russian question, and some very good people. It really is no good reinventing the wheel if it was a small inadequate one that only moved to the right, and was, in any case, irreparably smashed with the fall of the Berlin wall.
Jim Higgins

Alison Macleod, *The Death of Uncle Joe*, Merlin Press, Rendlesham, 1997, pp269, £9.95

JUSTIFYING yet another memoir from the inglorious tradition of the Communist Party of Great Britain poses a lighter task now than it did a year or two back. As the Yeltsin era in Russia totters towards its end, Stalinism no longer appears the dead bird it was only five years ago. Shameless in their wooing of ultra-nationalist and anti-Semitic currents, Russian Communists look quite capable of making a full comeback amidst the ruins of the Russian economy and social fabric. And — if we don't watch our back-yard carefully — some significant satellite group may still emerge in Britain, their coffers suitably lubricated from abroad, without our quite being conscious of the new challenge. *Marxism Today* may have stepped back into a deserved obscurity only for *Stalinism Yesteryear* to pop out to take an unexpected late bow.

Alison Macleod's recollections of her 13 years at the *Daily Worker*, from 1944 to 1957, are, then, timely — a reminder of the true nature of the beast which dominated the British left for so many years, which exercised a hegemony over trade union militancy for some decades, and which can in no way be excluded from that causal chain which led to the present parlous state of British left-wing Socialism. These memoirs are no apologia for the CPGB or the author, no subtle Hobsbawmian essay dovetailing past mistakes with supposed achievements in order to foster the illusion of justification. Macleod, who is fully aware of her own unimportance (she was the *Worker*'s lowly TV reporter), kept daily notes of debates and conversations for the crucial period, culminating in the traumatic months of 1956, and has since checked her facts and anecdotes with surviving participants. Consequently, her work is a detailed narrative of the party monolith in action, of the British leadership resolutely mimicking, or seeking to interpret, the Moscow line. And heaven help them when the line changed too abruptly, or got confused, as in the period following Stalin's death! Such is Macleod's cruel method that the reader has no choice but to alternate between bouts of indignation and fits of uncontrollable laughter. The casuistry of the Jesuits, acquiring its polish over the centuries, no doubt has its attractions, but Stalinist pseudo-scientific casuistry, with its dialectical basis, has a distinct earthy charm all of its own!

For the evolution of British Trotskyism, the crisis of late 1956 in the CPGB was a moment of fundamental importance; and the historic rôle of Peter Fryer, a *Daily Worker* foreign correspondent, cannot be overstated. Fryer had joined the paper in 1947, and had covered the infamous Rajk trial in Budapest, swallowing as holy writ in the process Rajk's confession of being a Titoist agent intent on overthrowing the Hungarian regime. After Khrushchev's 'Secret Speech' to the Twentieth Congress in 1956, Fryer came to his senses, and being an honest man, and in no way a party time-server, he underwent a *mea culpa* phase: he admitted that he'd deceived the paper's readers on the Rajk trial, and attacked the rôle of the current Soviet leadership in the cult of personality surrounding Stalin. At the CPGB's congress, he asked the question: 'What solid guarantees are there that such a combination of circumstances so grievously harmful to the interests of the working-class movement shall never happen again?' On 24 July, the *Daily Worker* printed his article on the rehabilitation of 474 non-persons in Hungary, including Rajk. But since this was an approved party position, that was no great advance on the editor's part.

Tensions within the party could be glossed over for the time being by a few minor concessions to the critics. But the Hungarian uprising that began in the autumn blew the façade of party unity wide apart. Johnnie Campbell, the *Daily Worker* editor, made the mistake of sending Fryer to Hungary to cover events. Fryer's first article, in which he described witnessing 80 corpses of men, women and children shot down by the security police, remained unpublished. No less than 455 key words were cut out of his second despatch, whilst his third despatch was completely suppressed. David Ainley, the paper's Business Manager, justified censorship on the grounds of Fryer's hysterical tone, whilst damning Fryer's integrity with the jibe that he'd taken refuge in the British Embassy (in order to avoid being shot on the streets, be it said). Incidentally, this reviewer has his own axe to grind: Ainley was instrumental in my suspension from the 1960 Committee in the London Co-op in the late 1960s.

Fryer had long ago given notice of his intention to quit the *Daily Worker*, and it duly printed his letter of resignation. Not that it had much choice in the matter, for the letter was simultaneously published in the *Manchester Guardian*. Meanwhile, the anti-Fryer smear campaign was working at full throttle, saying that his resignation was brought on by his wife's hand being found caught in the till (a total Stalinist fabrication, needless to say). Fryer and his poisonous truths about Hungary had now to be fully isolated from the purview of the party faithful, and inevitably he was suspended from party membership on 26 November 1956. He was expelled by 486 votes to 31, with 11 abstentions, at the subsequent congress, the weakness of party dissidents being thoroughly exposed. Yet this result masks the fact that 7000 members, over 20 per cent of the total, had flocked out of the organisation in a few months.

By this time, Mephistopheles (that is, Gerry Healy) had caught up with Fryer. Healy the Pabloite had been busying himself with the Young Communist League, and Macleod notes Healy's lustrous presence at the YCL congress, where he 'sat visibly giving orders to some delegates'. The YCL's critical resolution on Hungary proving unwelcome to the party leadership, it naturally did not merit mention in the *Daily Worker*. By the time of Fryer's formal expulsion, Healy was producing Fryer's daily *Congress Special* intended for the edification of delegates, and had published in pamphlet form the text of his appeal. Macleod's analysis of Fryer's relations with Healy is a shrewd one: 'Peter was to realise within three years that Gerry Healy... had all the worst habits of the Communist Party leaders, such as rigging congresses, blackening the names of those who disagreed with him, and manipulating young people.' But Healy had offered the expellee 'a rational explanation', some way 'to make sense of the events which had hit us'. As with Brian Pearce (also on the *Daily Worker*) and Brian Behan, Fryer was drawn to Healy 'not only because he had been right about Stalin, but because he boasted of a historical theory which accounted for Stalinism'. And as Macleod says: 'The attraction of the Trotskyists, that winter, was not that their arguments were good. It was that they were prepared to argue at all. The orthodox were not.' As readers will already have guessed, Alison Macleod was never attracted by Trotskyism herself. She caustically cites Trotsky's *In Defence of Terrorism* as 'a do-it-yourself manual. It shows how to construct a morality which will destroy you.'

This is an indispensable memoir, the best of its genre I know. Replete with unique accounts of the thinking of the party leadership, it penetrates to the sordid reality of the CPGB at a historical watershed from which it never recovered in a way that can't be obtained by ploughing through the party's dusty archives. Macleod's shading in of how the leadership sought to withhold knowledge of Khrushchev's 'Secret Speech' from the membership is unsurpassed. Her account of the leadership's inability to come to terms with the fact of Soviet anti-Semitism highlights how institutional anti-Semitism in Moscow produced a satellite counterpart in London. But in one respect, Macleod fails the reader. The *Daily Worker* had a highly respected racing tipster. At no point does she explain why he so regularly backed the right horse whilst the party leadership was so regularly backing the wrong one.

Ron Heisler

Sam Deaderick and **Tamara Turner**, *Gay Resistance: The Hidden History*, Red Letter Press, Seattle, 1997, $7.00

THIS journal will, I hope, always be interested in hidden histories, and especially interested in publications which bring them to light. *Revolutionary History* has not had many opportunities to review documents on questions of sexual liberation; consequently a recent visit to London from a comrade in the Freedom Socialist Party (closely associated with the publishers) with copies of this pamphlet is to be welcomed. It is to be regretted that there is no UK outlet for FSP publications.

The pamphlet could be used as a case study in support of Peter Fryer's excellent advice to new writers: 'Lucid, vigorous and brief.' (So brief in fact that $7.00 may seem expensive for 50 pages of text.) As a political tool, it achieves its objective of placing gay struggles in an historical framework, of which class struggle is a main element. And no doubt it will raise the spirit of gay activists to be able to perceive themselves as part of a greater struggle, and defending an important heritage.

Both authors are, or were, associated with the FSP, which originated in a split from the US Socialist Workers Party (the FSP has for some years defined itself as Socialist-feminist). The text first appeared in their paper *Freedom Socialist* in the late 1970s, and subsequently in pamphlet form in 1978. The current pamphlet updates the accounts of radical gay and lesbian groups since then.

The argument of the opening sections of the pamphlet can be summarised thus. In ancient matriarchal societies there was complete sexual freedom, and this naturally extended to homosexual behaviour. This happy state of affairs was ended by the rise of patriarchy and monogamy, and led directly to the oppression of women and social hostility towards homosexuality. Classical Greece and Rome were well on the way to the full institutionalisation of patriarchy and monogamy, but retained some pre-civilisation freedoms. Asian cultures (with the exception of Zoroastrian Persia) and pre-Columbian American cultures remained free of these evils until they fell under the influence or control of Western culture. Ancient Judaism, seemingly another exception, generated the first legal prohibition against male homosexuality (in Leviticus), and its attitudes were adopted in their entirety, indeed developed further, by Christianity, and especially by the Pauline current.

Medieval European history was substantially shaped by the growing power and institutionalisation of Christianity. The centuries-long wars against heretics, witches and other dissident currents were the form taken by the growth of Christian power, and the means by which Christianity suppressed the residual sexual freedoms of the mass of the European populations. Homosexuality was a frequent accusation against the enemies of the Church. The heretics, however, were not fighting specifically in defence of homosexuality; rather they were defending the pre-Christian cultures and their freedoms as a whole. The objective of these long wars was the establishment of the nuclear, patriarchal family, which was essential to the orderly accumulation of capital.

The authors next present a brief account of the rise of movements for homosexual rights in the nineteenth and twentieth centuries, beginning with Hirschfield and the Scientific Humanitarian Committee in Germany in the 1860s. It mentions the defeat of those movements by the Nazis, touches on the Bolsheviks' reforms, and includes radicals such as Edward Carpenter and Havelock Ellis. The following section is devoted to a presentation of lesbian contributions to literature, arguing that they prepared the cultural ground for later explicitly political movements.

The emergence of 'liberal' homosexual rights organisations in the USA is sketched in the next section, showing the impetus to their growth given by Kinsey and other researchers, and the setbacks suffered under McCarthyism. Some mention is given to similar movements in Europe. (The Minority Rights Group will perhaps be surprised to learn that they have a programme similar to that of the Daughters of Bilitis.)

The 1969 Stonewall riot marked a turning point, after which the majority of new movements had a distinctly radical character, or even hyper-radical in the case of the separatists. With the exception of the late 1970s campaigns against anti-gay changes in the law, these new movements have proven to be fissiparous, whilst the more general movement has built significant social institutions such as Gay Pride, and an infrastructure of publications and organisations.

In the closing section, the authors recognise and applaud the growth of a new leadership amongst gays from ethnic minorities, and argue that these victims of multiple oppression are the most capable of perceiving that gay oppression is a component of the problem of alienated life under capitalism.

That is the argument. How does the history stand up? There is a bibliography, but the authors do not provide specific references in support of their statements. No doubt this helps to maintain the punchy readability, but it makes it difficult to check on things and resolve questions about what is being said. For example, in his introduction, Roger Simpson writes that Deaderick and Turner remind readers that 'oppression around sexual identity is as old as history'. By my reading, they argue only that it is as old as civilisation – a very different proposition.

I have practically no knowledge of ancient cultures, but I suspect that the very generalised claim made about them here – that they were all matriarchal and libertarian to an extreme degree – is a hostage to fortune which a hostile reviewer with special knowledge could assail. I don't understand how such claims can be made on the basis of no written history and very limited evidence in the form of artefacts. And from what little I know of contemporary cultures that have had limited contact with capitalism, they do not closely resemble the joyous matriarchies which the authors describe. Trotsky's reports of his escape from Siberia, for example, describe the most depressed and depressing pattern of life amongst the isolated tribes he encountered.

And I don't see that the demand for gay rights today is in any way dependent upon a 'golden age' theory. No golden age lies behind other democratic and transitional demands, at least not since the English working class abandoned the demand to 'throw off the Norman yoke', and Connolly's fables of primitive Irish democracy faded from view.

The section dealing with the Social Democratic parties and their response to homosexual rights campaigns seems to me to understate or neglect important elements of the Socialist response. Eduard Bernstein's 1895 articles were published in English in 1977 by the British and Irish Communist Organisation (Athol Books), together with a related article by Herzen. This publication is perhaps obscure today, but in 1978, when the FSP articles first appeared, it was widely discussed. The BICO had a habit of disagreeing with the historical figures whose work they published, such as Bukharin and Jim Larkin. They gave a grudging acceptance to Bernstein with the conclusion: 'Heterosexuality remains socially necessary and should be encouraged: homosexuality is fairly harmless and can be tolerated.' This alone ensured that the publication was widely discussed. I would have included it in the bibliography.

Similarly, in 1978 the authors might not have had access to the English translation of Kautsky's 1906 writings on Marxism and morality, which had been out of print for many years before it reappeared in Patrick Goode's selection in 1983. An earlier version could probably have been found in university libraries, but nobody read the 'renegade' in those days. But by 1997 they cannot be omitted from a Socialist examination of moral questions.

Oscar Wilde is given the briefest of mentions, and his essay *The Soul of Man Under Socialism* is not referred to. And for a 1997 revision not enthusiastically to recommend Richard Ellman's splendid biography of Wilde is difficult for this reviewer to believe.

In describing the suppression of the German homosexual rights movement by the Nazis, the authors do not deal with the question of homosexuality amongst the Brownshirts. A reference to a publication that deals with this would be useful – such as the 1979 Big Flame pamphlet *Sexuality and Fascism*.

I found the brief section on the Russian experience disappointing for its lack of detail and references. A caption to an illustration refers to Batkis, but his book is not included in the bibliography.

If it is right (and it is) to credit lesbian novelists such as Virginia Woolf with a rôle in changing the climate of opinion, how can it be right to omit any mention of the beats? Allen Ginsberg's courageous campaigning against the oppression of gays was even conducted in the heart of the Stalinist states, but he gets not the slightest nod of acknowledgement. Barry Miles's biography of Ginsberg deserves a place in the recommended reading.

No doubt every reader would be able to produce his or her own list of amendments to the literary aspects of this question. But there is a more important and more political omission to be rectified – that of organised labour. The unions are not mentioned until the last page of the pamphlet. I don't think this fairly reflects the politics of the FSP. *Freedom Socialist* regularly reports the active union work of FSP militants. The FSP played an honourable part in the work towards the foundation of the Labor Party in the USA. So it is puzzling to find no commentary on or assessment of the successes and failures over the last 20 years in winning support within the trade unions for gay struggles. (Let us recall how Tony Cliff hectored us in 1979 that 'we should look forward to the first leader of the London workers' council being a 19-year-old gay woman!')

There are other questions that one would like to debate with the FSP which are probably outside the scope of their pamphlet. The FSP does not call for political revolution in Cuba or China. Conditions for gays have improved somewhat over recent years in Cuba, but not at all in China (to the limited extent of the available information). Is sexual liberation, then, a reform which it is within the ability of those states to allow? If so, how can the demands best be advanced by oppressed gays in those countries, and by those in solidarity with them elsewhere? And if Stalinist states can accommodate gay liberation, why is it impossible to think of similar reforms without revolutionary overthrow in capitalist states? Does it seem likely today that homosexual business people would set out to subvert and disrupt the circulation and accumulation of capital by refusing to pass their assets when they die? By this, of course, I am seeking to clarify the status of the demand for gay rights within the Trotskyist programme. Is it an achievable reform, or a basis for mobilisations which will overthrow the power of capital? Deaderick and Turner do not, in my assessment, make a categorical case for the latter position.

JJ Plant

Riccardo Anfossi, *La Resistenza Spezzata*, Prospettiva Edizioni, Rome, 1995, pp171, Lit 24 000
Carlo Guerriero and **Fausto Rondinelli**, *La Volante Rossa*, Datanews Editrice, Rome, 1996, pp142, Lit 18 000
Tom Behan, *The Long Awaited Moment: The Working Class and the Italian Communist Party in Milan, 1943-1948*, Peter Lang, New York, 1997, pp310, $35
Elena Aga-Rossi and **Victor Zaslavsky**, *Togliatti e Stalin. Il PCI e la Politica Estera Staliniana negli Archivi di Mosca*, Il Mulino, Bologna, 1997, pp312, Lit 38 000

THESE books each deal with different aspects of the years immediately preceding and following the end of the Second World War in Italy. They are jointly reviewed here as they all seek to shed light on the Italian Resistance and its consequences after 25 April 1945, the official date of Italy's 'liberation' by the Allied forces, as well as on the policies embraced by the Italian Communist Party (PCI) and its rôle in the outcome of this historical period.

In the past decade or so, the treatment afforded to the Resistance by successive Italian governments, historians and intellectuals of both the left and right has undergone a notable development, symptomatic of a wider international trend towards the obliteration of any class analysis of historical events. So, whilst it is not uncommon to see the Resistance termed as a 'second Risorgimento', painting an idealised and grossly inaccurate picture of the Italian people fully united in an attempt to repel the Nazi invader, the parties of the Italian official left, and most notably the PCI, emphasise the contribution made by the highly 'democratically responsible' and 'nationally aware' working masses 'in guaranteeing Italy's future as a nation'.

In more principled quarters of the left, the Resistance has often been seen as an instance of the more general 'revolution betrayed'. So, in this interpretation we see an Italian working class politically conscious and developed, armed and poised for power, were it not for the betrayal of the PCI, which instructed it to surrender its weapons to the Allied Command, mainly thanks to the party's moral authority amongst the workers and the critical rôle played by Stalin, as well as the lack of preparation displayed by other possible alternative parties or groups to the left of the PCI. Whilst these factors contain some truth, for many, including the authors reviewed here, they are only part of the story.

Nevertheless, in times when speaking of a working class attracts accusations of hopeless anachronism, with repeated calls from left and right in Italy to 'forgive and forget' the excesses of a small number of 'hotheads' wearing black or red shirts, all in the name of 'national reconciliation' and 'looking to the future', any work which seriously tackles these issues and attempts to debunk the myths surrounding the Italian Resistance should be warmly welcomed.

Riccardo Anfossi's book, whose title means 'The Broken Resistance', is an important work in this respect, whether or not one agrees with all its thought-provoking arguments. The picture of the Resistance which emerges from it is far from comfortable and unproblematic, but it deserves careful consideration.

Anfossi's premises are categorical: 'One cannot... speak of a Resistance that has had all its premises betrayed, as some historians, coming above all from an Actionist [Partito d'Azione] background have done, for these premises had been clear from the outset, and the development and choices of a political line were therefore coherent with such premises.' The Resistance was 'limited from the start by its political line and by the immaturity of the consciousness of the proletariat which – willingly or more often than not otherwise – to varying degrees made this line its own' (p155-7).

The Resistance, which Anfossi sees as just a part of a Europe-wide largely spontaneous opposition 'from below', was by no means the determining factor behind the collapse of Fascism in Italy. Not only was Mussolini's fall decided by the monarchy and the army, with big capital withdrawing its support from the ailing Fascist party from 1943, it is not even possible to speak of a consciously mature workers' movement during the Resistance in Italy.

Anfossi warns against an essentially political reading of events during 1943-45 in Italy. He insists that the driving force behind class struggle and strikes in those years was not anti-Fascism or national liberation, but the boss and the factory, how to survive on an ever-decreasing pay, and how to procure food. He concedes that the strikes of March 1944 were clearly more political in nature, but this was partly due to the work carried out by the PCI, which meant that they took on an anti-German character and therefore linked in with the strivings of the anti-Fascist forces for national unity.

Although the massive strikes of 1944 have been hailed as a success because they showed the growing 'maturity' of the working class, their ultimately disappointing outcome was because the workers recognised that their daily struggle went beyond the programme of the strikes' organisers, and they viewed both the Nazis and the Italian ruling class as their enemy. Although the PCI and other anti-Fascist Resistance forces were unable to meet the challenge of this spontaneous action 'from below', the Italian workers' movement was unable to 'go beyond the factory gates' (p43). This was not merely due to the obstacles posed by Stalinism, as the problem ultimately relates to the immature consciousness of the working class.

Anfossi sees the partisan guerrillas as the driving force behind the Resistance, but warns that they again reflected the general characteristics of the Resistance. Their members mainly joined spontaneously and for the most diverse reasons, and they were from all walks of life. Militarily, the Resistance was 'totally subject to the requirements of war and to the political needs of the Anglo-American Command'. In general, partisans were organised in squads, and numerical estimates vary between 1500 and 9000 individuals at the outset, growing to between 50 000 to 70 000 in 1944, and approximately 100 000 by the end. Of these, Anfossi calculates that about 50 per cent were grouped in Communist brigades, and 20 per cent in Actionist brigades, whilst the remaining 30 per cent comprised squads of various allegiances. Partisan squads never reflected a 'clear political choice', but were loosely aligned with one particular party. The Allies favoured this, for they never envisaged any major military rôle for groups which could prove difficult to control. Although a genuine partisan war was waged, Anfossi reiterates that 'the war was won by the Allied forces, and the contribution of the partisan forces was absolutely secondary'. The Allies did not stifle the potential of the partisan Resistance, because it was 'conceived as a subordinate to the Anglo-American imperialist army, and became the military arm of the politics of national unity to free the country from the Germans and include Italy in the Western bloc' (pp56-8).

The partisan formations were brought under one command in 1944, both in the name of patriotism, and to prevent fraternisation between partisans and German soldiers. Allied control prevented them from acquiring any military significance, and the PCI disarmed them politically. The party's constant efforts to subordinate class struggle to the patriotic war for national liberation meant that – save for very few exceptions – the partisans merely replicated bourgeois relations and excluded any concrete control by the masses over the territories liberated in Italy during 1944.

The PCI's rôle in containing and channelling the radical demands of the working class cannot be underestimated. The various stages of this party's policy have already been outlined in this journal (see *Revolutionary History*, Volume 5, no 4, Spring 1995). What is important to emphasise is that the PCI's attempt to become, in Togliatti's words, 'an Italian national party' (p82), opposing any struggle aiming 'to bring about any social or political transformation in a Socialist or Communist sense' but 'fighting for national liberation and for a progressive democratic regime' (p80), precluded any other outcome for the Resistance. Exploiting its prestige within the working class as the party enjoying Stalin's approval, ruthlessly expelling and persecuting all opposition, using the pretext of the Allies' presence to rule out *a priori* any alternative course, and continuously promoting class collaboration, the PCI 'turned into a mass all-class party, a party of government' (p82), and subordinated all revolutionary demands to the reconstruction of the Italian state. The Italian proletariat was given the rôle of 'the national subject, the backbone of the democratic bourgeois reconstruction', able 'to overcome any selfishness in its demands and its specific interests, so as to make its contribution to the needs of the fatherland in difficult times' (p165), and to help restore Italy to its rightful position in the family of democratic nations.

Anfossi sees the Resistance as the spontaneous intervention of the Italian masses, the unifying character of which is – in the last analysis – a strong social and ethical protest against injustice, rather than a patriotic war of national liberation. He feels that these values must be understood and emphasised, as opposed to the mythologisation and cynical exploitation of the Resistance, most notably by the Italian left, for the purposes of the continuity of bourgeois rule, if we are to understand these crucial events in Italian history.

Notwithstanding the many valuable insights of this work and its various undoubtedly valid arguments about the Resistance, Anfossi leaves some crucial questions unresolved, and the issue of the immature consciousness of the Italian working class requires a much more detailed analysis. He says that the Italian proletariat was never able in a widespread sense to extend its struggles beyond the factories, and its demands became increasingly economic in nature. But is this a sign of its 'immaturity', or the effect of the workers' declining political horizons resulting from the PCI's increasingly evident renunciation of any political leadership, especially after the end of the war? It could be argued that Anfossi confuses the effect with the cause, as if he actually expected – in line with his party's recent and rather selective embracing of aspects of Rosa Luxemburg's thought – to find a class fully developed for a revolutionary struggle in the absence of any revolutionary vanguard, nay, often despite the conscious political betrayals of its supposed vanguard party.

Guerriero and Rondinelli review the history and vicissitudes of Milan's Volante Rossa – Martiri Partigiani (Red Flying Squad – Partisan Martyrs), a name deriving from the term used during the partisan war in Italy to denote small squads based in the mountains which carried out brief incursions onto the plains. The Volante Rossa was formed towards the end of 1945 by Giulio Paggio, known as 'Lieutenant Alvaro', himself a former member of a volante rossa and later of a partisan brigade, so that members could help each other, or 'find work for the unemployed... and take part, always united, in all kinds of patriotic events' (p12).

The group came to be comprised of up to about 50 men, mainly ex-partisan fighters, all of them working-class members of the PCI, from the many large and medium-sized factories which made Milan, with Turin and Genoa, part of Italy's 'industrial triangle'. Here, in the first three years after the end of the war, worked highly militant and radicalised workers, almost all unionised and politically quite conscious. The story of the Volante Rossa is the story of partisans and Communists who were reluctant and even unwilling to lay down their arms and put an end to the struggle that had been waged during the war.

The authors convincingly show that the Volante Rossa was no mere anachronism, no wishful thinking or nostalgia on the part of few men who simply could not come to terms with the fact that the 'victory' over the enemy did not become a victory for the Italian workers over their rulers. The bourgeoisie swiftly regained its control when the war officially ended in April 1945. To add insult to injury, a large number of former Fascists, from low-ranking officers to men responsible for the persecution, torture and killing of partisans and workers, were often given prominent positions, and as early as 22 June 1945 an amnesty had been granted to Fascist prisoners, which reduced by one-third their 'political' sentences, whilst absolving altogether those responsible for 'non-political' offences, such as organising Fascist squads, marching on Rome, and collaboration. PCI leader Togliatti aided this process, arguing in parliament in February 1949 that such men 'had nevertheless a right to several mitigating circumstances, above all if we consider that we were then trying to provide the widest possible basis for the new republican state' (p19). Furthermore, the Italian right revived, the Movimento Sociale Italiano was legally formed in 1946, and elements in the higher echelons of the army and the *carabinieri*, the secret services and the police, aided by big business finance and the American secret service, provoked the working class with the aim of destabilising the country.

Unsurprisingly, despite the best efforts and propaganda by the left parties, the amnesty did nothing to calm the harsh protests of the partisans and the public. The partisans' numerous spontaneous reactions in those years were to prove a thorn in the side of the PCI leadership and its allies. The years following the end of the war were characterised by an extremely confrontational and highly charged climate. Faced with attacks from the right and a severe economic crisis, with rising unemployment, inflation and grossly inadequate wage levels, the working class responded with an almost uninterrupted series of strikes, demonstrations, occupations, meetings and protests. And workers were simply not ready to resume their jobs under bosses and managers who, but a few months before, were fighting in the opposite camp.

The Volante Rossa, far from being an extremist grouping involved in terrorism or armed actions divorced from the working class, invariably carried out its work within the ranks of the Milanese workers, and was highly respected by them. Its members adopted a uniform and distinctive insignia, and became highly visible participants on workers' marches, demonstrations and protests. Acting as a workers' defence force, the Volante Rossa undertook various tasks, including stewarding, acting as a rapid response unit, and intimidating and attacking Fascists or Fascist collaborators. The group came to be regarded as a force to be reckoned with, and was to be found in practically every action taken by Milanese workers during that time, until the fateful date of 27 January 1949, when two murders were attributed to the Volante Rossa, despite the style of action and choice of victims being atypical of the group. A highly publicised trial lasting until 1951 brought about the group's demise. Although Giulio Paggio and a few of the group's founders fled abroad, most members received prison sentences of varying severity.

The authors and some surviving members of the group do, however, readily recognise that the Volante Rossa had effectively ceased to exist by the summer of 1948, after the left's crushing defeat in the April election — the Christian Democrats (DC) won 48.5 per cent of the vote, as against 31 per cent for the PSI/PCI Fronte Popolare — the end of the government of 'national unity', and the failed attempt on Togliatti's life on 14 July 1948, with the spontaneous working-class rising being effectively contained by the PCI leadership. One Volante Rossa member bitterly remembers how, in the aftermath of the attempt on Togliatti, everyone was ready to rise in Milan, and the city could have easily been taken without much difficulty, given the relative lack of organisation of the police and the weaponry at the Volante's disposal. However, the PCI leadership wanted to avoid the outlawing of the party which would follow an armed insurrection. The leaders of the PCI branch in Milan intercepted the Volante men, and they were, as a Volante Rossa member said, 'swiftly stopped':

'... that was the end for us, because at that point we realised that the revolution would not be possible, whilst we had been thinking that we were on the eve of the working class taking power. It was clear that it was impossible. We had the chance to take power, but the situation did not allow it. The great majority of the party realised this, and at that point a cycle effectively came to an end. That blow plunged us into a crisis, so much so, that we asked ourselves what point there was in continuing the struggle at all.' (p50)

The crucial issue was the relationship between the Volante Rossa – and, by extension, the Milanese and Italian working class – and the leadership of the PCI. Since everyone in the Volante Rossa was a PCI member, and, as the authors convincingly show, the PCI always remained their reference point, what did the PCI really think of the Volante men?

Since the group was a constant feature in working-class activity of the time, much of which being either organised by the PCI or saw its participation, was the Volante Rossa the 'armed branch of the PCI' (p109)? Far from it. Its closest official involvement with the party leadership began with the series of protests in the autumn of 1947, and culminated with the PCI's Sixth Congress held in Milan in January 1948, when the Volante Rossa men were appointed as stewards, seemingly enjoying the approval of the party's leadership. It is also not unreasonable to concur with the authors' assumption that Paggio and his comrades could not have fled to Eastern Europe without the help of the PCI.

Nevertheless, the relationship between the Volante Rossa and the PCI was a troubled one, and it is more plausible that its apparent toleration by the party was a recognition of the group's high prestige amongst Milanese workers and its excellent local experience and organisational skills. This relationship can, however, be appreciated only in the wider context of the PCI's own national and international policy. The Volante Rossa was but another casualty of the course on which Togliatti and the party's leadership had embarked prior to the end of the war, and of its logical consequences.

However, it is too easy to fall into the trap of cynicism with the benefit of hindsight. For the various reasons explained in the books reviewed here, we cannot doubt the extremely high level of radicalisation of sections of the Italian working class in the first postwar years, or the sincerity and commitment of all those involved. What is all the more poignant is the crucial rôle played by the PCI – thanks to the enormous prestige it enjoyed amongst the workers – in thwarting any revolutionary outcome and in bringing its constituency into line, with its repeated calls for discipline, respect for 'democratic and republican legality', consideration for the PCI's constitutional partners, and so on.

In this light, it is not surprising that the partisan experience could not be absorbed into the party. So, from being 'political immature' individuals with a 'low ideological level' (p107), the partisans effectively became an enemy of the party. Togliatti argued as early as August 1945 that, to avoid possible provocations, the party 'should take a firm stand against any surviving partisan organisations'. In September 1946, Togliatti told a closed party meeting that they were agent provocateurs within the party. They may have had 'an honourable past' and 'actively participated in Communist organisations', but had 'now lost all links with the proletarian vanguard', and had 'become enslaved to foreign ideologies, if not servants of our worst enemies' (pp112-3).

And despite lively dissent at grassroots level, in a situation of worsening provocations and defeats suffered by workers in the factories, the PCI succeeded in containing the discontent and channelling working-class activity into national reconstruction.

With Tom Behan's book, we continue to analyse events in Milan, moving to the inner-city area of Porta Romana, perhaps more representative of the working-